MznLnx

Missing Links Exam Preps

Exam Prep for

The Changing Earth: Exploring Geology and Evolution

Monroe & Wicander, 4th Edition

The MznLnx Exam Prep is your link from the texbook and lecture to your exams.
The MznLnx Exam Preps are unauthorized and comprehensive reviews of your textbooks.

All material provided by MznLnx and Rico Publications (c) 2010
Textbook publishers and textbook authors do not particpate in or contribute to these reviews.

MznLnx

Rico Publications

Exam Prep for The Changing Earth: Exploring Geology and Evolution
4th Edition
Monroe & Wicander

Publisher: Raymond Houge
Assistant Editor: Michael Rouger
Text and Cover Designer: Lisa Buckner
Marketing Manager: Sara Swagger
Project Manager, Editorial Production: Jerry Emerson
Art Director: Vernon Lowerui

Product Manager: Dave Mason
Editorial Assitant: Rachel Guzmanji
Pedagogy: Debra Long
Cover Image: Jim Reed/Getty Images
Text and Cover Printer: City Printing, Inc.
Compositor: Media Mix, Inc.

(c) 2010 Rico Publications
ALL RIGHTS RESERVED. No part of this work
covered by the copyright may be reproduced or
used in any form or by an means--graphic, electronic,
or mechanical, including photocopying, recording,
taping, Web distribution, information storage, and
retrieval systems, or in any other manner--without the
written permission of the publisher.

Printed in the United States
ISBN:

For more information about our products, contact us at:
Dave.Mason@RicoPublications.com

For permission to use material from this text or
product, submit a request online to:
Dave.Mason@RicoPublications.com

Contents

CHAPTER 1
Understanding Earth: A Dynamic and Evolving Planet — 1

CHAPTER 2
Plate Tectonics: A Unifying Theory — 10

CHAPTER 3
Minerals—The Building Blocks of Rocks — 23

CHAPTER 4
Igneous Rocks and Intrusive Igneous Activity — 32

CHAPTER 5
Volcanism and Volcanoes — 45

CHAPTER 6
Weathering, Soil, and Sedimentary Rocks — 54

CHAPTER 7
Metamorphism and Metamorphic Rocks — 75

CHAPTER 8
Earthquakes and Earth Interior — 89

CHAPTER 9
The Seafloor — 101

CHAPTER 10
Deformation, Mountain Building, and the Continents — 115

CHAPTER 11
Mass Wasting — 130

CHAPTER 12
Running Water — 140

CHAPTER 13
Groundwater — 150

CHAPTER 14
Glaciers and Glaciation — 161

CHAPTER 15
The Work of Wind and Deserts — 175

CHAPTER 16
Shorelines and Shoreline Processes — 185

CHAPTER 17
Geologic Time: Concepts and Principles — 196

CHAPTER 18
Evolution— The Theory and Its Supporting Evidence — 207

CHAPTER 19
Precambrian Earth and Life History — 213

CHAPTER 20
Paleozoic Earth History — 229

Contents (Cont.)

CHAPTER 21
Paleozoic Life History — 247
CHAPTER 22
Mesozoic Earth and Life History — 256
CHAPTER 23
Cenozoic Earth and Life History — 271
CHAPTER 24
Physical and Historical Geology in Perspective — 291
ANSWER KEY — 294

TO THE STUDENT

COMPREHENSIVE

The *MznLnx* Exam Prep series is designed to help you pass your exams. Editors at MznLnx review your textbooks and then prepare these practice exams to help you master the textbook material. Unlike study guides, workbooks, and practice tests provided by the texbook publisher and textbook authors, *MznLnx* gives you **all** of the material in each chapter in exam form, not just samples, so you can be sure to nail your exam.

MECHANICAL

The MznLnx Exam Prep series creates exams that will help you learn the subject matter as well as test you on your understanding. Each question is designed to help you master the concept. Just working through the exams, you gain an understanding of the subject--its a simple mechanical process that produces success.

INTEGRATED STUDY GUIDE AND REVIEW

MznLnx is not just a set of exams designed to test you, its also a comprehensive review of the subject content. Each exam question is also a review of the concept, making sure that you will get the answer correct without having to go to other sources of material. You learn as you go! Its the easiest way to pass an exam.

HUMOR

Studying can be tedious and dry. MznLnx's instructional design includes moderate humor within the exam questions on occassion, to break the tedium and revitalize the brain

Chapter 1. Understanding Earth: A Dynamic and Evolving Planet　　　　1

1. In geology, _____ is a specific type of particle transport by fluids such as wind, or the denser fluid water. It occurs when loose material is removed from a bed and carried by the fluid, before being transported back to the surface. Examples include pebble transport by rivers, sand drift over desert surfaces, soil blowing over fields, or even snow drift over smooth surfaces such as those in the Arctic or Canadian Prairies.

   a. Transgression
   b. Hydrothermal circulation
   c. Permineralization
   d. Saltation

2. _____ is the use of the principles of geology to reconstruct and understand the history of the Earth . It focuses on geologic processes that change the Earth's surface and subsurface; and the use of stratigraphy, structural geology and paleontology to tell the sequence of these events. It also focuses on the evolution of plants and animals during different time periods in the geological timescale.

   a. Historical geology
   b. Rockall
   c. Valley glaciers
   d. Strike-slip faults

3. The _____ Era, is the most recent of the three classic geological eras and covers the period from 65.5 million years ago to the present. It is marked by the Cretaceous-Tertiary extinction event at the end of the Cretaceous that saw the demise of the last non-avian dinosaurs and the end of the Mesozoic Era. The _____ era is ongoing.

   a. 1509 Istanbul earthquake
   b. 1703 Genroku earthquake
   c. Cenozoic
   d. 1700 Cascadia earthquake

4. The _____ is a geological eon representing a period before the first abundant complex life on Earth. The _____ extended from 2500 Ma to 542.0 >± 1.0 Ma (million years ago), and is the most recent part of the old, informally named 'e;Precambrian'e; time.

The Proterozoic consists of 3 geologic eras, from oldest to youngest:

- Paleoproterozoic
- Mesoproterozoic
- Neoproterozoic

The well-identified events were:

- The transition to an oxygenated atmosphere during the Mesoproterozoic.
- Several glaciations, including the hypothesized Snowball Earth during the Cryogenian period in the late Neoproterozoic.
- The Ediacaran Period (635 to 542 Ma) which is characterized by the evolution of abundant soft-bodied multicellular organisms.

The geoloic record of the Proterozoic is much better than that for the preceding Archean. In contrast to the deep-water deposits of the Archean, the Proterozoic features many strata that were laid down in extensive shallow epicontinental seas; furthermore, many of these rocks are less metamorphosed than Archean-age ones, and plenty are unaltered.

   a. 1509 Istanbul earthquake
   b. 1700 Cascadia earthquake
   c. Proterozoic Eon
   d. 1703 Genroku earthquake

Chapter 1. Understanding Earth: A Dynamic and Evolving Planet

5. The _____ is a continental transform fault that runs a length of roughly 800 miles (1,300 km) through California in the United States. The fault's motion is right-lateral strike-slip (horizontal motion.) It forms the tectonic boundary between the Pacific Plate and the North American Plate.
   a. San Andreas fault
   b. 1703 Genroku earthquake
   c. 1700 Cascadia earthquake
   d. 1509 Istanbul earthquake

6. The _____ is the zone of the ocean floor that separates the thin oceanic crust from thick continental crust. Continental margins constitute about 28% of the oceanic area.

   The transition from continental to oceanic crust commonly occurs within the outer part of the margin, called continental rise.

   a. Longshore drift
   b. 1509 Istanbul earthquake
   c. Cuspate forelands
   d. Continental margin

7. An _____ is the result of a sudden release of energy in the Earth's crust that creates seismic waves. They are recorded with a seismometer or the related and mostly obsolete Richter magnitude, with a magnitude 3 or lower _____ being mostly imperceptible and magnitude 7 causing serious damage over large areas.
   a. AASHTO Soil Classification System
   b. Earthquake
   c. AL 333
   d. AL 129-1

8. In geology, a _____ or _____ line is a planar fracture in rock in which the rock on one side of the fracture has moved with respect to the rock on the other side. Large faults within the Earth's crust are the result of differential or shear motion and active _____ zones are the causal locations of most earthquakes. Earthquakes are caused by energy release during rapid slippage along a _____.
   a. Combe
   b. Stack
   c. Fault
   d. Dali

9. The _____ or the Dirty Thirties was a period of severe dust storms causing major ecological and agricultural damage to American and Canadian prairie lands from 1930 to 1936 (in some areas until 1940.) The phenomenon was caused by severe drought coupled with decades of extensive farming without crop rotation or other techniques to prevent erosion. Deep plowing of the virgin topsoil of the Great Plains had killed the natural grasses that normally kept the soil in place and trapped moisture even during periods of drought and high winds.
   a. Dust Bowl
   b. 1700 Cascadia earthquake
   c. 1703 Genroku earthquake
   d. 1509 Istanbul earthquake

10. _____ is water located beneath the ground surface in soil pore spaces and in the fractures of lithologic formations. A unit of rock or an unconsolidated deposit is called an aquifer when it can yield a usable quantity of water. The depth at which soil pore spaces or fractures and voids in rock become completely saturated with water is called the water table.
    a. Depression focused recharge
    b. 1509 Istanbul earthquake
    c. 1700 Cascadia earthquake
    d. Groundwater

Chapter 1. Understanding Earth: A Dynamic and Evolving Planet 3

11. _____ is the geomorphic process by which soil, regolith, and rock move downslope under the force of gravity. Types of _____ include creep, slides, flows, topples, and falls, each with its own characteristic features, and taking place over timescales from seconds to years. _____ occurs on both terrestrial and submarine slopes, and has been observed on Earth, Mars, and Venus.
  a. Soil liquefaction
  b. Mass wasting
  c. 1700 Cascadia earthquake
  d. 1509 Istanbul earthquake

12. The _____ is an informal name for the supereon comprising the eons of the geologic timescale that came before the current Phanerozoic eon. It spans from the formation of Earth around 4500 Mya (million years ago) to the evolution of abundant macroscopic hard-shelled animals, which marked the beginning of the Cambrian, the first period of the first era of the Phanerozoic eon, some 542 Mya. It is named after the Roman name for Wales - Cambria - where rocks from this age were first studied.
  a. 1509 Istanbul earthquake
  b. 1700 Cascadia earthquake
  c. 1703 Genroku earthquake
  d. Precambrian

13. The _____ is a cosmological model of the initial conditions and subsequent development of the universe. It is supported by the most comprehensive and accurate explanations from current scientific evidence and observation. As used by cosmologists, the term _____ generally refers to the idea that the universe has expanded from a primordial hot and dense initial condition at some finite time in the past, and continues to expand to this day.
  a. Big Bang
  b. 1703 Genroku earthquake
  c. 1509 Istanbul earthquake
  d. 1700 Cascadia earthquake

14. The _____ , usually abbreviated K for its German translation Kreide, is a geologic period and system from circa >145.5 >± 4 to >65.5 >± 0.3 million years ago . In the geologic timescale, the _____ follows on the Jurassic period and is followed by the Paleogene period. It is the youngest period of the Mesozoic era, and at 80 million years long, the longest period of the Phanerozoic eon. The end of the _____ defines the boundary between the Mesozoic and Cenozoic eras.
  a. Hauterivian
  b. Campanian
  c. Coniacian
  d. Cretaceous

15.

A widely accepted theory of planet formation, the so-called _____ hypothesis of Viktor Safronov, states that planets form out of dust grains that collide and stick to form larger and larger bodies. When the bodies reach sizes of approximately one kilometer, then they can attract each other directly through their mutual gravity, aiding further growth into moon-sized protoplanets enormously.

  a. 1703 Genroku earthquake
  b. Planetesimal
  c. 1509 Istanbul earthquake
  d. 1700 Cascadia earthquake

16. The _____, is a geologic eon before the Proterozoic and Paleoproterozoic, before 2.5 Ga (billion years ago, or 2,500 Ma.) Instead of being based on stratigraphy, this date is defined chronometrically. The lower boundary (starting point) has not been officially recognized by the International Commission on Stratigraphy, but it is usually set to 3.8 Ga, at the end of the Hadean eon.
  a. AASHTO Soil Classification System
  b. Archean
  c. AL 129-1
  d. AL 333

4 *Chapter 1. Understanding Earth: A Dynamic and Evolving Planet*

17. The _____ is the geologic eon before the Archean. It started at Earth's formation about 4.6 billion years ago (4,600 Ma), and ended roughly 3.8 billion years ago, though the latter date varies according to different sources.
   a. 1703 Genroku earthquake
   b. 1700 Cascadia earthquake
   c. 1509 Istanbul earthquake
   d. Hadean

18. The _____ Era is one of three geologic eras of the Phanerozoic eon. The division of time into eras dates back to Giovanni Arduino, in the 18th century, although his original name for the era now called the '_____' was 'Secondary' (making the modern era the 'Tertiary'.)

The _____ was a time of tectonic, climatic and evolutionary activity. The continents gradually shifted from a state of connectedness into their present configuration; the drifting provided for speciation and other important evolutionary developments.

   a. 1700 Cascadia earthquake
   b. 1703 Genroku earthquake
   c. 1509 Istanbul earthquake
   d. Mesozoic

19. The _____ is the earliest of three geologic eras of the Phanerozoic eon. The _____ spanned from roughly 542 to 251 million years ago (ICS, 2004), and is subdivided into six geologic periods; from oldest to youngest they are: the Cambrian, Ordovician, Silurian, Devonian, Carboniferous, and Permian.

The _____ covers the time from the first appearance of abundant, soft-shelled fossils to the time when the continents were beginning to be dominated by large, relatively sophisticated reptiles and modern plants. The lower (oldest) boundary was classically set at the first appearance of creatures known as trilobites and archeocyathids.

   a. 1703 Genroku earthquake
   b. 1700 Cascadia earthquake
   c. 1509 Istanbul earthquake
   d. Paleozoic

20. A _____ is a compound containing an anion in which one or more central silicon atoms are surrounded by electronegative ligands. This definition is broad enough to include species such as hexafluorosilicate ('fluorosilicate'), $[SiF_6]^{2-}$, but the _____ species that are encountered most often consist of silicon with oxygen as the ligand. _____ anions, with a negative net electrical charge, must have that charge balanced by other cations to make an electrically neutral compound.
   a. 1700 Cascadia earthquake
   b. 1703 Genroku earthquake
   c. 1509 Istanbul earthquake
   d. Silicate

21. The _____ make up the largest and most important class of rock-forming minerals, comprising approximately 90 percent of the crust of the Earth. They are classified based on the structure of their silicate group. _____ all contain silicon and oxygen.
   a. 1509 Istanbul earthquake
   b. 1700 Cascadia earthquake
   c. Mineraloid
   d. Silicate minerals

22. Two important classifications of weathering processes exist -- physical and _____. Mechanical or physical weathering involves the breakdown of rocks and soils through direct contact with atmospheric conditions, such as heat, water, ice and pressure. The second classification, _____, involves the direct effect of atmospheric chemicals or biologically produced chemicals (also known as biological weathering) in the breakdown of rocks, soils and minerals.

a. Physical weathering
b. 1509 Istanbul earthquake
c. Weathering
d. Chemical weathering

23. _____ is the decomposition of Earth rocks, soils and their minerals through direct contact with the planet's atmosphere. _____ occurs in situ, or 'with no movement', and thus should not be confused with erosion, which involves the movement of rocks and minerals by agents such as water, ice, wind and gravity.

Two important classifications of _____ processes exist -- physical and chemical _____.

a. 1509 Istanbul earthquake
b. Frost disintegration
c. Physical weathering
d. Weathering

24. The _____ is the epoch from 1.8 million to 11550 years BP covering the world's recent period of repeated glaciations. The _____ epoch follows the Pliocene epoch and is followed by the Holocene epoch. The _____ is the third epoch of the Neogene period or 6th epoch of the Cenozoic Era. The end of the _____ corresponds with the retreat of the last continental glacier. It also corresponds with the end of the Paleolithic age used in archaeology.

a. Late Pleistocene
b. Sicilian Stage
c. Tyrrhenian
d. Pleistocene

25. The _____ is the mechanically weak ductily-deforming region of the upper mantle of the Earth. It lies below the lithosphere, at depths between 100 and 200 km (~ 62 and 124 miles) below the surface, but perhaps extending as deep as 400 km (~ 249 miles.)

The _____ is a portion of the upper mantle just below the lithosphere that is involved in plate movements and isostatic adjustments. In spite of its heat, pressures keep it plastic, and it has a relatively low density. Seismic waves pass relatively slowly through the _____, compared to the overlying lithospheric mantle, thus it has been called the low-velocity zone. This was the observation that originally alerted seismologists to its presence and gave some information about its physical properties, as the speed of seismic waves decreases with decreasing rigidity.

a. AL 129-1
b. Asthenosphere
c. AASHTO Soil Classification System
d. AL 333

26. A _____ is a phenomenon of fluid dynamics that occurs in situations where there are temperature differences within a body of liquid or gas.

Fluids are materials that exhibit the property of flow. Both gases and liquids have fluid properties, and in sufficient quantity, even particulate solids such as salt, grain, and gravel show some fluid properties. When a volume of fluid is heated, it expands and becomes less dense and thus more buoyant than the surrounding fluid. The colder, denser fluid settles underneath the warmer, less dense fluid and forces it to rise. Such movement is called convection, and the moving body of liquid is referred to as a _____.

a. 1509 Istanbul earthquake
b. Convection cell
c. 1703 Genroku earthquake
d. 1700 Cascadia earthquake

27. The _____ is the rigid outermost shell of a rocky planet.

In the Earth, the _____ includes the crust and the uppermost mantle, which constitute the hard and rigid outer layer of the planet. The _____ is underlain by the asthenosphere, the weaker, hotter, and deeper part of the upper mantle.

   a. Continental drift
   b. Lithosphere
   c. Juan de Fuca Ridge
   d. Gorda Ridge

28. A _____ is a dense, coarse-grained igneous rock, consisting mostly of the minerals olivine and pyroxene. _____ is ultramafic, as the rock contains less than 45% silica. It is high in magnesium, reflecting the high proportions of magnesium-rich olivine, with appreciable iron.

_____ is the dominant rock of the upper part of the Earth's mantle. The compositions of _____ nodules found in certain basalts and diamond pipes (kimberlites) are of special interest, because they provide samples of the Earth's Mantle roots of continents brought up from depths from about 30 km or so to depths at least as great as about 200 km.

   a. 1703 Genroku earthquake
   b. Peridotite
   c. 1509 Istanbul earthquake
   d. 1700 Cascadia earthquake

29. _____, is the process of coastal sediments returning to the visible portion of a beach or foreshore following a submersion event. A sustainable beach or foreshore often goes through a cycle of submersion during rough weather then _____ during calmer periods. If a coastline is not in a healthy sustainable condition, then erosion can be more serious and _____ does not fully restore the original volume of the visible beach or foreshore leading to permanent beach or foreshore loss.

   a. AASHTO Soil Classification System
   b. AL 333
   c. Accretion
   d. AL 129-1

30. _____ is molten rock that is found beneath the surface of the Earth, and may also exist on other terrestrial planets. Besides molten rock, _____ may also contain suspended crystals and gas bubbles. _____ often collects in a _____ chamber inside a volcano. _____ is capable of intrusion into adjacent rocks, extrusion onto the surface as lava, and explosive ejection as tephra to form pyroclastic rock.

   a. Rock cycle
   b. Laccolith
   c. Volcanic rock
   d. Magma

31. The lithosphere is broken up into what are called _____. In the case of Earth, there are eight major and many minor plates The lithospheric plates ride on the asthenosphere. These plates move in relation to one another at one of three types of plate boundaries: convergent, or collisional boundaries; divergent boundaries, also called spreading centers; and transform boundaries.

   a. Gorda Ridge
   b. Copperbelt Province
   c. Tectonic plates
   d. Thrust fault

32. The _____ is the layer of igneous, sedimentary, and metamorphic rocks which form the continents and the areas of shallow seabed close to their shores, known as continental shelves. This layer is sometimes called sial due to more felsic, or granitic, bulk composition, which lies in contrast to the oceanic crust, called sima due to its mafic, or basaltic rock. (Based on the change in velocity of seismic waves, it is believed that at a certain depth sial becomes close in its physical properties to sima.
   a. Convergent boundary
   b. Nappe
   c. Tectonic plates
   d. Continental crust

33. _____ is the part of Earth's lithosphere that surfaces in the ocean basins. _____ is primarily composed of mafic rocks, or sima. It is thinner than continental crust, or sial, generally less than 10 kilometers thick, however it is denser, having a mean density of about 3.3 grams per cubic centimeter.
   a. AASHTO Soil Classification System
   b. AL 129-1
   c. AL 333
   d. Oceanic crust

34. _____ was the supercontinent that is theorized to have existed during the Paleozoic and Mesozoic eras about 250 million years ago, before the component continents were separated into their current configuration.

The name was first used by the German originator of the continental drift theory, Alfred Wegener, in the 1920 edition of his book The Origin of Continents and Oceans , in which a postulated supercontinent _____ played a key role.

The single enormous ocean which surrounded Pangaea is known as Panthalassa.

   a. 1700 Cascadia earthquake
   b. 1509 Istanbul earthquake
   c. Pangea
   d. 1703 Genroku earthquake

35. The _____ is the first geological period of the Phanerozoic eon, lasting from 542 ± 0.3 million years ago to 488.3 ± 1.7 million years ago (ICS, 2004); it is succeeded by the Ordovician. Its subdivisions, and indeed its base, are somewhat in flux. The period was established by Adam Sedgwick, who named it after Cambria, the classical name for Wales, where Britain's _____ rocks are best exposed.
   a. 1703 Genroku earthquake
   b. Cambrian
   c. 1509 Istanbul earthquake
   d. 1700 Cascadia earthquake

36. The _____ or Cambrian radiation was the seemingly rapid appearance of most major groups of complex animals around 530 million years ago, as evidenced by the fossil record. This was accompanied by a major diversification of other organisms, including animals, phytoplankton, and calcimicrobes. Before about 580 million years ago, most organisms were simple, composed of individual cells occasionally organized into colonies.
   a. Cambrian explosion
   b. Conodont Alteration Index
   c. Labyrinthodont
   d. Romer's Gap

37. _____ describes the large scale motions of Earth's lithosphere. The theory encompasses the older concepts of continental drift, developed during the first decades of the 20th century by Alfred Wegener, and seafloor spreading, understood during the 1960s.

The outermost part of the Earth's interior is made up of two layers: the lithosphere and the asthenosphere.

a. Thrust fault
c. Plate tectonics
b. Continental crust
d. Forearc

38. _____ defines an important group of generally dark-colored rock-forming inosilicate minerals, composed of double chain SiO_4 tetrahedra, linked at the vertices and generally containing ions of iron and/or magnesium in their structures. They crystallize into two crystal systems, monoclinic and orthorhombic. In chemical composition and general characteristics they are similar to the pyroxenes. They are minerals of either igneous or metamorphic origin; in the former case occurring as constituents (hornblende) of igneous rocks, such as granite, diorite, andesite and others. Those of metamorphic origin include examples such as those developed in limestones by contact metamorphism (tremolite) and those formed by the alteration of other ferromagnesian minerals (hornblende).
  a. AL 129-1
  b. AASHTO Soil Classification System
  c. AL 333
  d. Amphibole

39. _____ is one of the three main rock types (the others being sedimentary and metamorphic rock.) _____ is formed by magma (molten rock) being cooled and becoming solid . They may form with or without crystallization, either below the surface as intrusive (plutonic) rocks or on the surface as extrusive (volcanic) rocks. They make up approximately 95% of the upper part of the Earth's crust, but their great abundance is hidden on the Earth's surface by a relatively thin but widespread layer of sedimentary and metamorphic rocks.
  a. AL 129-1
  b. AL 333
  c. Igneous rock
  d. AASHTO Soil Classification System

40. _____ is the result of the transformation of an existing rock type, the protolith, in a process called metamorphism, which means 'change in form'. The protolith is subjected to heat and pressure (temperatures greater than 150 to 200 >°C and pressures of 1500 bars) causing profound physical and/or chemical change. The protolith may be sedimentary rock, igneous rock or another older _____.
  a. Sedimentary rock
  b. Metavolcanic rock
  c. Migmatite
  d. Metamorphic rock

41. _____ is the solid-state recrystallization of pre-existing rocks due to changes in physical and chemical conditions, primarily heat, pressure, and the introduction of chemically active fluids. Both mineralogical, chemical and crystallographic changes can occur during this process.

Three types of _____ exist: dynamic, contact and regional.

  a. Reading Prong
  b. Compression
  c. Detritus
  d. Metamorphism

42. _____ refers to natural mountain building, and may be studied as a tectonic structural event, (b) as a geographical event, and (c) a chronological event. Orogenic events (a) cause distinctive structural phenomena and related tectonic activity, (b) affect certain regions of rocks and crust, and (c) happen within a specific period of time.
  a. Antler orogeny
  b. Orogenesis
  c. Alice Springs Orogeny
  d. Orogeny

Chapter 1. Understanding Earth: A Dynamic and Evolving Planet

43. The _____ is a fundamental concept in geology that describes the dynamic transitions through geologic time among the three main rock types: sedimentary, metamorphic, and igneous. Each type of rock is altered or destroyed when it is forced out of its equilibrium conditions. An igneous rock such as basalt may break down and dissolve when exposed to the atmosphere, or melt as it is subducted under a continent.
 a. Petrology
 b. Laccolith
 c. Volcanic rock
 d. Rock cycle

44. The _____ is a chronologic schema (or idealized model) relating stratigraphy to time that is used by geologists, paleontologists and other earth scientists to describe the timing and relationships between events that have occurred during the history of the Earth. The table of geologic time spans presented here agrees with the dates and nomenclature proposed by the International Commission on Stratigraphy, and uses the standard color codes of the United States Geological Survey.

Evidence from radiometric dating indicates that the Earth is about 4.570 billion years old.

 a. 1700 Cascadia earthquake
 b. 1703 Genroku earthquake
 c. 1509 Istanbul earthquake
 d. Geologic time scale

45. _____ is a technique used to date materials, usually based on a comparison between the observed abundance of a naturally occurring radioactive isotope and its decay products, using known decay rates. It is the principal source of information about the absolute age of rocks and other geological features, including the age of the Earth itself, and can be used to date a wide range of natural and man-made materials. Together with stratigraphic principles, _____ methods are used in geochronology to establish the geological time scale.
 a. Chronozone
 b. Radiometric dating
 c. Global Standard Stratigraphic Age
 d. Paleomagnetism

46. _____ is the principle that the same scientific laws and processes are constant throughout space and time. It applies specifically to sciences that require a long timescale such as geology, astronomy, and paleontology. It was first defined by Charles Lyell (1797 - 1875), who incorporated James Hutton's gradualism into the idea of _____.
 a. Uniformitarianism
 b. AL 333
 c. AL 129-1
 d. AASHTO Soil Classification System

47. A _____ is a geological phenomenon which includes a wide range of ground movement, such as rock falls, deep failure of slopes and shallow debris flows, which can occur in offshore, coastal and onshore environments. Although the action of gravity is the primary driving force for a _____ to occur, there are other contributing factors affecting the original slope stability. Typically, pre-conditional factors build up specific sub-surface conditions that make the area/slope prone to failure, whereas the actual _____ often requires a trigger before being released.
 a. 1700 Cascadia earthquake
 b. Landslide
 c. Mass wasting
 d. 1509 Istanbul earthquake

48. A _____ or super volcanic eruption is a volcanic eruption which is substantially larger than any volcano in historic times (generally accepted to be greater than 1,000 cubic kilometres.) They occur when magma in the Earth rises into the crust from a hotspot but is unable to break through the crust. Pressure builds in a large and growing magma pool until the crust is unable to contain the pressure.
 a. Pit crater
 b. Volcanic ash
 c. Lapilli
 d. Supervolcano

Chapter 2. Plate Tectonics: A Unifying Theory

1. _____ is the movement of the Earth's continents relative to each other. The hypothesis that continents 'drift' was first put forward by Abraham Ortelius in 1596 and was fully developed by Alfred Wegener in 1912. However, it was not until the development of the theory of plate tectonics in the 1960s, that a sufficient geological explanation of that movement was found.
   a. Panthalassa
   b. Thrust fault
   c. Plate tectonics
   d. Continental drift

2. A _____ is a large, slow-moving mass of ice, formed from compacted layers of snow, that slowly deforms and flows in response to gravity and high pressure.

   _____ ice is the largest reservoir of fresh water on Earth, and second only to oceans as the largest reservoir of total water.

   a. Little Ice Age
   b. Keeling Curve
   c. Pacific Decadal Oscillation
   d. Glacier

3. _____ is the largest and best-known genus of the extinct order of seed ferns known as Glossopteridales (or in some cases as Arberiales or Dictyopteridiales.)

   The Glossopteridales arose around the beginning of the Permian on the great southern continent of Gondwana. These plants went on to become the dominant elements of the southern flora through the rest of the Permian but disappeared in almost all places at the end of the Permian.

   a. Glossopteris
   b. 1509 Istanbul earthquake
   c. Petrified wood
   d. Pteridospermatophyta

4. _____, originally Gondwanaland, is the name given to a southern precursor-supercontinent and then as a remnant separated from Laurasia 180-200 million years ago during the breakup of the Pangaea supercontinent that existed about 500 to 200 Ma ago into two large segments. While the corresponding northern hemisphere continent Laurasia moved further north, the nearly equal in area _____ included most of the landmasses in today's southern hemisphere, including Antarctica, South America, Africa, Madagascar, Australia-New Guinea, and New Zealand, as well as Arabia and the Indian subcontinent, which have now moved into the Northern Hemisphere.
   a. 1700 Cascadia earthquake
   b. 1509 Istanbul earthquake
   c. Laurasia
   d. Gondwana

5. The _____ is a mid-ocean ridge, a divergent tectonic plate boundary located along the floor of the Atlantic Ocean, and the longest mountain range in the world. It separates the Eurasian Plate and North American Plate in the North Atlantic, and the African Plate from the South American Plate in the South Atlantic. The MAR extends from a junction with the Gakkel Ridge (Mid-Arctic Ridge) northeast of Greenland southward to the Bouvet Triple Junction in the South Atlantic.
   a. 1700 Cascadia earthquake
   b. 1509 Istanbul earthquake
   c. 1703 Genroku earthquake
   d. Mid-Atlantic Ridge

6. The _____ is the earliest of three geologic eras of the Phanerozoic eon. The _____ spanned from roughly 542 to 251 million years ago (ICS, 2004), and is subdivided into six geologic periods; from oldest to youngest they are: the Cambrian, Ordovician, Silurian, Devonian, Carboniferous, and Permian.

The _____ covers the time from the first appearance of abundant, soft-shelled fossils to the time when the continents were beginning to be dominated by large, relatively sophisticated reptiles and modern plants. The lower (oldest) boundary was classically set at the first appearance of creatures known as trilobites and archeocyathids.

a. 1509 Istanbul earthquake
c. 1700 Cascadia earthquake

b. 1703 Genroku earthquake
d. Paleozoic

7. The _____ is a geological eon representing a period before the first abundant complex life on Earth. The _____ extended from 2500 Ma to 542.0 >± 1.0 Ma (million years ago), and is the most recent part of the old, informally named 'e;Precambrian'e; time.

The Proterozoic consists of 3 geologic eras, from oldest to youngest:

- Paleoproterozoic
- Mesoproterozoic
- Neoproterozoic

The well-identified events were:

- The transition to an oxygenated atmosphere during the Mesoproterozoic.
- Several glaciations, including the hypothesized Snowball Earth during the Cryogenian period in the late Neoproterozoic.
- The Ediacaran Period (635 to 542 Ma) which is characterized by the evolution of abundant soft-bodied multicellular organisms.

The geoloic record of the Proterozoic is much better than that for the preceding Archean. In contrast to the deep-water deposits of the Archean, the Proterozoic features many strata that were laid down in extensive shallow epicontinental seas; furthermore, many of these rocks are less metamorphosed than Archean-age ones, and plenty are unaltered.

a. 1700 Cascadia earthquake
c. 1509 Istanbul earthquake

b. 1703 Genroku earthquake
d. Proterozoic Eon

8. In geology, a _____ is a landmass comprising more than one continental core, or craton. The assembly of cratons and accreted terranes that form Eurasia qualifies as a _____ today.

Most commonly, paleogeographers employ the term _____ to refer to a single landmass consisting of all the modern continents.

a. 1509 Istanbul earthquake
c. Supercontinent

b. 1700 Cascadia earthquake
d. 1703 Genroku earthquake

Chapter 2. Plate Tectonics: A Unifying Theory

9. The _____ is the zone of the ocean floor that separates the thin oceanic crust from thick continental crust. Continental margins constitute about 28% of the oceanic area.

The transition from continental to oceanic crust commonly occurs within the outer part of the margin, called continental rise.

- a. Cuspate forelands
- b. Longshore drift
- c. 1509 Istanbul earthquake
- d. Continental margin

10. In geology, _____ is transported rock debris overlying the solid bedrock. The term is also sometimes refers to organic debris so-transported. In the largest sense, it refers to the material left behind by retreating continental glaciers.
- a. Geodiversity
- b. Platform cover
- c. Patterned ground
- d. Drift

11. An _____ is the result of a sudden release of energy in the Earth's crust that creates seismic waves. They are recorded with a seismometer or the related and mostly obsolete Richter magnitude, with a magnitude 3 or lower _____ being mostly imperceptible and magnitude 7 causing serious damage over large areas.
- a. Earthquake
- b. AL 129-1
- c. AASHTO Soil Classification System
- d. AL 333

12. The _____ is the rigid outermost shell of a rocky planet.

In the Earth, the _____ includes the crust and the uppermost mantle, which constitute the hard and rigid outer layer of the planet. The _____ is underlain by the asthenosphere, the weaker, hotter, and deeper part of the upper mantle.

- a. Gorda Ridge
- b. Continental drift
- c. Lithosphere
- d. Juan de Fuca Ridge

13. _____ is molten rock that is found beneath the surface of the Earth, and may also exist on other terrestrial planets. Besides molten rock, _____ may also contain suspended crystals and gas bubbles. _____ often collects in a _____ chamber inside a volcano. _____ is capable of intrusion into adjacent rocks, extrusion onto the surface as lava, and explosive ejection as tephra to form pyroclastic rock.
- a. Volcanic rock
- b. Laccolith
- c. Magma
- d. Rock cycle

14. An _____ is a type of rock that contains minerals such as gemstones and metals that can be extracted through mining and refined for use. Samples of _____ in the form of exceptionally beautiful crystals, exotic layering visible when sectioned or polished or metallic presentations such as large nuggets or crystalline formations of metals such as gold or copper may command a value far beyond their value as mere _____ or raw metal for subsequent reduction to utilitarian purposes.

The grade or concentration of an _____ mineral, or metal, as well as its form of occurrence, will directly affect the costs associated with mining the _____.

a. Ore
b. AL 129-1
c. Ore genesis
d. AASHTO Soil Classification System

15. The lithosphere is broken up into what are called _____. In the case of Earth, there are eight major and many minor plates The lithospheric plates ride on the asthenosphere. These plates move in relation to one another at one of three types of plate boundaries: convergent, or collisional boundaries; divergent boundaries, also called spreading centers; and transform boundaries.
   a. Thrust fault
   b. Gorda Ridge
   c. Copperbelt Province
   d. Tectonic plates

16. The _____ Era, is the most recent of the three classic geological eras and covers the period from 65.5 million years ago to the present. It is marked by the Cretaceous-Tertiary extinction event at the end of the Cretaceous that saw the demise of the last non-avian dinosaurs and the end of the Mesozoic Era. The _____ era is ongoing.
   a. Cenozoic
   b. 1703 Genroku earthquake
   c. 1509 Istanbul earthquake
   d. 1700 Cascadia earthquake

17. The _____ , usually abbreviated K for its German translation Kreide, is a geologic period and system from circa >145.5 >± 4 to >65.5 >± 0.3 million years ago . In the geologic timescale, the _____ follows on the Jurassic period and is followed by the Paleogene period. It is the youngest period of the Mesozoic era, and at 80 million years long, the longest period of the Phanerozoic eon. The end of the _____ defines the boundary between the Mesozoic and Cenozoic eras.
   a. Hauterivian
   b. Campanian
   c. Coniacian
   d. Cretaceous

18. The _____ or the Dirty Thirties was a period of severe dust storms causing major ecological and agricultural damage to American and Canadian prairie lands from 1930 to 1936 (in some areas until 1940.) The phenomenon was caused by severe drought coupled with decades of extensive farming without crop rotation or other techniques to prevent erosion. Deep plowing of the virgin topsoil of the Great Plains had killed the natural grasses that normally kept the soil in place and trapped moisture even during periods of drought and high winds.
   a. 1703 Genroku earthquake
   b. 1700 Cascadia earthquake
   c. 1509 Istanbul earthquake
   d. Dust Bowl

19. The _____ Era is one of three geologic eras of the Phanerozoic eon. The division of time into eras dates back to Giovanni Arduino, in the 18th century, although his original name for the era now called the '_____' was 'Secondary' (making the modern era the 'Tertiary'.)

The _____ was a time of tectonic, climatic and evolutionary activity. The continents gradually shifted from a state of connectedness into their present configuration; the drifting provided for speciation and other important evolutionary developments.

   a. 1509 Istanbul earthquake
   b. 1703 Genroku earthquake
   c. 1700 Cascadia earthquake
   d. Mesozoic

20. _____ was the supercontinent that is theorized to have existed during the Paleozoic and Mesozoic eras about 250 million years ago, before the component continents were separated into their current configuration.

The name was first used by the German originator of the continental drift theory, Alfred Wegener, in the 1920 edition of his book The Origin of Continents and Oceans , in which a postulated supercontinent _____ played a key role.

The single enormous ocean which surrounded Pangaea is known as Panthalassa.

  a. 1509 Istanbul earthquake
  b. 1703 Genroku earthquake
  c. 1700 Cascadia earthquake
  d. Pangea

21. _____ was a supercontinent that most recently existed as a part of the split of the Pangaean supercontinent in the late Mesozoic era. It included most of the landmasses which make up today's continents of the northern hemisphere, chiefly Laurentia (the name given to the North American craton), Baltica, Siberia, Kazakhstania, and the North China and East China cratons.
  a. Laurasia
  b. 1700 Cascadia earthquake
  c. Rodinia
  d. 1509 Istanbul earthquake

22. The _____ was a cratonic sequence that extended from the end of the Mississippian through the Permian periods. It is the unconformity between this sequence and the preceding Kaskaskia that divides the Carboniferous into the Mississippian and Pennsylvanian periods in North America.

Like the Kaskaskia sequence, Absaroka sedimentary deposits were dominated by detrital or siliclastic rocks.

  a. Absaroka sequence
  b. AL 333
  c. AASHTO Soil Classification System
  d. AL 129-1

23. The _____ is a geologic subperiod and stratigraphic subsystem of the Carboniferous Period. It is the later subperiod of the Carboniferous, lasting from roughly 318.1>± 1.3 to 299>± 0.8 Ma (million years ago.) As with most other geochronologic units, the rock beds that define the _____ are well identified, but the exact date of the start and end are uncertain by a few million years.
  a. Dinantian
  b. Pennsylvanian
  c. Calciferous sandstone
  d. Mississippian

24. _____, is the process of coastal sediments returning to the visible portion of a beach or foreshore following a submersion event. A sustainable beach or foreshore often goes through a cycle of submersion during rough weather then _____ during calmer periods. If a coastline is not in a healthy sustainable condition, then erosion can be more serious and _____ does not fully restore the original volume of the visible beach or foreshore leading to permanent beach or foreshore loss.
  a. AASHTO Soil Classification System
  b. AL 129-1
  c. AL 333
  d. Accretion

25. The _____ is the first geological period of the Phanerozoic eon, lasting from 542 ± 0.3 million years ago to 488.3 ± 1.7 million years ago (ICS, 2004); it is succeeded by the Ordovician. Its subdivisions, and indeed its base, are somewhat in flux. The period was established by Adam Sedgwick, who named it after Cambria, the classical name for Wales, where Britain's _____ rocks are best exposed.

Chapter 2. Plate Tectonics: A Unifying Theory   15

a. 1509 Istanbul earthquake
b. 1703 Genroku earthquake
c. Cambrian
d. 1700 Cascadia earthquake

26. The _____ or Cambrian radiation was the seemingly rapid appearance of most major groups of complex animals around 530 million years ago, as evidenced by the fossil record. This was accompanied by a major diversification of other organisms, including animals, phytoplankton, and calcimicrobes. Before about 580 million years ago, most organisms were simple, composed of individual cells occasionally organized into colonies.

a. Labyrinthodont
b. Conodont Alteration Index
c. Romer's Gap
d. Cambrian explosion

27. The _____ is a geologic period and system that extends from about 251 to 199 Mya (million years ago.) As the first period of the Mesozoic Era, the _____ follows the Permian and is followed by the Jurassic. Both the start and end of the _____ are marked by major extinction events.

a. Triassic
b. Rhaetian
c. 1700 Cascadia earthquake
d. 1509 Istanbul earthquake

28. _____ are the preserved remains or traces of animals, plants, and other organisms from the remote past. The totality of _____, both discovered and undiscovered, and their placement in fossiliferous rock formations and sedimentary layers (strata) is known as the fossil record. The study of _____ across geological time, how they were formed, and the evolutionary relationships between taxa (phylogeny) are some of the most important functions of the science of paleontology.

a. 1700 Cascadia earthquake
b. 1703 Genroku earthquake
c. 1509 Istanbul earthquake
d. Fossils

29. _____ is the study of the record of the Earth's magnetic field preserved in various magnetic minerals through time. The study of _____ has demonstrated that the Earth's magnetic field varies substantially in both orientation and intensity through time. <

a. Chronozone
b. Law of superposition
c. Paleomagnetism
d. Stage

30. _____ is the part of Earth's lithosphere that surfaces in the ocean basins. _____ is primarily composed of mafic rocks, or sima. It is thinner than continental crust, or sial, generally less than 10 kilometers thick, however it is denser, having a mean density of about 3.3 grams per cubic centimeter.

a. AL 333
b. AASHTO Soil Classification System
c. AL 129-1
d. Oceanic crust

31. A _____ is a special-purpose map made to show geological features.

The stratigraphic contour lines are drawn on the surface of a selected deep stratum, so that they can show the topographic trends of the strata under the ground. It is not always possible to properly show this when the strata are extremely fractured, mixed, in some discontinuities, or where they are otherwise disturbed.

a. 1509 Istanbul earthquake
b. 1703 Genroku earthquake
c. Geologic map
d. 1700 Cascadia earthquake

32. _____ refers to natural mountain building, and may be studied as a tectonic structural event, (b) as a geographical event, and (c) a chronological event. Orogenic events (a) cause distinctive structural phenomena and related tectonic activity, (b) affect certain regions of rocks and crust, and (c) happen within a specific period of time.
- a. Alice Springs Orogeny
- b. Orogenesis
- c. Antler orogeny
- d. Orogeny

33. _____ occurs at mid-ocean ridges, where new oceanic crust is formed through volcanic activity and then gradually moves away from the ridge. _____ helps explain continental drift in the theory of plate tectonics.

Earlier theories (e.g., by Alfred Wegener) of continental drift were that continents 'plowed' through the sea. The idea that the seafloor itself moves (and carries the continents with it) as it expands from a central axis was proposed by Harry Hess from Princeton University in the 1960s. The theory is well-accepted now, and the phenomenon is known to be caused by convection currents in the plastic, very weak upper mantle, or asthenosphere.

- a. Deposition
- b. Diagenesis
- c. Saltation
- d. Seafloor spreading

34. The _____ is the geologic eon before the Archean. It started at Earth's formation about 4.6 billion years ago (4,600 Ma), and ended roughly 3.8 billion years ago, though the latter date varies according to different sources.
- a. 1509 Istanbul earthquake
- b. Hadean
- c. 1700 Cascadia earthquake
- d. 1703 Genroku earthquake

35. A _____ column (or _____) is a column of rising air in the lower altitudes of the Earth's atmosphere. They are created by the uneven heating of the Earth's surface from solar radiation, and an example of convection. The Sun warms the ground, which in turn warms the air directly above it.
- a. Thermal
- b. 1700 Cascadia earthquake
- c. 1509 Istanbul earthquake
- d. 1703 Genroku earthquake

36. A _____ is a phenomenon of fluid dynamics that occurs in situations where there are temperature differences within a body of liquid or gas.

Fluids are materials that exhibit the property of flow. Both gases and liquids have fluid properties, and in sufficient quantity, even particulate solids such as salt, grain, and gravel show some fluid properties. When a volume of fluid is heated, it expands and becomes less dense and thus more buoyant than the surrounding fluid. The colder, denser fluid settles underneath the warmer, less dense fluid and forces it to rise. Such movement is called convection, and the moving body of liquid is referred to as a _____.

- a. 1700 Cascadia earthquake
- b. 1703 Genroku earthquake
- c. Convection cell
- d. 1509 Istanbul earthquake

37. _____ is a technique used to date materials, usually based on a comparison between the observed abundance of a naturally occurring radioactive isotope and its decay products, using known decay rates. It is the principal source of information about the absolute age of rocks and other geological features, including the age of the Earth itself, and can be used to date a wide range of natural and man-made materials. Together with stratigraphic principles, _____ methods are used in geochronology to establish the geological time scale.

a. Paleomagnetism
b. Radiometric dating
c. Chronozone
d. Global Standard Stratigraphic Age

38. _____ is any particulate matter that can be transported by fluid flow, and which eventually is deposited.

They are most often transported by water (fluvial processes) transported by wind (aeolian processes) and glaciers. Beach sands and river channel deposits are examples of fluvial transport and deposition, though _____ also often settles out of slow-moving or standing water in lakes and oceans.

a. Brickearth
b. Bovey Beds
c. Quicksand
d. Sediment

39. The _____ is the mechanically weak ductily-deforming region of the upper mantle of the Earth. It lies below the lithosphere, at depths between 100 and 200 km (~ 62 and 124 miles) below the surface, but perhaps extending as deep as 400 km (~ 249 miles.)

The _____ is a portion of the upper mantle just below the lithosphere that is involved in plate movements and isostatic adjustments. In spite of its heat, pressures keep it plastic, and it has a relatively low density. Seismic waves pass relatively slowly through the _____, compared to the overlying lithospheric mantle, thus it has been called the low-velocity zone. This was the observation that originally alerted seismologists to its presence and gave some information about its physical properties, as the speed of seismic waves decreases with decreasing rigidity.

a. AL 333
b. AL 129-1
c. AASHTO Soil Classification System
d. Asthenosphere

40. In geology, a _____ is a location on the Earth's surface that has experienced active volcanism for a long period of time.

J. Tuzo Wilson came up with the idea in 1963 that volcanic chains like the Hawaiian Islands result from the slow movement of a tectonic plate across a 'fixed' _____ deep beneath the surface of the planet.

a. 1703 Genroku earthquake
b. 1509 Istanbul earthquake
c. 1700 Cascadia earthquake
d. Hotspot

41. _____ is molten rock expelled by a volcano during eruption. When first expelled from a volcanic vent, it is a liquid at temperatures from 700 >°C to 1,200 >°C (1,300 >°F to 2,200 >°F.) Although _____ is quite viscous, with about 100,000 times the viscosity of water, it can flow great distances before cooling and solidifying, because of both its thixotropic and shear thinning properties.

a. Supervolcano
b. Pit crater
c. Volcanic ash
d. Lava

42. The _____, is a geologic eon before the Proterozoic and Paleoproterozoic, before 2.5 Ga (billion years ago, or 2,500 Ma.) Instead of being based on stratigraphy, this date is defined chronometrically. The lower boundary (starting point) has not been officially recognized by the International Commission on Stratigraphy, but it is usually set to 3.8 Ga, at the end of the Hadean eon.

a. Archean
c. AL 333

b. AASHTO Soil Classification System
d. AL 129-1

43. In geology, a _____ is a place where the Earth's crust and lithosphere are being pulled apart and is an example of extensional tectonics.

Typical _____ features are a central linear downdropped fault segment, called a graben, with parallel normal faulting and _____-flank uplifts on either side forming a _____ valley, where the _____ remains above sea level. The axis of the _____ area commonly contains volcanic rocks and active volcanism is a part of many, but not all active _____ systems.

a. 1700 Cascadia earthquake
c. 1509 Istanbul earthquake

b. Rift
d. 1703 Genroku earthquake

44. A _____ is a mountain rising from the ocean seafloor that does not reach to the water's surface (sea level), and thus is not an island. These are typically formed from extinct volcanoes, that rise abruptly and are usually found rising from a seafloor of 1,000-4,000 meters depth. They are defined by oceanographers as independent features that rise to at least 1,000 meters above the seafloor.

a. 1700 Cascadia earthquake
c. 1509 Istanbul earthquake

b. 1703 Genroku earthquake
d. Seamount

45. A _____ or dyke in geology is a type of sheet intrusion referring to any geologic body that cuts discordantly across

- planar wall rock structures, such as bedding or foliation
- massive rock formations, like igneous/magmatic intrusions and salt diapirs.

They can therefore be either intrusive or sedimentary in origin.

An intrusive _____ is an igneous body with a very high aspect ratio, which means that its thickness is usually much smaller than the other two dimensions. Thickness can vary from sub-centimeter scale to many meters and the lateral dimensions can extend over many kilometers. A _____ is an intrusion into an opening cross-cutting fissure, shouldering aside other pre-existing layers or bodies of rock; this implies that a _____ is always younger than the rocks that contain it.

a. Schmidt hammer
c. Geopetal

b. Pneumatolysis
d. Dike

46. In geology, a _____ or _____ line is a planar fracture in rock in which the rock on one side of the fracture has moved with respect to the rock on the other side. Large faults within the Earth's crust are the result of differential or shear motion and active _____ zones are the causal locations of most earthquakes. Earthquakes are caused by energy release during rapid slippage along a _____.

a. Stack
c. Dali

b. Combe
d. Fault

Chapter 2. Plate Tectonics: A Unifying Theory

47. The _____ is a continental transform fault that runs a length of roughly 800 miles (1,300 km) through California in the United States. The fault's motion is right-lateral strike-slip (horizontal motion.) It forms the tectonic boundary between the Pacific Plate and the North American Plate.
    a. 1700 Cascadia earthquake
    b. 1703 Genroku earthquake
    c. 1509 Istanbul earthquake
    d. San Andreas fault

48. _____ occurs typically around intrusive igneous rocks as a result of the temperature increase caused by the intrusion of magma into cooler country rock. The area surrounding the intrusion (called aureoles) where the _____ effects are present is called the metamorphic aureole. Contact metamorphic rocks are usually known as hornfels.
    a. Gibraltar Arc
    b. Paralithic
    c. Contact metamorphism
    d. Perched coastline

49. _____ is the solid-state recrystallization of pre-existing rocks due to changes in physical and chemical conditions, primarily heat, pressure, and the introduction of chemically active fluids. Both mineralogical, chemical and crystallographic changes can occur during this process.

    Three types of _____ exist: dynamic, contact and regional.

    a. Detritus
    b. Reading Prong
    c. Compression
    d. Metamorphism

50. _____ is an igneous, volcanic rock, of intermediate composition, with aphanitic to porphyritic texture. The mineral assemblage is typically dominated by plagioclase plus pyroxene and/or hornblende. Magnetite, zircon, apatite, ilmenite, biotite, and garnet are common accessory minerals.
    a. AL 129-1
    b. AL 333
    c. AASHTO Soil Classification System
    d. Andesite

51. The _____ is a name given in the late 19th century by British explorer John Walter Gregory to the continuous geographic trough, approximately 6,000 kilometres (3,700 mi) in length, that runs from northern Syria in Southwest Asia to central Mozambique in East Africa. The name continues in some usages, although it is today considered geologically imprecise as it includes what are today regarded as separate, since 1869 due to the Suez Canal Company project, although related rift and fault systems. Today, the term is most often used to refer to the valley of the East African Rift, the divergent plate boundary which extends from the Afar Triple Junction southward across eastern Africa, and is in the process of splitting the African Plate into two new separate plates.
    a. Great Rift Valley
    b. 1509 Istanbul earthquake
    c. 1703 Genroku earthquake
    d. 1700 Cascadia earthquake

52. A _____ is a compound containing an anion in which one or more central silicon atoms are surrounded by electronegative ligands. This definition is broad enough to include species such as hexafluorosilicate ('fluorosilicate'), $[SiF_6]^{2-}$, but the _____ species that are encountered most often consist of silicon with oxygen as the ligand. _____ anions, with a negative net electrical charge, must have that charge balanced by other cations to make an electrically neutral compound.
    a. 1703 Genroku earthquake
    b. 1509 Istanbul earthquake
    c. 1700 Cascadia earthquake
    d. Silicate

Chapter 2. Plate Tectonics: A Unifying Theory

53. The _____ make up the largest and most important class of rock-forming minerals, comprising approximately 90 percent of the crust of the Earth. They are classified based on the structure of their silicate group. _____ all contain silicon and oxygen.
   a. Silicate minerals
   b. 1700 Cascadia earthquake
   c. Mineraloid
   d. 1509 Istanbul earthquake

54. In geology, _____ is the process that takes place at convergent boundaries by which one tectonic plate moves under another tectonic plate, sinking into the Earth's mantle, as the plates converge. A _____ zone is an area on Earth where two tectonic plates move towards one another and _____ occurs. Rates of _____ are typically measured in centimeters per year, with the average rate of convergence being approximately 2 to 8 centimeters per year (about the rate a fingernail grows.)
   a. Divergent boundary
   b. Forearc
   c. Motagua Fault
   d. Subduction

55. _____ defines an important group of generally dark-colored rock-forming inosilicate minerals, composed of double chain SiO_4 tetrahedra, linked at the vertices and generally containing ions of iron and/or magnesium in their structures. They crystallize into two crystal systems, monoclinic and orthorhombic. In chemical composition and general characteristics they are similar to the pyroxenes. They are minerals of either igneous or metamorphic origin; in the former case occurring as constituents (hornblende) of igneous rocks, such as granite, diorite, andesite and others. Those of metamorphic origin include examples such as those developed in limestones by contact metamorphism (tremolite) and those formed by the alteration of other ferromagnesian minerals (hornblende).
   a. Amphibole
   b. AL 129-1
   c. AASHTO Soil Classification System
   d. AL 333

56. The _____ is an oceanic tectonic plate in the eastern Pacific Ocean basin off the west coast of South America.

The eastern margin is a convergent boundary subduction zone under the South American Plate and the Andes Mountains, forming the Peru-Chile Trench. The southern side is a divergent boundary with the Antarctic Plate, the Chile Rise, where seafloor spreading permits magma to rise.

   a. Juan de Fuca Plate
   b. Conway Reef Plate
   c. Timor Plate
   d. Nazca plate

57. A _____ is a chain of volcanic islands or mountains formed by plate tectonics as an oceanic tectonic plate subducts under another tectonic plate and produces magma. There are two types of these: oceanic arcs (commonly called island arcs, a type of archipelago) and continental arcs. In the former, oceanic crust subducts beneath other oceanic crust on an adjacent plate, while in the latter case the oceanic crust subducts beneath continental crust. In some situations, a single subduction zone may show both aspects along its length, as part of a plate subducts beneath a continent and part beneath adjacent oceanic crust.
   a. 1509 Istanbul earthquake
   b. Volcanic arc
   c. 1700 Cascadia earthquake
   d. 1703 Genroku earthquake

58. _____ refers to a large group of dark, coarse-grained, intrusive igneous rocks chemically equivalent to basalt. The rocks are plutonic, formed when molten magma is trapped beneath the Earth's surface and cools into a crystalline mass.

The vast majority of the Earth's surface is underlain by _____ within the oceanic crust, produced by basalt magmatism at mid-ocean ridges.

  a. Gabbro
  b. 1509 Istanbul earthquake
  c. 1703 Genroku earthquake
  d. 1700 Cascadia earthquake

59. A _____ is a dense, coarse-grained igneous rock, consisting mostly of the minerals olivine and pyroxene. _____ is ultramafic, as the rock contains less than 45% silica. It is high in magnesium, reflecting the high proportions of magnesium-rich olivine, with appreciable iron.

_____ is the dominant rock of the upper part of the Earth's mantle. The compositions of _____ nodules found in certain basalts and diamond pipes (kimberlites) are of special interest, because they provide samples of the Earth's Mantle roots of continents brought up from depths from about 30 km or so to depths at least as great as about 200 km.

  a. 1703 Genroku earthquake
  b. 1509 Istanbul earthquake
  c. 1700 Cascadia earthquake
  d. Peridotite

60. A _____ or transform boundary is a fault which runs along the boundary of a tectonic plate. The relative motion of such plates is horizontal in either sinistral or dextral direction. Typically, some vertical motion may also exist, but the principal vectors in a _____ are oriented horizontally.
  a. Sag pond
  b. Crenulation
  c. Transform fault
  d. Graben

61. The _____ is a tectonic plate arising from the Juan de Fuca Ridge, and subducting under the northerly portion of the western side of the North American Plate at the Cascadia subduction zone. It is bounded on the south by the Blanco Fracture Zone, on the north by the Nootka Fault, and along the west by the Pacific Plate. The _____ was originally part of the once-vast Farallon Plate, now largely subducted under the North American Plate, and has since fractured into three pieces.
  a. Kermadec Plate
  b. North American Plate
  c. Lhasa Plate
  d. Juan de Fuca plate

62. _____ is an active undersea volcano that lies approximately 48 km (30 mi) off the southeast coast of the island of Hawai>Ê»i. It is located on the flank of Mauna Loa, the largest shield volcano on Earth. _____ is the newest volcano in the Hawaiian-Emperor seamount chain, a string of volcanoes that stretches over 5,800 km (3,604 mi) northwest of LÅ >Ê»ihi and the island of Hawai>Ê»i. In 1996, Loihi was the site of the first ever directly observed eruption of an active underwater volcano in Hawai>Ê»i.
  a. Principle of inclusions and components
  b. Pahoehoe lava
  c. Loihi Seamount
  d. Rockall

63. A _____ is an upwelling of abnormally hot rock within the Earth's mantle. As the heads of mantle plumes can partly melt when they reach shallow depths, they are thought to be the cause of volcanic centers known as hotspots and probably also to have caused flood basalts. It is a secondary way that Earth loses heat, much less important in this regard than is heat loss at plate margins.

a. Seismic refraction
b. Mazuku
c. Strainmeter
d. Mantle plume

64. The _____ is a tectonic plate covering most of North America, Greenland and part of Siberia. It extends eastward to the Mid-Atlantic Ridge and westward to the Chersky Range in eastern Siberia. The plate includes both continental and oceanic crust. The interior of the main continental landmass includes an extensive granitic core called a craton. Along most of the edges of this craton are fragments of crustal material called terranes, accreted to the craton by tectonic actions over the long span of geologic time. It is believed that much of North America west of the Rockies is composed of such terranes.
   a. Philippine Sea Plate
   b. Burma Plate
   c. Kermadec Plate
   d. North American plate

65. The _____ is an oceanic tectonic plate beneath the Pacific Ocean.

To the north the easterly side is a divergent boundary with the Explorer Plate, the Juan de Fuca Plate and the Gorda Plate forming respectively the Explorer Ridge, the Juan de Fuca Ridge and the Gorda Ridge. In the middle the easterly side is a transform boundary with the North American Plate along the San Andreas Fault and a boundary with the Cocos Plate.

   a. Somali Plate
   b. Gorda Plate
   c. Conway Reef Plate
   d. Pacific plate

66. A _____ is in geology an area where, as a result of metamorphism, the same combination of minerals occur in the bed rocks. These zones occur because most metamorphic minerals are only stable in certain intervals of temperature and pressure.

The temperature and pressure at which the mineralogical composition of a rock equilibrated can vary laterally through a metamorphic terrane.

   a. Tephra
   b. Magma
   c. Metamorphic rock
   d. Metamorphic zone

67. The _____ was a period of mountain building in western North America, which started in the Late Cretaceous, 70 to 80 million years ago, and ended 35 to 55 million years ago. The exact duration and ages of beginning and end of the orogeny are in dispute, as is the cause. The _____ occurred in a series of pulses, with quiescent phases intervening. The major feature that was created by this orogeny was the Rocky Mountains, but evidence of this orogeny can be found from Alaska to northern Mexico, with the easternmost extent of the mountain-building represented by the Black Hills of South Dakota.
   a. Pan-African orogeny
   b. Kaikoura Orogeny
   c. Sevier orogeny
   d. Laramide orogeny

Chapter 3. Minerals—The Building Blocks of Rocks

1. _____ is fossil tree resin, which is appreciated for its color and beauty. Good quality _____ is used for the manufacture of ornamental objects and jewelry. Although not mineralized, it is often classified as a gemstone.

A common misconception is that _____ is made of tree sap; it is not. Sap is the fluid that circulates through a plant's vascular system, while resin is the semi-solid amorphous organic substance secreted in pockets and canals through epithelial cells of the plant.

   a. AASHTO Soil Classification System
   c. AL 333
   b. AL 129-1
   d. Amber

2. The _____, is a geologic eon before the Proterozoic and Paleoproterozoic, before 2.5 Ga (billion years ago, or 2,500 Ma.) Instead of being based on stratigraphy, this date is defined chronometrically. The lower boundary (starting point) has not been officially recognized by the International Commission on Stratigraphy, but it is usually set to 3.8 Ga, at the end of the Hadean eon.
   a. AL 129-1
   c. AL 333
   b. AASHTO Soil Classification System
   d. Archean

3. _____ are a group of rock-forming tectosilicate minerals which make up as much as 60% of the Earth's crust.

_____ crystallize from magma in both intrusive and extrusive igneous rocks, as veins, and are also present in many types of metamorphic rock. Rock formed entirely of plagioclase feldspar is known as anorthosite.

   a. Feldspars
   c. 1509 Istanbul earthquake
   b. 1700 Cascadia earthquake
   d. 1703 Genroku earthquake

4. _____ is a common and widely occurring type of intrusive, felsic, igneous rock. _____ has a medium to coarse texture, occasionally with some individual crystals larger than the groundmass forming a rock known as porphyry. Granites can be pink to dark gray or even black, depending on their chemistry and mineralogy.
   a. 1700 Cascadia earthquake
   c. 1703 Genroku earthquake
   b. 1509 Istanbul earthquake
   d. Granite

5. A _____ is a compound containing an anion in which one or more central silicon atoms are surrounded by electronegative ligands. This definition is broad enough to include species such as hexafluorosilicate ('fluorosilicate'), $[SiF_6]^{2-}$, but the _____ species that are encountered most often consist of silicon with oxygen as the ligand. _____ anions, with a negative net electrical charge, must have that charge balanced by other cations to make an electrically neutral compound.
   a. 1703 Genroku earthquake
   c. 1509 Istanbul earthquake
   b. 1700 Cascadia earthquake
   d. Silicate

6. The _____ make up the largest and most important class of rock-forming minerals, comprising approximately 90 percent of the crust of the Earth. They are classified based on the structure of their silicate group. _____ all contain silicon and oxygen.
   a. Mineraloid
   c. Silicate minerals
   b. 1700 Cascadia earthquake
   d. 1509 Istanbul earthquake

Chapter 3. Minerals—The Building Blocks of Rocks

7. _____ defines an important group of generally dark-colored rock-forming inosilicate minerals, composed of double chain SiO$_4$ tetrahedra, linked at the vertices and generally containing ions of iron and/or magnesium in their structures. They crystallize into two crystal systems, monoclinic and orthorhombic. In chemical composition and general characteristics they are similar to the pyroxenes. They are minerals of either igneous or metamorphic origin; in the former case occurring as constituents (hornblende) of igneous rocks, such as granite, diorite, andesite and others. Those of metamorphic origin include examples such as those developed in limestones by contact metamorphism (tremolite) and those formed by the alteration of other ferromagnesian minerals (hornblende).

   a. AL 129-1
   b. AASHTO Soil Classification System
   c. AL 333
   d. Amphibole

8. In geology, _____ is transported rock debris overlying the solid bedrock. The term is also sometimes refers to organic debris so-transported. In the largest sense, it refers to the material left behind by retreating continental glaciers.

   a. Patterned ground
   b. Geodiversity
   c. Platform cover
   d. Drift

9. A _____ or gem is a piece of attractive mineral, which -- when cut and polished -- is used to make jewelry or other adornments. However certain rocks, and organic materials are not minerals, but are still used for jewelry, and are therefore often considered to be gemstones as well. Most gemstones are hard, but some soft minerals are used in jewelry because of their lustre or other physical properties that have aesthetic value.

   a. Gemstone
   b. 1509 Istanbul earthquake
   c. 1703 Genroku earthquake
   d. 1700 Cascadia earthquake

10. A _____ is in geology an area where, as a result of metamorphism, the same combination of minerals occur in the bed rocks. These zones occur because most metamorphic minerals are only stable in certain intervals of temperature and pressure.

The temperature and pressure at which the mineralogical composition of a rock equilibrated can vary laterally through a metamorphic terrane.

   a. Magma
   b. Metamorphic rock
   c. Metamorphic zone
   d. Tephra

11. An _____ is a type of rock that contains minerals such as gemstones and metals that can be extracted through mining and refined for use. Samples of _____ in the form of exceptionally beautiful crystals, exotic layering visible when sectioned or polished or metallic presentations such as large nuggets or crystalline formations of metals such as gold or copper may command a value far beyond their value as mere _____ or raw metal for subsequent reduction to utilitarian purposes.

The grade or concentration of an _____ mineral, or metal, as well as its form of occurrence, will directly affect the costs associated with mining the _____.

   a. Ore genesis
   b. AL 129-1
   c. AASHTO Soil Classification System
   d. Ore

Chapter 3. Minerals—The Building Blocks of Rocks

12. _____ is the second most abundant mineral in the Earth's continental crust . It is made up of a framework of silicon-oxygen tetrahedra SiO_4, with each silicon shared between two oxygens to give the overall formula SiO_2. _____ has a hardness of 7 on the Mohs scale and a density of 2.65 g/cmÂ³.

   a. 1700 Cascadia earthquake
   b. Quartz
   c. 1509 Istanbul earthquake
   d. 1703 Genroku earthquake

13. A _____ is a free neutron that is Boltzmann distributed with kT = 0.024 eV (4.0×10^{-21} J) at room temperature. This gives characteristic (not average, or median) speed of 2.2 km/s. The name 'thermal' comes from their energy being that of the room temperature gas or material they are permeating.

   a. 1703 Genroku earthquake
   b. 1700 Cascadia earthquake
   c. 1509 Istanbul earthquake
   d. Thermal neutron

14. _____ is the electromagnetic interaction between delocalized electrons, called conduction electrons, and the metallic nuclei within metals. Understood as the sharing of 'free' electrons among a lattice of positively-charged ions (cations), _____ is sometimes compared with that of molten salts; however, this simplistic view holds true for very few metals. In a more quantum-mechanical view, the conduction electrons divide their density equally over all atoms that function as neutral (non-charged) entities.

   a. Metallic bonding
   b. 1703 Genroku earthquake
   c. 1509 Istanbul earthquake
   d. 1700 Cascadia earthquake

15. _____, in structural geology and related disciplines, describes the tendency of a rock to break along preferred planes of weakness.

Rocks deformed under very low to low metamorphic grade often develop planes along which the rock can easily be split. Slates are an example of a rock with a penetrative _____ caused partly by the realignment of phyllosilicate minerals with increasing flattening strain.

   a. Combe
   b. Cleavage
   c. Compaction
   d. Drainage system

16. The mineral _____ is a magnesium iron silicate with the formula $(Mg,Fe)_2SiO_4$. It is one of the most common minerals on Earth, and has also been identified in meteorites and on the Moon, Mars, and comet Wild 2.

The ratio of magnesium and iron varies between the two endmembers of the solid solution series: forsterite (Mg-endmember) and fayalite (Fe-endmember.)

   a. AL 333
   b. AL 129-1
   c. AASHTO Soil Classification System
   d. Olivine

17. _____ is an important tectosilicate mineral which forms igneous rock. The name is from the Greek for 'straight fracture,' because its two cleavage planes are at right angles to each other. An alternate name is alkali feldspar.

_____ is a common constituent of most granites and other felsic igneous rocks and often forms huge crystals and masses in pegmatite.

a. AL 333
b. AASHTO Soil Classification System
c. Orthoclase
d. AL 129-1

18. The _____ is the layer of igneous, sedimentary, and metamorphic rocks which form the continents and the areas of shallow seabed close to their shores, known as continental shelves. This layer is sometimes called sial due to more felsic, or granitic, bulk composition, which lies in contrast to the oceanic crust, called sima due to its mafic, or basaltic rock. (Based on the change in velocity of seismic waves, it is believed that at a certain depth sial becomes close in its physical properties to sima.
   a. Tectonic plates
   b. Continental crust
   c. Convergent boundary
   d. Nappe

19. _____ is the part of Earth's lithosphere that surfaces in the ocean basins. _____ is primarily composed of mafic rocks, or sima. It is thinner than continental crust, or sial, generally less than 10 kilometers thick, however it is denser, having a mean density of about 3.3 grams per cubic centimeter.
   a. AL 129-1
   b. AL 333
   c. AASHTO Soil Classification System
   d. Oceanic crust

20. Two important classifications of weathering processes exist -- physical and _____. Mechanical or physical weathering involves the breakdown of rocks and soils through direct contact with atmospheric conditions, such as heat, water, ice and pressure. The second classification, _____, involves the direct effect of atmospheric chemicals or biologically produced chemicals (also known as biological weathering) in the breakdown of rocks, soils and minerals.
   a. 1509 Istanbul earthquake
   b. Physical weathering
   c. Chemical weathering
   d. Weathering

21. _____ is the decomposition of Earth rocks, soils and their minerals through direct contact with the planet's atmosphere. _____ occurs in situ, or 'with no movement', and thus should not be confused with erosion, which involves the movement of rocks and minerals by agents such as water, ice, wind and gravity.

Two important classifications of _____ processes exist -- physical and chemical _____.

   a. Frost disintegration
   b. Weathering
   c. 1509 Istanbul earthquake
   d. Physical weathering

22. In chemistry, a _____ is a salt or ester of carbonic acid.

To test for the presence of the _____ anion in a salt, the addition of dilute mineral acid (e.g. hydrochloric acid) will yield carbon dioxide gas.

_____-containing salts are industrially and mineralogically ubiquitous.

   a. 1703 Genroku earthquake
   b. 1509 Istanbul earthquake
   c. Carbonate
   d. 1700 Cascadia earthquake

23. The _____ is the geologic eon before the Archean. It started at Earth's formation about 4.6 billion years ago (4,600 Ma), and ended roughly 3.8 billion years ago, though the latter date varies according to different sources.

Chapter 3. Minerals—The Building Blocks of Rocks

a. 1703 Genroku earthquake
b. 1509 Istanbul earthquake
c. 1700 Cascadia earthquake
d. Hadean

24. The chemical compound silicon dioxide, also known as _____ , is an oxide of silicon with a chemical formula of SiO_2 and has been known for its hardness since antiquity. _____ is most commonly found in nature as sand or quartz, as well as in the cell walls of diatoms. It is a principal component of most types of glass and substances such as concrete.
    a. Silica
    b. 1703 Genroku earthquake
    c. 1509 Istanbul earthquake
    d. 1700 Cascadia earthquake

25. _____ is a common phyllosilicate mineral within the mica group, with the approximate chemical formula K(Mg, Fe)$_3$AlSi$_3$O$_{10}$(F, OH)$_2$. More generally, it refers to the dark mica series, primarily a solid-solution series between the iron-endmember annite, and the magnesium-endmember phlogopite; more aluminous endmembers include siderophyllite.
    a. 1700 Cascadia earthquake
    b. 1703 Genroku earthquake
    c. 1509 Istanbul earthquake
    d. Biotite

26. _____ is a naturally occurring material composed primarily of fine-grained minerals, which show plasticity through a variable range of water content, and which can be hardened when dried and/or fired. _____ deposits are mostly composed of _____ minerals (phyllosilicate minerals), minerals which impart plasticity and harden when fired and/or dried, and variable amounts of water trapped in the mineral structure by polar attraction. Organic materials which do not impart plasticity may also be a part of _____ deposits.
    a. 1703 Genroku earthquake
    b. 1509 Istanbul earthquake
    c. 1700 Cascadia earthquake
    d. Clay

27. _____ are hydrous aluminium phyllosilicates, sometimes with variable amounts of iron, magnesium, alkali metals, alkaline earths and other cations. Clays have structures similar to the micas and therefore form flat hexagonal sheets. _____ are common weathering products (including weathering of feldspar) and low temperature hydrothermal alteration products.
    a. 1700 Cascadia earthquake
    b. Kaolinite
    c. Clay minerals
    d. 1509 Istanbul earthquake

28. _____ is a carbonate mineral and the most stable polymorph of calcium carbonate ($CaCO_3$.) The other polymorphs are the minerals aragonite and vaterite. Aragonite will change to _____ at 470>°C, and vaterite is even less stable.

_____ is a common constituent of sedimentary rocks, limestone in particular, much of which is formed from the shells of dead marine organisms. Approximately 10% of sedimentary rock is limestone.

   a. Calcite
   b. 1509 Istanbul earthquake
   c. 1703 Genroku earthquake
   d. 1700 Cascadia earthquake

29. _____ is the name of a sedimentary carbonate rock and a mineral, both composed of calcium magnesium carbonate CaMg$_2$ found in crystals.

_____ rock (also dolostone) is composed predominantly of the mineral _____. Limestone that is partially replaced by _____ is referred to as dolomitic limestone, or in old U.S. geologic literature as magnesian limestone.

a. Porcellanite
b. Metasediment
c. Dolostone
d. Dolomite

30. _____ or dolomite rock is a sedimentary carbonate rock that contains a high percentage of the mineral dolomite. In old U.S.G.S. publications it was referred to as magnesian limestone. Most _____ formed as a magnesium replacement of limestone or lime mud prior to lithification.
   a. Pelagic sediments
   b. Jasperoid
   c. Lithification
   d. Dolostone

31. _____ is a mineral composed of calcium fluoride, CaF_2. It is an isometric mineral with a cubic habit, though octahedral and more complex isometric forms are not uncommon. Cubic crystals up to 20 cm across have been found at Dalnegorsk, Russia.

_____ may occur as a vein deposit, especially with metallic minerals, where it often forms a part of the gangue (the worthless 'host-rock' in which valuable minerals occur) and may be associated with galena, sphalerite, barite, quartz, and calcite. It is a common mineral in deposits of hydrothermal origin and has been noted as a primary mineral in granites and other igneous rocks and as a common minor constituent of dolostone and limestone.

   a. 1509 Istanbul earthquake
   b. 1703 Genroku earthquake
   c. 1700 Cascadia earthquake
   d. Fluorite

32. _____ is a sedimentary rock composed largely of the mineral calcite (calcium carbonate: $CaCO_3$.) The deposition of _____ strata is often a by-product and indicator of biological activity in the geologic record. Calcium (along with nitrogen, phosphorus, and potassium) is a key mineral to plant nutrition: soils overlying _____ bedrock tend to be pre-fertilized with calcium.
   a. 1700 Cascadia earthquake
   b. 1509 Istanbul earthquake
   c. 1703 Genroku earthquake
   d. Limestone

33. The _____ Era, is the most recent of the three classic geological eras and covers the period from 65.5 million years ago to the present. It is marked by the Cretaceous-Tertiary extinction event at the end of the Cretaceous that saw the demise of the last non-avian dinosaurs and the end of the Mesozoic Era. The _____ era is ongoing.
   a. 1509 Istanbul earthquake
   b. 1700 Cascadia earthquake
   c. 1703 Genroku earthquake
   d. Cenozoic

34. _____ is a very coarse-grained igneous rock that has a grain size of 20 mm or more; such rocks are referred to as pegmatitic.

Most _____ is composed of quartz, feldspar and mica; in essence a 'granite'. Rarer 'intermediate' and 'mafic' _____ containing amphibole, Ca-plagioclase feldspar, pyroxene and other minerals are known, found in recrystallised zones and apophyses associated with large layered intrusions.

   a. 1509 Istanbul earthquake
   b. 1703 Genroku earthquake
   c. 1700 Cascadia earthquake
   d. Pegmatite

Chapter 3. Minerals—The Building Blocks of Rocks

35. The _____ characterizes the scratch resistance of various minerals through the ability of a harder material to scratch a softer material. It was created in 1812 by the German mineralogist Friedrich Mohs and is one of several definitions of hardness in materials science. The method, however, is of great antiquity, having first been mentioned by Theophrastus in his treatise On Stones in ca 300 BC, followed by Pliny the Elder in his Naturalis Historia circa A.D.
   a. 1509 Istanbul earthquake
   b. 1700 Cascadia earthquake
   c. 1703 Genroku earthquake
   d. Mohs scale of mineral hardness

36. _____ is defined as the ratio of the density of a given solid or liquid substance to the density of water at a specific temperature and pressure, typically at 4 >°C (39 >°F) and 1 atm (760.00 mmHg) , making it a dimensionless quantity Substances with a _____ greater than one are denser than water, and so (ignoring surface tension effects) will sink in it, and those with a _____ of less than one are less dense than water, and so will float in it. _____ is a special case of, or in some usages synonymous with, relative density, with the latter term often preferred in modern scientific writing.
   a. 1509 Istanbul earthquake
   b. 1700 Cascadia earthquake
   c. 1703 Genroku earthquake
   d. Specific gravity

37. An _____ is a confined aquifer containing groundwater that will flow upward through a well without the need for pumping. Water may even reach the ground surface if the natural pressure is high enough, in which case the well is called a flowing artesian well. An aquifer provides the water for an artesian well.
   a. AL 129-1
   b. AL 333
   c. AASHTO Soil Classification System
   d. Artesian aquifer

38. _____ is a common extrusive volcanic rock. It is usually grey to black and fine-grained due to rapid cooling of lava at the surface of a planet. It may be porphyritic containing larger crystals in a fine matrix, or vesicular, or frothy scoria.
   a. 1703 Genroku earthquake
   b. 1509 Istanbul earthquake
   c. 1700 Cascadia earthquake
   d. Basalt

39. _____ is molten rock expelled by a volcano during eruption. When first expelled from a volcanic vent, it is a liquid at temperatures from 700 >°C to 1,200 >°C (1,300 >°F to 2,200 >°F.) Although _____ is quite viscous, with about 100,000 times the viscosity of water, it can flow great distances before cooling and solidifying, because of both its thixotropic and shear thinning properties.
   a. Pit crater
   b. Lava
   c. Volcanic ash
   d. Supervolcano

40. _____ is a naturally occurring glass formed as an extrusive igneous rock. It is produced when felsic lava extruded from a volcano cools without crystal growth. _____ is commonly found within the margins of rhyolitic lava flows known as _____ flows, where the chemical composition (high silica content) induces a high viscosity and polymerization degree of the lava.
   a. AL 129-1
   b. AL 333
   c. Obsidian
   d. AASHTO Soil Classification System

41. The _____ is the earliest of three geologic eras of the Phanerozoic eon. The _____ spanned from roughly 542 to 251 million years ago (ICS, 2004), and is subdivided into six geologic periods; from oldest to youngest they are: the Cambrian, Ordovician, Silurian, Devonian, Carboniferous, and Permian.

The _____ covers the time from the first appearance of abundant, soft-shelled fossils to the time when the continents were beginning to be dominated by large, relatively sophisticated reptiles and modern plants. The lower (oldest) boundary was classically set at the first appearance of creatures known as trilobites and archeocyathids.

a. 1509 Istanbul earthquake
c. 1700 Cascadia earthquake
b. 1703 Genroku earthquake
d. Paleozoic

42. The _____ is a geological eon representing a period before the first abundant complex life on Earth. The _____ extended from 2500 Ma to 542.0 >± 1.0 Ma (million years ago), and is the most recent part of the old, informally named 'e;Precambrian'e; time.

The Proterozoic consists of 3 geologic eras, from oldest to youngest:

- Paleoproterozoic
- Mesoproterozoic
- Neoproterozoic

The well-identified events were:

- The transition to an oxygenated atmosphere during the Mesoproterozoic.
- Several glaciations, including the hypothesized Snowball Earth during the Cryogenian period in the late Neoproterozoic.
- The Ediacaran Period (635 to 542 Ma) which is characterized by the evolution of abundant soft-bodied multicellular organisms.

The geoloic record of the Proterozoic is much better than that for the preceding Archean. In contrast to the deep-water deposits of the Archean, the Proterozoic features many strata that were laid down in extensive shallow epicontinental seas; furthermore, many of these rocks are less metamorphosed than Archean-age ones, and plenty are unaltered.

a. 1509 Istanbul earthquake
c. 1703 Genroku earthquake
b. 1700 Cascadia earthquake
d. Proterozoic Eon

43. _____ is one of the three main rock types (the others being sedimentary and metamorphic rock.) _____ is formed by magma (molten rock) being cooled and becoming solid . They may form with or without crystallization, either below the surface as intrusive (plutonic) rocks or on the surface as extrusive (volcanic) rocks. They make up approximately 95% of the upper part of the Earth's crust, but their great abundance is hidden on the Earth's surface by a relatively thin but widespread layer of sedimentary and metamorphic rocks.

a. AL 333
c. AASHTO Soil Classification System
b. AL 129-1
d. Igneous rock

Chapter 3. Minerals—The Building Blocks of Rocks

44. _____ is molten rock that is found beneath the surface of the Earth, and may also exist on other terrestrial planets. Besides molten rock, _____ may also contain suspended crystals and gas bubbles. _____ often collects in a _____ chamber inside a volcano. _____ is capable of intrusion into adjacent rocks, extrusion onto the surface as lava, and explosive ejection as tephra to form pyroclastic rock.
   - a. Volcanic rock
   - b. Laccolith
   - c. Rock cycle
   - d. Magma

45. _____ refers to natural mountain building, and may be studied as a tectonic structural event, (b) as a geographical event, and (c) a chronological event. Orogenic events (a) cause distinctive structural phenomena and related tectonic activity, (b) affect certain regions of rocks and crust, and (c) happen within a specific period of time.
   - a. Orogeny
   - b. Orogenesis
   - c. Antler orogeny
   - d. Alice Springs Orogeny

46. _____ is a silvery white and ductile member of the boron group of chemical elements. It has the symbol Al; its atomic number is 13. It is not soluble in water under normal circumstances. _____ is the most abundant metal in the Earth's crust, and the third most abundant element therein, after oxygen and silicon. It makes up about 8% by weight of the Earth'e;s solid surface.
   - a. AL 333
   - b. Aluminum
   - c. AASHTO Soil Classification System
   - d. AL 129-1

Chapter 4. Igneous Rocks and Intrusive Igneous Activity

1. A _____ is an opening in a planet's surface or crust, which allows hot, molten rock, ash, and gases to escape from below the surface. Volcanic activity involving the extrusion of rock tends to form mountains or features like mountains over a period of time.
   - a. 1509 Istanbul earthquake
   - b. 1703 Genroku earthquake
   - c. 1700 Cascadia earthquake
   - d. Volcano

2. A _____ is a pyroclastic material. They are extrusive igneous rocks, and are similar to pumice, which has so many cavities and is such low-density that it can float on water.
   - a. Wadati-Benioff zone
   - b. Pit crater
   - c. Cinder
   - d. Pyroclastic flow

3. A _____ or scoria cone is a steep conical hill of volcanic fragments that accumulate around and downwind from a volcanic vent. The rock fragments, often called cinders or scoria, are glassy and contain numerous gas bubbles 'frozen' into place as magma exploded into the air and then cooled quickly. Cinder cones range in size from tens to hundreds of meters tall.
   - a. 1509 Istanbul earthquake
   - b. 1703 Genroku earthquake
   - c. Cinder cone
   - d. 1700 Cascadia earthquake

4. The _____ is the zone of the ocean floor that separates the thin oceanic crust from thick continental crust. Continental margins constitute about 28% of the oceanic area.

   The transition from continental to oceanic crust commonly occurs within the outer part of the margin, called continental rise.
   - a. Cuspate forelands
   - b. Continental margin
   - c. Longshore drift
   - d. 1509 Istanbul earthquake

5. A _____ is a special-purpose map made to show geological features.

   The stratigraphic contour lines are drawn on the surface of a selected deep stratum, so that they can show the topographic trends of the strata under the ground. It is not always possible to properly show this when the strata are extremely fractured, mixed, in some discontinuities, or where they are otherwise disturbed.
   - a. 1700 Cascadia earthquake
   - b. 1509 Istanbul earthquake
   - c. Geologic map
   - d. 1703 Genroku earthquake

6. _____ is one of the three main rock types (the others being sedimentary and metamorphic rock.) _____ is formed by magma (molten rock) being cooled and becoming solid . They may form with or without crystallization, either below the surface as intrusive (plutonic) rocks or on the surface as extrusive (volcanic) rocks. They make up approximately 95% of the upper part of the Earth's crust, but their great abundance is hidden on the Earth's surface by a relatively thin but widespread layer of sedimentary and metamorphic rocks.
   - a. AL 333
   - b. AASHTO Soil Classification System
   - c. AL 129-1
   - d. Igneous rock

7. The _____ is the rigid outermost shell of a rocky planet.

In the Earth, the _____ includes the crust and the uppermost mantle, which constitute the hard and rigid outer layer of the planet. The _____ is underlain by the asthenosphere, the weaker, hotter, and deeper part of the upper mantle.

   a. Juan de Fuca Ridge   b. Continental drift
   c. Lithosphere   d. Gorda Ridge

8. _____ is molten rock that is found beneath the surface of the Earth, and may also exist on other terrestrial planets. Besides molten rock, _____ may also contain suspended crystals and gas bubbles. _____ often collects in a _____ chamber inside a volcano. _____ is capable of intrusion into adjacent rocks, extrusion onto the surface as lava, and explosive ejection as tephra to form pyroclastic rock.
   a. Laccolith   b. Rock cycle
   c. Volcanic rock   d. Magma

9. A _____ is in geology an area where, as a result of metamorphism, the same combination of minerals occur in the bed rocks. These zones occur because most metamorphic minerals are only stable in certain intervals of temperature and pressure.

The temperature and pressure at which the mineralogical composition of a rock equilibrated can vary laterally through a metamorphic terrane.

   a. Metamorphic rock   b. Magma
   c. Tephra   d. Metamorphic zone

10. _____ refers to natural mountain building, and may be studied as a tectonic structural event, (b) as a geographical event, and (c) a chronological event. Orogenic events (a) cause distinctive structural phenomena and related tectonic activity, (b) affect certain regions of rocks and crust, and (c) happen within a specific period of time.
   a. Orogeny   b. Antler orogeny
   c. Alice Springs Orogeny   d. Orogenesis

11. The lithosphere is broken up into what are called _____. In the case of Earth, there are eight major and many minor plates The lithospheric plates ride on the asthenosphere. These plates move in relation to one another at one of three types of plate boundaries: convergent, or collisional boundaries; divergent boundaries, also called spreading centers; and transform boundaries.
   a. Thrust fault   b. Gorda Ridge
   c. Copperbelt Province   d. Tectonic plates

12. A _____ in geology is an intrusive igneous rock body that crystallized from a magma slowly cooling below the surface of the Earth. Plutons include batholiths, dikes, sills, laccoliths, lopoliths, and other igneous bodies. In practice, '_____' usually refers to a distinctive mass of igneous rock, typically kilometers in dimension, without a tabular shape like those of dikes and sills.
   a. Migmatite   b. Vesicular texture
   c. Metamorphic zone   d. Pluton

Chapter 4. Igneous Rocks and Intrusive Igneous Activity

13. The _____, is a geologic eon before the Proterozoic and Paleoproterozoic, before 2.5 Ga (billion years ago, or 2,500 Ma.) Instead of being based on stratigraphy, this date is defined chronometrically. The lower boundary (starting point) has not been officially recognized by the International Commission on Stratigraphy, but it is usually set to 3.8 Ga, at the end of the Hadean eon.
    a. AASHTO Soil Classification System
    b. AL 129-1
    c. AL 333
    d. Archean

14. The _____ Era, is the most recent of the three classic geological eras and covers the period from 65.5 million years ago to the present. It is marked by the Cretaceous-Tertiary extinction event at the end of the Cretaceous that saw the demise of the last non-avian dinosaurs and the end of the Mesozoic Era. The _____ era is ongoing.
    a. Cenozoic
    b. 1700 Cascadia earthquake
    c. 1509 Istanbul earthquake
    d. 1703 Genroku earthquake

15. _____ are a group of rock-forming tectosilicate minerals which make up as much as 60% of the Earth's crust.

    _____ crystallize from magma in both intrusive and extrusive igneous rocks, as veins, and are also present in many types of metamorphic rock. Rock formed entirely of plagioclase feldspar is known as anorthosite.

    a. 1703 Genroku earthquake
    b. Feldspars
    c. 1700 Cascadia earthquake
    d. 1509 Istanbul earthquake

16. _____ is a term used in geology to refer to silicate minerals, magma, and rocks which are enriched in the lighter elements such as silicon, oxygen, aluminium, sodium, and potassium. _____ minerals are usually light in color and have specific gravities less than 3. Common _____ minerals include quartz, muscovite, orthoclase, and the sodium-rich plagioclase feldspars.
    a. Felsic
    b. Laccolith
    c. Magma
    d. Tephra

17. The _____ is the geologic eon before the Archean. It started at Earth's formation about 4.6 billion years ago (4,600 Ma), and ended roughly 3.8 billion years ago, though the latter date varies according to different sources.
    a. 1703 Genroku earthquake
    b. Hadean
    c. 1700 Cascadia earthquake
    d. 1509 Istanbul earthquake

18. _____ is molten rock expelled by a volcano during eruption. When first expelled from a volcanic vent, it is a liquid at temperatures from 700 >°C to 1,200 >°C (1,300 >°F to 2,200 >°F.) Although _____ is quite viscous, with about 100,000 times the viscosity of water, it can flow great distances before cooling and solidifying, because of both its thixotropic and shear thinning properties.
    a. Supervolcano
    b. Volcanic ash
    c. Pit crater
    d. Lava

19. _____ is an adjective describing a silicate mineral or rock that is rich in magnesium and iron; the term was derived by contracting 'magnesium' and 'ferric'. Most _____ minerals are dark in color and the specific gravity is greater than 3. Common rock-forming _____ minerals include olivine, pyroxene, amphibole, and biotite.

_____ lava, before cooling, has a low viscosity, in comparison to felsic lava, due to the lower silica content in _____ magma. Water and other volatiles can more easily and gradually escape from _____ lava, so eruptions of volcanoes made of _____ lavas are less explosively violent than felsic lava eruptions.

a. 1700 Cascadia earthquake

b. 1703 Genroku earthquake

c. Mafic

d. 1509 Istanbul earthquake

20. A _____ is a large emplacement of igneous intrusive rock that forms from cooled magma deep in the Earth's crust. they are almost always made mostly of felsic or intermediate rock-types, such as granite, quartz monzonite, or diorite

Although they may appear uniform, batholiths are in fact structures with complex histories and compositions.

a. Batholith

b. Tuff

c. Flood basalt

d. Great Dyke

21. The _____ is a geological eon representing a period before the first abundant complex life on Earth. The _____ extended from 2500 Ma to 542.0 >± 1.0 Ma (million years ago), and is the most recent part of the old, informally named 'e;Precambrian'e; time.

The Proterozoic consists of 3 geologic eras, from oldest to youngest:

- Paleoproterozoic
- Mesoproterozoic
- Neoproterozoic

The well-identified events were:

- The transition to an oxygenated atmosphere during the Mesoproterozoic.
- Several glaciations, including the hypothesized Snowball Earth during the Cryogenian period in the late Neoproterozoic.
- The Ediacaran Period (635 to 542 Ma) which is characterized by the evolution of abundant soft-bodied multicellular organisms.

The geoloic record of the Proterozoic is much better than that for the preceding Archean. In contrast to the deep-water deposits of the Archean, the Proterozoic features many strata that were laid down in extensive shallow epicontinental seas; furthermore, many of these rocks are less metamorphosed than Archean-age ones, and plenty are unaltered.

a. 1700 Cascadia earthquake

b. Proterozoic Eon

c. 1703 Genroku earthquake

d. 1509 Istanbul earthquake

22. The chemical compound silicon dioxide, also known as _____ , is an oxide of silicon with a chemical formula of SiO_2 and has been known for its hardness since antiquity. _____ is most commonly found in nature as sand or quartz, as well as in the cell walls of diatoms. It is a principal component of most types of glass and substances such as concrete.

Chapter 4. Igneous Rocks and Intrusive Igneous Activity

    a. 1703 Genroku earthquake
    c. 1509 Istanbul earthquake
    b. 1700 Cascadia earthquake
    d. Silica

23. A _____ is a compound containing an anion in which one or more central silicon atoms are surrounded by electronegative ligands. This definition is broad enough to include species such as hexafluorosilicate ('fluorosilicate'), $[SiF_6]^{2-}$, but the _____ species that are encountered most often consist of silicon with oxygen as the ligand. _____ anions, with a negative net electrical charge, must have that charge balanced by other cations to make an electrically neutral compound.
    a. 1703 Genroku earthquake
    c. 1509 Istanbul earthquake
    b. 1700 Cascadia earthquake
    d. Silicate

24. The _____ make up the largest and most important class of rock-forming minerals, comprising approximately 90 percent of the crust of the Earth. They are classified based on the structure of their silicate group. _____ all contain silicon and oxygen.
    a. Mineraloid
    c. 1509 Istanbul earthquake
    b. 1700 Cascadia earthquake
    d. Silicate minerals

25. _____ is an igneous rock of volcanic origin.

They are usually fine-grained or aphanitic to glassy in texture. They often contain clasts of other rocks and phenocrysts.

    a. Petrology
    c. Large igneous provinces
    b. Volcanic rock
    d. Serpentinite

26. _____ defines an important group of generally dark-colored rock-forming inosilicate minerals, composed of double chain SiO_4 tetrahedra, linked at the vertices and generally containing ions of iron and/or magnesium in their structures. They crystallize into two crystal systems, monoclinic and orthorhombic. In chemical composition and general characteristics they are similar to the pyroxenes. They are minerals of either igneous or metamorphic origin; in the former case occurring as constituents (hornblende) of igneous rocks, such as granite, diorite, andesite and others. Those of metamorphic origin include examples such as those developed in limestones by contact metamorphism (tremolite) and those formed by the alteration of other ferromagnesian minerals (hornblende).
    a. AL 333
    c. AASHTO Soil Classification System
    b. AL 129-1
    d. Amphibole

27. Two important classifications of weathering processes exist -- physical and _____. Mechanical or physical weathering involves the breakdown of rocks and soils through direct contact with atmospheric conditions, such as heat, water, ice and pressure. The second classification, _____, involves the direct effect of atmospheric chemicals or biologically produced chemicals (also known as biological weathering) in the breakdown of rocks, soils and minerals.
    a. Weathering
    c. Chemical weathering
    b. Physical weathering
    d. 1509 Istanbul earthquake

28. _____ is the decomposition of Earth rocks, soils and their minerals through direct contact with the planet's atmosphere. _____ occurs in situ, or 'with no movement', and thus should not be confused with erosion, which involves the movement of rocks and minerals by agents such as water, ice, wind and gravity.

Two important classifications of _____ processes exist -- physical and chemical _____.

a. 1509 Istanbul earthquake
b. Weathering
c. Physical weathering
d. Frost disintegration

29. The _____ Era is one of three geologic eras of the Phanerozoic eon. The division of time into eras dates back to Giovanni Arduino, in the 18th century, although his original name for the era now called the '_____' was 'Secondary' (making the modern era the 'Tertiary'.)

The _____ was a time of tectonic, climatic and evolutionary activity. The continents gradually shifted from a state of connectedness into their present configuration; the drifting provided for speciation and other important evolutionary developments.

a. 1700 Cascadia earthquake
b. 1509 Istanbul earthquake
c. 1703 Genroku earthquake
d. Mesozoic

30. _____ is a measure of the resistance of a fluid which is being deformed by either shear stress or extensional stress. In everyday terms (and for fluids only), _____ is 'thickness'. Thus, water is 'thin', having a lower _____, while honey is 'thick' having a higher _____.

a. Tensile stress
b. Thixotropy
c. Shear stress
d. Viscosity

31. _____ is a common phyllosilicate mineral within the mica group, with the approximate chemical formula $K(Mg, Fe)_3AlSi_3O_{10}(F, OH)_2$. More generally, it refers to the dark mica series, primarily a solid-solution series between the iron-endmember annite, and the magnesium-endmember phlogopite; more aluminous endmembers include siderophyllite.

a. 1509 Istanbul earthquake
b. 1703 Genroku earthquake
c. 1700 Cascadia earthquake
d. Biotite

32. The mineral _____ is a magnesium iron silicate with the formula $(Mg,Fe)_2SiO_4$. It is one of the most common minerals on Earth, and has also been identified in meteorites and on the Moon, Mars, and comet Wild 2.

The ratio of magnesium and iron varies between the two endmembers of the solid solution series: forsterite (Mg-endmember) and fayalite (Fe-endmember.)

a. AL 333
b. AL 129-1
c. AASHTO Soil Classification System
d. Olivine

33. The _____ are a group of important rock-forming silicate minerals found in many igneous and metamorphic rocks. They share a common structure consisting of single chains of silica tetrahedra and they crystallize in the monoclinic and orthorhombic systems. _____ have the general formula $XY(Si,Al)_2O_6$ (where X represents calcium, sodium, iron^{+2} and magnesium and more rarely zinc, manganese and lithium and Y represents ions of smaller size, such as chromium, aluminium, iron^{+3}, magnesium, manganese, scandium, titanium, vanadium and even iron^{+2}).

a. 1703 Genroku earthquake
b. 1700 Cascadia earthquake
c. Pyroxenes
d. 1509 Istanbul earthquake

Chapter 4. Igneous Rocks and Intrusive Igneous Activity

34. An _____ is the result of a sudden release of energy in the Earth's crust that creates seismic waves. They are recorded with a seismometer or the related and mostly obsolete Richter magnitude, with a magnitude 3 or lower _____ being mostly imperceptible and magnitude 7 causing serious damage over large areas.
   a. AASHTO Soil Classification System
   b. AL 333
   c. AL 129-1
   d. Earthquake

35. In geology, _____ refers to heat sources within the planet. _____ is technically an adjective (e.g., _____ energy) but in U.S. English the word has attained frequent use as a noun.

The planet's internal heat was originally generated during its accretion, due to gravitational binding energy, and since then additional heat has continued to be generated by decay heat from the radioactive decay of elements.

   a. Dali
   b. Diamond Head
   c. Stratification
   d. Geothermal

36. The _____ is the rate of increase in temperature per unit depth in the Earth. It varies with location and is typically measured by determining the bottom open-hole temperature after borehole drilling. To achieve accuracy the drilling fluid needs time to reach the ambient temperature.
   a. Geothermal heat pump
   b. Geothermal power
   c. Geothermal desalination
   d. Geothermal gradient

37. _____ is an important tectosilicate mineral which forms igneous rock. The name is from the Greek for 'straight fracture,' because its two cleavage planes are at right angles to each other. An alternate name is alkali feldspar.

_____ is a common constituent of most granites and other felsic igneous rocks and often forms huge crystals and masses in pegmatite.

   a. AASHTO Soil Classification System
   b. Orthoclase
   c. AL 333
   d. AL 129-1

38. _____ is a process of melting that takes place in the Earth's mantle. The melting temperatures are unlikely high enough to melt the entire source rock, and only portions of or some of the minerals they contain melt.
   a. Volcanic blocks
   b. Raton hotspot
   c. Submarine eruption
   d. Partial melting

39. The _____ is an informal name for the supereon comprising the eons of the geologic timescale that came before the current Phanerozoic eon. It spans from the formation of Earth around 4500 Mya (million years ago) to the evolution of abundant macroscopic hard-shelled animals, which marked the beginning of the Cambrian, the first period of the first era of the Phanerozoic eon, some 542 Mya. It is named after the Roman name for Wales - Cambria - where rocks from this age were first studied.
   a. Precambrian
   b. 1700 Cascadia earthquake
   c. 1509 Istanbul earthquake
   d. 1703 Genroku earthquake

40. _____ are igneous and meta-igneous rocks with very low silica content (less than 45%), generally >18% MgO, high FeO, low potassium, and are composed of usually greater than 90% mafic minerals (dark colored, high magnesium and iron content.) The Earth's mantle is considered to be composed of _____.

Chapter 4. Igneous Rocks and Intrusive Igneous Activity

a. AASHTO Soil Classification System
c. Ultramafic rocks
b. AL 129-1
d. AL 333

41. The _____ is the mechanically weak ductily-deforming region of the upper mantle of the Earth. It lies below the lithosphere, at depths between 100 and 200 km (~ 62 and 124 miles) below the surface, but perhaps extending as deep as 400 km (~ 249 miles.)

The _____ is a portion of the upper mantle just below the lithosphere that is involved in plate movements and isostatic adjustments. In spite of its heat, pressures keep it plastic, and it has a relatively low density. Seismic waves pass relatively slowly through the _____, compared to the overlying lithospheric mantle, thus it has been called the low-velocity zone. This was the observation that originally alerted seismologists to its presence and gave some information about its physical properties, as the speed of seismic waves decreases with decreasing rigidity.

a. AL 129-1
c. AL 333
b. AASHTO Soil Classification System
d. Asthenosphere

42. The _____ was a period of mountain building in western North America, which started in the Late Cretaceous, 70 to 80 million years ago, and ended 35 to 55 million years ago. The exact duration and ages of beginning and end of the orogeny are in dispute, as is the cause. The _____ occurred in a series of pulses, with quiescent phases intervening. The major feature that was created by this orogeny was the Rocky Mountains, but evidence of this orogeny can be found from Alaska to northern Mexico, with the easternmost extent of the mountain-building represented by the Black Hills of South Dakota.

a. Sevier orogeny
c. Pan-African orogeny
b. Laramide orogeny
d. Kaikoura Orogeny

43. _____ is the part of Earth's lithosphere that surfaces in the ocean basins. _____ is primarily composed of mafic rocks, or sima. It is thinner than continental crust, or sial, generally less than 10 kilometers thick, however it is denser, having a mean density of about 3.3 grams per cubic centimeter.

a. AL 333
c. AASHTO Soil Classification System
b. Oceanic crust
d. AL 129-1

44. _____ is a common and widely occurring type of intrusive, felsic, igneous rock. _____ has a medium to coarse texture, occasionally with some individual crystals larger than the groundmass forming a rock known as porphyry. Granites can be pink to dark gray or even black, depending on their chemistry and mineralogy.

a. 1703 Genroku earthquake
c. 1700 Cascadia earthquake
b. 1509 Istanbul earthquake
d. Granite

45. _____ is a naturally occurring glass formed as an extrusive igneous rock. It is produced when felsic lava extruded from a volcano cools without crystal growth. _____ is commonly found within the margins of rhyolitic lava flows known as _____ flows, where the chemical composition (high silica content) induces a high viscosity and polymerization degree of the lava.

a. AL 333
c. Obsidian
b. AASHTO Soil Classification System
d. AL 129-1

Chapter 4. Igneous Rocks and Intrusive Igneous Activity

46. The _____ is the earliest of three geologic eras of the Phanerozoic eon. The _____ spanned from roughly 542 to 251 million years ago (ICS, 2004), and is subdivided into six geologic periods; from oldest to youngest they are: the Cambrian, Ordovician, Silurian, Devonian, Carboniferous, and Permian.

The _____ covers the time from the first appearance of abundant, soft-shelled fossils to the time when the continents were beginning to be dominated by large, relatively sophisticated reptiles and modern plants. The lower (oldest) boundary was classically set at the first appearance of creatures known as trilobites and archeocyathids.

- a. 1509 Istanbul earthquake
- b. 1700 Cascadia earthquake
- c. 1703 Genroku earthquake
- d. Paleozoic

47. _____ is a term usually used to refer to igneous rock grain size. It means that the size of matrix grains in the rock are large enough to be distinguished with the unaided eye as opposed to aphanitic This texture forms by slow cooling of magma deep underground in the plutonic environment.
- a. 1700 Cascadia earthquake
- b. Petrified forest
- c. 1509 Istanbul earthquake
- d. Phaneritic

48. _____ is a volcanic rock texture characterised by, or containing many vesicles. The texture is often found in extrusive aphanitic igneous rock. The vesicles are small cavities formed by the expansion of bubbles of gas or steam during the solidification of the rock.
- a. Migmatite
- b. Laccolith
- c. Magma
- d. Vesicular texture

49. _____ is an igneous, volcanic rock, of intermediate composition, with aphanitic to porphyritic texture. The mineral assemblage is typically dominated by plagioclase plus pyroxene and/or hornblende. Magnetite, zircon, apatite, ilmenite, biotite, and garnet are common accessory minerals.
- a. AASHTO Soil Classification System
- b. AL 333
- c. AL 129-1
- d. Andesite

50. _____ is a common extrusive volcanic rock. It is usually grey to black and fine-grained due to rapid cooling of lava at the surface of a planet. It may be porphyritic containing larger crystals in a fine matrix, or vesicular, or frothy scoria.
- a. 1509 Istanbul earthquake
- b. Basalt
- c. 1703 Genroku earthquake
- d. 1700 Cascadia earthquake

51. _____ refers to a large group of dark, coarse-grained, intrusive igneous rocks chemically equivalent to basalt. The rocks are plutonic, formed when molten magma is trapped beneath the Earth's surface and cools into a crystalline mass.

The vast majority of the Earth's surface is underlain by _____ within the oceanic crust, produced by basalt magmatism at mid-ocean ridges.

- a. 1509 Istanbul earthquake
- b. 1703 Genroku earthquake
- c. Gabbro
- d. 1700 Cascadia earthquake

Chapter 4. Igneous Rocks and Intrusive Igneous Activity 41

52. A _____ is a dense, coarse-grained igneous rock, consisting mostly of the minerals olivine and pyroxene. _____ is ultramafic, as the rock contains less than 45% silica. It is high in magnesium, reflecting the high proportions of magnesium-rich olivine, with appreciable iron.

_____ is the dominant rock of the upper part of the Earth's mantle. The compositions of _____ nodules found in certain basalts and diamond pipes (kimberlites) are of special interest, because they provide samples of the Earth's Mantle roots of continents brought up from depths from about 30 km or so to depths at least as great as about 200 km.

a. 1703 Genroku earthquake
b. 1700 Cascadia earthquake
c. 1509 Istanbul earthquake
d. Peridotite

53. _____ is an igneous, volcanic (extrusive) rock, of felsic (silicon-rich) composition. It may have any texture from aphanitic to porphyritic. The mineral assemblage is usually quartz, alkali feldspar and plagioclase. Biotite and hornblende are common accessory minerals.

_____ can be considered as the extrusive equivalent to the plutonic granite rock, and consequently, outcroppings of it often bear a resemblance to granite. Due to their high content of silica and low iron and magnesium contents, _____ melts are highly polymerized and form highly viscous lavas.

a. Rhyolite
b. 1703 Genroku earthquake
c. 1509 Istanbul earthquake
d. 1700 Cascadia earthquake

54. _____ is the second most abundant mineral in the Earth's continental crust . It is made up of a framework of silicon-oxygen tetrahedra SiO_4, with each silicon shared between two oxygens to give the overall formula SiO_2. _____ has a hardness of 7 on the Mohs scale and a density of 2.65 g/cmÂ³.

a. 1700 Cascadia earthquake
b. 1703 Genroku earthquake
c. 1509 Istanbul earthquake
d. Quartz

55. _____ is a very coarse-grained igneous rock that has a grain size of 20 mm or more; such rocks are referred to as pegmatitic.

Most _____ is composed of quartz, feldspar and mica; in essence a 'granite'. Rarer 'intermediate' and 'mafic' _____ containing amphibole, Ca-plagioclase feldspar, pyroxene and other minerals are known, found in recrystallised zones and apophyses associated with large layered intrusions.

a. 1700 Cascadia earthquake
b. 1703 Genroku earthquake
c. Pegmatite
d. 1509 Istanbul earthquake

56. _____ is a rock composed of angular fragments of minerals or rocks in a matrix (cementing material), that may be similar or different in composition to the fragments. A _____ may have a variety of different origins, as indicated by the named types including sedimentary _____, tectonic _____, igneous _____, impact _____ and hydrothermal _____.

Sedimentary breccias are a type of clastic sedimentary rock which are composed of angular to subangular, randomly oriented clasts of other sedimentary rocks.

   a. 1509 Istanbul earthquake   b. Fault breccia
   c. Breccia   d. Ventifacts

57. _____ is a type of rock consisting of consolidated volcanic ash ejected from vents during a volcanic eruption. _____ is sometimes called tufa, particularly when used as construction material, although tufa also refers to a quite different rock.

The products of a volcanic eruption are volcanic gases, lava, steam, and tephra. Magma is blown apart when it interacts violently with volcanic gases and steam. Solid material produced and thrown into the air by such volcanic eruptions is called tephra, regardless of composition or fragment size. If the resulting pieces of ejecta are small enough, the material is called volcanic ash, defined as such particles less than 2 mm in diameter, sand-sized or smaller.

   a. Pyroclastic rocks   b. Coldwell Complex
   c. Country rock   d. Tuff

58. A _____ or dyke in geology is a type of sheet intrusion referring to any geologic body that cuts discordantly across

- planar wall rock structures, such as bedding or foliation
- massive rock formations, like igneous/magmatic intrusions and salt diapirs.

They can therefore be either intrusive or sedimentary in origin.

An intrusive _____ is an igneous body with a very high aspect ratio, which means that its thickness is usually much smaller than the other two dimensions. Thickness can vary from sub-centimeter scale to many meters and the lateral dimensions can extend over many kilometers. A _____ is an intrusion into an opening cross-cutting fissure, shouldering aside other pre-existing layers or bodies of rock; this implies that a _____ is always younger than the rocks that contain it.

   a. Schmidt hammer   b. Geopetal
   c. Pneumatolysis   d. Dike

59. _____ occurs typically around intrusive igneous rocks as a result of the temperature increase caused by the intrusion of magma into cooler country rock. The area surrounding the intrusion (called aureoles) where the _____ effects are present is called the metamorphic aureole. Contact metamorphic rocks are usually known as hornfels.
   a. Paralithic   b. Perched coastline
   c. Gibraltar Arc   d. Contact metamorphism

60. _____ is the removal of solids (sediment, soil, rock and other particles) in the natural environment. It usually occurs due to transport by wind, water, or ice; by down-slope creep of soil and other material under the force of gravity; or by living organisms, such as burrowing animals, in the case of bioerosion.

Chapter 4. Igneous Rocks and Intrusive Igneous Activity

_____ is distinguished from weathering, which is the process of chemical or physical breakdown of the minerals in the rocks, although the two processes may occur concurrently.

- a. Erosion
- b. AASHTO Soil Classification System
- c. AL 333
- d. AL 129-1

61. _____ is the solid-state recrystallization of pre-existing rocks due to changes in physical and chemical conditions, primarily heat, pressure, and the introduction of chemically active fluids. Both mineralogical, chemical and crystallographic changes can occur during this process.

Three types of _____ exist: dynamic, contact and regional.

- a. Detritus
- b. Reading Prong
- c. Compression
- d. Metamorphism

62. _____ is a region of the Colorado Plateau characterized by a cluster of vast and iconic sandstone buttes, the largest reaching 1,000 ft (300 m) above the valley floor. It is located on the southern border of Utah with northern Arizona (around >>36>°59>'N 110>°6>'W'#20;/'#20;>36.983>°N 110.1>°W>'#20;/'#20;36.983; -110.1), near the Four Corners area. The valley lies within the range of the Navajo Nation Reservation, and is accessible from U.S. Highway 163.

- a. Thirtynine Mile volcanic field
- b. Rano Kau
- c. Monument Valley
- d. 1509 Istanbul earthquake

63. A _____ is a volcanic landform created when magma hardens within a vent on an active volcano. When forming, a _____ can cause an extreme build-up of pressure if volatile-charged magma is trapped beneath it, and this can sometimes lead to an explosive eruption. If a plug is preserved, erosion may remove the surrounding rock while the erosion-resistant plug remains, producing a distinctive landform.

- a. 1509 Istanbul earthquake
- b. 1700 Cascadia earthquake
- c. 1703 Genroku earthquake
- d. Volcanic plug

64. A _____ is an igneous intrusion (or concordant pluton) that has been injected between two layers of sedimentary rock. The pressure of the magma is high enough that the overlying strata are forced upward, giving the _____ a dome or mushroom-like form with a generally planar base.

They tend to form at relatively shallow depths and are typically formed by relatively viscous magmas, such as those that crystallize to diorite, granodiorite, and granite. Cooling underground takes place slowly, giving time for larger crystals to form in the cooling magma. The surface rock above the _____ often erodes away completely, leaving the core mound of igneous rock.

- a. Serpentinite
- b. Rock cycle
- c. Volcanic rock
- d. Laccolith

65. The _____ was the earliest of the six cratonic sequences that have occurred during the Phanerozoic (followed by the Tippecanoe, Kaskaskia, Absaroka, Zu>ñi, and Tejas.) It dates from the late Proterozoic through the early Ordovician, though the marine transgression did not begin in earnest until the middle Cambrian.

Chapter 4. Igneous Rocks and Intrusive Igneous Activity

At its peak, most of North America was covered by the shallow Sauk Sea, save for parts of the Canadian Shield and the islands of the Transcontinental Arch.

a. 1509 Istanbul earthquake
b. Sauk sequence
c. Tippecanoe sequence
d. 1700 Cascadia earthquake

66. _____ is a fine-grained sedimentary rock whose original constituents were clay minerals or muds. It is characterized by thin laminae breaking with an irregular curving fracture, often splintery and usually parallel to the often-indistinguishable bedding plane. This property is called fissility.
a. Pelagic sediments
b. Mudstone
c. Metasediment
d. Shale

67. _____, (Navajo: >Ts>é Bit'a'>í, 'rock with wings' or 'winged rock') is a rock formation rising nearly 1,800 feet (550 m) above the high-desert plain on the Navajo Nation and in San Juan County, New Mexico.

_____ is composed of fractured volcanic breccia and black dikes of igneous rock called 'minette'. It is the erosional remnant of the throat of a volcano, and the volcanic breccia formed in a diatreme. The exposed rock probably was originally formed 2,500-3000 feet (750-1,000 meters) below the earth's surface, but it was exposed after millions of years of erosion. Wall-like sheets of minette, known as dikes, radiate away from the central formation. Radiometric age determinations of the minette establish that these volcanic rocks solidified about 27 million years ago.

a. 1700 Cascadia earthquake
b. 1509 Istanbul earthquake
c. 1703 Genroku earthquake
d. Shiprock

68. The _____ was a major mountain building event that took place along the western edge of ancient North America between the Mid to Late Jurassic (between about 180 and 140 million years ago.) The _____ was the first of three major mountain building episodes to transform Western North America between the Late Mesozoic and Early Cenozoic Eras, the latter two being the Sevier and Laramide orogeny, chronologically. Much like the two orogenies that followed, the Nevadan was caused by the subduction of oceanic lithosphere at a subduction zone running along the edge of the North American continent.
a. Sevier orogeny
b. Kaikoura Orogeny
c. Pan-African orogeny
d. Nevadan orogeny

69. _____ is a process accommodating the ascent of magmatic bodies from their sources in the mantle (geology) or lower crust to the surface. The process involves the mechanical disintegration of the surrounding country/host rock, typically through fracturing due to pressure increases associated with thermal expansion of the host rock in proximity of the interface with the melt. Once fractures are formed, melt and/or volatiles will typically invade, widening the fracture and promoting the foundering of host rock blocks (i.e. stoped blocks.)
a. Spheroidal weathering
b. Wave pounding
c. Stoping
d. Transgression

Chapter 5. Volcanism and Volcanoes

1. A _____ is a type of mudflow or landslide composed of pyroclastic material and water that flows down from a volcano, typically along a river valley. The term '_____' originated in the Javanese language of Indonesia. They can be best described as volcanic mudflows. They may not necessarily be caused by volcanic activity, but at the very least do originate from some type of volcanism.
   a. 1703 Genroku earthquake
   b. 1509 Istanbul earthquake
   c. Lahar
   d. 1700 Cascadia earthquake

2. A _____ or mudslide is the most rapid (up to 80 km/h, or 50 mph) and fluid type of downhill mass wasting. It is a rapid movement of a large mass of mud formed from loose earth and water. Similar terms are mudslide (not very liquid), mud stream, debris flow (e.g. in high mountains), j>ökulhlaup, and lahar
   a. 1700 Cascadia earthquake
   b. Mudflow
   c. 1703 Genroku earthquake
   d. 1509 Istanbul earthquake

3. The _____ is the earliest of three geologic eras of the Phanerozoic eon. The _____ spanned from roughly 542 to 251 million years ago (ICS, 2004), and is subdivided into six geologic periods; from oldest to youngest they are: the Cambrian, Ordovician, Silurian, Devonian, Carboniferous, and Permian.

   The _____ covers the time from the first appearance of abundant, soft-shelled fossils to the time when the continents were beginning to be dominated by large, relatively sophisticated reptiles and modern plants. The lower (oldest) boundary was classically set at the first appearance of creatures known as trilobites and archeocyathids.

   a. 1700 Cascadia earthquake
   b. 1703 Genroku earthquake
   c. 1509 Istanbul earthquake
   d. Paleozoic

4. The _____ is an informal name for the supereon comprising the eons of the geologic timescale that came before the current Phanerozoic eon. It spans from the formation of Earth around 4500 Mya (million years ago) to the evolution of abundant macroscopic hard-shelled animals, which marked the beginning of the Cambrian, the first period of the first era of the Phanerozoic eon, some 542 Mya. It is named after the Roman name for Wales - Cambria - where rocks from this age were first studied.
   a. 1509 Istanbul earthquake
   b. 1703 Genroku earthquake
   c. 1700 Cascadia earthquake
   d. Precambrian

5. An _____ is the result of a sudden release of energy in the Earth's crust that creates seismic waves. They are recorded with a seismometer or the related and mostly obsolete Richter magnitude, with a magnitude 3 or lower _____ being mostly imperceptible and magnitude 7 causing serious damage over large areas.
   a. AASHTO Soil Classification System
   b. Earthquake
   c. AL 333
   d. AL 129-1

6. The lithosphere is broken up into what are called _____. In the case of Earth, there are eight major and many minor plates The lithospheric plates ride on the asthenosphere. These plates move in relation to one another at one of three types of plate boundaries: convergent, or collisional boundaries; divergent boundaries, also called spreading centers; and transform boundaries.
   a. Thrust fault
   b. Copperbelt Province
   c. Gorda Ridge
   d. Tectonic plates

Chapter 5. Volcanism and Volcanoes

7. A _____ is an opening in a planet's surface or crust, which allows hot, molten rock, ash, and gases to escape from below the surface. Volcanic activity involving the extrusion of rock tends to form mountains or features like mountains over a period of time.
   - a. 1703 Genroku earthquake
   - b. Volcano
   - c. 1509 Istanbul earthquake
   - d. 1700 Cascadia earthquake

8. _____ is a term used in geology to refer to silicate minerals, magma, and rocks which are enriched in the lighter elements such as silicon, oxygen, aluminium, sodium, and potassium. _____ minerals are usually light in color and have specific gravities less than 3. Common _____ minerals include quartz, muscovite, orthoclase, and the sodium-rich plagioclase feldspars.
   - a. Felsic
   - b. Tephra
   - c. Laccolith
   - d. Magma

9. The _____ is the geologic eon before the Archean. It started at Earth's formation about 4.6 billion years ago (4,600 Ma), and ended roughly 3.8 billion years ago, though the latter date varies according to different sources.
   - a. 1509 Istanbul earthquake
   - b. 1703 Genroku earthquake
   - c. 1700 Cascadia earthquake
   - d. Hadean

10. _____ is an adjective describing a silicate mineral or rock that is rich in magnesium and iron; the term was derived by contracting 'magnesium' and 'ferric'. Most _____ minerals are dark in color and the specific gravity is greater than 3. Common rock-forming _____ minerals include olivine, pyroxene, amphibole, and biotite.

    _____ lava, before cooling, has a low viscosity, in comparison to felsic lava, due to the lower silica content in _____ magma. Water and other volatiles can more easily and gradually escape from _____ lava, so eruptions of volcanoes made of _____ lavas are less explosively violent than felsic lava eruptions.

    - a. 1509 Istanbul earthquake
    - b. 1700 Cascadia earthquake
    - c. 1703 Genroku earthquake
    - d. Mafic

11. The _____ Era is one of three geologic eras of the Phanerozoic eon. The division of time into eras dates back to Giovanni Arduino, in the 18th century, although his original name for the era now called the '_____' was 'Secondary' (making the modern era the 'Tertiary'.)

    The _____ was a time of tectonic, climatic and evolutionary activity. The continents gradually shifted from a state of connectedness into their present configuration; the drifting provided for speciation and other important evolutionary developments.

    - a. Mesozoic
    - b. 1703 Genroku earthquake
    - c. 1700 Cascadia earthquake
    - d. 1509 Istanbul earthquake

12. The _____ is a geological eon representing a period before the first abundant complex life on Earth. The _____ extended from 2500 Ma to 542.0 >± 1.0 Ma (million years ago), and is the most recent part of the old, informally named 'e;Precambrian'e; time.

Chapter 5. Volcanism and Volcanoes

The Proterozoic consists of 3 geologic eras, from oldest to youngest:

- Paleoproterozoic
- Mesoproterozoic
- Neoproterozoic

The well-identified events were:

- The transition to an oxygenated atmosphere during the Mesoproterozoic.
- Several glaciations, including the hypothesized Snowball Earth during the Cryogenian period in the late Neoproterozoic.
- The Ediacaran Period (635 to 542 Ma) which is characterized by the evolution of abundant soft-bodied multicellular organisms.

The geoloic record of the Proterozoic is much better than that for the preceding Archean. In contrast to the deep-water deposits of the Archean, the Proterozoic features many strata that were laid down in extensive shallow epicontinental seas; furthermore, many of these rocks are less metamorphosed than Archean-age ones, and plenty are unaltered.

    a. 1703 Genroku earthquake   b. 1509 Istanbul earthquake
    c. Proterozoic Eon   d. 1700 Cascadia earthquake

13. The _____ is a geologic period and system that extends from about 251 to 199 Mya (million years ago.) As the first period of the Mesozoic Era, the _____ follows the Permian and is followed by the Jurassic. Both the start and end of the _____ are marked by major extinction events.
    a. 1509 Istanbul earthquake   b. 1700 Cascadia earthquake
    c. Triassic   d. Rhaetian

14. _____ is a measure of the resistance of a fluid which is being deformed by either shear stress or extensional stress. In everyday terms (and for fluids only), _____ is 'thickness'. Thus, water is 'thin', having a lower _____, while honey is 'thick' having a higher _____.
    a. Viscosity   b. Thixotropy
    c. Shear stress   d. Tensile stress

15. _____ is molten rock expelled by a volcano during eruption. When first expelled from a volcanic vent, it is a liquid at temperatures from 700 >°C to 1,200 >°C (1,300 >°F to 2,200 >°F.) Although _____ is quite viscous, with about 100,000 times the viscosity of water, it can flow great distances before cooling and solidifying, because of both its thixotropic and shear thinning properties.
    a. Pit crater   b. Volcanic ash
    c. Supervolcano   d. Lava

Chapter 5. Volcanism and Volcanoes

16. _____ is molten rock that is found beneath the surface of the Earth, and may also exist on other terrestrial planets. Besides molten rock, _____ may also contain suspended crystals and gas bubbles. _____ often collects in a _____ chamber inside a volcano. _____ is capable of intrusion into adjacent rocks, extrusion onto the surface as lava, and explosive ejection as tephra to form pyroclastic rock.
   a. Volcanic rock
   b. Rock cycle
   c. Laccolith
   d. Magma

17. The _____ Era, is the most recent of the three classic geological eras and covers the period from 65.5 million years ago to the present. It is marked by the Cretaceous-Tertiary extinction event at the end of the Cretaceous that saw the demise of the last non-avian dinosaurs and the end of the Mesozoic Era. The _____ era is ongoing.
   a. 1703 Genroku earthquake
   b. Cenozoic
   c. 1509 Istanbul earthquake
   d. 1700 Cascadia earthquake

18. _____ are natural conduits through which lava travels beneath the surface of a lava flow, expelled by a volcano during an eruption. They can be actively draining lava from a source, or can be extinct, meaning the lava flow has ceased and the rock has cooled and left a long, cave-like channel.

_____ are formed when an active low-viscosity lava flow develops a continuous and hard crust, which thickens and forms a roof above the still-flowing lava stream.

   a. 1509 Istanbul earthquake
   b. 1700 Cascadia earthquake
   c. 1703 Genroku earthquake
   d. Lava tubes

19. _____ are pillow-shaped structures sometimes seen in lavas and are attributed to the congealment of lava under water, or subaqeous extrusion. A pillow structure in certain extrusive igneous rock is characterized by discontinuous pillow-shaped masses, commonly up to 1 metre in diameter. _____ commonly occur at Constructive plate boundaries, forming part of a mid-ocean ridge.
   a. Mineral hydration
   b. Fahlband
   c. Pillow lava
   d. Pumice raft

20. In geology, a _____ is a place where the Earth's crust and lithosphere are being pulled apart and is an example of extensional tectonics.

Typical _____ features are a central linear downdropped fault segment, called a graben, with parallel normal faulting and _____-flank uplifts on either side forming a _____ valley, where the _____ remains above sea level. The axis of the _____ area commonly contains volcanic rocks and active volcanism is a part of many, but not all active _____ systems.

   a. 1509 Istanbul earthquake
   b. 1700 Cascadia earthquake
   c. 1703 Genroku earthquake
   d. Rift

21. A _____ is a mountain rising from the ocean seafloor that does not reach to the water's surface (sea level), and thus is not an island. These are typically formed from extinct volcanoes, that rise abruptly and are usually found rising from a seafloor of 1,000-4,000 meters depth. They are defined by oceanographers as independent features that rise to at least 1,000 meters above the seafloor.

a. Seamount
b. 1509 Istanbul earthquake
c. 1703 Genroku earthquake
d. 1700 Cascadia earthquake

22. A _____ is a cauldron-like volcanic feature usually formed by the collapse of land following a volcanic eruption such as the one at Yellowstone National Park. They are sometimes confused with volcanic craters.
   a. 1703 Genroku earthquake
   b. Caldera
   c. 1509 Istanbul earthquake
   d. 1700 Cascadia earthquake

23. _____ is a caldera lake located in the U.S. state of Oregon. It is the main feature of _____ National Park and famous for its deep blue color and water clarity. The lake partly fills a nearly 1,958 foot (597 m) deep caldera that was formed around 7,700 (>± 150) BC by the collapse of the volcano Mount Mazama.
   a. 1700 Cascadia earthquake
   b. 1509 Istanbul earthquake
   c. 1703 Genroku earthquake
   d. Crater Lake

24. _____ is a size classification term for tephra, which is material that falls out of the air during a volcanic eruption. They are in some senses similar to ooids or pisoids in calcareous sediments.

By definition _____ range in size from 2 mm to 64 mm in diameter. A pyroclastic particle greater than 64 mm in diameter is correctly known as a volcanic bomb when molten, or a volcanic block when solid.

   a. Lapilli
   b. Pyroclastic flow
   c. Lava
   d. Pit crater

25. A _____ is a pyroclastic material. They are extrusive igneous rocks, and are similar to pumice, which has so many cavities and is such low-density that it can float on water.
   a. Cinder
   b. Pyroclastic flow
   c. Wadati-Benioff zone
   d. Pit crater

26. A _____ or scoria cone is a steep conical hill of volcanic fragments that accumulate around and downwind from a volcanic vent. The rock fragments, often called cinders or scoria, are glassy and contain numerous gas bubbles 'frozen' into place as magma exploded into the air and then cooled quickly. Cinder cones range in size from tens to hundreds of meters tall.
   a. 1700 Cascadia earthquake
   b. 1703 Genroku earthquake
   c. Cinder cone
   d. 1509 Istanbul earthquake

27. A _____, sometimes called a composite volcano, is a tall, conical volcano with many layers (strata) of hardened lava, tephra, and volcanic ash. They are characterized by a steep profile and periodic, explosive eruptions. The lava that flows from a _____ tends to be viscous; it cools and hardens before spreading far.
   a. Mount Overlord
   b. Broken Top
   c. Mount Baker
   d. Stratovolcano

28. _____ is the largest volcano on earth in terms of area covered and one of five volcanoes that form the Island of Hawaii in the U.S. state of Hawai>Ê»i in the Pacific Ocean. It is an active shield volcano, with a volume estimated at approximately 18,000 cubic miles (75,000 kmÂ³), although its peak is about 120 feet (37 m) lower than that of its neighbor, Mauna Kea. The Hawaiian name '_____' means 'Long Mountain'.

Chapter 5. Volcanism and Volcanoes

a. 1703 Genroku earthquake
b. 1509 Istanbul earthquake
c. 1700 Cascadia earthquake
d. Mauna Loa

29. _____ is a common extrusive volcanic rock. It is usually grey to black and fine-grained due to rapid cooling of lava at the surface of a planet. It may be porphyritic containing larger crystals in a fine matrix, or vesicular, or frothy scoria.

a. 1509 Istanbul earthquake
b. Basalt
c. 1703 Genroku earthquake
d. 1700 Cascadia earthquake

30. _____ is water located beneath the ground surface in soil pore spaces and in the fractures of lithologic formations. A unit of rock or an unconsolidated deposit is called an aquifer when it can yield a usable quantity of water. The depth at which soil pore spaces or fractures and voids in rock become completely saturated with water is called the water table.

a. 1509 Istanbul earthquake
b. 1700 Cascadia earthquake
c. Depression focused recharge
d. Groundwater

31. _____ was the supercontinent that is theorized to have existed during the Paleozoic and Mesozoic eras about 250 million years ago, before the component continents were separated into their current configuration.

The name was first used by the German originator of the continental drift theory, Alfred Wegener, in the 1920 edition of his book The Origin of Continents and Oceans , in which a postulated supercontinent _____ played a key role.

The single enormous ocean which surrounded Pangaea is known as Panthalassa.

a. 1703 Genroku earthquake
b. 1509 Istanbul earthquake
c. 1700 Cascadia earthquake
d. Pangea

32. A _____ is generally a large area of exposed Precambrian crystalline igneous and high-grade metamorphic rocks that form tectonically stable areas. In all cases, the age of these rocks is greater than 570 million years and sometimes dates back 2 to 3.5 billion years. They have been little affected by tectonic events following the end of the Precambrian Era, and are relatively flat regions where mountain building, faulting, and other tectonic processes are greatly diminished compared with the activity that occurs at the margins of the shields and the boundaries between tectonic plates.

a. Shield
b. 1509 Istanbul earthquake
c. 1700 Cascadia earthquake
d. 1703 Genroku earthquake

33. A _____ is a large volcano with shallow-sloping sides.

They are formed by lava flows of low viscosity - lava that flows easily. Consequently, a volcanic mountain having a broad profile is built up over time by flow after flow of relatively fluid basaltic lava issuing from vents or fissures on the surface of the volcano

a. 1703 Genroku earthquake
b. 1700 Cascadia earthquake
c. 1509 Istanbul earthquake
d. Shield volcano

Chapter 5. Volcanism and Volcanoes 51

34. _____ is a carbonate mineral and the most stable polymorph of calcium carbonate (CaCO₃.) The other polymorphs are the minerals aragonite and vaterite. Aragonite will change to _____ at 470>°C, and vaterite is even less stable.

_____ is a common constituent of sedimentary rocks, limestone in particular, much of which is formed from the shells of dead marine organisms. Approximately 10% of sedimentary rock is limestone.

a. 1703 Genroku earthquake
b. 1509 Istanbul earthquake
c. 1700 Cascadia earthquake
d. Calcite

35. _____ is the name of a sedimentary carbonate rock and a mineral, both composed of calcium magnesium carbonate CaMg₂ found in crystals.

_____ rock (also dolostone) is composed predominantly of the mineral _____. Limestone that is partially replaced by _____ is referred to as dolomitic limestone, or in old U.S. geologic literature as magnesian limestone.

a. Metasediment
b. Dolomite
c. Porcellanite
d. Dolostone

36. _____ is a depression in eastern California that is adjacent to Mammoth Mountain. The valley is one of the largest calderas on earth, measuring about 32 kilometres (20 mi) long (east-west) and 17 kilometres (11 mi) wide (north-south.) The elevation of the floor of the caldera is 6,500 feet (2,000 m) in the east and 8,500 feet (2,600 m) in the west.

a. 1700 Cascadia earthquake
b. Long Valley caldera
c. 1509 Istanbul earthquake
d. 1703 Genroku earthquake

37. _____ is a type of rock consisting of consolidated volcanic ash ejected from vents during a volcanic eruption. _____ is sometimes called tufa, particularly when used as construction material, although tufa also refers to a quite different rock.

The products of a volcanic eruption are volcanic gases, lava, steam, and tephra. Magma is blown apart when it interacts violently with volcanic gases and steam. Solid material produced and thrown into the air by such volcanic eruptions is called tephra, regardless of composition or fragment size. If the resulting pieces of ejecta are small enough, the material is called volcanic ash, defined as such particles less than 2 mm in diameter, sand-sized or smaller.

a. Pyroclastic rocks
b. Coldwell Complex
c. Country rock
d. Tuff

38. A _____ is a geological phenomenon which includes a wide range of ground movement, such as rock falls, deep failure of slopes and shallow debris flows, which can occur in offshore, coastal and onshore environments. Although the action of gravity is the primary driving force for a _____ to occur, there are other contributing factors affecting the original slope stability. Typically, pre-conditional factors build up specific sub-surface conditions that make the area/slope prone to failure, whereas the actual _____ often requires a trigger before being released.

Chapter 5. Volcanism and Volcanoes

    a. 1509 Istanbul earthquake
    c. 1700 Cascadia earthquake
    b. Mass wasting
    d. Landslide

39. The _____, also known as the local magnitude (M_L) scale, assigns a single number to quantify the amount of seismic energy released by an earthquake. It is a base-10 logarithmic scale obtained by calculating the logarithm of the combined horizontal amplitude of the largest displacement from zero on a Wood-Anderson torsion seismometer output. So, for example, an earthquake that measures 5.0 on the Richter scale has a shaking amplitude 10 times larger than one that measures 4.0.
    a. China Seismic Intensity Scale
    c. Medvedev-Sponheuer-Karnik scale
    b. Moment magnitude scale
    d. Richter Magnitude Scale

40. _____ describes a long-duration release of seismic energy with distinct spectral (harmonic) lines that and often precedes or accompanies volcanic eruptions. More generally, volcanic tremor, is a sustained signal that may or may not possess these harmonic spectral features.

_____ is a sustained release of seismic and/or infrasonic energy typically associated with the underground movement or venting of magma and/or volcanic gases.

    a. Rayleigh waves
    c. Tornillo event
    b. Meizoseismal area
    d. Harmonic tremor

41. A _____ is an instrument designed to measure very small changes from the horizontal level, either on the ground or in structures. A similar term, in less common usage, is the inclinometer. They are used extensively for monitoring volcanos, the response of dams to filling, the small movements of potential landslides, the orientation and volume of hydraulic fractures, and the response of structures to various influences such as loading and foundation settlement.
    a. 1703 Genroku earthquake
    c. 1700 Cascadia earthquake
    b. 1509 Istanbul earthquake
    d. Tiltmeter

42. The _____ of Thera, also referred to as the Thera eruption or Santorini eruption, was a major catastrophic volcanic eruption (Volcanic Explosivity Index (VEI) = 6 or 7, Dense-rock equivalent (DRE) = 60 km^3) which is estimated to have occurred in the mid second millennium BCE. The eruption was one of the largest volcanic events on Earth in recorded history. The eruption devastated the island of Thera (also called Santorini), including the Minoan settlement at Akrotiri as well as communities and agricultural areas on nearby islands and on the coast of Crete.
    a. 1700 Cascadia earthquake
    c. 1703 Genroku earthquake
    b. 1509 Istanbul earthquake
    d. Minoan eruption

43. The _____ is a mid-oceanic ridge, a divergent tectonic plate boundary located along the floor of the Pacific Ocean. It separates the Pacific Plate to the west from (north to south) the North American Plate, the Rivera Plate, the Cocos Plate, the Nazca Plate, and the Antarctic Plate. It runs from an undefined point near Antarctica in the south northward to its termination at the northern end of the Gulf of California in the Salton Sea basin in southern California.
    a. Azores-Gibraltar Transform Fault
    c. Obduction
    b. Elastic rebound theory
    d. East Pacific Rise

44. _____ refers to a large group of dark, coarse-grained, intrusive igneous rocks chemically equivalent to basalt. The rocks are plutonic, formed when molten magma is trapped beneath the Earth's surface and cools into a crystalline mass.

Chapter 5. Volcanism and Volcanoes

The vast majority of the Earth's surface is underlain by _____ within the oceanic crust, produced by basalt magmatism at mid-ocean ridges.

a. 1509 Istanbul earthquake
c. 1703 Genroku earthquake

b. Gabbro
d. 1700 Cascadia earthquake

45. The _____ is a mid-ocean ridge, a divergent tectonic plate boundary located along the floor of the Atlantic Ocean, and the longest mountain range in the world. It separates the Eurasian Plate and North American Plate in the North Atlantic, and the African Plate from the South American Plate in the South Atlantic. The MAR extends from a junction with the Gakkel Ridge (Mid-Arctic Ridge) northeast of Greenland southward to the Bouvet Triple Junction in the South Atlantic.

a. 1509 Istanbul earthquake
c. 1700 Cascadia earthquake

b. 1703 Genroku earthquake
d. Mid-Atlantic Ridge

46. The _____ is a tectonic plate covering the continent of South America and extending eastward to the Mid-Atlantic Ridge.

The easterly side is a divergent boundary with the African Plate forming the southern part of the Mid-Atlantic Ridge. The southerly side is a complex boundary with the Antarctic Plate and the Scotia Plate.

a. Lhasa Plate
c. Mariana Plate

b. South American plate
d. Juan de Fuca Plate

47. _____ is the movement of the Earth's continents relative to each other. The hypothesis that continents 'drift' was first put forward by Abraham Ortelius in 1596 and was fully developed by Alfred Wegener in 1912. However, it was not until the development of the theory of plate tectonics in the 1960s, that a sufficient geological explanation of that movement was found.

a. Plate tectonics
c. Thrust fault

b. Continental drift
d. Panthalassa

48. In geology, _____ is transported rock debris overlying the solid bedrock. The term is also sometimes refers to organic debris so-transported. In the largest sense, it refers to the material left behind by retreating continental glaciers.

a. Geodiversity
c. Patterned ground

b. Drift
d. Platform cover

Chapter 6. Weathering, Soil, and Sedimentary Rocks

1. The _____, is a geologic eon before the Proterozoic and Paleoproterozoic, before 2.5 Ga (billion years ago, or 2,500 Ma.) Instead of being based on stratigraphy, this date is defined chronometrically. The lower boundary (starting point) has not been officially recognized by the International Commission on Stratigraphy, but it is usually set to 3.8 Ga, at the end of the Hadean eon.

   a. AL 129-1
   b. AASHTO Soil Classification System
   c. AL 333
   d. Archean

2. The _____ Era, is the most recent of the three classic geological eras and covers the period from 65.5 million years ago to the present. It is marked by the Cretaceous-Tertiary extinction event at the end of the Cretaceous that saw the demise of the last non-avian dinosaurs and the end of the Mesozoic Era. The _____ era is ongoing.

   a. 1703 Genroku earthquake
   b. 1700 Cascadia earthquake
   c. 1509 Istanbul earthquake
   d. Cenozoic

3. _____ is the geological process by which material is added to a landform or land mass. Fluids such as wind and water, as well as sediment gravity flows, transport previously eroded sediment, which, at the loss of enough kinetic energy in the fluid, is deposited, building up layers of sediment.

_____ occurs when the forces responsible for sediment transportation are no longer sufficient to overcome the forces of particle weight and friction, which resist motion.

   a. Diagenesis
   b. Downcutting
   c. Deposition
   d. Headward erosion

4. _____ is a common and widely occurring type of intrusive, felsic, igneous rock. _____ has a medium to coarse texture, occasionally with some individual crystals larger than the groundmass forming a rock known as porphyry. Granites can be pink to dark gray or even black, depending on their chemistry and mineralogy.

   a. Granite
   b. 1703 Genroku earthquake
   c. 1700 Cascadia earthquake
   d. 1509 Istanbul earthquake

5. The _____ was a cratonic sequence that began in the mid-Devonian, peaked early in the Mississippian, and ended by mid-Mississippian time. A major unconformity separates it from the lower Tippecanoe sequence.

The basal-that is, the lowest and oldest-units of the Kaskaskia consist of clean quartz sandstones eroded from the Appalachian orogenic belt to the east, the Ozark Dome in the center of the continent, and south from the Canadian Shield.

   a. Sauk sequence
   b. 1700 Cascadia earthquake
   c. 1509 Istanbul earthquake
   d. Kaskaskia sequence

6. _____ is the result of the transformation of an existing rock type, the protolith, in a process called metamorphism, which means 'change in form'. The protolith is subjected to heat and pressure (temperatures greater than 150 to 200 >°C and pressures of 1500 bars) causing profound physical and/or chemical change. The protolith may be sedimentary rock, igneous rock or another older _____.

   a. Sedimentary rock
   b. Metavolcanic rock
   c. Migmatite
   d. Metamorphic rock

Chapter 6. Weathering, Soil, and Sedimentary Rocks

7. The _____ is an informal name for the supereon comprising the eons of the geologic timescale that came before the current Phanerozoic eon. It spans from the formation of Earth around 4500 Mya (million years ago) to the evolution of abundant macroscopic hard-shelled animals, which marked the beginning of the Cambrian, the first period of the first era of the Phanerozoic eon, some 542 Mya. It is named after the Roman name for Wales - Cambria - where rocks from this age were first studied.
    a. Precambrian
    b. 1509 Istanbul earthquake
    c. 1703 Genroku earthquake
    d. 1700 Cascadia earthquake

8. The _____ was the earliest of the six cratonic sequences that have occurred during the Phanerozoic (followed by the Tippecanoe, Kaskaskia, Absaroka, Zu>ñi, and Tejas.) It dates from the late Proterozoic through the early Ordovician, though the marine transgression did not begin in earnest until the middle Cambrian.

At its peak, most of North America was covered by the shallow Sauk Sea, save for parts of the Canadian Shield and the islands of the Transcontinental Arch.

    a. 1509 Istanbul earthquake
    b. 1700 Cascadia earthquake
    c. Tippecanoe sequence
    d. Sauk sequence

9. _____ is the naturally occurring, unconsolidated or loose covering on the Earth's surface. _____ is composed of particles of broken rock that have been altered by chemical, biological and environmental processes including weathering and erosion. _____ is different from its parent rock(s) source(s), altered by interactions between the lithosphere, hydrosphere, atmosphere, and the biosphere.
    a. Topsoil
    b. Soil
    c. 1509 Istanbul earthquake
    d. Slump

10. _____ is the decomposition of Earth rocks, soils and their minerals through direct contact with the planet's atmosphere. _____ occurs in situ, or 'with no movement', and thus should not be confused with erosion, which involves the movement of rocks and minerals by agents such as water, ice, wind and gravity.

Two important classifications of _____ processes exist -- physical and chemical _____.

    a. Weathering
    b. Physical weathering
    c. 1509 Istanbul earthquake
    d. Frost disintegration

11. _____ are flat or very gently sloping areas of the deep ocean basin floor. They are among the Earth's flattest and smoothest regions and the least explored. _____ cover approximately 40% of the ocean floor and reach depths between 2,200 and 5,500 m (7,200 and 18,000 ft.)
    a. Eutrophication
    b. AASHTO Soil Classification System
    c. Intertidal
    d. Abyssal plains

12. _____ is the removal of solids (sediment, soil, rock and other particles) in the natural environment. It usually occurs due to transport by wind, water, or ice; by down-slope creep of soil and other material under the force of gravity; or by living organisms, such as burrowing animals, in the case of bioerosion.

_____ is distinguished from weathering, which is the process of chemical or physical breakdown of the minerals in the rocks, although the two processes may occur concurrently.

Chapter 6. Weathering, Soil, and Sedimentary Rocks

  a. AL 129-1
  c. AL 333

  b. AASHTO Soil Classification System
  d. Erosion

13. A _____ is a large, slow-moving mass of ice, formed from compacted layers of snow, that slowly deforms and flows in response to gravity and high pressure.

_____ ice is the largest reservoir of fresh water on Earth, and second only to oceans as the largest reservoir of total water.

  a. Glacier
  c. Little Ice Age

  b. Keeling Curve
  d. Pacific Decadal Oscillation

14. The lithosphere is broken up into what are called _____. In the case of Earth, there are eight major and many minor plates The lithospheric plates ride on the asthenosphere. These plates move in relation to one another at one of three types of plate boundaries: convergent, or collisional boundaries; divergent boundaries, also called spreading centers; and transform boundaries.
  a. Copperbelt Province
  c. Gorda Ridge

  b. Thrust fault
  d. Tectonic plates

15. _____ is one of the three main rock types (the others being igneous and metamorphic rock.) _____ is formed by deposition and consolidation of mineral and organic material and from precipitation of minerals from solution. The processes that form _____ occur at the surface of the Earth and within bodies of water.
  a. Serpentinite
  c. Petrology

  b. Sedimentary rock
  d. Rock cycle

16. The _____ was a cratonic sequence that extended from the end of the Mississippian through the Permian periods. It is the unconformity between this sequence and the preceding Kaskaskia that divides the Carboniferous into the Mississippian and Pennsylvanian periods in North America.

Like the Kaskaskia sequence, Absaroka sedimentary deposits were dominated by detrital or siliclastic rocks.

  a. AL 129-1
  c. AASHTO Soil Classification System

  b. AL 333
  d. Absaroka sequence

17. _____ is a silvery white and ductile member of the boron group of chemical elements. It has the symbol Al; its atomic number is 13. It is not soluble in water under normal circumstances. _____ is the most abundant metal in the Earth's crust, and the third most abundant element therein, after oxygen and silicon. It makes up about 8% by weight of the Earth'e;s solid surface.
  a. AL 333
  c. Aluminum

  b. AL 129-1
  d. AASHTO Soil Classification System

18. _____ is a common phyllosilicate mineral within the mica group, with the approximate chemical formula K(Mg, Fe)$_3$AlSi$_3$O$_{10}$(F, OH)$_2$. More generally, it refers to the dark mica series, primarily a solid-solution series between the iron-endmember annite, and the magnesium-endmember phlogopite; more aluminous endmembers include siderophyllite.

a. 1509 Istanbul earthquake
b. Biotite
c. 1703 Genroku earthquake
d. 1700 Cascadia earthquake

19. Two important classifications of weathering processes exist -- physical and _____. Mechanical or physical weathering involves the breakdown of rocks and soils through direct contact with atmospheric conditions, such as heat, water, ice and pressure. The second classification, _____, involves the direct effect of atmospheric chemicals or biologically produced chemicals (also known as biological weathering) in the breakdown of rocks, soils and minerals.
   a. Weathering
   b. 1509 Istanbul earthquake
   c. Physical weathering
   d. Chemical weathering

20. _____ can also be called frost shattering or frost-wedging. This type of weathering is common in mountain areas where the temperature is around freezing point. Frost induced weathering, although often attributed to the expansion of freezing water captured in cracks, is generally independent of the water-to-ice expansion. It has long been known that moist soils expand or frost heave upon freezing as a result of water migrating along from unfrozen areas via thin films to collect at growing ice lenses. This same phenomena occurs within pore spaces of rocks.
   a. Weathering
   b. 1509 Istanbul earthquake
   c. Physical weathering
   d. Frost disintegration

21. The _____ is the geologic eon before the Archean. It started at Earth's formation about 4.6 billion years ago (4,600 Ma), and ended roughly 3.8 billion years ago, though the latter date varies according to different sources.
   a. 1703 Genroku earthquake
   b. Hadean
   c. 1509 Istanbul earthquake
   d. 1700 Cascadia earthquake

22. A _____ is a tall thin spire of rock that protrudes from the bottom of an arid drainage basin or badland. Hoodoos are composed of soft sedimentary rock and are topped by a piece of harder, less easily-eroded stone that protects the column from the elements.

They are mainly located in the desert in dry, hot areas.

   a. 1509 Istanbul earthquake
   b. 1703 Genroku earthquake
   c. 1700 Cascadia earthquake
   d. Hoodoo

23. Two important classifications of weathering processes exist -- _____ and chemical weathering. Mechanical or _____ involves the breakdown of rocks and soils through direct contact with atmospheric conditions, such as heat, water, ice and pressure. The second classification, chemical weathering, involves the direct effect of atmospheric chemicals or biologically produced chemicals (also known as biological weathering) in the breakdown of rocks, soils and minerals.
   a. Frost disintegration
   b. Physical weathering
   c. Weathering
   d. 1509 Istanbul earthquake

24. The _____ is the earliest of three geologic eras of the Phanerozoic eon. The _____ spanned from roughly 542 to 251 million years ago (ICS, 2004), and is subdivided into six geologic periods; from oldest to youngest they are: the Cambrian, Ordovician, Silurian, Devonian, Carboniferous, and Permian.

The _____ covers the time from the first appearance of abundant, soft-shelled fossils to the time when the continents were beginning to be dominated by large, relatively sophisticated reptiles and modern plants. The lower (oldest) boundary was classically set at the first appearance of creatures known as trilobites and archeocyathids.

- a. 1509 Istanbul earthquake
- c. 1703 Genroku earthquake
- b. 1700 Cascadia earthquake
- d. Paleozoic

25. The _____ is a geological eon representing a period before the first abundant complex life on Earth. The _____ extended from 2500 Ma to 542.0 >± 1.0 Ma (million years ago), and is the most recent part of the old, informally named 'e;Precambrian'e; time.

The Proterozoic consists of 3 geologic eras, from oldest to youngest:

- Paleoproterozoic
- Mesoproterozoic
- Neoproterozoic

The well-identified events were:

- The transition to an oxygenated atmosphere during the Mesoproterozoic.
- Several glaciations, including the hypothesized Snowball Earth during the Cryogenian period in the late Neoproterozoic.
- The Ediacaran Period (635 to 542 Ma) which is characterized by the evolution of abundant soft-bodied multicellular organisms.

The geoloic record of the Proterozoic is much better than that for the preceding Archean. In contrast to the deep-water deposits of the Archean, the Proterozoic features many strata that were laid down in extensive shallow epicontinental seas; furthermore, many of these rocks are less metamorphosed than Archean-age ones, and plenty are unaltered.

- a. 1509 Istanbul earthquake
- c. 1703 Genroku earthquake
- b. Proterozoic Eon
- d. 1700 Cascadia earthquake

26. _____ or sheet joints are surface-parallel fracture systems in rock often leading to erosion of concentric slabs.
- a. Exfoliation joints
- c. AASHTO Soil Classification System
- b. AL 129-1
- d. AL 333

27. _____ is a term given to an accumulation of broken rock fragments at the base of crags, mountain cliffs, or valley shoulders. Landforms associated with these materials are sometimes called _____ slopes or talus piles. These deposits typically have a concave upwards form, while the maximum inclination of such deposits corresponds to the angle of repose of the mean debris size.

Chapter 6. Weathering, Soil, and Sedimentary Rocks

a. 1700 Cascadia earthquake
c. 1509 Istanbul earthquake

b. 1703 Genroku earthquake
d. Scree

28. The _____ was the cratonic sequence--that is, the marine transgression--that followed the Sauk sequence; it extended from roughly the middle Ordovician to the early Devonian.

After the regression of the Sauk Sea early in the Ordovician, the exposed craton for a time underwent vigorous erosion, due to being located in a tropical climate; indeed, at this point in the Phanerozoic the North American continent roughly straddled the equator.

The Tippecanoe transgression ended this period of erosion, beginning with the deposition of clean sandstones across the craton, followed by abundant carbonate deposition.

a. Tippecanoe sequence
c. 1700 Cascadia earthquake

b. 1509 Istanbul earthquake
d. Sauk sequence

29. _____ are a group of rock-forming tectosilicate minerals which make up as much as 60% of the Earth's crust.

_____ crystallize from magma in both intrusive and extrusive igneous rocks, as veins, and are also present in many types of metamorphic rock. Rock formed entirely of plagioclase feldspar is known as anorthosite.

a. 1700 Cascadia earthquake
c. 1703 Genroku earthquake

b. 1509 Istanbul earthquake
d. Feldspars

30. _____ is the second most abundant mineral in the Earth's continental crust. It is made up of a framework of silicon-oxygen tetrahedra SiO_4, with each silicon shared between two oxygens to give the overall formula SiO_2. _____ has a hardness of 7 on the Mohs scale and a density of 2.65 g/cm³.

a. 1700 Cascadia earthquake
c. 1703 Genroku earthquake

b. 1509 Istanbul earthquake
d. Quartz

31. _____ is a naturally occurring material composed primarily of fine-grained minerals, which show plasticity through a variable range of water content, and which can be hardened when dried and/or fired. _____ deposits are mostly composed of _____ minerals (phyllosilicate minerals), minerals which impart plasticity and harden when fired and/or dried, and variable amounts of water trapped in the mineral structure by polar attraction. Organic materials which do not impart plasticity may also be a part of _____ deposits.

a. 1509 Istanbul earthquake
c. Clay

b. 1700 Cascadia earthquake
d. 1703 Genroku earthquake

32. _____ are hydrous aluminium phyllosilicates, sometimes with variable amounts of iron, magnesium, alkali metals, alkaline earths and other cations. Clays have structures similar to the micas and therefore form flat hexagonal sheets.
_____ are common weathering products (including weathering of feldspar) and low temperature hydrothermal alteration products.

a. 1509 Istanbul earthquake
c. Kaolinite

b. Clay minerals
d. 1700 Cascadia earthquake

Chapter 6. Weathering, Soil, and Sedimentary Rocks

33. The _____ , usually abbreviated K for its German translation Kreide, is a geologic period and system from circa >145.5 >± 4 to >65.5 >± 0.3 million years ago . In the geologic timescale, the _____ follows on the Jurassic period and is followed by the Paleogene period. It is the youngest period of the Mesozoic era, and at 80 million years long, the longest period of the Phanerozoic eon. The end of the _____ defines the boundary between the Mesozoic and Cenozoic eras.
   a. Coniacian
   b. Hauterivian
   c. Campanian
   d. Cretaceous

34. _____ is a sedimentary rock composed mainly of sand-size mineral or rock grains. Most _____ is composed of quartz and/or feldspar because these are the most common minerals in the Earth's crust. Like sand, _____ may be any color, but the most common colors are tan, brown, yellow, red, gray and white.
   a. Sandstone
   b. Dolostone
   c. Lithification
   d. Porcellanite

35. A _____ is a compound containing an anion in which one or more central silicon atoms are surrounded by electronegative ligands. This definition is broad enough to include species such as hexafluorosilicate ('fluorosilicate'), $[SiF_6]^{2-}$, but the _____ species that are encountered most often consist of silicon with oxygen as the ligand. _____ anions, with a negative net electrical charge, must have that charge balanced by other cations to make an electrically neutral compound.
   a. 1703 Genroku earthquake
   b. Silicate
   c. 1509 Istanbul earthquake
   d. 1700 Cascadia earthquake

36. The _____ make up the largest and most important class of rock-forming minerals, comprising approximately 90 percent of the crust of the Earth. They are classified based on the structure of their silicate group. _____ all contain silicon and oxygen.
   a. 1509 Istanbul earthquake
   b. Mineraloid
   c. 1700 Cascadia earthquake
   d. Silicate minerals

37. A _____ column (or _____) is a column of rising air in the lower altitudes of the Earth's atmosphere. They are created by the uneven heating of the Earth's surface from solar radiation, and an example of convection. The Sun warms the ground, which in turn warms the air directly above it.
   a. 1703 Genroku earthquake
   b. 1509 Istanbul earthquake
   c. Thermal
   d. 1700 Cascadia earthquake

38. _____ defines an important group of generally dark-colored rock-forming inosilicate minerals, composed of double chain SiO_4 tetrahedra, linked at the vertices and generally containing ions of iron and/or magnesium in their structures. They crystallize into two crystal systems, monoclinic and orthorhombic. In chemical composition and general characteristics they are similar to the pyroxenes. They are minerals of either igneous or metamorphic origin; in the former case occurring as constituents (hornblende) of igneous rocks, such as granite, diorite, andesite and others. Those of metamorphic origin include examples such as those developed in limestones by contact metamorphism (tremolite) and those formed by the alteration of other ferromagnesian minerals (hornblende).
   a. AL 129-1
   b. AL 333
   c. AASHTO Soil Classification System
   d. Amphibole

39. _____ is a carbonate mineral and the most stable polymorph of calcium carbonate ($CaCO_3$.) The other polymorphs are the minerals aragonite and vaterite. Aragonite will change to _____ at 470>°C, and vaterite is even less stable.

_____ is a common constituent of sedimentary rocks, limestone in particular, much of which is formed from the shells of dead marine organisms. Approximately 10% of sedimentary rock is limestone.

a. 1700 Cascadia earthquake
b. 1703 Genroku earthquake
c. 1509 Istanbul earthquake
d. Calcite

40. _____ is water located beneath the ground surface in soil pore spaces and in the fractures of lithologic formations. A unit of rock or an unconsolidated deposit is called an aquifer when it can yield a usable quantity of water. The depth at which soil pore spaces or fractures and voids in rock become completely saturated with water is called the water table.

a. Groundwater
b. 1509 Istanbul earthquake
c. 1700 Cascadia earthquake
d. Depression focused recharge

41. The mineral _____ is a magnesium iron silicate with the formula $(Mg,Fe)_2SiO_4$. It is one of the most common minerals on Earth, and has also been identified in meteorites and on the Moon, Mars, and comet Wild 2.

The ratio of magnesium and iron varies between the two endmembers of the solid solution series: forsterite (Mg-endmember) and fayalite (Fe-endmember.)

a. AL 333
b. AL 129-1
c. AASHTO Soil Classification System
d. Olivine

42. The _____ are a group of important rock-forming silicate minerals found in many igneous and metamorphic rocks. They share a common structure consisting of single chains of silica tetrahedra and they crystallize in the monoclinic and orthorhombic systems. _____ have the general formula $XY(Si,Al)_2O_6$ (where X represents calcium, sodium, iron^{+2} and magnesium and more rarely zinc, manganese and lithium and Y represents ions of smaller size, such as chromium, aluminium, iron^{+3}, magnesium, manganese, scandium, titanium, vanadium and even iron^{+2}).

a. Pyroxenes
b. 1703 Genroku earthquake
c. 1509 Istanbul earthquake
d. 1700 Cascadia earthquake

43. _____ is an important tectosilicate mineral which forms igneous rock. The name is from the Greek for 'straight fracture,' because its two cleavage planes are at right angles to each other. An alternate name is alkali feldspar.

_____ is a common constituent of most granites and other felsic igneous rocks and often forms huge crystals and masses in pegmatite.

a. AL 129-1
b. AASHTO Soil Classification System
c. AL 333
d. Orthoclase

44. _____ is a common extrusive volcanic rock. It is usually grey to black and fine-grained due to rapid cooling of lava at the surface of a planet. It may be porphyritic containing larger crystals in a fine matrix, or vesicular, or frothy scoria.

a. 1700 Cascadia earthquake
b. 1703 Genroku earthquake
c. 1509 Istanbul earthquake
d. Basalt

Chapter 6. Weathering, Soil, and Sedimentary Rocks

45. _____ is a hard metamorphic rock which was originally sandstone. Sandstone is converted into _____ through heating and pressure usually related to tectonic compression within orogenic belts. Pure _____ is usually white to grey, though quartzites often occur in various shades of pink and red due to varying amounts of iron oxide .
 a. Schist
 b. Metaconglomerate
 c. Foliation
 d. Quartzite

46. _____ is a layer of loose, heterogeneous material covering solid rock. It includes dust, soil, broken rock, and other related materials and is present on Earth, the Moon, some asteroids, and other planets. The term was first defined by George P. Merrill in 1897 who stated, 'In places this covering is made up of material originating through rock-weathering or plant growth in situ. In other instances it is of fragmental and more or less decomposed matter drifted by wind, water or ice from other sources. This entire mantle of unconsolidated material, whatever its nature or origin, it is proposed to call the _____.'
 a. 1509 Istanbul earthquake
 b. 1700 Cascadia earthquake
 c. 1703 Genroku earthquake
 d. Regolith

47. _____ is a type of chemical weathering that creates rounded boulders and helps to create domed monoliths. This should not be confused with stream abrasion, a physical process which also creates rounded rocks on a much smaller scale. A good example of _____ can be found in the Alabama Hills area of eastern California.
 a. Deposition
 b. Hydrothermal circulation
 c. Stoping
 d. Spheroidal weathering

48. '_____' is degraded organic material in soil, which causes some soil layers to be dark brown or black.

In soil science, _____ refers to any organic matter that has reached a point of stability, where it will break down no further and might, if conditions do not change, remain essentially as it is for centuries, if not millennia.

 a. 1509 Istanbul earthquake
 b. 1703 Genroku earthquake
 c. 1700 Cascadia earthquake
 d. Humus

49. _____ is soil or rock derived granular material of a grain size between sand and clay. _____ may occur as a soil or as suspended sediment in a surface water body. It may also exist as soil deposited at the bottom of a water body.
 a. Silt
 b. 1703 Genroku earthquake
 c. 1509 Istanbul earthquake
 d. 1700 Cascadia earthquake

50. A _____ is a specific layer in the soil which measures parallel to the soil surface and possesses physical characteristics which differ from the layers above and beneath. Horizon formation is a function of a range of geological, chemical, and biological processes and occurs over long time periods. Soils vary in the degree to which horizons are expressed.
 a. Vertisol
 b. Mollisols
 c. Laterite
 d. Soil horizon

51. _____ is any particulate matter that can be transported by fluid flow, and which eventually is deposited.

They are most often transported by water (fluvial processes) transported by wind (aeolian processes) and glaciers. Beach sands and river channel deposits are examples of fluvial transport and deposition, though _____ also often settles out of slow-moving or standing water in lakes and oceans.

Chapter 6. Weathering, Soil, and Sedimentary Rocks

a. Brickearth
c. Quicksand
b. Sediment
d. Bovey Beds

52. _____ is a sedimentary rock, a hardened deposit of calcium carbonate. This calcium carbonate cements together other materials, including gravel, sand, clay, and silt. It is found in aridisol and mollisol soil orders.
   a. 1509 Istanbul earthquake
   c. Caliche
   b. 1703 Genroku earthquake
   d. 1700 Cascadia earthquake

53. _____ is a surface formation in hot and wet tropical areas which is enriched in iron and aluminium and develops by intensive and long lasting weathering of the underlying parent rock. Nearly all kinds of rocks can be deeply decomposed by the action of high rainfall and elevated temperatures. The percolating rain water causes dissolution of primary rock minerals and decrease of easily soluble elements as sodium, potassium, calcium, magnesium and silicon.
   a. Paleosol
   c. Laterite
   b. Podsol
   d. Soil structure

54. The _____ is the epoch from 1.8 million to 11550 years BP covering the world's recent period of repeated glaciations. The _____ epoch follows the Pliocene epoch and is followed by the Holocene epoch. The _____ is the third epoch of the Neogene period or 6th epoch of the Cenozoic Era. The end of the _____ corresponds with the retreat of the last continental glacier. It also corresponds with the end of the Paleolithic age used in archaeology.
   a. Sicilian Stage
   c. Late Pleistocene
   b. Tyrrhenian
   d. Pleistocene

55. _____ is the upper, outermost layer of soil, usually the top 2 inches (5.1 cm) to 8 inches (20 cm.) It has the highest concentration of organic matter and microorganisms and is where most of the Earth's biological soil activity occurs. Plants generally concentrate their roots in and obtain most of their nutrients from this layer.
   a. 1509 Istanbul earthquake
   c. Slump
   b. Soil
   d. Topsoil

56. An _____ is a confined aquifer containing groundwater that will flow upward through a well without the need for pumping. Water may even reach the ground surface if the natural pressure is high enough, in which case the well is called a flowing artesian well. An aquifer provides the water for an artesian well.
   a. AASHTO Soil Classification System
   c. Artesian aquifer
   b. AL 333
   d. AL 129-1

57. _____ is the process by which soil is created. It is the major topic of the science of pedology, whose other aspects include the soil morphology, classification (taxonomy) of soils, and their distribution in nature, present and past (soil geography and paleopedology).
   a. Podsol
   c. Laterite
   b. Pedogenesis
   d. Soil structure

58. The _____ or the Dirty Thirties was a period of severe dust storms causing major ecological and agricultural damage to American and Canadian prairie lands from 1930 to 1936 (in some areas until 1940.) The phenomenon was caused by severe drought coupled with decades of extensive farming without crop rotation or other techniques to prevent erosion. Deep plowing of the virgin topsoil of the Great Plains had killed the natural grasses that normally kept the soil in place and trapped moisture even during periods of drought and high winds.

Chapter 6. Weathering, Soil, and Sedimentary Rocks

a. 1700 Cascadia earthquake
c. 1509 Istanbul earthquake
b. Dust Bowl
d. 1703 Genroku earthquake

59. In geology, _____ is transported rock debris overlying the solid bedrock. The term is also sometimes refers to organic debris so-transported. In the largest sense, it refers to the material left behind by retreating continental glaciers.
 a. Geodiversity
 b. Patterned ground
 c. Drift
 d. Platform cover

60. _____ in the French school of pedology are two regressive evolution processes associated with the loss of equilibrium of a stable soil. Retrogression is primarily due to erosion and corresponds to a phenomenon where succession reverts back to pioneer conditions (such as bare ground.) Degradation is an evolution, different of natural evolution, related to the locale climate and vegetation.
 a. Soils retrogression and degradation
 b. 1700 Cascadia earthquake
 c. 1703 Genroku earthquake
 d. 1509 Istanbul earthquake

61. A _____ is a narrow and shallow incision into soil resulting from erosion by overland flow that has been focused into a thin thread by soil surface roughness. Rilling, the process of _____ formation, is common on agricultural land and unvegetated ground.
 a. Planar deformation features
 b. Primordial water
 c. Salt tectonics
 d. Rill

62. _____ is the most important aluminium ore. It consists largely of the minerals gibbsite $Al(OH)_3$, boehmite >γ-AlO(OH), and diaspore >α-AlO(OH), together with the iron oxides goethite and hematite, the clay mineral kaolinite and small amounts of anatase TiO_2. It was named after the village Les Baux in southern France, where it was first discovered in 1821 by the geologist Pierre Berthier.
 a. 1703 Genroku earthquake
 b. Bauxite
 c. 1509 Istanbul earthquake
 d. 1700 Cascadia earthquake

63. _____ is a clay mineral with the chemical composition $Al_2Si_2O_5(OH)_4$. It is a layered silicate mineral, with one tetrahedral sheet linked through oxygen atoms to one octahedral sheet of alumina octahedra. Rocks that are rich in _____ are known as china clay or kaolin. _____ clay occurs in abundance in soils that have formed from the chemical weathering of rocks in hot, moist climates - for example in tropical rainforest areas
 a. 1700 Cascadia earthquake
 b. Kaolinite
 c. 1509 Istanbul earthquake
 d. Clay minerals

64. _____ is a method of farming used when a slope is too steep or too long, or when other types of farming may not prevent soil erosion. _____ alternates strips of closely sown crops such as hay, wheat, or other small grains with strips of row crops, such as corn, soybeans, cotton, or sugar beets. It is also known as strip cropping.

_____ helps to stop soil erosion by creating natural dams for water, helping to preserve the strength of the soil. Certain layers of plants will absorb minerals and water from the soil more effectively than others. When water reaches the weaker soil that lacks the minerals needed to make it stronger, it normally washes it away.

 a. 1509 Istanbul earthquake
 b. 1703 Genroku earthquake
 c. Strip farming
 d. 1700 Cascadia earthquake

Chapter 6. Weathering, Soil, and Sedimentary Rocks

65. The _____ is a fundamental concept in geology that describes the dynamic transitions through geologic time among the three main rock types: sedimentary, metamorphic, and igneous. Each type of rock is altered or destroyed when it is forced out of its equilibrium conditions. An igneous rock such as basalt may break down and dissolve when exposed to the atmosphere, or melt as it is subducted under a continent.
   a. Petrology
   b. Volcanic rock
   c. Laccolith
   d. Rock cycle

66. _____ is mechanical scraping of a rock surface by friction between rocks and moving particles during their transport in wind, glacier, waves, gravity or running water, after friction, the moving particles dislodge loose and weak debris from the side of the rock, these particles can be dissolved in the water source.

The intensity of _____ depends on the hardness, concentration, velocity and mass of moving particles.

A virtually smooth marine platform cut by the ocean waves at a coastline.

   a. AL 333
   b. AASHTO Soil Classification System
   c. AL 129-1
   d. Abrasion

67. _____ refers to the process by which a sediment progressively loses its porosity due to the effects of loading. This forms part of the process of lithification. When a layer of sediment is originally deposited, it contains an open framework of particles with the pore space being usually filled with water.
   a. Stack
   b. Compaction
   c. Platform
   d. Combe

68. _____ is a geological term used to describe particles of rock derived from pre-existing rock through processes of weathering and erosion. Thesel particles can consist of lithic fragments (particles of recognisable rock), or of monomineralic fragments (mineral grains.) These particles are often transported through sedimentary processes into depositional systems such as riverbeds, lakes or the ocean forming sedimentary successions.
   a. Detritus
   b. Medical geology
   c. Geomechanics
   d. Perched coastline

69. _____ is the process in which sediments compact under pressure, expel connate fluids, and gradually become solid rock. Essentially, _____ is a process of porosity destruction through compaction and cementation. _____ includes all the processes which convert unconsolidated sediments into sedimentary rocks.
   a. Jasperoid
   b. Metasediment
   c. Dolomite
   d. Lithification

70. _____ are waves that travel through the Earth or other elastic body, for example as the result of an earthquake, explosion, or some other process that imparts forces to the body. _____ are also continually excited on Earth by the incessant pounding of ocean waves (referred to as the microseism) and the wind. _____ are studied by seismologists, and measured by a seismograph, which records the output of a seismometer, or geophone.
   a. Harmonic tremor
   b. Seismic waves
   c. Maximum magnitude
   d. Shadow zone

Chapter 6. Weathering, Soil, and Sedimentary Rocks

71. _____ is caused by movement of ice, typically as glaciers. Glaciers erode predominantly by three different processes: abrasion/scouring, plucking, and ice thrusting. In an abrasion process, debris in the basal ice scrapes along the bed, polishing and gouging the underlying rocks, similar to sandpaper on wood. Glaciers can also cause pieces of bedrock to crack off in the process of plucking. In ice thrusting, the glacier freezes to its bed, then as it surges forward, it moves large sheets of frozen sediment at the base along with the glacier. This method produced some of the many thousands of lake basins that dot the edge of the Canadian Shield. These processes, combined with erosion and transport by the water network beneath the glacier, leave moraines, drumlins, eskers, ground moraine (till), kames, kame deltas, moulins, and glacial erratics in their wake, typically at the terminus or during glacier retreat.

    a. AL 129-1   b. AL 333
    c. AASHTO Soil Classification System   d. Ice erosion

72. _____ is the chemical element with the symbol Ca and atomic number 20. It has an atomic mass of 40.078 amu. _____ is a soft grey alkaline earth metal, and is the fifth most abundant element by mass in the Earth's crust.

    a. 1700 Cascadia earthquake   b. Calcium
    c. 1703 Genroku earthquake   d. 1509 Istanbul earthquake

73. _____ is a chemical compound with the chemical formula $CaCO_3$. It is a common substance found in rock in all parts of the world, and is the main component of shells of marine organisms, snails, pearls, and eggshells. _____ is the active ingredient in agricultural lime, and is usually the principal cause of hard water.

    a. 1509 Istanbul earthquake   b. 1703 Genroku earthquake
    c. 1700 Cascadia earthquake   d. Calcium carbonate

74. _____ is the process of determining a specific date for an archaeological or palaeontological site or artifact. Some archaeologists prefer the terms chronometric or calendar dating, as use of the word 'absolute' implies a certainty and precision that is rarely possible in archaeology. _____ is usually based on the physical or chemical properties of the materials of artifacts, buildings, or other items that have been modified by humans.

    a. AASHTO Soil Classification System   b. Uranium-lead dating
    c. Erathem   d. Absolute dating

75. In chemistry, a _____ is a salt or ester of carbonic acid.

To test for the presence of the _____ anion in a salt, the addition of dilute mineral acid (e.g. hydrochloric acid) will yield carbon dioxide gas.

_____-containing salts are industrially and mineralogically ubiquitous.

    a. Carbonate   b. 1700 Cascadia earthquake
    c. 1509 Istanbul earthquake   d. 1703 Genroku earthquake

76. _____ rocks are composed of fragments of pre-existing rock. The term is most commonly, but not uniquely, applied to sedimentary rocks.

_____ metamorphic rocks include breccias formed in faults, as well as some protomylonite and pseudotachylite.

Chapter 6. Weathering, Soil, and Sedimentary Rocks

a. 1700 Cascadia earthquake
b. 1509 Istanbul earthquake
c. 1703 Genroku earthquake
d. Clastic

77. A _____ is a rock consisting of individual stones that have become cemented together. They are sedimentary rocks consisting of rounded fragments and are thus differentiated from breccias, which consist of angular clasts. Both conglomerates and breccias are characterized by clasts larger than sand (>2 mm).
    a. Keystone
    b. Conglomerate
    c. Pelagic sediments
    d. Porcellanite

78. _____ is a rock composed of angular fragments of minerals or rocks in a matrix (cementing material), that may be similar or different in composition to the fragments. A _____ may have a variety of different origins, as indicated by the named types including sedimentary _____, tectonic _____, igneous _____, impact _____ and hydrothermal _____.

Sedimentary breccias are a type of clastic sedimentary rock which are composed of angular to subangular, randomly oriented clasts of other sedimentary rocks.

   a. Ventifacts
   b. Breccia
   c. 1509 Istanbul earthquake
   d. Fault breccia

79. _____ is one of the three main rock types (the others being sedimentary and metamorphic rock.) _____ is formed by magma (molten rock) being cooled and becoming solid. They may form with or without crystallization, either below the surface as intrusive (plutonic) rocks or on the surface as extrusive (volcanic) rocks. They make up approximately 95% of the upper part of the Earth's crust, but their great abundance is hidden on the Earth's surface by a relatively thin but widespread layer of sedimentary and metamorphic rocks.
    a. AL 129-1
    b. Igneous rock
    c. AASHTO Soil Classification System
    d. AL 333

80. _____ is a fine grained sedimentary rock whose original constituents were clays or muds. Grain size is up to 0.0625 mm with individual grains too small to be distinguished without a microscope. With increased pressure over time the platey clay minerals may become aligned, with the appearance of fissility or parallel layering.
    a. Jasperoid
    b. Diatomaceous earth
    c. Shale
    d. Mudstone

81. _____ is a fine-grained sedimentary rock whose original constituents were clay minerals or muds. It is characterized by thin laminae breaking with an irregular curving fracture, often splintery and usually parallel to the often-indistinguishable bedding plane. This property is called fissility.
    a. Mudstone
    b. Pelagic sediments
    c. Metasediment
    d. Shale

82. _____ is rock that is of a specific particle size range. Specifically, it is any loose rock that is larger than two millimeters (2mm) in its largest dimension (about 1/12 of an inch) and no more than 64 millimeters (about 2.5 inches.) The next smaller size class in geology is sand, which is >0.0625 mm to 2 mm in size.
    a. Gravel
    b. 1703 Genroku earthquake
    c. 1509 Istanbul earthquake
    d. 1700 Cascadia earthquake

Chapter 6. Weathering, Soil, and Sedimentary Rocks

83. _____ is the name of a sedimentary carbonate rock and a mineral, both composed of calcium magnesium carbonate $CaMg_2$ found in crystals.

_____ rock (also dolostone) is composed predominantly of the mineral _____. Limestone that is partially replaced by _____ is referred to as dolomitic limestone, or in old U.S. geologic literature as magnesian limestone.

a. Dolomite
b. Metasediment
c. Porcellanite
d. Dolostone

84. _____ or dolomite rock is a sedimentary carbonate rock that contains a high percentage of the mineral dolomite. In old U.S.G.S. publications it was referred to as magnesian limestone. Most _____ formed as a magnesium replacement of limestone or lime mud prior to lithification.

a. Jasperoid
b. Pelagic sediments
c. Lithification
d. Dolostone

85. _____ are water-soluble mineral sediments that result from the evaporation of bodies of surficial water. _____ are considered sedimentary rocks.

Although all water bodies on the surface and in aquifers contain dissolved salts, the water must evaporate into the atmosphere for the minerals to precipitate.

a. AASHTO Soil Classification System
b. AL 333
c. Evaporites
d. AL 129-1

86. _____ is a sedimentary rock composed largely of the mineral calcite (calcium carbonate: $CaCO_3$.) The deposition of _____ strata is often a by-product and indicator of biological activity in the geologic record. Calcium (along with nitrogen, phosphorus, and potassium) is a key mineral to plant nutrition: soils overlying _____ bedrock tend to be pre-fertilized with calcium.

a. Limestone
b. 1509 Istanbul earthquake
c. 1703 Genroku earthquake
d. 1700 Cascadia earthquake

87. _____ is a hard, compact variety of mineral coal that has a high lustre. It has the highest carbon count and contains the fewest impurities of all coals, despite its lower calorific content.

_____ is the highest of the metamorphic rank, in which the carbon content is between 92% and 98%.

a. AL 129-1
b. AASHTO Soil Classification System
c. AL 333
d. Anthracite

88. _____ is a relatively soft coal containing a tarlike substance called bitumen. It is of higher quality than lignite coal but of poorer quality than anthracite coal.

_____ is a sedimorphic rock formed by diagenetic and submetamorphic compression of peat bog material.

Chapter 6. Weathering, Soil, and Sedimentary Rocks

a. 1509 Istanbul earthquake
c. Bituminous coal
b. 1700 Cascadia earthquake
d. 1703 Genroku earthquake

89. _____ is a fine-grained silica-rich microcrystalline, cryptocrystalline or microfibrous sedimentary rock that may contain small fossils. It varies greatly in color (from white to black), but most often manifests as gray, brown, grayish brown and light green to rusty red; its color is an expression of trace elements present in the rock, and both red and green are most often related to traces of iron (in its oxidized and reduced forms respectively.)

_____ occurs as oval to irregular nodules in greensand, limestone, chalk, and dolostone formations as a replacement mineral, where it is formed as a result of some type of diagenesis.

a. 1700 Cascadia earthquake
c. 1703 Genroku earthquake
b. 1509 Istanbul earthquake
d. Chert

90. A _____ in petrology or mineralogy is a secondary structure, generally spherical or irregularly rounded in shape. They are typically solid replacement bodies of chert or iron oxides formed during diagenesis of a sedimentary rock. They may be hollow as geodes or vugs or filled with crystals and intricate geometric shrinkage patterns as in septarian nodules.
a. Nodule
c. Streak
b. Diamond Head
d. Combe

91. _____ is an accumulation of partially decayed vegetation matter. _____ forms in wetlands or peatlands, variously called bogs, moors, muskegs, pocosins, mires, and _____ swamp forests. By volume there are about 4 trillion mÂÅ³ of _____ in the world covering a total of around 2% of global land mass (about 3 million km²), containing about 8 billion terajoules of energy.
a. 1509 Istanbul earthquake
c. 1703 Genroku earthquake
b. 1700 Cascadia earthquake
d. Peat

92. In geology, _____ are a body of rock with specified characteristics. Ideally, a _____ is a distinctive rock unit that forms under certain conditions of sedimentation, reflecting a particular process or environment.

The term _____ was introduced by the Swiss geologist Amanz Gressly in 1838 and was part of his significant contribution to the foundations of modern stratigraphy, [Cross and Homewood (1997)] which replaced the earlier notions of Neptunism.

a. Mylonite
c. Facies
b. Granulites
d. Schist

93. _____ is a naturally occurring granular material composed of finely divided rock and mineral particles.

As the term is used by geologists, _____ particles range in diameter from 0.0625 (or >$^1\!/_{16}$ mm, or 62.5 micrometers) to 2 millimeters. An individual particle in this range size is termed a _____ grain.

a. 1509 Istanbul earthquake
c. Sand
b. 1703 Genroku earthquake
d. 1700 Cascadia earthquake

Chapter 6. Weathering, Soil, and Sedimentary Rocks

94. In chronostratigraphy, a _____ is a succession of rock strata laid down in an single age on the geologic timescale, which usually represents millions of years of deposition. A given _____ of rock and the corresponding age of time will by convention have the same name, and the same boundaries.
    a. Stage
    b. Relative dating
    c. Chronostratigraphy
    d. Geologic record

95. A _____ or sandbar is a somewhat linear landform within or extending into a body of water, typically composed of sand, silt or small pebbles. A bar is characteristically long and narrow and develops where a stream or ocean current promotes deposition of granular material, resulting in localized shallowing of the water. Bars can appear in the sea, in a lake, or in a river.

    The term _____ can be applied to larger geological units that form off a coastline as part of the process of coastal erosion. These include spits and baymouth bars that form across the front of embayments and rias. A tombolo is a bar that forms an isthmus between an island or offshore rock and a mainland shore.

    a. 1703 Genroku earthquake
    b. 1509 Istanbul earthquake
    c. 1700 Cascadia earthquake
    d. Shoal

96. In geology a _____ is the smallest division of a geologic formation or stratigraphic rock series marked by well-defined divisional planes (bedding planes) separating it from layers above and below. A _____ is the smallest lithostratigraphic unit, usually ranging in thickness from a centimeter to several meters and distinguishable from beds above and below it. Beds can be differentiated in various ways, including rock or mineral type and particle size.
    a. Biozones
    b. Sequence stratigraphy
    c. Bed
    d. Cyclostratigraphy

97. The _____ is a geologic formation that is spread across the U.S. states of northern Arizona, Nevada, Utah, western New Mexico, and western Colorado. The _____ is controversially considered to be synonymous to Dockum Group in eastern Colorado, eastern New Mexico, southwestern Kansas, the Oklahoma panhandle, and western Texas. The _____ is sometimes colloquially used as a geologic formation within the Dockum in New Mexico and occasionally in Texas.
    a. Diamond Head
    b. Cohesion
    c. Chinle
    d. Stack

98. In geology, _____ refers to inclined sedimentary structures in a horizontal unit of rock. These tilted structures are deposits from bedforms such as ripples and dunes, and they indicate that the depositional environment contained a flowing fluid (typically, water or wind.) This is a case in geology when original depositional layering is tilted, and that the tilting is not a result of post-depositional deformation.
    a. Geomicrobiology
    b. Cross-bedding
    c. Platform cover
    d. Schmidt hammer

99. _____ are those structures formed during sediment deposition.

    _____ such as cross bedding, graded bedding and ripple marks are utilized in stratigraphic studies to indicate original position of strata in geologically complex terranes.

    There are two kinds of flow regimes, which at varying speeds and velocities produce different structures.

Chapter 6. Weathering, Soil, and Sedimentary Rocks

a. 1509 Istanbul earthquake
c. 1703 Genroku earthquake
b. 1700 Cascadia earthquake
d. Sedimentary structures

100. _____ are the preserved remains or traces of animals, plants, and other organisms from the remote past. The totality of _____, both discovered and undiscovered, and their placement in fossiliferous rock formations and sedimentary layers (strata) is known as the fossil record. The study of _____ across geological time, how they were formed, and the evolutionary relationships between taxa (phylogeny) are some of the most important functions of the science of paleontology.

a. 1700 Cascadia earthquake
c. 1509 Istanbul earthquake
b. 1703 Genroku earthquake
d. Fossils

101. A _____ is a mountain rising from the ocean seafloor that does not reach to the water's surface (sea level), and thus is not an island. These are typically formed from extinct volcanoes, that rise abruptly and are usually found rising from a seafloor of 1,000-4,000 meters depth. They are defined by oceanographers as independent features that rise to at least 1,000 meters above the seafloor.

a. 1509 Istanbul earthquake
c. Seamount
b. 1700 Cascadia earthquake
d. 1703 Genroku earthquake

102. The _____ is a geologic period and system of the Paleozoic era spanning from >416 to 359.2 million years ago (ICS, 2004.).

During the _____ Period, which occurred in the Paleozoic era, the first fish evolved legsand started to walk on land as tetrapods around 365 Ma.

a. 1509 Istanbul earthquake
c. Xitun Formation
b. Gogo Formation
d. Devonian

103. In geology, _____ are sedimentary structures that indicate agitation by water (current or waves) or wind. _____ formed by water consist of two basic types:

1. Current _____ are asymmetrical in profile, with a gentle up-current slope and a steeper down-current slope. The down-current slope depends on the shape of the sediment, with 33>° being typical.
2. Wave-formed _____ have a symmetrical, almost sinusoidal profile; they indicate an environment with weak currents where water motion is dominated by wave oscillations.

Ripples will not form in sediment larger than course sand.

a. 1700 Cascadia earthquake
c. 1703 Genroku earthquake
b. 1509 Istanbul earthquake
d. Ripple marks

104. In geology, a _____ or _____ line is a planar fracture in rock in which the rock on one side of the fracture has moved with respect to the rock on the other side. Large faults within the Earth's crust are the result of differential or shear motion and active _____ zones are the causal locations of most earthquakes. Earthquakes are caused by energy release during rapid slippage along a _____.

Chapter 6. Weathering, Soil, and Sedimentary Rocks

    a. Dali
    b. Combe
    c. Stack
    d. Fault

105. The _____ is an Eocene geologic formation that records the sedimentation in a series of intermountain lakes. The sedimentary layers were formed in a large area of interconnecting lakes a tributary of the Colorado River. The area of the formation exists as three separate basins around the Uinta Mountains of northeastern Utah: an area in northwestern Colorado east of the Uintas, a larger area in the southwest corner of Wyoming just north of the Uintas known as Lake Gosiute, and the largest area, which lies in northeastern Utah and western Colorado south of the Uintas, known as Lake Uinta.
    a. 1700 Cascadia earthquake
    b. 1703 Genroku earthquake
    c. 1509 Istanbul earthquake
    d. Green River Formation

106. _____ is a mixture of organic chemical compounds that make up a portion of the organic matter in sedimentary rocks. It is insoluble in normal organic solvents because of the huge molecular weight (upwards of 1,000 Daltons) of its component compounds. The soluble portion is known as bitumen.
    a. 1509 Istanbul earthquake
    b. 1703 Genroku earthquake
    c. 1700 Cascadia earthquake
    d. Kerogen

107. _____ is an organic-rich fine-grained sedimentary rock. It contains significant amounts of kerogen, a solid mixture of organic chemical compounds from which liquid hydrocarbons can be extracted. Deposits of _____ occur around the world, including major deposits in the United States of America. Estimates of global deposits range from 2.8 trillion to 3.3 trillion barrels >(450 >× 10^9 to 520 >× 10^9 m^3) of recoverable oil.
    a. AASHTO Soil Classification System
    b. Oil shale
    c. AL 129-1
    d. AL 333

108. The _____ is a geologic subperiod and stratigraphic subsystem of the Carboniferous Period. It is the later subperiod of the Carboniferous, lasting from roughly 318.1>± 1.3 to 299>± 0.8 Ma (million years ago.) As with most other geochronologic units, the rock beds that define the _____ are well identified, but the exact date of the start and end are uncertain by a few million years.
    a. Calciferous sandstone
    b. Dinantian
    c. Mississippian
    d. Pennsylvanian

109. In geology, a _____ deposit or _____ is an accumulation of valuable minerals formed by deposition of dense mineral phases in a trap site. Types of _____ deposits include alluvium, eluvium, beach placers, and paleoplacers.

Typical locations for alluvial _____ deposits are on the inside bends of rivers and creeks, in natural hollows, at the break of slope on a stream, the base of an escarpment, waterfall or other barrier, within sand dunes, beach profiles or in gravel beds.

    a. 1509 Istanbul earthquake
    b. 1703 Genroku earthquake
    c. Placer
    d. 1700 Cascadia earthquake

110. The _____ is a continental transform fault that runs a length of roughly 800 miles (1,300 km) through California in the United States. The fault's motion is right-lateral strike-slip (horizontal motion.) It forms the tectonic boundary between the Pacific Plate and the North American Plate.

Chapter 6. Weathering, Soil, and Sedimentary Rocks 73

   a. 1703 Genroku earthquake
   b. 1509 Istanbul earthquake
   c. 1700 Cascadia earthquake
   d. San Andreas fault

111. _____ or extra heavy oil, is a type of bitumen deposit. The sands are naturally occurring mixtures of sand or clay, water and an extremely dense and viscous form of petroleum called bitumen. They are found in large amounts in many countries throughout the world, but are found in extremely large quantities in Canada and Venezuela.
   a. AASHTO Soil Classification System
   b. AL 129-1
   c. Oil sands
   d. AL 333

112. A _____ is an old and stable part of the continental crust that has survived the merging and splitting of continents and supercontinents for at least 500 million years. Some are over two billion years old. They are generally found in the interiors of continents and are characteristically composed of ancient crystalline basement crust of lightweight felsic igneous rock such as granite.
   a. Kalahari craton
   b. Craton
   c. Sebakwe proto-craton
   d. Superior craton

113. An _____ is a type of rock that contains minerals such as gemstones and metals that can be extracted through mining and refined for use. Samples of _____ in the form of exceptionally beautiful crystals, exotic layering visible when sectioned or polished or metallic presentations such as large nuggets or crystalline formations of metals such as gold or copper may command a value far beyond their value as mere _____ or raw metal for subsequent reduction to utilitarian purposes.

The grade or concentration of an _____ mineral, or metal, as well as its form of occurrence, will directly affect the costs associated with mining the _____.

   a. AL 129-1
   b. AASHTO Soil Classification System
   c. Ore genesis
   d. Ore

114. In geology, a _____ is a place where the Earth's crust and lithosphere are being pulled apart and is an example of extensional tectonics.

Typical _____ features are a central linear downdropped fault segment, called a graben, with parallel normal faulting and _____-flank uplifts on either side forming a _____ valley, where the _____ remains above sea level. The axis of the _____ area commonly contains volcanic rocks and active volcanism is a part of many, but not all active _____ systems.

   a. 1509 Istanbul earthquake
   b. Rift
   c. 1700 Cascadia earthquake
   d. 1703 Genroku earthquake

115. _____ are a distinctive type of rock often found in primordial sedimentary rocks. The structures consist of repeated thin layers of iron oxides, either magnetite or hematite, alternating with bands of iron-poor shale and chert. Some of the oldest known rock formations, formed around three thousand million years before present, include banded iron layers, and the banded layers are a common feature in sediments for much of the Earth's early history.
   a. Mudstone
   b. Jasperoid
   c. Superficial deposits
   d. Banded Iron Formations

116. The _____ is a physiographic region of the Intermontane Plateaus, roughly centered on the Four Corners region of the southwestern United States. The province covers an area of 337,000 km^2 within western Colorado, northwestern New Mexico, southern and eastern Utah, and northern Arizona. About 90% of the area is drained by the Colorado River and its main tributaries; the Green, San Juan and Little Colorado.

Development of the province has in large part been influenced by structural features in its oldest rocks. Part of the Wasatch Line and its various faults form the western edge of the province. Faults that run parallel to the Wasatch Fault that lies along the Wasatch Range form the boundaries between the plateaus in the High Plateaus Section. The Uinta Basin, Uncompahgre Uplift, and the Paradox Basin were also created by movement along structural weaknesses in the region's oldest rock.

a. 1703 Genroku earthquake
b. 1700 Cascadia earthquake
c. 1509 Istanbul earthquake
d. Colorado Plateau

Chapter 7. Metamorphism and Metamorphic Rocks

1. The _____ is the layer of igneous, sedimentary, and metamorphic rocks which form the continents and the areas of shallow seabed close to their shores, known as continental shelves. This layer is sometimes called sial due to more felsic, or granitic, bulk composition, which lies in contrast to the oceanic crust, called sima due to its mafic, or basaltic rock. (Based on the change in velocity of seismic waves, it is believed that at a certain depth sial becomes close in its physical properties to sima.
   a. Continental crust
   b. Tectonic plates
   c. Convergent boundary
   d. Nappe

2. The _____ is the geologic eon before the Archean. It started at Earth's formation about 4.6 billion years ago (4,600 Ma), and ended roughly 3.8 billion years ago, though the latter date varies according to different sources.
   a. 1703 Genroku earthquake
   b. 1700 Cascadia earthquake
   c. 1509 Istanbul earthquake
   d. Hadean

3. The _____ was a cratonic sequence that began in the mid-Devonian, peaked early in the Mississippian, and ended by mid-Mississippian time. A major unconformity separates it from the lower Tippecanoe sequence.

The basal-that is, the lowest and oldest-units of the Kaskaskia consist of clean quartz sandstones eroded from the Appalachian orogenic belt to the east, the Ozark Dome in the center of the continent, and south from the Canadian Shield.

   a. 1509 Istanbul earthquake
   b. 1700 Cascadia earthquake
   c. Sauk sequence
   d. Kaskaskia sequence

4. _____ is the result of the transformation of an existing rock type, the protolith, in a process called metamorphism, which means 'change in form'. The protolith is subjected to heat and pressure (temperatures greater than 150 to 200 >°C and pressures of 1500 bars) causing profound physical and/or chemical change. The protolith may be sedimentary rock, igneous rock or another older _____.
   a. Sedimentary rock
   b. Migmatite
   c. Metavolcanic rock
   d. Metamorphic rock

5. _____ is the solid-state recrystallization of pre-existing rocks due to changes in physical and chemical conditions, primarily heat, pressure, and the introduction of chemically active fluids. Both mineralogical, chemical and crystallographic changes can occur during this process.

Three types of _____ exist: dynamic, contact and regional.

   a. Metamorphism
   b. Reading Prong
   c. Compression
   d. Detritus

6. A _____ is generally a large area of exposed Precambrian crystalline igneous and high-grade metamorphic rocks that form tectonically stable areas. In all cases, the age of these rocks is greater than 570 million years and sometimes dates back 2 to 3.5 billion years. They have been little affected by tectonic events following the end of the Precambrian Era, and are relatively flat regions where mountain building, faulting, and other tectonic processes are greatly diminished compared with the activity that occurs at the margins of the shields and the boundaries between tectonic plates.
   a. 1509 Istanbul earthquake
   b. 1700 Cascadia earthquake
   c. 1703 Genroku earthquake
   d. Shield

Chapter 7. Metamorphism and Metamorphic Rocks

7. _____ is a fine-grained, foliated, homogeneous metamorphic rock derived from an original shale-type sedimentary rock composed of clay or volcanic ash through low grade regional metamorphism. The result is a foliated rock in which the foliation may not correspond to the original sedimentary layering. _____ is frequently grey in colour especially when seen en masse covering roofs.

- a. Hornfels
- b. Greenstone belts
- c. Talc carbonate
- d. Slate

8. _____ is the process of determining a specific date for an archaeological or palaeontological site or artifact. Some archaeologists prefer the terms chronometric or calendar dating, as use of the word 'absolute' implies a certainty and precision that is rarely possible in archaeology. _____ is usually based on the physical or chemical properties of the materials of artifacts, buildings, or other items that have been modified by humans.

- a. Erathem
- b. Uranium-lead dating
- c. AASHTO Soil Classification System
- d. Absolute dating

9. The _____ -- also called the Laurentian Plateau, or Bouclier Canadien -- is a massive geological shield covered by a thin layer of soil that forms the nucleus of the North American or Laurentia craton. It has a deep, common, joined bedrock region in eastern and central Canada and stretches North from the Great Lakes to the Arctic Ocean, covering over half of Canada; it also extends south into the northern reaches of the United States. Population is scarce, and industrial development is minimal, although the region has a large hydroelectric power potential.

- a. Canadian Shield
- b. Yilgarn Craton
- c. Gawler craton
- d. Grade

10. In geology, _____ is transported rock debris overlying the solid bedrock. The term is also sometimes refers to organic debris so-transported. In the largest sense, it refers to the material left behind by retreating continental glaciers.

- a. Drift
- b. Geodiversity
- c. Platform cover
- d. Patterned ground

11. _____ defines an important group of generally dark-colored rock-forming inosilicate minerals, composed of double chain SiO_4 tetrahedra, linked at the vertices and generally containing ions of iron and/or magnesium in their structures. They crystallize into two crystal systems, monoclinic and orthorhombic. In chemical composition and general characteristics they are similar to the pyroxenes. They are minerals of either igneous or metamorphic origin; in the former case occurring as constituents (hornblende) of igneous rocks, such as granite, diorite, andesite and others. Those of metamorphic origin include examples such as those developed in limestones by contact metamorphism (tremolite) and those formed by the alteration of other ferromagnesian minerals (hornblende).

- a. AL 333
- b. AASHTO Soil Classification System
- c. AL 129-1
- d. Amphibole

12. _____ or white asbestos is the most commonly encountered form of asbestos, accounting for approximately 95% of the asbestos in place in the United States and a similar proportion in other countries. It is a soft, fibrous silicate mineral in the serpentine group of phyllosilicates: as such, it is distinct from other asbestiform minerals in the amphibole group. Its idealized chemical formula is $Mg_3(Si_2O_5)(OH)_4$, in which some of the magnesium ions may be substituted by iron or other cations.

- a. Clay minerals
- b. Chrysotile
- c. 1700 Cascadia earthquake
- d. 1509 Istanbul earthquake

Chapter 7. Metamorphism and Metamorphic Rocks

13. A _____ is a compound containing an anion in which one or more central silicon atoms are surrounded by electronegative ligands. This definition is broad enough to include species such as hexafluorosilicate ('fluorosilicate'), $[SiF_6]^{2-}$, but the _____ species that are encountered most often consist of silicon with oxygen as the ligand. _____ anions, with a negative net electrical charge, must have that charge balanced by other cations to make an electrically neutral compound.
    a. Silicate
    b. 1700 Cascadia earthquake
    c. 1509 Istanbul earthquake
    d. 1703 Genroku earthquake

14. The _____ make up the largest and most important class of rock-forming minerals, comprising approximately 90 percent of the crust of the Earth. They are classified based on the structure of their silicate group. _____ all contain silicon and oxygen.
    a. 1509 Istanbul earthquake
    b. Mineraloid
    c. 1700 Cascadia earthquake
    d. Silicate minerals

15. The _____ is a chronologic schema (or idealized model) relating stratigraphy to time that is used by geologists, paleontologists and other earth scientists to describe the timing and relationships between events that have occurred during the history of the Earth. The table of geologic time spans presented here agrees with the dates and nomenclature proposed by the International Commission on Stratigraphy, and uses the standard color codes of the United States Geological Survey.

Evidence from radiometric dating indicates that the Earth is about 4.570 billion years old.

    a. 1703 Genroku earthquake
    b. 1700 Cascadia earthquake
    c. 1509 Istanbul earthquake
    d. Geologic time scale

16. In geology, _____ refers to heat sources within the planet. _____ is technically an adjective (e.g., _____ energy) but in U.S. English the word has attained frequent use as a noun.

The planet's internal heat was originally generated during its accretion, due to gravitational binding energy, and since then additional heat has continued to be generated by decay heat from the radioactive decay of elements.

    a. Diamond Head
    b. Dali
    c. Stratification
    d. Geothermal

17. The _____ is the rate of increase in temperature per unit depth in the Earth. It varies with location and is typically measured by determining the bottom open-hole temperature after borehole drilling. To achieve accuracy the drilling fluid needs time to reach the ambient temperature.
    a. Geothermal power
    b. Geothermal gradient
    c. Geothermal desalination
    d. Geothermal heat pump

18. _____ is water located beneath the ground surface in soil pore spaces and in the fractures of lithologic formations. A unit of rock or an unconsolidated deposit is called an aquifer when it can yield a usable quantity of water. The depth at which soil pore spaces or fractures and voids in rock become completely saturated with water is called the water table.
    a. Depression focused recharge
    b. 1509 Istanbul earthquake
    c. 1700 Cascadia earthquake
    d. Groundwater

Chapter 7. Metamorphism and Metamorphic Rocks

19. The _____ was a period of mountain building in western North America, which started in the Late Cretaceous, 70 to 80 million years ago, and ended 35 to 55 million years ago. The exact duration and ages of beginning and end of the orogeny are in dispute, as is the cause. The _____ occurred in a series of pulses, with quiescent phases intervening. The major feature that was created by this orogeny was the Rocky Mountains, but evidence of this orogeny can be found from Alaska to northern Mexico, with the easternmost extent of the mountain-building represented by the Black Hills of South Dakota.

a. Laramide orogeny
b. Kaikoura Orogeny
c. Sevier orogeny
d. Pan-African orogeny

20. _____ is molten rock expelled by a volcano during eruption. When first expelled from a volcanic vent, it is a liquid at temperatures from 700 >°C to 1,200 >°C (1,300 >°F to 2,200 >°F.) Although _____ is quite viscous, with about 100,000 times the viscosity of water, it can flow great distances before cooling and solidifying, because of both its thixotropic and shear thinning properties.

a. Supervolcano
b. Lava
c. Volcanic ash
d. Pit crater

21. Overburden pressure, _____, and vertical stress are terms that denote the pressure or stress imposed on a layer of soil or rock by the weight of overlying material.

The overburden pressure at a depth z is given by

where >ρ(z) is the density of the overlying rock at depth z and g is the acceleration due to gravity. p_0 is the datum pressure, like the pressure at the surface.

a. Transition zone
b. Sclavia craton
c. Marine clay
d. Lithostatic pressure

22. A _____ or mudslide is the most rapid (up to 80 km/h, or 50 mph) and fluid type of downhill mass wasting. It is a rapid movement of a large mass of mud formed from loose earth and water. Similar terms are mudslide (not very liquid), mud stream, debris flow (e.g. in high mountains), j>ökulhlaup, and lahar

a. 1700 Cascadia earthquake
b. 1703 Genroku earthquake
c. 1509 Istanbul earthquake
d. Mudflow

23. In geology, solid-state _____ is a metamorphic process that occurs under situations of intense temperature and pressure where grains, atoms or molecules of a rock or mineral are packed closer together, creating a new crystal structure. The basic composition remains the same. This process can be illustrated by observing how snow recrystallizes to ice without melting.

a. 1509 Istanbul earthquake
b. Recrystallization
c. 1703 Genroku earthquake
d. 1700 Cascadia earthquake

Chapter 7. Metamorphism and Metamorphic Rocks

24. Two important classifications of weathering processes exist -- physical and _____. Mechanical or physical weathering involves the breakdown of rocks and soils through direct contact with atmospheric conditions, such as heat, water, ice and pressure. The second classification, _____, involves the direct effect of atmospheric chemicals or biologically produced chemicals (also known as biological weathering) in the breakdown of rocks, soils and minerals.
   a. 1509 Istanbul earthquake
   b. Physical weathering
   c. Weathering
   d. Chemical weathering

25. _____ is one of the three main rock types (the others being sedimentary and metamorphic rock.) _____ is formed by magma (molten rock) being cooled and becoming solid . They may form with or without crystallization, either below the surface as intrusive (plutonic) rocks or on the surface as extrusive (volcanic) rocks. They make up approximately 95% of the upper part of the Earth's crust, but their great abundance is hidden on the Earth's surface by a relatively thin but widespread layer of sedimentary and metamorphic rocks.
   a. AL 129-1
   b. AASHTO Soil Classification System
   c. AL 333
   d. Igneous rock

26. A _____ is in geology an area where, as a result of metamorphism, the same combination of minerals occur in the bed rocks. These zones occur because most metamorphic minerals are only stable in certain intervals of temperature and pressure.

The temperature and pressure at which the mineralogical composition of a rock equilibrated can vary laterally through a metamorphic terrane.

   a. Metamorphic rock
   b. Metamorphic zone
   c. Tephra
   d. Magma

27. _____ refers to natural mountain building, and may be studied as a tectonic structural event, (b) as a geographical event, and (c) a chronological event. Orogenic events (a) cause distinctive structural phenomena and related tectonic activity, (b) affect certain regions of rocks and crust, and (c) happen within a specific period of time.
   a. Antler orogeny
   b. Orogeny
   c. Alice Springs Orogeny
   d. Orogenesis

28. _____ is the decomposition of Earth rocks, soils and their minerals through direct contact with the planet's atmosphere. _____ occurs in situ, or 'with no movement', and thus should not be confused with erosion, which involves the movement of rocks and minerals by agents such as water, ice, wind and gravity.

Two important classifications of _____ processes exist -- physical and chemical _____.

   a. Physical weathering
   b. 1509 Istanbul earthquake
   c. Weathering
   d. Frost disintegration

29. The _____, is a geologic eon before the Proterozoic and Paleoproterozoic, before 2.5 Ga (billion years ago, or 2,500 Ma.) Instead of being based on stratigraphy, this date is defined chronometrically. The lower boundary (starting point) has not been officially recognized by the International Commission on Stratigraphy, but it is usually set to 3.8 Ga, at the end of the Hadean eon.

Chapter 7. Metamorphism and Metamorphic Rocks

a. AL 333
b. AASHTO Soil Classification System
c. AL 129-1
d. Archean

30. The _____ Era, is the most recent of the three classic geological eras and covers the period from 65.5 million years ago to the present. It is marked by the Cretaceous-Tertiary extinction event at the end of the Cretaceous that saw the demise of the last non-avian dinosaurs and the end of the Mesozoic Era. The _____ era is ongoing.
    a. 1509 Istanbul earthquake
    b. 1703 Genroku earthquake
    c. 1700 Cascadia earthquake
    d. Cenozoic

31. _____ occurs typically around intrusive igneous rocks as a result of the temperature increase caused by the intrusion of magma into cooler country rock. The area surrounding the intrusion (called aureoles) where the _____ effects are present is called the metamorphic aureole. Contact metamorphic rocks are usually known as hornfels.
    a. Paralithic
    b. Contact metamorphism
    c. Perched coastline
    d. Gibraltar Arc

32. A _____ or dyke in geology is a type of sheet intrusion referring to any geologic body that cuts discordantly across

- planar wall rock structures, such as bedding or foliation
- massive rock formations, like igneous/magmatic intrusions and salt diapirs.

They can therefore be either intrusive or sedimentary in origin.

An intrusive _____ is an igneous body with a very high aspect ratio, which means that its thickness is usually much smaller than the other two dimensions. Thickness can vary from sub-centimeter scale to many meters and the lateral dimensions can extend over many kilometers. A _____ is an intrusion into an opening cross-cutting fissure, shouldering aside other pre-existing layers or bodies of rock; this implies that a _____ is always younger than the rocks that contain it.

a. Geopetal
b. Schmidt hammer
c. Pneumatolysis
d. Dike

33. _____ is a term used in geology to refer to silicate minerals, magma, and rocks which are enriched in the lighter elements such as silicon, oxygen, aluminium, sodium, and potassium. _____ minerals are usually light in color and have specific gravities less than 3. Common _____ minerals include quartz, muscovite, orthoclase, and the sodium-rich plagioclase feldspars.
    a. Tephra
    b. Magma
    c. Laccolith
    d. Felsic

34. _____ is an adjective describing a silicate mineral or rock that is rich in magnesium and iron; the term was derived by contracting 'magnesium' and 'ferric'. Most _____ minerals are dark in color and the specific gravity is greater than 3. Common rock-forming _____ minerals include olivine, pyroxene, amphibole, and biotite.

_____ lava, before cooling, has a low viscosity, in comparison to felsic lava, due to the lower silica content in _____ magma. Water and other volatiles can more easily and gradually escape from _____ lava, so eruptions of volcanoes made of _____ lavas are less explosively violent than felsic lava eruptions.

a. 1703 Genroku earthquake
c. 1509 Istanbul earthquake
b. 1700 Cascadia earthquake
d. Mafic

35. The _____ Era is one of three geologic eras of the Phanerozoic eon. The division of time into eras dates back to Giovanni Arduino, in the 18th century, although his original name for the era now called the '_____' was 'Secondary' (making the modern era the 'Tertiary'.)

The _____ was a time of tectonic, climatic and evolutionary activity. The continents gradually shifted from a state of connectedness into their present configuration; the drifting provided for speciation and other important evolutionary developments.

a. 1509 Istanbul earthquake
c. 1703 Genroku earthquake
b. 1700 Cascadia earthquake
d. Mesozoic

36. The _____ is a geological eon representing a period before the first abundant complex life on Earth. The _____ extended from 2500 Ma to 542.0 >± 1.0 Ma (million years ago), and is the most recent part of the old, informally named 'e;Precambrian'e; time.

The Proterozoic consists of 3 geologic eras, from oldest to youngest:

- Paleoproterozoic
- Mesoproterozoic
- Neoproterozoic

The well-identified events were:

- The transition to an oxygenated atmosphere during the Mesoproterozoic.
- Several glaciations, including the hypothesized Snowball Earth during the Cryogenian period in the late Neoproterozoic.
- The Ediacaran Period (635 to 542 Ma) which is characterized by the evolution of abundant soft-bodied multicellular organisms.

The geoloic record of the Proterozoic is much better than that for the preceding Archean. In contrast to the deep-water deposits of the Archean, the Proterozoic features many strata that were laid down in extensive shallow epicontinental seas; furthermore, many of these rocks are less metamorphosed than Archean-age ones, and plenty are unaltered.

a. 1703 Genroku earthquake
c. 1509 Istanbul earthquake
b. 1700 Cascadia earthquake
d. Proterozoic Eon

37. The _____ is the zone of the ocean floor that separates the thin oceanic crust from thick continental crust. Continental margins constitute about 28% of the oceanic area.

The transition from continental to oceanic crust commonly occurs within the outer part of the margin, called continental rise.

a. Cuspate forelands
b. Longshore drift
c. 1509 Istanbul earthquake
d. Continental margin

38. A _____ is an old and stable part of the continental crust that has survived the merging and splitting of continents and supercontinents for at least 500 million years. Some are over two billion years old. They are generally found in the interiors of continents and are characteristically composed of ancient crystalline basement crust of lightweight felsic igneous rock such as granite.
    a. Craton
    b. Kalahari craton
    c. Sebakwe proto-craton
    d. Superior craton

39. _____ is molten rock that is found beneath the surface of the Earth, and may also exist on other terrestrial planets. Besides molten rock, _____ may also contain suspended crystals and gas bubbles. _____ often collects in a _____ chamber inside a volcano. _____ is capable of intrusion into adjacent rocks, extrusion onto the surface as lava, and explosive ejection as tephra to form pyroclastic rock.
    a. Volcanic rock
    b. Rock cycle
    c. Laccolith
    d. Magma

40. _____ or dolomite rock is a sedimentary carbonate rock that contains a high percentage of the mineral dolomite. In old U.S.G.S. publications it was referred to as magnesian limestone. Most _____ formed as a magnesium replacement of limestone or lime mud prior to lithification.
    a. Pelagic sediments
    b. Jasperoid
    c. Dolostone
    d. Lithification

41. In geology, a _____ or _____ line is a planar fracture in rock in which the rock on one side of the fracture has moved with respect to the rock on the other side. Large faults within the Earth's crust are the result of differential or shear motion and active _____ zones are the causal locations of most earthquakes. Earthquakes are caused by energy release during rapid slippage along a _____.
    a. Dali
    b. Stack
    c. Fault
    d. Combe

42. _____ is a fine grained sedimentary rock whose original constituents were clays or muds. Grain size is up to 0.0625 mm with individual grains too small to be distinguished without a microscope. With increased pressure over time the platey clay minerals may become aligned, with the appearance of fissility or parallel layering.
    a. Shale
    b. Mudstone
    c. Jasperoid
    d. Diatomaceous earth

43. The _____ is a continental transform fault that runs a length of roughly 800 miles (1,300 km) through California in the United States. The fault's motion is right-lateral strike-slip (horizontal motion.) It forms the tectonic boundary between the Pacific Plate and the North American Plate.
    a. 1509 Istanbul earthquake
    b. 1700 Cascadia earthquake
    c. 1703 Genroku earthquake
    d. San Andreas fault

44. _____ is a sedimentary rock composed mainly of sand-size mineral or rock grains. Most _____ is composed of quartz and/or feldspar because these are the most common minerals in the Earth's crust. Like sand, _____ may be any color, but the most common colors are tan, brown, yellow, red, gray and white.

a. Dolostone	b. Sandstone
c. Porcellanite	d. Lithification

45. _____ is a fine-grained sedimentary rock whose original constituents were clay minerals or muds. It is characterized by thin laminae breaking with an irregular curving fracture, often splintery and usually parallel to the often-indistinguishable bedding plane. This property is called fissility.

a. Mudstone	b. Metasediment
c. Pelagic sediments	d. Shale

46. An _____ is a type of rock that contains minerals such as gemstones and metals that can be extracted through mining and refined for use. Samples of _____ in the form of exceptionally beautiful crystals, exotic layering visible when sectioned or polished or metallic presentations such as large nuggets or crystalline formations of metals such as gold or copper may command a value far beyond their value as mere _____ or raw metal for subsequent reduction to utilitarian purposes.

The grade or concentration of an _____ mineral, or metal, as well as its form of occurrence, will directly affect the costs associated with mining the _____.

a. AASHTO Soil Classification System	b. AL 129-1
c. Ore genesis	d. Ore

47. The lithosphere is broken up into what are called _____. In the case of Earth, there are eight major and many minor plates The lithospheric plates ride on the asthenosphere. These plates move in relation to one another at one of three types of plate boundaries: convergent, or collisional boundaries; divergent boundaries, also called spreading centers; and transform boundaries.

a. Tectonic plates	b. Thrust fault
c. Gorda Ridge	d. Copperbelt Province

48. In geology, a _____ is a place where the Earth's crust and lithosphere are being pulled apart and is an example of extensional tectonics.

Typical _____ features are a central linear downdropped fault segment, called a graben, with parallel normal faulting and _____-flank uplifts on either side forming a _____ valley, where the _____ remains above sea level. The axis of the _____ area commonly contains volcanic rocks and active volcanism is a part of many, but not all active _____ systems.

a. 1700 Cascadia earthquake	b. 1509 Istanbul earthquake
c. 1703 Genroku earthquake	d. Rift

49. An _____ is used in geology to determine the degree of metamorphism a rock has experienced. Depending on the original composition of and the pressure and temperature experienced by the protolith (parent rock), chemical reactions between minerals in the solid state produce new minerals. When an _____ is found in a metamorphosed rock, it indicates the minimum pressure and temperature the protolith must have achieved in order for that mineral to form.

a. Index mineral	b. AL 333
c. AASHTO Soil Classification System	d. AL 129-1

Chapter 7. Metamorphism and Metamorphic Rocks

50. _____ is a fine-grained, compact rock produced by dynamic crystallization of the constituent minerals resulting in a reduction of the grain size of the rock. It is classified as a metamorphic rock. _____ can have many different mineralogical compositions; it is a classification based on the textural appearance of the rock.
   a. Mylonite
   b. Hornfels
   c. Metaconglomerate
   d. Shock metamorphism

51. The _____ is the earliest of three geologic eras of the Phanerozoic eon. The _____ spanned from roughly 542 to 251 million years ago (ICS, 2004), and is subdivided into six geologic periods; from oldest to youngest they are: the Cambrian, Ordovician, Silurian, Devonian, Carboniferous, and Permian.

The _____ covers the time from the first appearance of abundant, soft-shelled fossils to the time when the continents were beginning to be dominated by large, relatively sophisticated reptiles and modern plants. The lower (oldest) boundary was classically set at the first appearance of creatures known as trilobites and archeocyathids.

   a. 1509 Istanbul earthquake
   b. 1703 Genroku earthquake
   c. 1700 Cascadia earthquake
   d. Paleozoic

52. _____ is the name of a sedimentary carbonate rock and a mineral, both composed of calcium magnesium carbonate $CaMg_2$ found in crystals.

_____ rock (also dolostone) is composed predominantly of the mineral _____. Limestone that is partially replaced by _____ is referred to as dolomitic limestone, or in old U.S. geologic literature as magnesian limestone.

   a. Metasediment
   b. Porcellanite
   c. Dolostone
   d. Dolomite

53. _____ are a group of rock-forming tectosilicate minerals which make up as much as 60% of the Earth's crust.

_____ crystallize from magma in both intrusive and extrusive igneous rocks, as veins, and are also present in many types of metamorphic rock. Rock formed entirely of plagioclase feldspar is known as anorthosite.

   a. Feldspars
   b. 1703 Genroku earthquake
   c. 1509 Istanbul earthquake
   d. 1700 Cascadia earthquake

54. The _____ is an informal name for the supereon comprising the eons of the geologic timescale that came before the current Phanerozoic eon. It spans from the formation of Earth around 4500 Mya (million years ago) to the evolution of abundant macroscopic hard-shelled animals, which marked the beginning of the Cambrian, the first period of the first era of the Phanerozoic eon, some 542 Mya. It is named after the Roman name for Wales - Cambria - where rocks from this age were first studied.
   a. 1700 Cascadia earthquake
   b. 1703 Genroku earthquake
   c. 1509 Istanbul earthquake
   d. Precambrian

55. _____ is a feature of rocks containing platy minerals. Platy minerals include clay minerals and micas, with a long thin shape. When these align, they form a series of planes along which the rock tends to split.

a. Slaty cleavage	b. Marine clay
c. Salt tectonics	d. Bediasite

56. _____, in structural geology and related disciplines, describes the tendency of a rock to break along preferred planes of weakness.

Rocks deformed under very low to low metamorphic grade often develop planes along which the rock can easily be split. Slates are an example of a rock with a penetrative _____ caused partly by the realignment of phyllosilicate minerals with increasing flattening strain.

a. Combe	b. Compaction
c. Cleavage	d. Drainage system

57. _____ is a type of foliated metamorphic rock primarily composed of quartz, sericite mica, and chlorite; the rock represents a gradation in the degree of metamorphism between slate and mica schist. Minute crystals of graphite, sericite, or chlorite impart a silky, sometimes golden sheen to the surfaces of cleavage (or schistosity.) _____ is formed from the continued metamorphism of slate.

a. 1703 Genroku earthquake	b. Phyllite
c. 1509 Istanbul earthquake	d. 1700 Cascadia earthquake

58. _____ forms a group of medium-grade metamorphic rocks, chiefly notable for the preponderance of lamellar minerals such as micas, chlorite, talc, hornblende, graphite, and others. Quartz often occurs in drawn-out grains to such an extent that a particular form called quartz _____ is produced. By definition, _____ contains more than 50% platy and elongated minerals, often finely interleaved with quartz and feldspar.

a. Metasomatism	b. Metaconglomerate
c. Granoblastic	d. Schist

59. _____ is a common and widely distributed type of rock formed by high-grade regional metamorphic processes from pre-existing formations that were originally either igneous or sedimentary rocks. Gneissic rocks are usually medium to coarse foliated and largely recrystallized but do not carry large quantities of micas, chlorite or other platy minerals. Gneisses that are metamorphosed igneous rocks or their equivalent are termed granite gneisses, diorite gneisses, etc.

a. 1509 Istanbul earthquake	b. 1703 Genroku earthquake
c. 1700 Cascadia earthquake	d. Gneiss

60. _____ is any penetrative planar fabric present in rocks. _____ is common to rocks affected by regional metamorphic compression typical of orogenic belts. Rocks exhibiting _____ include the typical metamorphic rock sequence of slate, phyllite, schist and gneiss.

a. Foliation	b. Hornfels
c. Porphyroblast	d. Shock metamorphism

61. _____ is the name given to a rock consisting mainly of hornblende amphibole, the use of the term being restricted, however, to metamorphic rocks. The modern terminology for a holocrystalline plutonic igneous rocks composed primarily of hornblende amphibole is a hornblendite, which are usually crystal cumulates. Rocks with >90% amphibole which have a feldspar groundmass may be a lamprophyre.

Chapter 7. Metamorphism and Metamorphic Rocks

a. AL 129-1
c. AL 333
b. AASHTO Soil Classification System
d. Amphibolite

62. _____ is a common phyllosilicate mineral within the mica group, with the approximate chemical formula $K(Mg, Fe)_3AlSi_3O_{10}(F, OH)_2$. More generally, it refers to the dark mica series, primarily a solid-solution series between the iron-endmember annite, and the magnesium-endmember phlogopite; more aluminous endmembers include siderophyllite.
   a. 1703 Genroku earthquake
   c. 1509 Istanbul earthquake
   b. 1700 Cascadia earthquake
   d. Biotite

63. _____ is a common and widely occurring type of intrusive, felsic, igneous rock. _____ has a medium to coarse texture, occasionally with some individual crystals larger than the groundmass forming a rock known as porphyry. Granites can be pink to dark gray or even black, depending on their chemistry and mineralogy.
   a. 1700 Cascadia earthquake
   c. 1509 Istanbul earthquake
   b. 1703 Genroku earthquake
   d. Granite

64. _____ is a rock at the frontier between igneous and metamorphic rocks. They can also be known as diatexite.

_____ forms under extreme temperature conditions during prograde metamorphism, where partial melting occurs in pre-existing rocks.

   a. Metamorphic zone
   c. Petrology
   b. Magma
   d. Migmatite

65. _____ - also known as greenstone - is a general field petrologic term applied to metamorphic and/or altered mafic volcanic rock. The green is due to abundant green chlorite, actinolite and epidote minerals that dominate the rock. However, basalts may remain quite black if primary pyroxene does not revert to chlorite or actinolite.
   a. Supracrustal rocks
   c. Greenschist
   b. Metamorphic facies
   d. Hornfels

66. _____ is the group designation for a series of contact metamorphic rocks that have been baked and indurated by the heat of intrusive igneous masses and have been rendered massive, hard, splintery, and in some cases exceedingly tough and durable. Most _____ are fine-grained, and while the original rocks may have been more or less fissile owing to the presence of bedding or cleavage planes, this structure is effaced or rendered inoperative in the _____. Though they may show banding, due to bedding, etc., they break across this as readily as along it; in fact, they tend to separate into cubical fragments rather than into thin plates.
   a. Hornfels
   c. Schist
   b. Talc carbonate
   d. Metasomatism

67. _____ is the second most abundant mineral in the Earth's continental crust. It is made up of a framework of silicon-oxygen tetrahedra SiO_4, with each silicon shared between two oxygens to give the overall formula SiO_2. _____ has a hardness of 7 on the Mohs scale and a density of 2.65 g/cmÂ³.
   a. 1700 Cascadia earthquake
   c. 1509 Istanbul earthquake
   b. Quartz
   d. 1703 Genroku earthquake

Chapter 7. Metamorphism and Metamorphic Rocks

68. _____ is a hard metamorphic rock which was originally sandstone. Sandstone is converted into _____ through heating and pressure usually related to tectonic compression within orogenic belts. Pure _____ is usually white to grey, though quartzites often occur in various shades of pink and red due to varying amounts of iron oxide .
   a. Quartzite
   b. Schist
   c. Metaconglomerate
   d. Foliation

69. _____ is a hard, compact variety of mineral coal that has a high lustre. It has the highest carbon count and contains the fewest impurities of all coals, despite its lower calorific content.

_____ is the highest of the metamorphic rank, in which the carbon content is between 92% and 98%.

   a. AL 333
   b. Anthracite
   c. AASHTO Soil Classification System
   d. AL 129-1

70. _____ are fine to medium-grained metamorphic rocks that have experienced high temperatures of metamorphism, composed mainly of feldspars sometimes associated with quartz and anhydrous ferromagnesian minerals, with granoblastic texture and gneissose to massive structure. They are of particular interest to geologists because many _____ represent samples of the deep continental crust. Some _____ experienced decompression from deep in the Earth to shallower crustal levels at high temperature; others cooled while remaining at depth in the Earth.
   a. Slate
   b. Geothermobarometry
   c. Granulites
   d. Metasomatism

71. In geology, an _____ is a plane of constant metamorphic grade in the field; it separates metamorphic zones of different metamorphic index minerals. On geologic maps focusing on metamorphic terranes (or landscapes underlain by metamorphic rocks), the boundaries between rocks of different metamorphic grade are commonly demarcated by _____ lines. The garnet _____, for example, would mark the first occurrence of garnet in the rocks.
   a. Isograd
   b. Ostwald ripening
   c. Espresso crema effect
   d. Exner equation

72. The _____ are groups of mineral compositions in metamorphic rocks, that are typical for a certain field in pressure-temperature space. Rocks which contain certain minerals can therefore be linked to certain tectonic settings.

The name facies was first used for specific sedimentary environments in sedimentary rocks by Swiss geologist Amanz Gressly in 1838.

   a. Greenstone belts
   b. Mylonite
   c. Supracrustal rocks
   d. Metamorphic facies

73. In geology, _____ are a body of rock with specified characteristics. Ideally, a _____ is a distinctive rock unit that forms under certain conditions of sedimentation, reflecting a particular process or environment.

The term _____ was introduced by the Swiss geologist Amanz Gressly in 1838 and was part of his significant contribution to the foundations of modern stratigraphy, [Cross and Homewood (1997)] which replaced the earlier notions of Neptunism.

a. Facies
b. Granulites
c. Mylonite
d. Schist

74. _____ is a rock that forms by the metamorphism of basalt and rocks with similar composition at high pressures and low temperatures, approximately corresponding to a depth of 15 to 30 kilometers and 200 to ~500 degrees Celsius. The blue color of the rock comes from the presence of the mineral glaucophane.

They are typically found within orogenic belts as terranes of lithology in faulted contact with greenschist or rarely eclogite facies rocks.

a. Metamorphic facies
b. Talc carbonate
c. Mylonite
d. Blueschist

Chapter 8. Earthquakes and Earth Interior   89

1. An _____ is the result of a sudden release of energy in the Earth's crust that creates seismic waves. They are recorded with a seismometer or the related and mostly obsolete Richter magnitude, with a magnitude 3 or lower _____ being mostly imperceptible and magnitude 7 causing serious damage over large areas.
   a. AL 129-1
   b. AL 333
   c. Earthquake
   d. AASHTO Soil Classification System

2. An _____ is an earthquake that occurs after a previous earthquake (the main shock.) An _____ is in the same region of the main shock but is always of smaller magnitude strength. If an _____ is larger than the main shock, the _____ is redesignated as the main shock and the original main shock is redesignated as a foreshock.
   a. AL 333
   b. AL 129-1
   c. AASHTO Soil Classification System
   d. Aftershock

3. The _____ Era, is the most recent of the three classic geological eras and covers the period from 65.5 million years ago to the present. It is marked by the Cretaceous-Tertiary extinction event at the end of the Cretaceous that saw the demise of the last non-avian dinosaurs and the end of the Mesozoic Era. The _____ era is ongoing.
   a. Cenozoic
   b. 1703 Genroku earthquake
   c. 1509 Istanbul earthquake
   d. 1700 Cascadia earthquake

4. In geology, a _____ or _____ line is a planar fracture in rock in which the rock on one side of the fracture has moved with respect to the rock on the other side. Large faults within the Earth's crust are the result of differential or shear motion and active _____ zones are the causal locations of most earthquakes. Earthquakes are caused by energy release during rapid slippage along a _____.
   a. Combe
   b. Stack
   c. Fault
   d. Dali

5. The _____ is a continental transform fault that runs a length of roughly 800 miles (1,300 km) through California in the United States. The fault's motion is right-lateral strike-slip (horizontal motion.) It forms the tectonic boundary between the Pacific Plate and the North American Plate.
   a. 1700 Cascadia earthquake
   b. 1509 Istanbul earthquake
   c. San Andreas fault
   d. 1703 Genroku earthquake

6. In geology, a _____ is a place where the Earth's crust and lithosphere are being pulled apart and is an example of extensional tectonics.

Typical _____ features are a central linear downdropped fault segment, called a graben, with parallel normal faulting and _____-flank uplifts on either side forming a _____ valley, where the _____ remains above sea level. The axis of the _____ area commonly contains volcanic rocks and active volcanism is a part of many, but not all active _____ systems.

   a. 1509 Istanbul earthquake
   b. 1703 Genroku earthquake
   c. Rift
   d. 1700 Cascadia earthquake

7. The _____ is an explanation for how energy is spread during earthquakes. As plates shift on opposite sides of a fault are subjected to force, they accumulate energy and slowly deform until their internal strength is exceeded. At that time, a sudden movement occurs along the fault, releasing the accumulated energy, and the rocks snap back to their original undeformed shape.

a. Azores-Gibraltar Transform Fault
b. Obduction
c. East Pacific Rise
d. Elastic rebound theory

8. _____ is the scientific study of earthquakes and the propagation of elastic waves through the Earth. The field also includes studies of earthquake effects, such as tsunamis as well as diverse seismic sources such as volcanic, tectonic, oceanic, atmospheric, and artificial processes . A related field that uses geology to infer information regarding past earthquakes is paleoseismology.
   a. 1703 Genroku earthquake
   b. 1509 Istanbul earthquake
   c. Seismology
   d. 1700 Cascadia earthquake

9. The _____ or epicentre is the point on the Earth's surface that is directly above the hypocenter or focus, the point where an earthquake or underground explosion originates.

The _____ is usually the location of greatest damage. However, in some cases the _____ is above the start of a much larger event.

   a. AL 129-1
   b. AL 333
   c. AASHTO Soil Classification System
   d. Epicenter

10. The _____, refers to the site of an earthquake or to that of a nuclear explosion. In the former, it is a synonym of the focus; in the latter, of ground zero.

The location of an earthquake's _____ is the position where the energy stored in the strain in the rock is released, which occurs at the focal depth below the epicentre. The focal depth can be calculated from measurements based on seismic wave phenomena.

   a. Seismic waves
   b. Receiver function
   c. Harmonic tremor
   d. Hypocenter

11. _____ are waves that travel through the Earth or other elastic body, for example as the result of an earthquake, explosion, or some other process that imparts forces to the body. _____ are also continually excited on Earth by the incessant pounding of ocean waves (referred to as the microseism) and the wind. _____ are studied by seismologists, and measured by a seismograph, which records the output of a seismometer, or geophone.
   a. Shadow zone
   b. Harmonic tremor
   c. Maximum magnitude
   d. Seismic waves

12. An _____ is a confined aquifer containing groundwater that will flow upward through a well without the need for pumping. Water may even reach the ground surface if the natural pressure is high enough, in which case the well is called a flowing artesian well. An aquifer provides the water for an artesian well.
   a. AL 333
   b. AASHTO Soil Classification System
   c. Artesian aquifer
   d. AL 129-1

13. A _____ is a deep active seismic area in a subduction zone. Differential motion along the zone produces deep-seated earthquakes, the foci of which may be as deep as about 700 kilometres (435 miles.) They develop beneath volcanic island arcs and continental margins above active subduction zones.

a. Pit crater
b. Wadati-Benioff zone
c. Lava
d. Pyroclastic flow

14. A _____ is a mountain rising from the ocean seafloor that does not reach to the water's surface (sea level), and thus is not an island. These are typically formed from extinct volcanoes, that rise abruptly and are usually found rising from a seafloor of 1,000-4,000 meters depth. They are defined by oceanographers as independent features that rise to at least 1,000 meters above the seafloor.
  a. 1700 Cascadia earthquake
  b. 1703 Genroku earthquake
  c. 1509 Istanbul earthquake
  d. Seamount

15. The _____ is the rigid outermost shell of a rocky planet.

In the Earth, the _____ includes the crust and the uppermost mantle, which constitute the hard and rigid outer layer of the planet. The _____ is underlain by the asthenosphere, the weaker, hotter, and deeper part of the upper mantle.

  a. Gorda Ridge
  b. Continental drift
  c. Lithosphere
  d. Juan de Fuca Ridge

16. The lithosphere is broken up into what are called _____. In the case of Earth, there are eight major and many minor plates The lithospheric plates ride on the asthenosphere. These plates move in relation to one another at one of three types of plate boundaries: convergent, or collisional boundaries; divergent boundaries, also called spreading centers; and transform boundaries.
  a. Thrust fault
  b. Gorda Ridge
  c. Copperbelt Province
  d. Tectonic plates

17. A _____ is a chain of volcanic islands or mountains formed by plate tectonics as an oceanic tectonic plate subducts under another tectonic plate and produces magma. There are two types of these: oceanic arcs (commonly called island arcs, a type of archipelago) and continental arcs. In the former, oceanic crust subducts beneath other oceanic crust on an adjacent plate, while in the latter case the oceanic crust subducts beneath continental crust. In some situations, a single subduction zone may show both aspects along its length, as part of a plate subducts beneath a continent and part beneath adjacent oceanic crust.
  a. 1703 Genroku earthquake
  b. 1509 Istanbul earthquake
  c. Volcanic arc
  d. 1700 Cascadia earthquake

18. _____ are type of elastic wave, also called seismic waves, that can travel through gases, elastic solids and liquids, including the Earth. _____ can be produced by earthquakes and recorded by seismometers.
  a. P-waves
  b. 1700 Cascadia earthquake
  c. 1509 Istanbul earthquake
  d. 1703 Genroku earthquake

19. In seismology, _____ are surface seismic waves that cause horizontal shifting of the earth during an earthquake. A.E.H. Love predicted the existence of _____ mathematically in 1911. They form a distinct class, different from other types of seismic waves, such as P-waves and S-waves (both body waves), or Rayleigh waves (another type of surface wave). _____ travel with a slower velocity than P- or S- waves, but faster than Rayleigh waves.

a. Strainmeter
c. Seismic refraction
b. Mazuku
d. Love waves

20. _____ are a type of elastic surface wave that travel on solids. They are produced on the Earth by earthquakes, in which case they are also known as 'ground roll', or by other sources of seismic energy such as an explosion or even a sledgehammer impact. They are also produced in materials by acoustic transducers, and are used in non-destructive testing for detecting defects.
   a. Seismic waves
   b. Maximum magnitude
   c. Tornillo event
   d. Rayleigh waves

21. A type of seismic wave, the _____, secondary wave or shear wave (sometimes called an elastic _____) is one of the two main types of elastic body waves, so named because they move through the body of an object, unlike surface waves.

The _____ move as a shear or transverse wave, so motion is perpendicular to the direction of wave propagation: S-waves, like waves in a rope, as opposed to waves moving through a slinky, the P-wave. The wave moves through elastic media, and the main restoring force comes from shear effects.

   a. 1509 Istanbul earthquake
   b. 1700 Cascadia earthquake
   c. 1703 Genroku earthquake
   d. S-wave

22. Study of geological _____ is related to the study of structural geology, rock microstructure or rock texture and fault mechanics.

_____ is the response of a rock to deformation usually by compressive stress and forms particular textures. _____ can be homogeneous or non-homogeneous, and may be pure _____ or simple _____.

   a. Sag pond
   b. Crenulation
   c. Molasse basin
   d. Shear

23. In physics, a _____ is a mechanical wave that propagates along the interface between differing media, usually two fluids with different densities. A _____ can also be an electromagnetic wave guided by a refractive index gradient. In radio transmission, a ground wave is a _____ that propagates close to the surface of the Earth.
   a. 1703 Genroku earthquake
   b. 1509 Istanbul earthquake
   c. 1700 Cascadia earthquake
   d. Surface wave

24. The _____ is a scale used for measuring the intensity of an earthquake. The scale quantifies the effects of an earthquake on the Earth's surface, humans, objects of nature, and man-made structures on a scale of I through XII, with I denoting not felt, and XII one that causes almost complete destruction. The values will differ based on the distance to the earthquake, with the highest intensities being around the epicentral area.
   a. Seismic scale
   b. China Seismic Intensity Scale
   c. Richter magnitude scale
   d. Mercalli Intensity Scale

Chapter 8. Earthquakes and Earth Interior

25. The _____, also known as the local magnitude (M_L) scale, assigns a single number to quantify the amount of seismic energy released by an earthquake. It is a base-10 logarithmic scale obtained by calculating the logarithm of the combined horizontal amplitude of the largest displacement from zero on a Wood-Anderson torsion seismometer output. So, for example, an earthquake that measures 5.0 on the Richter scale has a shaking amplitude 10 times larger than one that measures 4.0.
   a. Medvedev-Sponheuer-Karnik scale
   b. Richter Magnitude Scale
   c. Moment magnitude scale
   d. China Seismic Intensity Scale

26. In stratigraphy, _____ is the native consolidated rock underlying the surface of a terrestrial planet, usually the Earth. Above the _____ is usually an area of broken and weathered unconsolidated rock in the basal subsoil. The top of the _____ is known as rockhead and identifying this, via excavations, drilling or geophysical methods, is an important task in most civil engineering projects.
   a. Bedrock
   b. Biozones
   c. Polystrate
   d. Sequence stratigraphy

27. _____ is water located beneath the ground surface in soil pore spaces and in the fractures of lithologic formations. A unit of rock or an unconsolidated deposit is called an aquifer when it can yield a usable quantity of water. The depth at which soil pore spaces or fractures and voids in rock become completely saturated with water is called the water table.
   a. Depression focused recharge
   b. 1509 Istanbul earthquake
   c. 1700 Cascadia earthquake
   d. Groundwater

28. _____ is the naturally occurring, unconsolidated or loose covering on the Earth's surface. _____ is composed of particles of broken rock that have been altered by chemical, biological and environmental processes including weathering and erosion. _____ is different from its parent rock(s) source(s), altered by interactions between the lithosphere, hydrosphere, atmosphere, and the biosphere.
   a. Slump
   b. 1509 Istanbul earthquake
   c. Topsoil
   d. Soil

29. A _____ is a geological phenomenon which includes a wide range of ground movement, such as rock falls, deep failure of slopes and shallow debris flows, which can occur in offshore, coastal and onshore environments. Although the action of gravity is the primary driving force for a _____ to occur, there are other contributing factors affecting the original slope stability. Typically, pre-conditional factors build up specific sub-surface conditions that make the area/slope prone to failure, whereas the actual _____ often requires a trigger before being released.
   a. 1700 Cascadia earthquake
   b. 1509 Istanbul earthquake
   c. Landslide
   d. Mass wasting

30. _____ is the geomorphic process by which soil, regolith, and rock move downslope under the force of gravity. Types of _____ include creep, slides, flows, topples, and falls, each with its own characteristic features, and taking place over timescales from seconds to years. _____ occurs on both terrestrial and submarine slopes, and has been observed on Earth, Mars, and Venus.
   a. 1700 Cascadia earthquake
   b. 1509 Istanbul earthquake
   c. Soil liquefaction
   d. Mass wasting

Chapter 8. Earthquakes and Earth Interior

31. The _____ is a tectonic plate covering most of North America, Greenland and part of Siberia. It extends eastward to the Mid-Atlantic Ridge and westward to the Chersky Range in eastern Siberia. The plate includes both continental and oceanic crust. The interior of the main continental landmass includes an extensive granitic core called a craton. Along most of the edges of this craton are fragments of crustal material called terranes, accreted to the craton by tectonic actions over the long span of geologic time. It is believed that much of North America west of the Rockies is composed of such terranes.
    a. Kermadec Plate
    b. Burma Plate
    c. North American plate
    d. Philippine Sea Plate

32. The _____ is an oceanic tectonic plate beneath the Pacific Ocean.

To the north the easterly side is a divergent boundary with the Explorer Plate, the Juan de Fuca Plate and the Gorda Plate forming respectively the Explorer Ridge, the Juan de Fuca Ridge and the Gorda Ridge. In the middle the easterly side is a transform boundary with the North American Plate along the San Andreas Fault and a boundary with the Cocos Plate.

    a. Gorda Plate
    b. Somali Plate
    c. Conway Reef Plate
    d. Pacific plate

33. When building a house, regional _____ maps are used to find the best (or the worst) place to locate for earthquake shaking. Although greatly confused with its sister, seismic risk, _____ is the study of expected earthquake ground motions at any point on the earth. Surface motion map for a hypothetical earthquake on the northern portion of the Hayward Fault Zone and its presumed northern extension, the Rodgers Creek Fault Zone

The calculations for _____ can be quite complex.

    a. Seismic risk
    b. Seismic Hazard
    c. 1700 Cascadia earthquake
    d. 1509 Istanbul earthquake

34. _____ uses the results of a seismic hazard analysis, and includes both consequence and probability. _____ has been defined, for most management purposes, as the potential economic, social and environmental consequences of hazardous events that may occur in a specified period of time. A building located in a region of high seismic hazard is at lower risk if it is built to sound seismic engineering principles.
    a. 1509 Istanbul earthquake
    b. Seismic risk
    c. 1700 Cascadia earthquake
    d. Seismic microzonation

35. A _____ is an instrument designed to measure very small changes from the horizontal level, either on the ground or in structures. A similar term, in less common usage, is the inclinometer. They are used extensively for monitoring volcanos, the response of dams to filling, the small movements of potential landslides, the orientation and volume of hydraulic fractures, and the response of structures to various influences such as loading and foundation settlement.
    a. 1509 Istanbul earthquake
    b. 1700 Cascadia earthquake
    c. 1703 Genroku earthquake
    d. Tiltmeter

36. A _____ is a segment of an active fault that has not slipped in an unusually long time when compared with other segments along the same structure. _____ hypothesis/theory states that, over long periods of time, the displacement on any segment must be equal to that experienced by all the other parts of the fault. Any large and longstanding gap is therefore considered to be the fault segment most likely to suffer future earthquakes.

a. Harmonic tremor
b. Paleoliquefaction
c. Seismic gap
d. Teleseism

37. _____ is a common and widely distributed type of rock formed by high-grade regional metamorphic processes from pre-existing formations that were originally either igneous or sedimentary rocks. Gneissic rocks are usually medium to coarse foliated and largely recrystallized but do not carry large quantities of micas, chlorite or other platy minerals. Gneisses that are metamorphosed igneous rocks or their equivalent are termed granite gneisses, diorite gneisses, etc.
   a. 1700 Cascadia earthquake
   b. Gneiss
   c. 1703 Genroku earthquake
   d. 1509 Istanbul earthquake

38. The _____ is the geologic eon before the Archean. It started at Earth's formation about 4.6 billion years ago (4,600 Ma), and ended roughly 3.8 billion years ago, though the latter date varies according to different sources.
   a. 1703 Genroku earthquake
   b. 1700 Cascadia earthquake
   c. 1509 Istanbul earthquake
   d. Hadean

39. The _____ is an informal name for the supereon comprising the eons of the geologic timescale that came before the current Phanerozoic eon. It spans from the formation of Earth around 4500 Mya (million years ago) to the evolution of abundant macroscopic hard-shelled animals, which marked the beginning of the Cambrian, the first period of the first era of the Phanerozoic eon, some 542 Mya. It is named after the Roman name for Wales - Cambria - where rocks from this age were first studied.
   a. 1509 Istanbul earthquake
   b. 1700 Cascadia earthquake
   c. 1703 Genroku earthquake
   d. Precambrian

40. The _____ is the earliest of three geologic eras of the Phanerozoic eon. The _____ spanned from roughly 542 to 251 million years ago (ICS, 2004), and is subdivided into six geologic periods; from oldest to youngest they are: the Cambrian, Ordovician, Silurian, Devonian, Carboniferous, and Permian.

The _____ covers the time from the first appearance of abundant, soft-shelled fossils to the time when the continents were beginning to be dominated by large, relatively sophisticated reptiles and modern plants. The lower (oldest) boundary was classically set at the first appearance of creatures known as trilobites and archeocyathids.

   a. 1700 Cascadia earthquake
   b. 1703 Genroku earthquake
   c. 1509 Istanbul earthquake
   d. Paleozoic

41. The _____ is a geological eon representing a period before the first abundant complex life on Earth. The _____ extended from 2500 Ma to 542.0 >± 1.0 Ma (million years ago), and is the most recent part of the old, informally named 'e;Precambrian'e; time.

The Proterozoic consists of 3 geologic eras, from oldest to youngest:

- Paleoproterozoic
- Mesoproterozoic
- Neoproterozoic

The well-identified events were:

- The transition to an oxygenated atmosphere during the Mesoproterozoic.
- Several glaciations, including the hypothesized Snowball Earth during the Cryogenian period in the late Neoproterozoic.
- The Ediacaran Period (635 to 542 Ma) which is characterized by the evolution of abundant soft-bodied multicellular organisms.

The geoloic record of the Proterozoic is much better than that for the preceding Archean. In contrast to the deep-water deposits of the Archean, the Proterozoic features many strata that were laid down in extensive shallow epicontinental seas; furthermore, many of these rocks are less metamorphosed than Archean-age ones, and plenty are unaltered.

a. 1700 Cascadia earthquake
b. Proterozoic Eon
c. 1703 Genroku earthquake
d. 1509 Istanbul earthquake

42. _____ is one of the three main rock types (the others being igneous and metamorphic rock.) _____ is formed by deposition and consolidation of mineral and organic material and from precipitation of minerals from solution. The processes that form _____ occur at the surface of the Earth and within bodies of water.
    a. Rock cycle
    b. Petrology
    c. Serpentinite
    d. Sedimentary rock

43. _____ is the part of Earth's lithosphere that surfaces in the ocean basins. _____ is primarily composed of mafic rocks, or sima. It is thinner than continental crust, or sial, generally less than 10 kilometers thick, however it is denser, having a mean density of about 3.3 grams per cubic centimeter.
    a. Oceanic crust
    b. AL 333
    c. AASHTO Soil Classification System
    d. AL 129-1

44. A _____ is an area in which an S-Wave (secondary seismic wave) is not detected due to it not being able to pass through the outer core of the earth due to it being liquid. When an earthquake occurs, seismographs near the epicenter, out to about 90° distance, are able to record both Primary and Secondary waves, but those at a greater distance no longer detect the S-wave. This is because shear waves cannot pass through liquids.
    a. Tornillo event
    b. Receiver function
    c. Shadow zone
    d. Maximum magnitude

45. The _____ is the mechanically weak ductily-deforming region of the upper mantle of the Earth. It lies below the lithosphere, at depths between 100 and 200 km (~ 62 and 124 miles) below the surface, but perhaps extending as deep as 400 km (~ 249 miles.)

Chapter 8. Earthquakes and Earth Interior

The _____ is a portion of the upper mantle just below the lithosphere that is involved in plate movements and isostatic adjustments. In spite of its heat, pressures keep it plastic, and it has a relatively low density. Seismic waves pass relatively slowly through the _____, compared to the overlying lithospheric mantle, thus it has been called the low-velocity zone. This was the observation that originally alerted seismologists to its presence and gave some information about its physical properties, as the speed of seismic waves decreases with decreasing rigidity.

a. AASHTO Soil Classification System
b. Asthenosphere
c. AL 333
d. AL 129-1

46. The _____, usually referred to as the Moho, is the boundary between the Earth's crust and the mantle. The Moho serves to separate both oceanic crust and continental crust from underlying mantle. The Moho mostly lies entirely within the lithosphere; only beneath mid-ocean ridges does it define the lithosphere-asthenosphere boundary.
a. Gorda Ridge
b. Mohorovičić discontinuity
c. Panthalassa
d. Copperbelt Province

47. A _____ is a compound containing an anion in which one or more central silicon atoms are surrounded by electronegative ligands. This definition is broad enough to include species such as hexafluorosilicate ('fluorosilicate'), $[SiF_6]^{2-}$, but the _____ species that are encountered most often consist of silicon with oxygen as the ligand. _____ anions, with a negative net electrical charge, must have that charge balanced by other cations to make an electrically neutral compound.
a. 1703 Genroku earthquake
b. 1700 Cascadia earthquake
c. 1509 Istanbul earthquake
d. Silicate

48. The _____ make up the largest and most important class of rock-forming minerals, comprising approximately 90 percent of the crust of the Earth. They are classified based on the structure of their silicate group. _____ all contain silicon and oxygen.
a. Mineraloid
b. 1700 Cascadia earthquake
c. Silicate minerals
d. 1509 Istanbul earthquake

49. _____ defines an important group of generally dark-colored rock-forming inosilicate minerals, composed of double chain SiO_4 tetrahedra, linked at the vertices and generally containing ions of iron and/or magnesium in their structures. They crystallize into two crystal systems, monoclinic and orthorhombic. In chemical composition and general characteristics they are similar to the pyroxenes. They are minerals of either igneous or metamorphic origin; in the former case occurring as constituents (hornblende) of igneous rocks, such as granite, diorite, andesite and others. Those of metamorphic origin include examples such as those developed in limestones by contact metamorphism (tremolite) and those formed by the alteration of other ferromagnesian minerals (hornblende).
a. AL 129-1
b. AL 333
c. AASHTO Soil Classification System
d. Amphibole

50. _____ is a type of potassic volcanic rock best known for sometimes containing diamonds. It is named after the town of Kimberley in South Africa, where the discovery of an 83.5 carats (16.7 g) diamond in 1871 spawned a diamond rush, eventually creating the Big Hole.

_____ occurs in the Earth's crust in vertical structures known as _____ pipes.

a. 1700 Cascadia earthquake
b. 1509 Istanbul earthquake
c. 1703 Genroku earthquake
d. Kimberlite

51. A _____ is a dense, coarse-grained igneous rock, consisting mostly of the minerals olivine and pyroxene. _____ is ultramafic, as the rock contains less than 45% silica. It is high in magnesium, reflecting the high proportions of magnesium-rich olivine, with appreciable iron.

_____ is the dominant rock of the upper part of the Earth's mantle. The compositions of _____ nodules found in certain basalts and diamond pipes (kimberlites) are of special interest, because they provide samples of the Earth's Mantle roots of continents brought up from depths from about 30 km or so to depths at least as great as about 200 km.

a. 1509 Istanbul earthquake
b. 1703 Genroku earthquake
c. Peridotite
d. 1700 Cascadia earthquake

52. The _____ is part of the Earth's mantle, and is located between the lower mantle and the upper mantle, between a depth of 410 and 660 km. The Earth's mantle, including the _____, consists primarily of peridotite, a course grained, ultramafic, igneous rock.

The mantle was divided into the upper mantle, _____, and lower mantle as a result of sudden seismic-velocity discontinuities at depths of 410 and 660 km.

a. Dissolved load
b. Subfossil
c. Transition zone
d. Teilzone

53. In geology, _____ refers to heat sources within the planet. _____ is technically an adjective (e.g., _____ energy) but in U.S. English the word has attained frequent use as a noun .

The planet's internal heat was originally generated during its accretion, due to gravitational binding energy, and since then additional heat has continued to be generated by decay heat from the radioactive decay of elements.

a. Stratification
b. Diamond Head
c. Dali
d. Geothermal

54. The _____ is the rate of increase in temperature per unit depth in the Earth. It varies with location and is typically measured by determining the bottom open-hole temperature after borehole drilling. To achieve accuracy the drilling fluid needs time to reach the ambient temperature.

a. Geothermal desalination
b. Geothermal heat pump
c. Geothermal power
d. Geothermal gradient

55. In geology, a _____ deposit or _____ is an accumulation of valuable minerals formed by deposition of dense mineral phases in a trap site. Types of _____ deposits include alluvium, eluvium, beach placers, and paleoplacers.

Typical locations for alluvial _____ deposits are on the inside bends of rivers and creeks, in natural hollows, at the break of slope on a stream, the base of an escarpment, waterfall or other barrier, within sand dunes, beach profiles or in gravel beds.

a. Placer
c. 1509 Istanbul earthquake
b. 1703 Genroku earthquake
d. 1700 Cascadia earthquake

56. _____ is a common extrusive volcanic rock. It is usually grey to black and fine-grained due to rapid cooling of lava at the surface of a planet. It may be porphyritic containing larger crystals in a fine matrix, or vesicular, or frothy scoria.

a. 1703 Genroku earthquake
c. 1509 Istanbul earthquake
b. Basalt
d. 1700 Cascadia earthquake

57. _____ is a geologic term for a type of topography characterized by a series of separate and parallel mountain ranges with broad valleys interposed, extending over a more or less wide area. It is typified by the topography found in the Great Basin in the western United States, which is part of a larger regional topography known as the _____ Province. _____ topography results from crustal extension.

a. Tidal scour
c. Zechstein
b. Basin and Range
d. Rill

58. The _____ is a large geologic province which includes parts of the southwestern United States and northwestern Mexico, typified by basin and range topography.

The topography of the _____ is a result of crustal extension within this part of the North American Plate. The cause of this extension is as yet not fully understood, although several hypotheses have been offered. The crust here has been stretched up to 100% of its original width. In fact, the crust underneath the _____, especially under the Great Basin, is some of the thinnest in the world.

a. Quaternary
c. Canadian Shield
b. Yilgarn Craton
d. Basin and Range Province

59. _____ refers to a large group of dark, coarse-grained, intrusive igneous rocks chemically equivalent to basalt. The rocks are plutonic, formed when molten magma is trapped beneath the Earth's surface and cools into a crystalline mass.

The vast majority of the Earth's surface is underlain by _____ within the oceanic crust, produced by basalt magmatism at mid-ocean ridges.

a. 1700 Cascadia earthquake
c. 1509 Istanbul earthquake
b. 1703 Genroku earthquake
d. Gabbro

60. The _____ Era is one of three geologic eras of the Phanerozoic eon. The division of time into eras dates back to Giovanni Arduino, in the 18th century, although his original name for the era now called the '_____' was 'Secondary' (making the modern era the 'Tertiary'.)

The _____ was a time of tectonic, climatic and evolutionary activity. The continents gradually shifted from a state of connectedness into their present configuration; the drifting provided for speciation and other important evolutionary developments.

a. Mesozoic
b. 1509 Istanbul earthquake
c. 1703 Genroku earthquake
d. 1700 Cascadia earthquake

61. The _____ is the layer of igneous, sedimentary, and metamorphic rocks which form the continents and the areas of shallow seabed close to their shores, known as continental shelves. This layer is sometimes called sial due to more felsic, or granitic, bulk composition, which lies in contrast to the oceanic crust, called sima due to its mafic, or basaltic rock. (Based on the change in velocity of seismic waves, it is believed that at a certain depth sial becomes close in its physical properties to sima.

a. Tectonic plates
b. Nappe
c. Continental crust
d. Convergent boundary

62. An _____ is a type of rock that contains minerals such as gemstones and metals that can be extracted through mining and refined for use. Samples of _____ in the form of exceptionally beautiful crystals, exotic layering visible when sectioned or polished or metallic presentations such as large nuggets or crystalline formations of metals such as gold or copper may command a value far beyond their value as mere _____ or raw metal for subsequent reduction to utilitarian purposes.

The grade or concentration of an _____ mineral, or metal, as well as its form of occurrence, will directly affect the costs associated with mining the _____.

a. AASHTO Soil Classification System
b. AL 129-1
c. Ore genesis
d. Ore

Chapter 9. The Seafloor

1. The _____ is a mid-ocean ridge, a divergent tectonic plate boundary located along the floor of the Atlantic Ocean, and the longest mountain range in the world. It separates the Eurasian Plate and North American Plate in the North Atlantic, and the African Plate from the South American Plate in the South Atlantic. The MAR extends from a junction with the Gakkel Ridge (Mid-Arctic Ridge) northeast of Greenland southward to the Bouvet Triple Junction in the South Atlantic.
   a. 1509 Istanbul earthquake
   b. 1703 Genroku earthquake
   c. 1700 Cascadia earthquake
   d. Mid-Atlantic Ridge

2. _____ is the movement of the Earth's continents relative to each other. The hypothesis that continents 'drift' was first put forward by Abraham Ortelius in 1596 and was fully developed by Alfred Wegener in 1912. However, it was not until the development of the theory of plate tectonics in the 1960s, that a sufficient geological explanation of that movement was found.
   a. Panthalassa
   b. Plate tectonics
   c. Thrust fault
   d. Continental drift

3. In geology, _____ is transported rock debris overlying the solid bedrock. The term is also sometimes refers to organic debris so-transported. In the largest sense, it refers to the material left behind by retreating continental glaciers.
   a. Geodiversity
   b. Patterned ground
   c. Drift
   d. Platform cover

4. _____ is molten rock expelled by a volcano during eruption. When first expelled from a volcanic vent, it is a liquid at temperatures from 700 >°C to 1,200 >°C (1,300 >°F to 2,200 >°F.) Although _____ is quite viscous, with about 100,000 times the viscosity of water, it can flow great distances before cooling and solidifying, because of both its thixotropic and shear thinning properties.
   a. Pit crater
   b. Supervolcano
   c. Lava
   d. Volcanic ash

5. _____ are pillow-shaped structures sometimes seen in lavas and are attributed to the congealment of lava under water, or subaqeous extrusion. A pillow structure in certain extrusive igneous rock is characterized by discontinuous pillow-shaped masses, commonly up to 1 metre in diameter. _____ commonly occur at Constructive plate boundaries, forming part of a mid-ocean ridge.
   a. Fahlband
   b. Pumice raft
   c. Pillow lava
   d. Mineral hydration

6. The _____, is a geologic eon before the Proterozoic and Paleoproterozoic, before 2.5 Ga (billion years ago, or 2,500 Ma.) Instead of being based on stratigraphy, this date is defined chronometrically. The lower boundary (starting point) has not been officially recognized by the International Commission on Stratigraphy, but it is usually set to 3.8 Ga, at the end of the Hadean eon.
   a. AL 333
   b. AL 129-1
   c. AASHTO Soil Classification System
   d. Archean

7. The _____ is the layer of igneous, sedimentary, and metamorphic rocks which form the continents and the areas of shallow seabed close to their shores, known as continental shelves. This layer is sometimes called sial due to more felsic, or granitic, bulk composition, which lies in contrast to the oceanic crust, called sima due to its mafic, or basaltic rock. (Based on the change in velocity of seismic waves, it is believed that at a certain depth sial becomes close in its physical properties to sima.
   a. Convergent boundary
   b. Nappe
   c. Tectonic plates
   d. Continental crust

Chapter 9. The Seafloor

8. The _____ is the zone of the ocean floor that separates the thin oceanic crust from thick continental crust. Continental margins constitute about 28% of the oceanic area.

The transition from continental to oceanic crust commonly occurs within the outer part of the margin, called continental rise.

- a. 1509 Istanbul earthquake
- b. Cuspate forelands
- c. Longshore drift
- d. Continental margin

9. The _____ Era is one of three geologic eras of the Phanerozoic eon. The division of time into eras dates back to Giovanni Arduino, in the 18th century, although his original name for the era now called the '_____' was 'Secondary' (making the modern era the 'Tertiary'.)

The _____ was a time of tectonic, climatic and evolutionary activity. The continents gradually shifted from a state of connectedness into their present configuration; the drifting provided for speciation and other important evolutionary developments.

- a. 1703 Genroku earthquake
- b. 1509 Istanbul earthquake
- c. Mesozoic
- d. 1700 Cascadia earthquake

10. _____ is the part of Earth's lithosphere that surfaces in the ocean basins. _____ is primarily composed of mafic rocks, or sima. It is thinner than continental crust, or sial, generally less than 10 kilometers thick, however it is denser, having a mean density of about 3.3 grams per cubic centimeter.
- a. Oceanic crust
- b. AL 129-1
- c. AASHTO Soil Classification System
- d. AL 333

11. The _____ is the earliest of three geologic eras of the Phanerozoic eon. The _____ spanned from roughly 542 to 251 million years ago (ICS, 2004), and is subdivided into six geologic periods; from oldest to youngest they are: the Cambrian, Ordovician, Silurian, Devonian, Carboniferous, and Permian.

The _____ covers the time from the first appearance of abundant, soft-shelled fossils to the time when the continents were beginning to be dominated by large, relatively sophisticated reptiles and modern plants. The lower (oldest) boundary was classically set at the first appearance of creatures known as trilobites and archeocyathids.

- a. 1509 Istanbul earthquake
- b. 1703 Genroku earthquake
- c. 1700 Cascadia earthquake
- d. Paleozoic

12. _____ was the supercontinent that is theorized to have existed during the Paleozoic and Mesozoic eras about 250 million years ago, before the component continents were separated into their current configuration.

The name was first used by the German originator of the continental drift theory, Alfred Wegener, in the 1920 edition of his book The Origin of Continents and Oceans , in which a postulated supercontinent _____ played a key role.

The single enormous ocean which surrounded Pangaea is known as Panthalassa.

- a. 1509 Istanbul earthquake
- b. 1700 Cascadia earthquake
- c. 1703 Genroku earthquake
- d. Pangea

13. The _____ is an informal name for the supereon comprising the eons of the geologic timescale that came before the current Phanerozoic eon. It spans from the formation of Earth around 4500 Mya (million years ago) to the evolution of abundant macroscopic hard-shelled animals, which marked the beginning of the Cambrian, the first period of the first era of the Phanerozoic eon, some 542 Mya. It is named after the Roman name for Wales - Cambria - where rocks from this age were first studied.

- a. 1700 Cascadia earthquake
- b. Precambrian
- c. 1703 Genroku earthquake
- d. 1509 Istanbul earthquake

14. The _____ is a geological eon representing a period before the first abundant complex life on Earth. The _____ extended from 2500 Ma to 542.0 >± 1.0 Ma (million years ago), and is the most recent part of the old, informally named 'e;Precambrian'e; time.

The Proterozoic consists of 3 geologic eras, from oldest to youngest:

- Paleoproterozoic
- Mesoproterozoic
- Neoproterozoic

The well-identified events were:

- The transition to an oxygenated atmosphere during the Mesoproterozoic.
- Several glaciations, including the hypothesized Snowball Earth during the Cryogenian period in the late Neoproterozoic.
- The Ediacaran Period (635 to 542 Ma) which is characterized by the evolution of abundant soft-bodied multicellular organisms.

The geoloic record of the Proterozoic is much better than that for the preceding Archean. In contrast to the deep-water deposits of the Archean, the Proterozoic features many strata that were laid down in extensive shallow epicontinental seas; furthermore, many of these rocks are less metamorphosed than Archean-age ones, and plenty are unaltered.

- a. Proterozoic Eon
- b. 1703 Genroku earthquake
- c. 1509 Istanbul earthquake
- d. 1700 Cascadia earthquake

15. An _____ is the result of a sudden release of energy in the Earth's crust that creates seismic waves. They are recorded with a seismometer or the related and mostly obsolete Richter magnitude, with a magnitude 3 or lower _____ being mostly imperceptible and magnitude 7 causing serious damage over large areas.

Chapter 9. The Seafloor

    a. Earthquake
    b. AL 333
    c. AASHTO Soil Classification System
    d. AL 129-1

16. The lithosphere is broken up into what are called _____. In the case of Earth, there are eight major and many minor plates The lithospheric plates ride on the asthenosphere. These plates move in relation to one another at one of three types of plate boundaries: convergent, or collisional boundaries; divergent boundaries, also called spreading centers; and transform boundaries.
    a. Gorda Ridge
    b. Copperbelt Province
    c. Thrust fault
    d. Tectonic plates

17. _____ is any particulate matter that can be transported by fluid flow, and which eventually is deposited.

They are most often transported by water (fluvial processes) transported by wind (aeolian processes) and glaciers. Beach sands and river channel deposits are examples of fluvial transport and deposition, though _____ also often settles out of slow-moving or standing water in lakes and oceans.

    a. Brickearth
    b. Bovey Beds
    c. Quicksand
    d. Sediment

18. The _____ is the first geological period of the Phanerozoic eon, lasting from 542 ± 0.3 million years ago to 488.3 ± 1.7 million years ago (ICS, 2004); it is succeeded by the Ordovician. Its subdivisions, and indeed its base, are somewhat in flux. The period was established by Adam Sedgwick, who named it after Cambria, the classical name for Wales, where Britain's _____ rocks are best exposed.
    a. 1509 Istanbul earthquake
    b. Cambrian
    c. 1703 Genroku earthquake
    d. 1700 Cascadia earthquake

19. The _____ or Cambrian radiation was the seemingly rapid appearance of most major groups of complex animals around 530 million years ago, as evidenced by the fossil record. This was accompanied by a major diversification of other organisms, including animals, phytoplankton, and calcimicrobes. Before about 580 million years ago, most organisms were simple, composed of individual cells occasionally organized into colonies.
    a. Conodont Alteration Index
    b. Cambrian explosion
    c. Labyrinthodont
    d. Romer's Gap

20. The _____ Era, is the most recent of the three classic geological eras and covers the period from 65.5 million years ago to the present. It is marked by the Cretaceous-Tertiary extinction event at the end of the Cretaceous that saw the demise of the last non-avian dinosaurs and the end of the Mesozoic Era. The _____ era is ongoing.
    a. 1703 Genroku earthquake
    b. Cenozoic
    c. 1509 Istanbul earthquake
    d. 1700 Cascadia earthquake

21. _____ is a common extrusive volcanic rock. It is usually grey to black and fine-grained due to rapid cooling of lava at the surface of a planet. It may be porphyritic containing larger crystals in a fine matrix, or vesicular, or frothy scoria.
    a. Basalt
    b. 1700 Cascadia earthquake
    c. 1509 Istanbul earthquake
    d. 1703 Genroku earthquake

Chapter 9. The Seafloor

22. In geology, a _____ or _____ line is a planar fracture in rock in which the rock on one side of the fracture has moved with respect to the rock on the other side. Large faults within the Earth's crust are the result of differential or shear motion and active _____ zones are the causal locations of most earthquakes. Earthquakes are caused by energy release during rapid slippage along a _____.
   a. Dali
   b. Stack
   c. Fault
   d. Combe

23. _____ refers to a large group of dark, coarse-grained, intrusive igneous rocks chemically equivalent to basalt. The rocks are plutonic, formed when molten magma is trapped beneath the Earth's surface and cools into a crystalline mass.

The vast majority of the Earth's surface is underlain by _____ within the oceanic crust, produced by basalt magmatism at mid-ocean ridges.

   a. 1703 Genroku earthquake
   b. Gabbro
   c. 1700 Cascadia earthquake
   d. 1509 Istanbul earthquake

24. The _____ is the geologic eon before the Archean. It started at Earth's formation about 4.6 billion years ago (4,600 Ma), and ended roughly 3.8 billion years ago, though the latter date varies according to different sources.
   a. 1700 Cascadia earthquake
   b. 1509 Istanbul earthquake
   c. 1703 Genroku earthquake
   d. Hadean

25. The _____ is a continental transform fault that runs a length of roughly 800 miles (1,300 km) through California in the United States. The fault's motion is right-lateral strike-slip (horizontal motion.) It forms the tectonic boundary between the Pacific Plate and the North American Plate.
   a. 1509 Istanbul earthquake
   b. San Andreas fault
   c. 1700 Cascadia earthquake
   d. 1703 Genroku earthquake

26. A _____ is a type of fault in which rocks of lower stratigraphic position are pushed up and over higher strata. They are often recognized because they place older rocks above younger. Thrust faults are the result of compressional forces.
   a. Juan de Fuca Ridge
   b. Subduction
   c. Thrust fault
   d. Convergent boundary

27. In geology, a _____ is a place where the Earth's crust and lithosphere are being pulled apart and is an example of extensional tectonics.

Typical _____ features are a central linear downdropped fault segment, called a graben, with parallel normal faulting and _____-flank uplifts on either side forming a _____ valley, where the _____ remains above sea level. The axis of the _____ area commonly contains volcanic rocks and active volcanism is a part of many, but not all active _____ systems.

   a. 1700 Cascadia earthquake
   b. 1509 Istanbul earthquake
   c. 1703 Genroku earthquake
   d. Rift

28. The _____ is the extended perimeter of each continent and associated coastal plain, and was part of the continent during the glacial periods, but is undersea during interglacial periods such as the current epoch by relatively shallow seas (known as shelf seas) and gulfs.

The continental rise is below the slope, but landward of the abyssal plains. Its gradient is intermediate between the slope and the shelf, on the order of 0.5-1°.

a. 1700 Cascadia earthquake
c. 1509 Istanbul earthquake
b. 1703 Genroku earthquake
d. Continental shelf

29. _____ is molten rock that is found beneath the surface of the Earth, and may also exist on other terrestrial planets. Besides molten rock, _____ may also contain suspended crystals and gas bubbles. _____ often collects in a _____ chamber inside a volcano. _____ is capable of intrusion into adjacent rocks, extrusion onto the surface as lava, and explosive ejection as tephra to form pyroclastic rock.

a. Magma
c. Laccolith
b. Volcanic rock
d. Rock cycle

30. A _____ is a dense, coarse-grained igneous rock, consisting mostly of the minerals olivine and pyroxene. _____ is ultramafic, as the rock contains less than 45% silica. It is high in magnesium, reflecting the high proportions of magnesium-rich olivine, with appreciable iron.

_____ is the dominant rock of the upper part of the Earth's mantle. The compositions of _____ nodules found in certain basalts and diamond pipes (kimberlites) are of special interest, because they provide samples of the Earth's Mantle roots of continents brought up from depths from about 30 km or so to depths at least as great as about 200 km.

a. 1703 Genroku earthquake
c. Peridotite
b. 1700 Cascadia earthquake
d. 1509 Istanbul earthquake

31. _____ is a rock composed of one or more serpentine minerals. Minerals in this group are formed by serpentinization, a hydration and metamorphic transformation of ultramafic rock from the Earth's mantle. The alteration is particularly important at the sea floor at tectonic plate boundaries.

a. Metamorphic zone
c. Vesicular texture
b. Rock cycle
d. Serpentinite

32. _____ are the collective effect of changes in the Earth's movements upon its climate axial tilt, and precession of the Earth's orbit determined climatic patterns on Earth, resulting in 100,000-year ice age cycles of the Quaternary glaciation over the last few million years. The Earth's axis completes one full cycle of precession approximately every 26,000 years. At the same time, the elliptical orbit rotates, more slowly, leading to a 23,000-year cycle between the seasons and the orbit.

a. Geologic record
c. Global Standard Stratigraphic Age
b. Milankovitch theory
d. Stage

33. The _____ is the epoch from 1.8 million to 11550 years BP covering the world's recent period of repeated glaciations. The _____ epoch follows the Pliocene epoch and is followed by the Holocene epoch. The _____ is the third epoch of the Neogene period or 6th epoch of the Cenozoic Era. The end of the _____ corresponds with the retreat of the last continental glacier. It also corresponds with the end of the Paleolithic age used in archaeology.

a. Sicilian Stage
b. Late Pleistocene
c. Pleistocene
d. Tyrrhenian

34. The _____ was the earliest of the six cratonic sequences that have occurred during the Phanerozoic (followed by the Tippecanoe, Kaskaskia, Absaroka, Zu>ñi, and Tejas.) It dates from the late Proterozoic through the early Ordovician, though the marine transgression did not begin in earnest until the middle Cambrian.

At its peak, most of North America was covered by the shallow Sauk Sea, save for parts of the Canadian Shield and the islands of the Transcontinental Arch.

a. 1509 Istanbul earthquake
b. Tippecanoe sequence
c. 1700 Cascadia earthquake
d. Sauk sequence

35. _____ are waves that travel through the Earth or other elastic body, for example as the result of an earthquake, explosion, or some other process that imparts forces to the body. _____ are also continually excited on Earth by the incessant pounding of ocean waves (referred to as the microseism) and the wind. _____ are studied by seismologists, and measured by a seismograph, which records the output of a seismometer, or geophone.

a. Harmonic tremor
b. Maximum magnitude
c. Shadow zone
d. Seismic waves

36. _____ is the geological process by which material is added to a landform or land mass. Fluids such as wind and water, as well as sediment gravity flows, transport previously eroded sediment, which, at the loss of enough kinetic energy in the fluid, is deposited, building up layers of sediment.

_____ occurs when the forces responsible for sediment transportation are no longer sufficient to overcome the forces of particle weight and friction, which resist motion.

a. Deposition
b. Headward erosion
c. Diagenesis
d. Downcutting

37. A _____ is a large, slow-moving mass of ice, formed from compacted layers of snow, that slowly deforms and flows in response to gravity and high pressure.

_____ ice is the largest reservoir of fresh water on Earth, and second only to oceans as the largest reservoir of total water.

a. Pacific Decadal Oscillation
b. Little Ice Age
c. Keeling Curve
d. Glacier

38. _____ are flat or very gently sloping areas of the deep ocean basin floor. They are among the Earth's flattest and smoothest regions and the least explored. _____ cover approximately 40% of the ocean floor and reach depths between 2,200 and 5,500 m (7,200 and 18,000 ft.)

a. Abyssal plains
b. Eutrophication
c. Intertidal
d. AASHTO Soil Classification System

39. In geology, _____ is the process that takes place at convergent boundaries by which one tectonic plate moves under another tectonic plate, sinking into the Earth's mantle, as the plates converge. A _____ zone is an area on Earth where two tectonic plates move towards one another and _____ occurs. Rates of _____ are typically measured in centimeters per year, with the average rate of convergence being approximately 2 to 8 centimeters per year (about the rate a fingernail grows.)
   a. Divergent boundary
   b. Forearc
   c. Motagua Fault
   d. Subduction

40. The _____ is the deepest surveyed point in the oceans, with a depth of about 11,000 metres (estimated 36,198 ft.) The exact depth is unknown. It is located in the Mariana Islands group at the southern end of the Mariana Trench.
   a. Mariana Trough
   b. 1509 Istanbul earthquake
   c. 1700 Cascadia earthquake
   d. Challenger Deep

41. A _____ is a fissure in a planet's surface from which geothermally heated water issues. they are commonly found near volcanically active places, areas where tectonic plates are moving apart, ocean basins, and hotspots.

They are locally very common because the earth is both geologically active and has large amounts of water on its surface and within its crust. Common land types include hot springs, fumaroles and geysers. The most famous _____ system on land is probably within Yellowstone National Park in the United States.

   a. 1700 Cascadia earthquake
   b. 1509 Istanbul earthquake
   c. 1703 Genroku earthquake
   d. Hydrothermal vent

42. A _____ is a deep active seismic area in a subduction zone. Differential motion along the zone produces deep-seated earthquakes, the foci of which may be as deep as about 700 kilometres (435 miles.) They develop beneath volcanic island arcs and continental margins above active subduction zones.
   a. Pit crater
   b. Wadati-Benioff zone
   c. Pyroclastic flow
   d. Lava

43. The _____ , usually abbreviated K for its German translation Kreide, is a geologic period and system from circa >145.5 >± 4 to >65.5 >± 0.3 million years ago . In the geologic timescale, the _____ follows on the Jurassic period and is followed by the Paleogene period. It is the youngest period of the Mesozoic era, and at 80 million years long, the longest period of the Phanerozoic eon. The end of the _____ defines the boundary between the Mesozoic and Cenozoic eras.
   a. Coniacian
   b. Campanian
   c. Hauterivian
   d. Cretaceous

44. The _____ is a mid-oceanic ridge, a divergent tectonic plate boundary located along the floor of the Pacific Ocean. It separates the Pacific Plate to the west from (north to south) the North American Plate, the Rivera Plate, the Cocos Plate, the Nazca Plate, and the Antarctic Plate. It runs from an undefined point near Antarctica in the south northward to its termination at the northern end of the Gulf of California in the Salton Sea basin in southern California.
   a. Obduction
   b. East Pacific Rise
   c. Azores-Gibraltar Transform Fault
   d. Elastic rebound theory

Chapter 9. The Seafloor

45. The _____ is a tectonic spreading center located off the coasts of the state of Washington in the United States and the province of British Columbia in Canada. It runs northward from a transform boundary, the Blanco Fracture Zone, to a triple junction with the Nootka Fault and the Sovanco Fracture Zone. To its east is the Juan de Fuca Plate, which together with the Gorda Plate to its south and the Explorer Plate to its north, is what remains of the once-vast Farallon Plate which has been largely subducted under the North American Plate.
    a. Lithosphere
    b. Nappe
    c. Divergent boundary
    d. Juan de Fuca Ridge

46. _____ are natural conduits through which lava travels beneath the surface of a lava flow, expelled by a volcano during an eruption. They can be actively draining lava from a source, or can be extinct, meaning the lava flow has ceased and the rock has cooled and left a long, cave-like channel.

    _____ are formed when an active low-viscosity lava flow develops a continuous and hard crust, which thickens and forms a roof above the still-flowing lava stream.

    a. 1509 Istanbul earthquake
    b. Lava tubes
    c. 1703 Genroku earthquake
    d. 1700 Cascadia earthquake

47. A _____ is a mountain rising from the ocean seafloor that does not reach to the water's surface (sea level), and thus is not an island. These are typically formed from extinct volcanoes, that rise abruptly and are usually found rising from a seafloor of 1,000-4,000 meters depth. They are defined by oceanographers as independent features that rise to at least 1,000 meters above the seafloor.
    a. 1509 Istanbul earthquake
    b. 1703 Genroku earthquake
    c. Seamount
    d. 1700 Cascadia earthquake

48. A _____ or transform boundary is a fault which runs along the boundary of a tectonic plate. The relative motion of such plates is horizontal in either sinistral or dextral direction. Typically, some vertical motion may also exist, but the principal vectors in a _____ are oriented horizontally.
    a. Crenulation
    b. Graben
    c. Sag pond
    d. Transform fault

49. An _____ is a confined aquifer containing groundwater that will flow upward through a well without the need for pumping. Water may even reach the ground surface if the natural pressure is high enough, in which case the well is called a flowing artesian well. An aquifer provides the water for an artesian well.
    a. AL 333
    b. AL 129-1
    c. AASHTO Soil Classification System
    d. Artesian aquifer

50. A _____ is in geology an area where, as a result of metamorphism, the same combination of minerals occur in the bed rocks. These zones occur because most metamorphic minerals are only stable in certain intervals of temperature and pressure.

The temperature and pressure at which the mineralogical composition of a rock equilibrated can vary laterally through a metamorphic terrane.

Chapter 9. The Seafloor

a. Metamorphic rock
b. Metamorphic zone
c. Tephra
d. Magma

51. In geology, a _____ is a location on the Earth's surface that has experienced active volcanism for a long period of time.

J. Tuzo Wilson came up with the idea in 1963 that volcanic chains like the Hawaiian Islands result from the slow movement of a tectonic plate across a 'fixed' _____ deep beneath the surface of the planet.

a. 1703 Genroku earthquake
b. 1509 Istanbul earthquake
c. 1700 Cascadia earthquake
d. Hotspot

52. _____ are rock concretions on the sea bottom formed of concentric layers of iron and manganese hydroxides around a core. The core may be microscopically small and is sometimes completely transformed into manganese minerals by crystallization. When visible to the naked eye, it can be a small test of a microfossil, a phosphatized shark tooth, basalt debris or even fragments of earlier nodules.

a. 1703 Genroku earthquake
b. 1509 Istanbul earthquake
c. 1700 Cascadia earthquake
d. Polymetallic nodules

53. _____, partially synonymous with microcontinents, are fragments of continents thought to have been broken off from the main continental mass forming distinct islands, possibly several hundred kilometers from their place of origin. All continents are fragments; the terms 'continental fragment' and 'microcontinent' are restricted to those smaller than Sahul (Australia-New Guinea.) Other than perhaps Zealandia, they are not known to contain a craton or fragment of a craton.

a. 1703 Genroku earthquake
b. 1700 Cascadia earthquake
c. 1509 Istanbul earthquake
d. Continental crustal fragments

54. _____ is an ocean ridge in the southern Atlantic Ocean, extending for thousands of miles, off the coast of southwest Africa. Both it and the Rio Grande Rise originated from hotspot volcanism now occurring at the islands of Tristan da Cunha (the Tristan hotspot), 300 kilometres east of the crest of the Mid-Atlantic Ridge. The eastern section of the ridge is thought to have been created in the Middle Cretaceous period, between 120 and 80 million years ago.

a. Walvis Ridge
b. 1509 Istanbul earthquake
c. 1700 Cascadia earthquake
d. 1703 Genroku earthquake

55. _____ is a naturally occurring material composed primarily of fine-grained minerals, which show plasticity through a variable range of water content, and which can be hardened when dried and/or fired. _____ deposits are mostly composed of _____ minerals (phyllosilicate minerals), minerals which impart plasticity and harden when fired and/or dried, and variable amounts of water trapped in the mineral structure by polar attraction. Organic materials which do not impart plasticity may also be a part of _____ deposits.

a. 1509 Istanbul earthquake
b. 1703 Genroku earthquake
c. 1700 Cascadia earthquake
d. Clay

56. _____ is the removal of solids (sediment, soil, rock and other particles) in the natural environment. It usually occurs due to transport by wind, water, or ice; by down-slope creep of soil and other material under the force of gravity; or by living organisms, such as burrowing animals, in the case of bioerosion.

Chapter 9. The Seafloor

_____ is distinguished from weathering, which is the process of chemical or physical breakdown of the minerals in the rocks, although the two processes may occur concurrently.

a. AL 129-1
c. Erosion

b. AASHTO Soil Classification System
d. AL 333

57. A _____ in petrology or mineralogy is a secondary structure, generally spherical or irregularly rounded in shape. They are typically solid replacement bodies of chert or iron oxides formed during diagenesis of a sedimentary rock. They may be hollow as geodes or vugs or filled with crystals and intricate geometric shrinkage patterns as in septarian nodules.

a. Nodule
c. Diamond Head

b. Combe
d. Streak

58. A _____ is an opening in a planet's surface or crust, which allows hot, molten rock, ash, and gases to escape from below the surface. Volcanic activity involving the extrusion of rock tends to form mountains or features like mountains over a period of time.

a. Volcano
c. 1700 Cascadia earthquake

b. 1509 Istanbul earthquake
d. 1703 Genroku earthquake

59. The _____ was a cratonic sequence that extended from the end of the Mississippian through the Permian periods. It is the unconformity between this sequence and the preceding Kaskaskia that divides the Carboniferous into the Mississippian and Pennsylvanian periods in North America.

Like the Kaskaskia sequence, Absaroka sedimentary deposits were dominated by detrital or siliclastic rocks.

a. Absaroka sequence
c. AL 333

b. AASHTO Soil Classification System
d. AL 129-1

60. _____ refers to a sediment, sedimentary rock, or soil type which is formed from or contains a high proportion of calcium carbonate in the form of calcite or aragonite.

It can also be used as an adjectival term applied to anatomical structures which are made of calcium carbonate in animals such as gastropods, when referring to such structures as the operculum, the clausilium, and the love dart.

_____ sediments are usually deposited in shallow water near land, since the carbonate is precipitated by marine organisms that need land-derived nutrients.

a. 1700 Cascadia earthquake
c. 1703 Genroku earthquake

b. 1509 Istanbul earthquake
d. Calcareous

61. _____ is a geological term used to describe particles of rock derived from pre-existing rock through processes of weathering and erosion. Thesel particles can consist of lithic fragments (particles of recognisable rock), or of monomineralic fragments (mineral grains.) These particles are often transported through sedimentary processes into depositional systems such as riverbeds, lakes or the ocean forming sedimentary successions.

Chapter 9. The Seafloor

a. Medical geology
c. Geomechanics
b. Detritus
d. Perched coastline

62. The _____ is a geologic period and system of the Paleozoic era spanning from >416 to 359.2 million years ago (ICS, 2004.).

During the _____ Period, which occurred in the Paleozoic era, the first fish evolved legsand started to walk on land as tetrapods around 365 Ma.

a. Gogo Formation
c. Xitun Formation
b. 1509 Istanbul earthquake
d. Devonian

63. The _____ was a cratonic sequence that began in the mid-Devonian, peaked early in the Mississippian, and ended by mid-Mississippian time. A major unconformity separates it from the lower Tippecanoe sequence.

The basal-that is, the lowest and oldest-units of the Kaskaskia consist of clean quartz sandstones eroded from the Appalachian orogenic belt to the east, the Ozark Dome in the center of the continent, and south from the Canadian Shield.

a. 1700 Cascadia earthquake
c. Kaskaskia sequence
b. 1509 Istanbul earthquake
d. Sauk sequence

64. The _____ was the cratonic sequence--that is, the marine transgression--that followed the Sauk sequence; it extended from roughly the middle Ordovician to the early Devonian.

After the regression of the Sauk Sea early in the Ordovician, the exposed craton for a time underwent vigorous erosion, due to being located in a tropical climate; indeed, at this point in the Phanerozoic the North American continent roughly straddled the equator.

The Tippecanoe transgression ended this period of erosion, beginning with the deposition of clean sandstones across the craton, followed by abundant carbonate deposition.

a. Sauk sequence
c. 1700 Cascadia earthquake
b. 1509 Istanbul earthquake
d. Tippecanoe sequence

65. _____ is a sedimentary rock composed largely of the mineral calcite (calcium carbonate: $CaCO_3$.) The deposition of _____ strata is often a by-product and indicator of biological activity in the geologic record. Calcium (along with nitrogen, phosphorus, and potassium) is a key mineral to plant nutrition: soils overlying _____ bedrock tend to be pre-fertilized with calcium.

a. Limestone
c. 1509 Istanbul earthquake
b. 1700 Cascadia earthquake
d. 1703 Genroku earthquake

66. _____ is a term given to an accumulation of broken rock fragments at the base of crags, mountain cliffs, or valley shoulders. Landforms associated with these materials are sometimes called _____ slopes or talus piles. These deposits typically have a concave upwards form, while the maximum inclination of such deposits corresponds to the angle of repose of the mean debris size.

Chapter 9. The Seafloor

a. 1509 Istanbul earthquake
c. 1700 Cascadia earthquake
b. 1703 Genroku earthquake
d. Scree

67. _____ are single-celled algae, protists and phytoplankton belonging to the division haptophytes. They are distinguished by special calcium carbonate plates of uncertain function called coccoliths, which are important microfossils. _____ are almost exclusively marine and are found in large numbers throughout the surface euphotic zone of the ocean.
   a. 1703 Genroku earthquake
   c. 1700 Cascadia earthquake
   b. Coccolithophores
   d. 1509 Istanbul earthquake

68. The _____ is a tectonic spreading center located off the coast of Oregon and northern California north of Cape Mendocino. It runs from a triple junction with the San Andreas Fault and the Mendocino Fracture Zone northward to another transform boundary, the Blanco Fracture Zone. To its east is the Gorda Plate, which together with the Juan de Fuca Plate to its north, is what remains of the once-vast Farallon Plate which has been largely subducted under the North American Plate.
   a. Thrust fault
   c. Motagua Fault
   b. Panthalassa
   d. Gorda Ridge

69. The _____, together with its northern extension towards Europe, the North Atlantic Drift, is a powerful, warm, and swift Atlantic ocean current that originates in the Gulf of Mexico, exits through the Strait of Florida, and follows the eastern coastlines of the United States and Newfoundland before crossing the Atlantic Ocean. The process of western intensification causes the _____ to be a northward accelerating current offshore the east coast of North America. At about 30>°W, 40>°N, it splits in two, with the northern stream crossing to northern Europe and the southern stream recirculating off West Africa.
   a. 1509 Istanbul earthquake
   c. Gulf Stream
   b. 1700 Cascadia earthquake
   d. 1703 Genroku earthquake

70. The _____ is an extinct member of the Homo genus that is known from Pleistocene specimens found in Europe and parts of western and central Asia. Neanderthals are either classified as a subspecies of humans (Homo sapiens neanderthalensis) or as a separate species (Homo neanderthalensis.) The first proto-_____ traits appeared in Europe as early as 600,000-350,000 years ago.
   a. 1700 Cascadia earthquake
   c. 1703 Genroku earthquake
   b. 1509 Istanbul earthquake
   d. Neanderthal

71. An _____ is an oceanographic phenomenon that involves wind-driven motion of dense, cooler, and usually nutrient-rich water towards the ocean surface, replacing the warmer, usually nutrient-depleted surface water. There are at least five types of _____: coastal _____, large-scale wind-driven _____ in the ocean interior, _____ associated with eddies, topographically-associated _____, and broad-diffusive _____ in the ocean interior.

Coastal _____ is the best known type of _____, and the most closely related to human activities as it supports some of the most productive fisheries in the world, like small pelagics (sardines, anchovies, etc.).

   a. AL 129-1
   c. AASHTO Soil Classification System
   b. Upwelling
   d. AL 333

72. In geology, a _____ deposit or _____ is an accumulation of valuable minerals formed by deposition of dense mineral phases in a trap site. Types of _____ deposits include alluvium, eluvium, beach placers, and paleoplacers.

Typical locations for alluvial _____ deposits are on the inside bends of rivers and creeks, in natural hollows, at the break of slope on a stream, the base of an escarpment, waterfall or other barrier, within sand dunes, beach profiles or in gravel beds.

a. 1509 Istanbul earthquake
b. 1703 Genroku earthquake
c. 1700 Cascadia earthquake
d. Placer

Chapter 10. Deformation, Mountain Building, and the Continents

1. _____ forms a group of medium-grade metamorphic rocks, chiefly notable for the preponderance of lamellar minerals such as micas, chlorite, talc, hornblende, graphite, and others. Quartz often occurs in drawn-out grains to such an extent that a particular form called quartz _____ is produced. By definition, _____ contains more than 50% platy and elongated minerals, often finely interleaved with quartz and feldspar.
   a. Granoblastic
   b. Metasomatism
   c. Metaconglomerate
   d. Schist

2. The _____, is a geologic eon before the Proterozoic and Paleoproterozoic, before 2.5 Ga (billion years ago, or 2,500 Ma.) Instead of being based on stratigraphy, this date is defined chronometrically. The lower boundary (starting point) has not been officially recognized by the International Commission on Stratigraphy, but it is usually set to 3.8 Ga, at the end of the Hadean eon.
   a. AL 333
   b. AASHTO Soil Classification System
   c. AL 129-1
   d. Archean

3. The _____ Era, is the most recent of the three classic geological eras and covers the period from 65.5 million years ago to the present. It is marked by the Cretaceous-Tertiary extinction event at the end of the Cretaceous that saw the demise of the last non-avian dinosaurs and the end of the Mesozoic Era. The _____ era is ongoing.
   a. Cenozoic
   b. 1509 Istanbul earthquake
   c. 1703 Genroku earthquake
   d. 1700 Cascadia earthquake

4. The _____ is the zone of the ocean floor that separates the thin oceanic crust from thick continental crust. Continental margins constitute about 28% of the oceanic area.

   The transition from continental to oceanic crust commonly occurs within the outer part of the margin, called continental rise.

   a. Longshore drift
   b. Cuspate forelands
   c. 1509 Istanbul earthquake
   d. Continental margin

5. An _____ is the result of a sudden release of energy in the Earth's crust that creates seismic waves. They are recorded with a seismometer or the related and mostly obsolete Richter magnitude, with a magnitude 3 or lower _____ being mostly imperceptible and magnitude 7 causing serious damage over large areas.
   a. AASHTO Soil Classification System
   b. AL 333
   c. AL 129-1
   d. Earthquake

6. The _____ Era is one of three geologic eras of the Phanerozoic eon. The division of time into eras dates back to Giovanni Arduino, in the 18th century, although his original name for the era now called the '_____' was 'Secondary' (making the modern era the 'Tertiary'.)

   The _____ was a time of tectonic, climatic and evolutionary activity. The continents gradually shifted from a state of connectedness into their present configuration; the drifting provided for speciation and other important evolutionary developments.

   a. Mesozoic
   b. 1703 Genroku earthquake
   c. 1700 Cascadia earthquake
   d. 1509 Istanbul earthquake

116   Chapter 10. Deformation, Mountain Building, and the Continents

7. The _____ is the earliest of three geologic eras of the Phanerozoic eon. The _____ spanned from roughly 542 to 251 million years ago (ICS, 2004), and is subdivided into six geologic periods; from oldest to youngest they are: the Cambrian, Ordovician, Silurian, Devonian, Carboniferous, and Permian.

The _____ covers the time from the first appearance of abundant, soft-shelled fossils to the time when the continents were beginning to be dominated by large, relatively sophisticated reptiles and modern plants. The lower (oldest) boundary was classically set at the first appearance of creatures known as trilobites and archeocyathids.

   a. 1509 Istanbul earthquake
   c. 1703 Genroku earthquake
   b. 1700 Cascadia earthquake
   d. Paleozoic

8. A _____ is an opening in a planet's surface or crust, which allows hot, molten rock, ash, and gases to escape from below the surface. Volcanic activity involving the extrusion of rock tends to form mountains or features like mountains over a period of time.
   a. 1703 Genroku earthquake
   c. 1700 Cascadia earthquake
   b. 1509 Istanbul earthquake
   d. Volcano

9. _____, is the process of coastal sediments returning to the visible portion of a beach or foreshore following a submersion event. A sustainable beach or foreshore often goes through a cycle of submersion during rough weather then _____ during calmer periods. If a coastline is not in a healthy sustainable condition, then erosion can be more serious and _____ does not fully restore the original volume of the visible beach or foreshore leading to permanent beach or foreshore loss.
   a. AASHTO Soil Classification System
   c. Accretion
   b. AL 333
   d. AL 129-1

10. An _____ is a confined aquifer containing groundwater that will flow upward through a well without the need for pumping. Water may even reach the ground surface if the natural pressure is high enough, in which case the well is called a flowing artesian well. An aquifer provides the water for an artesian well.
    a. AL 333
    c. AL 129-1
    b. AASHTO Soil Classification System
    d. Artesian aquifer

11. A _____ is a pyroclastic material. They are extrusive igneous rocks, and are similar to pumice, which has so many cavities and is such low-density that it can float on water.
    a. Wadati-Benioff zone
    c. Pit crater
    b. Cinder
    d. Pyroclastic flow

12. A _____ or scoria cone is a steep conical hill of volcanic fragments that accumulate around and downwind from a volcanic vent. The rock fragments, often called cinders or scoria, are glassy and contain numerous gas bubbles 'frozen' into place as magma exploded into the air and then cooled quickly. Cinder cones range in size from tens to hundreds of meters tall.
    a. 1509 Istanbul earthquake
    c. 1703 Genroku earthquake
    b. Cinder cone
    d. 1700 Cascadia earthquake

Chapter 10. Deformation, Mountain Building, and the Continents

13. A _____ is an old and stable part of the continental crust that has survived the merging and splitting of continents and supercontinents for at least 500 million years. Some are over two billion years old. They are generally found in the interiors of continents and are characteristically composed of ancient crystalline basement crust of lightweight felsic igneous rock such as granite.

   a. Craton
   b. Superior craton
   c. Sebakwe proto-craton
   d. Kalahari craton

14. The lithosphere is broken up into what are called _____. In the case of Earth, there are eight major and many minor plates The lithospheric plates ride on the asthenosphere. These plates move in relation to one another at one of three types of plate boundaries: convergent, or collisional boundaries; divergent boundaries, also called spreading centers; and transform boundaries.

   a. Thrust fault
   b. Gorda Ridge
   c. Copperbelt Province
   d. Tectonic plates

15. In geology the term _____ refers to the system of forces that tend to decrease the volume of or shorten rocks. Compressive strength refers to the maximum compressive stress that can be applied to a material before failure occurs. In tectonics, plates are always subjected to compressive stress.

   a. Seismic to simulation
   b. Metamorphic reaction
   c. Seismic inversion
   d. Compression

16. Study of geological _____ is related to the study of structural geology, rock microstructure or rock texture and fault mechanics.

   _____ is the response of a rock to deformation usually by compressive stress and forms particular textures. _____ can be homogeneous or non-homogeneous, and may be pure _____ or simple _____.

   a. Shear
   b. Crenulation
   c. Molasse basin
   d. Sag pond

17. A _____, denoted τ (tau), is defined as a stress which is applied parallel or tangential to a face of a material, as opposed to a normal stress which is applied perpendicularly. In other words, considering that weight is a force, hanging something from a wall creates a _____ on the wall, since the weight of the object is acting parallel to the wall, as opposed to hanging something from the ceiling which creates a normal stress on the ceiling, since the weight is acting perpendicular to the ceiling.

The formula to calculate average _____ is:

where

>τ = the _____
F = the force applied
A = the cross sectional area

Beam shear is defined as the internal _____ of a beam caused by the shear force applied to the beam.

a. Tensile stress
c. Viscosity
b. Shear stress
d. Thixotropy

18. The _____ is a chronologic schema (or idealized model) relating stratigraphy to time that is used by geologists, paleontologists and other earth scientists to describe the timing and relationships between events that have occurred during the history of the Earth. The table of geologic time spans presented here agrees with the dates and nomenclature proposed by the International Commission on Stratigraphy, and uses the standard color codes of the United States Geological Survey.

Evidence from radiometric dating indicates that the Earth is about 4.570 billion years old.

a. Geologic time scale
c. 1700 Cascadia earthquake
b. 1509 Istanbul earthquake
d. 1703 Genroku earthquake

19. The _____ is an informal name for the supereon comprising the eons of the geologic timescale that came before the current Phanerozoic eon. It spans from the formation of Earth around 4500 Mya (million years ago) to the evolution of abundant macroscopic hard-shelled animals, which marked the beginning of the Cambrian, the first period of the first era of the Phanerozoic eon, some 542 Mya. It is named after the Roman name for Wales - Cambria - where rocks from this age were first studied.

a. 1700 Cascadia earthquake
c. 1509 Istanbul earthquake
b. 1703 Genroku earthquake
d. Precambrian

20. _____ is the solid-state recrystallization of pre-existing rocks due to changes in physical and chemical conditions, primarily heat, pressure, and the introduction of chemically active fluids. Both mineralogical, chemical and crystallographic changes can occur during this process.

Three types of _____ exist: dynamic, contact and regional.

a. Detritus
c. Compression
b. Reading Prong
d. Metamorphism

21. The _____ was proposed by the Danish geological pioneer Nicholas Steno (1638-1686.) This principle states that layers of sediment are originally deposited horizontally. The principle is important to the analysis of folded and tilted strata.
a. Key bed
c. Cyclostratigraphy
b. Principle of original horizontality
d. Bedrock

Chapter 10. Deformation, Mountain Building, and the Continents

22. In structural geology, an _____ is a fold that is convex up and has its oldest beds at its core. The term is not to be confused with antiform, which is a purely descriptive term for any fold that is convex up. Therefore if age relationships (i.e. younging direction) between various strata are unknown, the term antiform must be used.
    a. AL 129-1
    b. Anticline
    c. AASHTO Soil Classification System
    d. AL 333

23. The _____ is the layer of igneous, sedimentary, and metamorphic rocks which form the continents and the areas of shallow seabed close to their shores, known as continental shelves. This layer is sometimes called sial due to more felsic, or granitic, bulk composition, which lies in contrast to the oceanic crust, called sima due to its mafic, or basaltic rock. (Based on the change in velocity of seismic waves, it is believed that at a certain depth sial becomes close in its physical properties to sima.
    a. Continental crust
    b. Nappe
    c. Convergent boundary
    d. Tectonic plates

24. The term _____ is used in geology when one or a stack of originally flat and planar surfaces, such as sedimentary strata, are bent or curved as a result of plastic (i.e. permanent) deformation. Synsedimentary folds are those due to slumping of sedimentary material before it is lithified. Folds in rocks vary in size from microscopic crinkles to mountain-sized folds.
    a. 1509 Istanbul earthquake
    b. 1700 Cascadia earthquake
    c. 1703 Genroku earthquake
    d. Fold

25. A _____ is a special-purpose map made to show geological features.

The stratigraphic contour lines are drawn on the surface of a selected deep stratum, so that they can show the topographic trends of the strata under the ground. It is not always possible to properly show this when the strata are extremely fractured, mixed, in some discontinuities, or where they are otherwise disturbed.

    a. 1700 Cascadia earthquake
    b. Geologic map
    c. 1703 Genroku earthquake
    d. 1509 Istanbul earthquake

26. _____ is the part of Earth's lithosphere that surfaces in the ocean basins. _____ is primarily composed of mafic rocks, or sima. It is thinner than continental crust, or sial, generally less than 10 kilometers thick, however it is denser, having a mean density of about 3.3 grams per cubic centimeter.
    a. AASHTO Soil Classification System
    b. AL 129-1
    c. Oceanic crust
    d. AL 333

27. In structural geology, a _____ is a downward-curving fold, with layers that dip toward the center of the structure. A synclinorium is a large _____ with superimposed smaller folds.

On a geologic map, they are recognized by a sequence of rock layers that grow progressively younger, followed by the youngest layer at the fold's center or hinge, and by a reverse sequence of the same rock layers on the opposite side of the hinge.

    a. Petermann Orogeny
    b. Shear
    c. Syncline
    d. Michoud fault

Chapter 10. Deformation, Mountain Building, and the Continents

28. _____ is one of the three main rock types (the others being sedimentary and metamorphic rock.) _____ is formed by magma (molten rock) being cooled and becoming solid . They may form with or without crystallization, either below the surface as intrusive (plutonic) rocks or on the surface as extrusive (volcanic) rocks. They make up approximately 95% of the upper part of the Earth's crust, but their great abundance is hidden on the Earth's surface by a relatively thin but widespread layer of sedimentary and metamorphic rocks.
    a. Igneous rock
    b. AASHTO Soil Classification System
    c. AL 333
    d. AL 129-1

29. _____ is the result of the transformation of an existing rock type, the protolith, in a process called metamorphism, which means 'change in form'. The protolith is subjected to heat and pressure (temperatures greater than 150 to 200 >°C and pressures of 1500 bars) causing profound physical and/or chemical change. The protolith may be sedimentary rock, igneous rock or another older _____.
    a. Metamorphic rock
    b. Migmatite
    c. Metavolcanic rock
    d. Sedimentary rock

30. In geology, a _____ is a large sheetlike body of rock that has been moved more than 2 km (1.2 miles) from its original position. Nappes form during continental plate collisions, when folds are sheared so much that they fold back over on themselves and break apart. The resulting structure is a large-scale recumbent fold.
    a. Forearc
    b. Gorda Ridge
    c. Copperbelt Province
    d. Nappe

31. _____ is one of the three main rock types (the others being igneous and metamorphic rock.) _____ is formed by deposition and consolidation of mineral and organic material and from precipitation of minerals from solution. The processes that form _____ occur at the surface of the Earth and within bodies of water.
    a. Serpentinite
    b. Sedimentary rock
    c. Rock cycle
    d. Petrology

32. In geology, a _____ or _____ line is a planar fracture in rock in which the rock on one side of the fracture has moved with respect to the rock on the other side. Large faults within the Earth's crust are the result of differential or shear motion and active _____ zones are the causal locations of most earthquakes. Earthquakes are caused by energy release during rapid slippage along a _____.
    a. Stack
    b. Fault
    c. Dali
    d. Combe

33. _____, or tectonic breccia is a breccia (a rock type consisting of angular clasts) that was formed by tectonic forces. _____ has no cohesion, it is normally an unconsolidated rock type, unless cementation took place at a later stage. Sometimes a distinction is made between fault gouge and _____, the first has a smaller grain size.
    a. Ventifacts
    b. 1509 Istanbul earthquake
    c. Fault breccia
    d. Coprolite

34. A _____ is the topographic expression of faulting attributed to the displacement of the land surface by movement along the fault. It can be caused by differential erosion along an old inactive geologic fault (a sort of old rupture) with hard and weak rock, or by a movement on an active fault. In many cases, bluffs form from the upthrown block and can be very steep.
    a. Fault scarp
    b. Bradyseism
    c. Gravitational erosion
    d. Rejuvenated

Chapter 10. Deformation, Mountain Building, and the Continents 121

35. Since faults do not usually consist of a single, clean fracture, the term fault zone is used when referring to the zone of complex deformation that is associated with the fault plane. The two sides of a non-vertical fault are called the _____ and footwall. By definition, the _____ occurs above the fault and the footwall occurs below the fault.
   a. 1509 Istanbul earthquake
   b. Reverse fault
   c. 1700 Cascadia earthquake
   d. Hanging wall

36. The _____ is a continental transform fault that runs a length of roughly 800 miles (1,300 km) through California in the United States. The fault's motion is right-lateral strike-slip (horizontal motion.) It forms the tectonic boundary between the Pacific Plate and the North American Plate.
   a. 1509 Istanbul earthquake
   b. 1700 Cascadia earthquake
   c. 1703 Genroku earthquake
   d. San Andreas fault

37. _____ or sheet joints are surface-parallel fracture systems in rock often leading to erosion of concentric slabs.
   a. Exfoliation joints
   b. AL 129-1
   c. AASHTO Soil Classification System
   d. AL 333

38. _____ is a rock composed of angular fragments of minerals or rocks in a matrix (cementing material), that may be similar or different in composition to the fragments. A _____ may have a variety of different origins, as indicated by the named types including sedimentary _____, tectonic _____, igneous _____, impact _____ and hydrothermal _____.

Sedimentary breccias are a type of clastic sedimentary rock which are composed of angular to subangular, randomly oriented clasts of other sedimentary rocks.

   a. Ventifacts
   b. Fault breccia
   c. 1509 Istanbul earthquake
   d. Breccia

39. In geology, a _____ is a place where the Earth's crust and lithosphere are being pulled apart and is an example of extensional tectonics.

Typical _____ features are a central linear downdropped fault segment, called a graben, with parallel normal faulting and _____-flank uplifts on either side forming a _____ valley, where the _____ remains above sea level. The axis of the _____ area commonly contains volcanic rocks and active volcanism is a part of many, but not all active _____ systems.

   a. 1703 Genroku earthquake
   b. 1700 Cascadia earthquake
   c. Rift
   d. 1509 Istanbul earthquake

40. The _____ was a cratonic sequence that extended from the end of the Mississippian through the Permian periods. It is the unconformity between this sequence and the preceding Kaskaskia that divides the Carboniferous into the Mississippian and Pennsylvanian periods in North America.

Like the Kaskaskia sequence, Absaroka sedimentary deposits were dominated by detrital or siliclastic rocks.

a. AL 333
c. AL 129-1
b. AASHTO Soil Classification System
d. Absaroka sequence

41. _____ is a geologic term for a type of topography characterized by a series of separate and parallel mountain ranges with broad valleys interposed, extending over a more or less wide area. It is typified by the topography found in the Great Basin in the western United States, which is part of a larger regional topography known as the _____ Province. _____ topography results from crustal extension.
   a. Rill
   c. Basin and Range
   b. Zechstein
   d. Tidal scour

42. The _____ is a large geologic province which includes parts of the southwestern United States and northwestern Mexico, typified by basin and range topography.

The topography of the _____ is a result of crustal extension within this part of the North American Plate. The cause of this extension is as yet not fully understood, although several hypotheses have been offered. The crust here has been stretched up to 100% of its original width. In fact, the crust underneath the _____, especially under the Great Basin, is some of the thinnest in the world.

   a. Quaternary
   c. Canadian Shield
   b. Basin and Range Province
   d. Yilgarn Craton

43. _____ can be again classified into the types 'reverse' and 'normal'. A normal fault occurs when the crust is extended. Alternatively such a fault can be called an extensional fault.
   a. Hanging wall
   c. 1700 Cascadia earthquake
   b. 1509 Istanbul earthquake
   d. Dip-slip faults

44. _____ is the removal of solids (sediment, soil, rock and other particles) in the natural environment. It usually occurs due to transport by wind, water, or ice; by down-slope creep of soil and other material under the force of gravity; or by living organisms, such as burrowing animals, in the case of bioerosion.

_____ is distinguished from weathering, which is the process of chemical or physical breakdown of the minerals in the rocks, although the two processes may occur concurrently.

   a. AASHTO Soil Classification System
   c. AL 129-1
   b. AL 333
   d. Erosion

45. The _____ is a geologic fault structure of the Rocky Mountains within Glacier National Park in Montana, USA and Waterton Lakes National Park in Alberta, Canada, as well as into Lewis and Clark National Forest. It provides scientific insight into geologic processes happening in other parts of the world, like the Andes and the Himalaya Mountains. Scientific study of this region is practical because the original rock characteristics were well-preserved and recently sculptured by glaciers.
   a. Lewis overthrust
   c. 1703 Genroku earthquake
   b. 1509 Istanbul earthquake
   d. 1700 Cascadia earthquake

46. A _____ is the opposite of a normal fault -- the hanging wall moves up relative to the footwall. They are indicative of shortening of the crust. The dip of a _____ is relatively steep, greater than 45>°.

Chapter 10. Deformation, Mountain Building, and the Continents

a. Reverse fault
b. Hanging wall
c. 1700 Cascadia earthquake
d. 1509 Istanbul earthquake

47. The fault surface of _____ is usually near vertical and the footwall moves either left or right or laterally with very little vertical motion. _____ with left-lateral motion are also known as sinistral faults. Those with right-lateral motion are also known as dextral faults.
   a. Valley glaciers
   b. Principle of inclusions and components
   c. Pahoehoe lava
   d. Strike-slip faults

48. A _____ is a type of fault in which rocks of lower stratigraphic position are pushed up and over higher strata. They are often recognized because they place older rocks above younger. Thrust faults are the result of compressional forces.
   a. Convergent boundary
   b. Subduction
   c. Juan de Fuca Ridge
   d. Thrust fault

49. A _____ or transform boundary is a fault which runs along the boundary of a tectonic plate. The relative motion of such plates is horizontal in either sinistral or dextral direction. Typically, some vertical motion may also exist, but the principal vectors in a _____ are oriented horizontally.
   a. Sag pond
   b. Crenulation
   c. Transform fault
   d. Graben

50. In geology, a _____ is a location on the Earth's surface that has experienced active volcanism for a long period of time.

J. Tuzo Wilson came up with the idea in 1963 that volcanic chains like the Hawaiian Islands result from the slow movement of a tectonic plate across a 'fixed' _____ deep beneath the surface of the planet.

   a. 1509 Istanbul earthquake
   b. 1703 Genroku earthquake
   c. 1700 Cascadia earthquake
   d. Hotspot

51. The _____ was a cratonic sequence that began in the mid-Devonian, peaked early in the Mississippian, and ended by mid-Mississippian time. A major unconformity separates it from the lower Tippecanoe sequence.

The basal-that is, the lowest and oldest-units of the Kaskaskia consist of clean quartz sandstones eroded from the Appalachian orogenic belt to the east, the Ozark Dome in the center of the continent, and south from the Canadian Shield.

   a. Sauk sequence
   b. 1509 Istanbul earthquake
   c. 1700 Cascadia earthquake
   d. Kaskaskia sequence

52. _____ is the decomposition of Earth rocks, soils and their minerals through direct contact with the planet's atmosphere. _____ occurs in situ, or 'with no movement', and thus should not be confused with erosion, which involves the movement of rocks and minerals by agents such as water, ice, wind and gravity.

Two important classifications of _____ processes exist -- physical and chemical _____.

a. Physical weathering
b. Frost disintegration
c. Weathering
d. 1509 Istanbul earthquake

53. A _____ is a depressed block of land bordered by parallel faults.

A _____ is the result of a block of land being downthrown producing a valley with a distinct scarp on each side.

_____ are produced from parallel normal faults, where the hanging wall is downthrown and the footwall is upthrown. The faults typically dip toward the center of the _____ from both sides.

a. Tectonites
b. Crenulation
c. Shear
d. Graben

54. The _____ is a geological eon representing a period before the first abundant complex life on Earth. The _____ extended from 2500 Ma to 542.0 >± 1.0 Ma (million years ago), and is the most recent part of the old, informally named 'e;Precambrian'e; time.

The Proterozoic consists of 3 geologic eras, from oldest to youngest:

- Paleoproterozoic
- Mesoproterozoic
- Neoproterozoic

The well-identified events were:

- The transition to an oxygenated atmosphere during the Mesoproterozoic.
- Several glaciations, including the hypothesized Snowball Earth during the Cryogenian period in the late Neoproterozoic.
- The Ediacaran Period (635 to 542 Ma) which is characterized by the evolution of abundant soft-bodied multicellular organisms.

The geoloic record of the Proterozoic is much better than that for the preceding Archean. In contrast to the deep-water deposits of the Archean, the Proterozoic features many strata that were laid down in extensive shallow epicontinental seas; furthermore, many of these rocks are less metamorphosed than Archean-age ones, and plenty are unaltered.

a. 1700 Cascadia earthquake
b. 1509 Istanbul earthquake
c. 1703 Genroku earthquake
d. Proterozoic Eon

55. _____ is a geological term referring to the appearance of bedrock or superficial deposits exposed at the surface of the Earth. In most places the bedrock or superficial deposits are covered by a mantle of soil and vegetation and cannot be seen or examined closely. However in places where the overlying cover is removed through erosion, the rock may be exposed, or crop out.

Chapter 10. Deformation, Mountain Building, and the Continents

    a. AASHTO Soil Classification System   b. AL 129-1
    c. AL 333   d. Outcrop

56. A _____ or mudslide is the most rapid (up to 80 km/h, or 50 mph) and fluid type of downhill mass wasting. It is a rapid movement of a large mass of mud formed from loose earth and water. Similar terms are mudslide (not very liquid), mud stream, debris flow (e.g. in high mountains), jökulhlaup, and lahar
    a. 1700 Cascadia earthquake   b. 1509 Istanbul earthquake
    c. 1703 Genroku earthquake   d. Mudflow

57. The _____ is a geologic period and system that extends from about 251 to 199 Mya (million years ago.) As the first period of the Mesozoic Era, the _____ follows the Permian and is followed by the Jurassic. Both the start and end of the _____ are marked by major extinction events.
    a. Rhaetian   b. 1509 Istanbul earthquake
    c. 1700 Cascadia earthquake   d. Triassic

58. An _____ or accretionary prism is formed from sediments that are accreted onto the non-subducting tectonic plate at a convergent plate boundary. Most of the material in the _____ consists of marine sediments scraped off from the downgoing slab of oceanic crust but in some cases includes the erosional products of volcanic island arcs formed on the overriding plate.

The internal structure of an _____ is similar to that found in a thin-skinned foreland thrust belt.

    a. AL 333   b. AL 129-1
    c. AASHTO Soil Classification System   d. Accretionary wedge

59. _____, originally Gondwanaland, is the name given to a southern precursor-supercontinent and then as a remnant separated from Laurasia 180-200 million years ago during the breakup of the Pangaea supercontinent that existed about 500 to 200 Ma ago into two large segments. While the corresponding northern hemisphere continent Laurasia moved further north, the nearly equal in area _____ included most of the landmasses in today's southern hemisphere, including Antarctica, South America, Africa, Madagascar, Australia-New Guinea, and New Zealand, as well as Arabia and the Indian subcontinent, which have now moved into the Northern Hemisphere.
    a. Gondwana   b. 1509 Istanbul earthquake
    c. Laurasia   d. 1700 Cascadia earthquake

60. The _____ is the geologic eon before the Archean. It started at Earth's formation about 4.6 billion years ago (4,600 Ma), and ended roughly 3.8 billion years ago, though the latter date varies according to different sources.
    a. Hadean   b. 1509 Istanbul earthquake
    c. 1700 Cascadia earthquake   d. 1703 Genroku earthquake

61. A _____ is a mountain rising from the ocean seafloor that does not reach to the water's surface (sea level), and thus is not an island. These are typically formed from extinct volcanoes, that rise abruptly and are usually found rising from a seafloor of 1,000-4,000 meters depth. They are defined by oceanographers as independent features that rise to at least 1,000 meters above the seafloor.
    a. 1509 Istanbul earthquake   b. 1700 Cascadia earthquake
    c. 1703 Genroku earthquake   d. Seamount

62. _____ is the geomorphic process by which soil, regolith, and rock move downslope under the force of gravity. Types of _____ include creep, slides, flows, topples, and falls, each with its own characteristic features, and taking place over timescales from seconds to years. _____ occurs on both terrestrial and submarine slopes, and has been observed on Earth, Mars, and Venus.
 a. Soil liquefaction
 b. 1700 Cascadia earthquake
 c. Mass wasting
 d. 1509 Istanbul earthquake

63. The _____ was a period of mountain building in western North America, which started in the Late Cretaceous, 70 to 80 million years ago, and ended 35 to 55 million years ago. The exact duration and ages of beginning and end of the orogeny are in dispute, as is the cause. The _____ occurred in a series of pulses, with quiescent phases intervening. The major feature that was created by this orogeny was the Rocky Mountains, but evidence of this orogeny can be found from Alaska to northern Mexico, with the easternmost extent of the mountain-building represented by the Black Hills of South Dakota.
 a. Pan-African orogeny
 b. Kaikoura Orogeny
 c. Laramide orogeny
 d. Sevier orogeny

64. _____ refers to natural mountain building, and may be studied as a tectonic structural event, (b) as a geographical event, and (c) a chronological event. Orogenic events (a) cause distinctive structural phenomena and related tectonic activity, (b) affect certain regions of rocks and crust, and (c) happen within a specific period of time.
 a. Orogenesis
 b. Alice Springs Orogeny
 c. Orogeny
 d. Antler orogeny

65. _____ is an igneous, volcanic rock, of intermediate composition, with aphanitic to porphyritic texture. The mineral assemblage is typically dominated by plagioclase plus pyroxene and/or hornblende. Magnetite, zircon, apatite, ilmenite, biotite, and garnet are common accessory minerals.
 a. Andesite
 b. AASHTO Soil Classification System
 c. AL 129-1
 d. AL 333

66. _____ is a term used in geology to refer to silicate minerals, magma, and rocks which are enriched in the lighter elements such as silicon, oxygen, aluminium, sodium, and potassium. _____ minerals are usually light in color and have specific gravities less than 3. Common _____ minerals include quartz, muscovite, orthoclase, and the sodium-rich plagioclase feldspars.
 a. Laccolith
 b. Magma
 c. Tephra
 d. Felsic

67. _____ is molten rock that is found beneath the surface of the Earth, and may also exist on other terrestrial planets. Besides molten rock, _____ may also contain suspended crystals and gas bubbles. _____ often collects in a _____ chamber inside a volcano. _____ is capable of intrusion into adjacent rocks, extrusion onto the surface as lava, and explosive ejection as tephra to form pyroclastic rock.
 a. Magma
 b. Rock cycle
 c. Volcanic rock
 d. Laccolith

68. The _____ is a tectonic plate which includes most of the continent of Eurasia (a landmass consisting of the traditional continents of Europe and Asia), with the notable exceptions of the Indian subcontinent, the Arabian subcontinent, and the area east of the Chersky Range in East Siberia. It also includes oceanic crust extending westward to the Mid-Atlantic Ridge and northward to the Gakkel Ridge.

Chapter 10. Deformation, Mountain Building, and the Continents

The easterly side is a boundary with the North American Plate to the north and a boundary with the Philippine Mobile Belt and the Philippine Sea Plate to the south, and possibly with the Okhotsk Plate and the Amurian Plate.

a. Antarctic Plate
b. Intermontane Plate
c. Arabian Plate
d. Eurasian plate

69. The _____ is a tectonic plate that was originally a part of the ancient continent of Gondwanaland from which it split off, eventually becoming a major plate. About 50 to 55 million years ago, it fused with the adjacent Australian Plate. It is today part of the major Indo-Australian Plate, and includes the subcontinent of India and a portion of the basin under the Indian Ocean.
a. AL 129-1
b. AL 333
c. AASHTO Soil Classification System
d. Indian plate

70. _____ is a common extrusive volcanic rock. It is usually grey to black and fine-grained due to rapid cooling of lava at the surface of a planet. It may be porphyritic containing larger crystals in a fine matrix, or vesicular, or frothy scoria.
a. 1509 Istanbul earthquake
b. 1703 Genroku earthquake
c. 1700 Cascadia earthquake
d. Basalt

71. _____ refers to a large group of dark, coarse-grained, intrusive igneous rocks chemically equivalent to basalt. The rocks are plutonic, formed when molten magma is trapped beneath the Earth's surface and cools into a crystalline mass.

The vast majority of the Earth's surface is underlain by _____ within the oceanic crust, produced by basalt magmatism at mid-ocean ridges.

a. 1703 Genroku earthquake
b. 1509 Istanbul earthquake
c. Gabbro
d. 1700 Cascadia earthquake

72. _____ is a common and widely occurring type of intrusive, felsic, igneous rock. _____ has a medium to coarse texture, occasionally with some individual crystals larger than the groundmass forming a rock known as porphyry. Granites can be pink to dark gray or even black, depending on their chemistry and mineralogy.
a. 1700 Cascadia earthquake
b. 1509 Istanbul earthquake
c. 1703 Genroku earthquake
d. Granite

73. _____ is a term used in geology to refer to the state of gravitational equilibrium between the earth's lithosphere and asthenosphere such that the tectonic plates 'float' at an elevation which depends on their thickness and density. This concept is invoked to explain how different topographic heights can exist at the Earth's surface. When a certain area of lithosphere reaches the state of _____, it is said to be in isostatic equilibrium.
a. Economic geology
b. Isostasy
c. Isograd
d. Orientation Tensor

Chapter 10. Deformation, Mountain Building, and the Continents

74. An _____ is a type of rock that contains minerals such as gemstones and metals that can be extracted through mining and refined for use. Samples of _____ in the form of exceptionally beautiful crystals, exotic layering visible when sectioned or polished or metallic presentations such as large nuggets or crystalline formations of metals such as gold or copper may command a value far beyond their value as mere _____ or raw metal for subsequent reduction to utilitarian purposes.

The grade or concentration of an _____ mineral, or metal, as well as its form of occurrence, will directly affect the costs associated with mining the _____.

a. AASHTO Soil Classification System
b. Ore genesis
c. AL 129-1
d. Ore

75. A type of seismic wave, the _____, secondary wave or shear wave (sometimes called an elastic _____) is one of the two main types of elastic body waves, so named because they move through the body of an object, unlike surface waves.

The _____ move as a shear or transverse wave, so motion is perpendicular to the direction of wave propagation: S-waves, like waves in a rope, as opposed to waves moving through a slinky, the P-wave. The wave moves through elastic media, and the main restoring force comes from shear effects.

a. 1509 Istanbul earthquake
b. 1703 Genroku earthquake
c. 1700 Cascadia earthquake
d. S-wave

76. _____ are waves that travel through the Earth or other elastic body, for example as the result of an earthquake, explosion, or some other process that imparts forces to the body. _____ are also continually excited on Earth by the incessant pounding of ocean waves (referred to as the microseism) and the wind. _____ are studied by seismologists, and measured by a seismograph, which records the output of a seismometer, or geophone.

a. Harmonic tremor
b. Maximum magnitude
c. Shadow zone
d. Seismic waves

77. _____ is the geological process by which material is added to a landform or land mass. Fluids such as wind and water, as well as sediment gravity flows, transport previously eroded sediment, which, at the loss of enough kinetic energy in the fluid, is deposited, building up layers of sediment.

_____ occurs when the forces responsible for sediment transportation are no longer sufficient to overcome the forces of particle weight and friction, which resist motion.

a. Headward erosion
b. Diagenesis
c. Downcutting
d. Deposition

78. _____ are flat or very gently sloping areas of the deep ocean basin floor. They are among the Earth's flattest and smoothest regions and the least explored. _____ cover approximately 40% of the ocean floor and reach depths between 2,200 and 5,500 m (7,200 and 18,000 ft.)

a. AASHTO Soil Classification System
b. Eutrophication
c. Intertidal
d. Abyssal plains

79. A _____ in geology is an intrusive igneous rock body that crystallized from a magma slowly cooling below the surface of the Earth. Plutons include batholiths, dikes, sills, laccoliths, lopoliths, and other igneous bodies. In practice, '_____' usually refers to a distinctive mass of igneous rock, typically kilometers in dimension, without a tabular shape like those of dikes and sills.
  a. Pluton
  b. Vesicular texture
  c. Metamorphic zone
  d. Migmatite

Chapter 11. Mass Wasting

1. _____ is water located beneath the ground surface in soil pore spaces and in the fractures of lithologic formations. A unit of rock or an unconsolidated deposit is called an aquifer when it can yield a usable quantity of water. The depth at which soil pore spaces or fractures and voids in rock become completely saturated with water is called the water table.
   a. Depression focused recharge
   b. Groundwater
   c. 1700 Cascadia earthquake
   d. 1509 Istanbul earthquake

2. The _____ was a cratonic sequence that began in the mid-Devonian, peaked early in the Mississippian, and ended by mid-Mississippian time. A major unconformity separates it from the lower Tippecanoe sequence.

   The basal-that is, the lowest and oldest-units of the Kaskaskia consist of clean quartz sandstones eroded from the Appalachian orogenic belt to the east, the Ozark Dome in the center of the continent, and south from the Canadian Shield.

   a. 1509 Istanbul earthquake
   b. Sauk sequence
   c. 1700 Cascadia earthquake
   d. Kaskaskia sequence

3. A _____ is a geological phenomenon which includes a wide range of ground movement, such as rock falls, deep failure of slopes and shallow debris flows, which can occur in offshore, coastal and onshore environments. Although the action of gravity is the primary driving force for a _____ to occur, there are other contributing factors affecting the original slope stability. Typically, pre-conditional factors build up specific sub-surface conditions that make the area/slope prone to failure, whereas the actual _____ often requires a trigger before being released.
   a. 1509 Istanbul earthquake
   b. Landslide
   c. 1700 Cascadia earthquake
   d. Mass wasting

4. _____ is the geomorphic process by which soil, regolith, and rock move downslope under the force of gravity. Types of _____ include creep, slides, flows, topples, and falls, each with its own characteristic features, and taking place over timescales from seconds to years. _____ occurs on both terrestrial and submarine slopes, and has been observed on Earth, Mars, and Venus.
   a. 1700 Cascadia earthquake
   b. 1509 Istanbul earthquake
   c. Soil liquefaction
   d. Mass wasting

5. _____ refers to quantities of rock falling freely from a cliff face. A _____ is a fragment of rock (a block) detached by sliding, toppling, or falling, that falls along a vertical or sub-vertical cliff, proceeds down slope by bouncing and flying along ballistic trajectories or by rolling on talus or debris slopes,'e; (Varnes, 1978.) Alternatively, a '_____ is the natural downward motion of a detached block or series of blocks with a small volume involving free falling, bouncing, rolling, and sliding'.
   a. Predator trap
   b. Debris flow
   c. Solifluction
   d. Rockfall

6. The _____ is an engineering property of granular materials. The _____ is the maximum angle of a stable slope determined by friction, cohesion and the shapes of the particles.

   When bulk granular materials are poured onto a horizontal surface, a conical pile will form. The internal angle between the surface of the pile and the horizontal surface is known as the _____ and is related to the density, surface area, and coefficient of friction of the material.

Chapter 11. Mass Wasting

a. AASHTO Soil Classification System
c. Angle of repose
b. AL 129-1
d. AL 333

7. The _____ was the earliest of the six cratonic sequences that have occurred during the Phanerozoic (followed by the Tippecanoe, Kaskaskia, Absaroka, Zu>ñi, and Tejas.) It dates from the late Proterozoic through the early Ordovician, though the marine transgression did not begin in earnest until the middle Cambrian.

At its peak, most of North America was covered by the shallow Sauk Sea, save for parts of the Canadian Shield and the islands of the Transcontinental Arch.

a. 1700 Cascadia earthquake
c. 1509 Istanbul earthquake
b. Tippecanoe sequence
d. Sauk sequence

8. Study of geological _____ is related to the study of structural geology, rock microstructure or rock texture and fault mechanics.

_____ is the response of a rock to deformation usually by compressive stress and forms particular textures. _____ can be homogeneous or non-homogeneous, and may be pure _____ or simple _____.

a. Shear
c. Crenulation
b. Molasse basin
d. Sag pond

9. _____ in reference to soil is a term used to describe the maximum strength of soil at which point significant plastic deformation or yielding occurs due to an applied shear stress. There is no definitive '_____' of a soil as it depends on a number of factors affecting the soil at any given time and on the frame of reference, in particular the rate at which the shearing occurs.

Two theories are commonly used to estimate the _____ of a soil depending on the rate of shearing as a frame of reference.

a. Shear strength
c. Slope stability
b. Consolidation
d. Lateral earth pressure

10. The field of _____ encompasses the analysis of static and dynamic stability of slopes of earth and rock-fill dams, slopes of other types of embankments, excavated slopes, and natural slopes in soil and soft rock.

Earthen slopes can develop a cut-spherical weakness zone. The probability of this happening can be calculated in advance using a simple 2-D circular analysis package. A primary difficulty with analysis is locating the most-probable slip plane for any given situation. Many landslides have only been analyzed after the fact.

a. Slope stability
c. Groundwater-related subsidence
b. Vibro replacement stone columns
d. Pore water pressure

11. In geology, _____ is transported rock debris overlying the solid bedrock. The term is also sometimes refers to organic debris so-transported. In the largest sense, it refers to the material left behind by retreating continental glaciers.

Chapter 11. Mass Wasting

    a. Drift
    c. Geodiversity
    b. Patterned ground
    d. Platform cover

12. In stratigraphy, _____ is the native consolidated rock underlying the surface of a terrestrial planet, usually the Earth. Above the _____ is usually an area of broken and weathered unconsolidated rock in the basal subsoil. The top of the _____ is known as rockhead and identifying this, via excavations, drilling or geophysical methods, is an important task in most civil engineering projects.
    a. Biozones
    c. Sequence stratigraphy
    b. Polystrate
    d. Bedrock

13. _____ is a naturally occurring material composed primarily of fine-grained minerals, which show plasticity through a variable range of water content, and which can be hardened when dried and/or fired. _____ deposits are mostly composed of _____ minerals (phyllosilicate minerals), minerals which impart plasticity and harden when fired and/or dried, and variable amounts of water trapped in the mineral structure by polar attraction. Organic materials which do not impart plasticity may also be a part of _____ deposits.
    a. 1700 Cascadia earthquake
    c. 1703 Genroku earthquake
    b. Clay
    d. 1509 Istanbul earthquake

14. The _____ is the epoch from 1.8 million to 11550 years BP covering the world's recent period of repeated glaciations. The _____ epoch follows the Pliocene epoch and is followed by the Holocene epoch. The _____ is the third epoch of the Neogene period or 6th epoch of the Cenozoic Era. The end of the _____ corresponds with the retreat of the last continental glacier. It also corresponds with the end of the Paleolithic age used in archaeology.
    a. Sicilian Stage
    c. Late Pleistocene
    b. Tyrrhenian
    d. Pleistocene

15. _____ is a form of mass wasting event that occurs when loosely consolidated materials or rock layers move a short distance down a slope. The landmass and the surface it slumps upon is called a failure surface. When the movement occurs in soil, there is often a distinctive rotational movement to the mass, that cuts vertically through bedding planes (landslides take place along a bedding plane or fault). This rotational movement moves along a curved slip surface of regolith (the failure surface) which overlies bedrock. This results in internal deformation of the moving mass consisting chiefly of overturned folds called 'sheath folds.'
    a. Soil
    c. 1509 Istanbul earthquake
    b. Topsoil
    d. Slump

16. _____ is the naturally occurring, unconsolidated or loose covering on the Earth's surface. _____ is composed of particles of broken rock that have been altered by chemical, biological and environmental processes including weathering and erosion. _____ is different from its parent rock(s) source(s), altered by interactions between the lithosphere, hydrosphere, atmosphere, and the biosphere.
    a. Topsoil
    c. 1509 Istanbul earthquake
    b. Slump
    d. Soil

17. An _____ is a fan-shaped deposit formed where a fast flowing stream flattens, slows, and spreads typically at the exit of a canyon onto a flatter plain. A convergence of neighboring fans into a single apron of deposits against a slope is called a bajada, or compound _____.

Chapter 11. Mass Wasting

a. AASHTO Soil Classification System
b. AL 333
c. Alluvial fan
d. AL 129-1

18. A _____ or mudslide is the most rapid (up to 80 km/h, or 50 mph) and fluid type of downhill mass wasting. It is a rapid movement of a large mass of mud formed from loose earth and water. Similar terms are mudslide (not very liquid), mud stream, debris flow (e.g. in high mountains), j>ökulhlaup, and lahar

a. 1700 Cascadia earthquake
b. 1509 Istanbul earthquake
c. 1703 Genroku earthquake
d. Mudflow

19. An _____ is a rapid flow of snow down a slope, from either natural triggers or human activity. Typically occurring in mountainous terrain, an _____ can mix air and water with the descending snow. Powerful avalanches have the capability to entrain ice, rocks, trees, and other material on the slope; however avalanches are always initiated in snow, are primarily composed of flowing snow, and are distinct from mudslides, rock slides, rock avalanches, and serac collapses from an icefall.

a. Avalanche
b. AASHTO Soil Classification System
c. AL 333
d. AL 129-1

20. The _____ is the earliest of three geologic eras of the Phanerozoic eon. The _____ spanned from roughly 542 to 251 million years ago (ICS, 2004), and is subdivided into six geologic periods; from oldest to youngest they are: the Cambrian, Ordovician, Silurian, Devonian, Carboniferous, and Permian.

The _____ covers the time from the first appearance of abundant, soft-shelled fossils to the time when the continents were beginning to be dominated by large, relatively sophisticated reptiles and modern plants. The lower (oldest) boundary was classically set at the first appearance of creatures known as trilobites and archeocyathids.

a. 1703 Genroku earthquake
b. 1509 Istanbul earthquake
c. 1700 Cascadia earthquake
d. Paleozoic

21. _____ was the supercontinent that is theorized to have existed during the Paleozoic and Mesozoic eras about 250 million years ago, before the component continents were separated into their current configuration.

The name was first used by the German originator of the continental drift theory, Alfred Wegener, in the 1920 edition of his book The Origin of Continents and Oceans , in which a postulated supercontinent _____ played a key role.

The single enormous ocean which surrounded Pangaea is known as Panthalassa.

a. 1509 Istanbul earthquake
b. 1703 Genroku earthquake
c. 1700 Cascadia earthquake
d. Pangea

22. _____ is the decomposition of Earth rocks, soils and their minerals through direct contact with the planet's atmosphere. _____ occurs in situ, or 'with no movement', and thus should not be confused with erosion, which involves the movement of rocks and minerals by agents such as water, ice, wind and gravity.

Two important classifications of _____ processes exist -- physical and chemical _____.

a. Frost disintegration
c. Physical weathering
b. Weathering
d. 1509 Istanbul earthquake

23. An _____ is the result of a sudden release of energy in the Earth's crust that creates seismic waves. They are recorded with a seismometer or the related and mostly obsolete Richter magnitude, with a magnitude 3 or lower _____ being mostly imperceptible and magnitude 7 causing serious damage over large areas.
   a. AL 333
   b. Earthquake
   c. AASHTO Soil Classification System
   d. AL 129-1

24. A _____ or super volcanic eruption is a volcanic eruption which is substantially larger than any volcano in historic times (generally accepted to be greater than 1,000 cubic kilometres.) They occur when magma in the Earth rises into the crust from a hotspot but is unable to break through the crust. Pressure builds in a large and growing magma pool until the crust is unable to contain the pressure.
   a. Supervolcano
   b. Pit crater
   c. Volcanic ash
   d. Lapilli

25. In chemistry, a _____ is a salt or ester of carbonic acid.

To test for the presence of the _____ anion in a salt, the addition of dilute mineral acid (e.g. hydrochloric acid) will yield carbon dioxide gas.

_____-containing salts are industrially and mineralogically ubiquitous.

   a. 1509 Istanbul earthquake
   b. 1703 Genroku earthquake
   c. Carbonate
   d. 1700 Cascadia earthquake

26. Two important classifications of weathering processes exist -- physical and _____. Mechanical or physical weathering involves the breakdown of rocks and soils through direct contact with atmospheric conditions, such as heat, water, ice and pressure. The second classification, _____, involves the direct effect of atmospheric chemicals or biologically produced chemicals (also known as biological weathering) in the breakdown of rocks, soils and minerals.
   a. 1509 Istanbul earthquake
   b. Physical weathering
   c. Weathering
   d. Chemical weathering

27. _____ can also be called frost shattering or frost-wedging. This type of weathering is common in mountain areas where the temperature is around freezing point. Frost induced weathering, although often attributed to the expansion of freezing water captured in cracks, is generally independent of the water-to-ice expansion. It has long been known that moist soils expand or frost heave upon freezing as a result of water migrating along from unfrozen areas via thin films to collect at growing ice lenses. This same phenomena occurs within pore spaces of rocks.
   a. Physical weathering
   b. Frost disintegration
   c. 1509 Istanbul earthquake
   d. Weathering

28. The _____ is an informal name for the supereon comprising the eons of the geologic timescale that came before the current Phanerozoic eon. It spans from the formation of Earth around 4500 Mya (million years ago) to the evolution of abundant macroscopic hard-shelled animals, which marked the beginning of the Cambrian, the first period of the first era of the Phanerozoic eon, some 542 Mya. It is named after the Roman name for Wales - Cambria - where rocks from this age were first studied.

a. Precambrian
b. 1509 Istanbul earthquake
c. 1703 Genroku earthquake
d. 1700 Cascadia earthquake

29. _____ is a term given to an accumulation of broken rock fragments at the base of crags, mountain cliffs, or valley shoulders. Landforms associated with these materials are sometimes called _____ slopes or talus piles. These deposits typically have a concave upwards form, while the maximum inclination of such deposits corresponds to the angle of repose of the mean debris size.
   a. 1700 Cascadia earthquake
   b. 1509 Istanbul earthquake
   c. 1703 Genroku earthquake
   d. Scree

30. An _____ is a confined aquifer containing groundwater that will flow upward through a well without the need for pumping. Water may even reach the ground surface if the natural pressure is high enough, in which case the well is called a flowing artesian well. An aquifer provides the water for an artesian well.
   a. AL 333
   b. Artesian aquifer
   c. AASHTO Soil Classification System
   d. AL 129-1

31. A _____ is a fast moving mass of unconsolidated, saturated debris that looks like flowing concrete. They differentiate from a mudflow by terms of the viscosity of the flow. Flows can carry clasts ranging in size from clay particles to boulders, and also often contains a large amount of woody debris.
   a. Debris flow
   b. Geohazard
   c. Cryoseism
   d. Predator trap

32. _____ is a unique form of highly sensitive marine clay, with the tendency to change from a relatively stiff condition to a liquid mass when it is disturbed.

Undisturbed _____ resembles a water-saturated gel. When a mass of _____ undergoes sufficient stress, however, it instantly turns into a flowing ooze, a process known as liquefaction.

   a. Salt glacier
   b. Brickearth
   c. Quicksand
   d. Quick clay

33. In geology, _____ is a type of mass wasting where waterlogged sediment slowly moves downslope over impermeable material. It can occur in any climate where the ground is saturated by water, though it is most often found in periglacial environments where the ground is permanently frozen, under which conditions the process is often called gelifluction. During warm seasonal periods the surface layer melts and slides over the frozen underlayer, slowly moving downslope due to frost heave that occurs normal to the slope.
   a. Cryoseism
   b. Rockfall
   c. Solifluction
   d. Sturzstrom

34. A _____ is a large, slow-moving mass of ice, formed from compacted layers of snow, that slowly deforms and flows in response to gravity and high pressure.

_____ ice is the largest reservoir of fresh water on Earth, and second only to oceans as the largest reservoir of total water.

Chapter 11. Mass Wasting

  a. Keeling Curve   b. Pacific Decadal Oscillation
  c. Little Ice Age   d. Glacier

35. An _____ is a downslope viscous flow of fine grained materials that have been saturated with water, and moves under the pull of gravity. They are an intermediate type of mass wasting that is between downhill creep and mudflow. The types of materials that are susceptible to earthflows are clay, fine sand and silt, and fine-grained pyroclastic material.
  a. AASHTO Soil Classification System   b. Earthflow
  c. AL 333   d. AL 129-1

36. In geology, a _____ or _____ line is a planar fracture in rock in which the rock on one side of the fracture has moved with respect to the rock on the other side. Large faults within the Earth's crust are the result of differential or shear motion and active _____ zones are the causal locations of most earthquakes. Earthquakes are caused by energy release during rapid slippage along a _____.
  a. Dali   b. Stack
  c. Combe   d. Fault

37. The _____ is a continental transform fault that runs a length of roughly 800 miles (1,300 km) through California in the United States. The fault's motion is right-lateral strike-slip (horizontal motion.) It forms the tectonic boundary between the Pacific Plate and the North American Plate.
  a. 1700 Cascadia earthquake   b. San Andreas fault
  c. 1509 Istanbul earthquake   d. 1703 Genroku earthquake

38. In geology, a _____ is a place where the Earth's crust and lithosphere are being pulled apart and is an example of extensional tectonics.

Typical _____ features are a central linear downdropped fault segment, called a graben, with parallel normal faulting and _____-flank uplifts on either side forming a _____ valley, where the _____ remains above sea level. The axis of the _____ area commonly contains volcanic rocks and active volcanism is a part of many, but not all active _____ systems.

  a. 1700 Cascadia earthquake   b. Rift
  c. 1703 Genroku earthquake   d. 1509 Istanbul earthquake

39. The _____ is a geologic period and system of the Paleozoic era spanning from >416 to 359.2 million years ago (ICS, 2004.).

During the _____ Period, which occurred in the Paleozoic era, the first fish evolved legsand started to walk on land as tetrapods around 365 Ma.

  a. Xitun Formation   b. Devonian
  c. Gogo Formation   d. 1509 Istanbul earthquake

Chapter 11. Mass Wasting

40. _____ is a layer of loose, heterogeneous material covering solid rock. It includes dust, soil, broken rock, and other related materials and is present on Earth, the Moon, some asteroids, and other planets. The term was first defined by George P. Merrill in 1897 who stated, 'In places this covering is made up of material originating through rock-weathering or plant growth in situ. In other instances it is of fragmental and more or less decomposed matter drifted by wind, water or ice from other sources. This entire mantle of unconsolidated material, whatever its nature or origin, it is proposed to call the _____.'

   a. Regolith
   b. 1700 Cascadia earthquake
   c. 1509 Istanbul earthquake
   d. 1703 Genroku earthquake

41. _____ is a measure of the resistance of a fluid which is being deformed by either shear stress or extensional stress. In everyday terms (and for fluids only), _____ is 'thickness'. Thus, water is 'thin', having a lower _____, while honey is 'thick' having a higher _____.

   a. Thixotropy
   b. Shear stress
   c. Tensile stress
   d. Viscosity

42. The _____ is a geological eon representing a period before the first abundant complex life on Earth. The _____ extended from 2500 Ma to 542.0 >± 1.0 Ma (million years ago), and is the most recent part of the old, informally named 'e;Precambrian'e; time.

The Proterozoic consists of 3 geologic eras, from oldest to youngest:

- Paleoproterozoic
- Mesoproterozoic
- Neoproterozoic

The well-identified events were:

- The transition to an oxygenated atmosphere during the Mesoproterozoic.
- Several glaciations, including the hypothesized Snowball Earth during the Cryogenian period in the late Neoproterozoic.
- The Ediacaran Period (635 to 542 Ma) which is characterized by the evolution of abundant soft-bodied multicellular organisms.

The geoloic record of the Proterozoic is much better than that for the preceding Archean. In contrast to the deep-water deposits of the Archean, the Proterozoic features many strata that were laid down in extensive shallow epicontinental seas; furthermore, many of these rocks are less metamorphosed than Archean-age ones, and plenty are unaltered.

   a. 1700 Cascadia earthquake
   b. 1509 Istanbul earthquake
   c. 1703 Genroku earthquake
   d. Proterozoic Eon

43. The _____ is the geologic eon before the Archean. It started at Earth's formation about 4.6 billion years ago (4,600 Ma), and ended roughly 3.8 billion years ago, though the latter date varies according to different sources.

a. 1700 Cascadia earthquake
c. 1703 Genroku earthquake
b. 1509 Istanbul earthquake
d. Hadean

44. _____ are waves that travel through the Earth or other elastic body, for example as the result of an earthquake, explosion, or some other process that imparts forces to the body. _____ are also continually excited on Earth by the incessant pounding of ocean waves (referred to as the microseism) and the wind. _____ are studied by seismologists, and measured by a seismograph, which records the output of a seismometer, or geophone.
a. Seismic waves
c. Harmonic tremor
b. Shadow zone
d. Maximum magnitude

45. _____ is the geological process by which material is added to a landform or land mass. Fluids such as wind and water, as well as sediment gravity flows, transport previously eroded sediment, which, at the loss of enough kinetic energy in the fluid, is deposited, building up layers of sediment.

_____ occurs when the forces responsible for sediment transportation are no longer sufficient to overcome the forces of particle weight and friction, which resist motion.

a. Deposition
c. Downcutting
b. Headward erosion
d. Diagenesis

46. _____ is the removal of solids (sediment, soil, rock and other particles) in the natural environment. It usually occurs due to transport by wind, water, or ice; by down-slope creep of soil and other material under the force of gravity; or by living organisms, such as burrowing animals, in the case of bioerosion.

_____ is distinguished from weathering, which is the process of chemical or physical breakdown of the minerals in the rocks, although the two processes may occur concurrently.

a. AASHTO Soil Classification System
c. AL 129-1
b. AL 333
d. Erosion

47. The _____ Era, is the most recent of the three classic geological eras and covers the period from 65.5 million years ago to the present. It is marked by the Cretaceous-Tertiary extinction event at the end of the Cretaceous that saw the demise of the last non-avian dinosaurs and the end of the Mesozoic Era. The _____ era is ongoing.
a. 1509 Istanbul earthquake
c. Cenozoic
b. 1703 Genroku earthquake
d. 1700 Cascadia earthquake

48. In geology, _____ or _____ soil is soil at or below the freezing point of water (0 >°C or 32 >°F) for two or more years. Ice is not always present, as may be in the case of nonporous bedrock, but it frequently occurs and it may be in amounts exceeding the potential hydraulic saturation of the ground material. Most _____ is located in high latitudes (i.e. land in close proximity to the North and South poles), but alpine _____ may exist at high altitudes in much lower latitudes.
a. 1700 Cascadia earthquake
c. 1703 Genroku earthquake
b. 1509 Istanbul earthquake
d. Permafrost

Chapter 11. Mass Wasting

49. _____ in the earth sciences (commonly symbolized as κ a rock or k) is a measure of the ability of a material (typically unconsolidated material) to transmit fluids. It is of great importance in determining the flow characteristics of hydrocarbons in oil and gas reservoirs, and of groundwater in aquifers. It is typically measured in the lab by application of Darcy's law under steady state conditions or, more generally, by application of various solutions to the diffusion equation for unsteady flow conditions.

   a. Porosity
   b. Saltwater intrusion
   c. Phreatic zone
   d. Permeability

50. The _____ is the zone of the ocean floor that separates the thin oceanic crust from thick continental crust. Continental margins constitute about 28% of the oceanic area.

   The transition from continental to oceanic crust commonly occurs within the outer part of the margin, called continental rise.

   a. Longshore drift
   b. Cuspate forelands
   c. 1509 Istanbul earthquake
   d. Continental margin

51. _____ is the natural or artificial removal of surface and sub-surface water from an area. Many agricultural soils need _____ to improve production or to manage water supplies.

   The earliest archaeological record of an advanced system of _____ comes from the Indus Valley Civilization from around 3100 BC in what is now Pakistan and North India.

   a. 1700 Cascadia earthquake
   b. 1703 Genroku earthquake
   c. 1509 Istanbul earthquake
   d. Drainage

52. A _____ is a long anchor bolt, for stabilizing rock excavations, which may be tunnels or rock cuts. It transfers load from the unstable exterior, to the confined (and much stronger) interior of the rock mass.

   They were first used in mining starting in the 1890s, with systematic use documented at the St Joseph Lead Mine in the US in the 1920s.

   a. Rock bolt
   b. Wave equation analysis
   c. Dynamic load testing
   d. Nuclear Densometer Test

Chapter 12. Running Water

1. The _____, is a geologic eon before the Proterozoic and Paleoproterozoic, before 2.5 Ga (billion years ago, or 2,500 Ma.) Instead of being based on stratigraphy, this date is defined chronometrically. The lower boundary (starting point) has not been officially recognized by the International Commission on Stratigraphy, but it is usually set to 3.8 Ga, at the end of the Hadean eon.
    a. AASHTO Soil Classification System
    b. AL 333
    c. Archean
    d. AL 129-1

2. _____ is the geological process by which material is added to a landform or land mass. Fluids such as wind and water, as well as sediment gravity flows, transport previously eroded sediment, which, at the loss of enough kinetic energy in the fluid, is deposited, building up layers of sediment.

    _____ occurs when the forces responsible for sediment transportation are no longer sufficient to overcome the forces of particle weight and friction, which resist motion.

    a. Headward erosion
    b. Diagenesis
    c. Downcutting
    d. Deposition

3. _____ is water located beneath the ground surface in soil pore spaces and in the fractures of lithologic formations. A unit of rock or an unconsolidated deposit is called an aquifer when it can yield a usable quantity of water. The depth at which soil pore spaces or fractures and voids in rock become completely saturated with water is called the water table.
    a. 1509 Istanbul earthquake
    b. Depression focused recharge
    c. 1700 Cascadia earthquake
    d. Groundwater

4. The _____ describes the continuous movement of water on, above, and below the surface of the Earth. Since the _____ is truly a 'cycle,' there is no beginning or end. Water can change states among liquid, vapor, and ice at various places in the _____.
    a. Water cycle
    b. Cone of depression
    c. Vadose zone
    d. Hydraulic conductivity

5. The _____ is the earliest of three geologic eras of the Phanerozoic eon. The _____ spanned from roughly 542 to 251 million years ago (ICS, 2004), and is subdivided into six geologic periods; from oldest to youngest they are: the Cambrian, Ordovician, Silurian, Devonian, Carboniferous, and Permian.

    The _____ covers the time from the first appearance of abundant, soft-shelled fossils to the time when the continents were beginning to be dominated by large, relatively sophisticated reptiles and modern plants. The lower (oldest) boundary was classically set at the first appearance of creatures known as trilobites and archeocyathids.

    a. 1700 Cascadia earthquake
    b. Paleozoic
    c. 1703 Genroku earthquake
    d. 1509 Istanbul earthquake

6. _____ was the supercontinent that is theorized to have existed during the Paleozoic and Mesozoic eras about 250 million years ago, before the component continents were separated into their current configuration.

The name was first used by the German originator of the continental drift theory, Alfred Wegener, in the 1920 edition of his book The Origin of Continents and Oceans, in which a postulated supercontinent _____ played a key role.

The single enormous ocean which surrounded Pangaea is known as Panthalassa.

a. 1700 Cascadia earthquake
c. Pangea

b. 1703 Genroku earthquake
d. 1509 Istanbul earthquake

7. The _____ is an informal name for the supereon comprising the eons of the geologic timescale that came before the current Phanerozoic eon. It spans from the formation of Earth around 4500 Mya (million years ago) to the evolution of abundant macroscopic hard-shelled animals, which marked the beginning of the Cambrian, the first period of the first era of the Phanerozoic eon, some 542 Mya. It is named after the Roman name for Wales - Cambria - where rocks from this age were first studied.

a. 1703 Genroku earthquake
c. 1700 Cascadia earthquake

b. 1509 Istanbul earthquake
d. Precambrian

8. The _____ is a geological eon representing a period before the first abundant complex life on Earth. The _____ extended from 2500 Ma to 542.0 >± 1.0 Ma (million years ago), and is the most recent part of the old, informally named 'e;Precambrian'e; time.

The Proterozoic consists of 3 geologic eras, from oldest to youngest:

- Paleoproterozoic
- Mesoproterozoic
- Neoproterozoic

The well-identified events were:

- The transition to an oxygenated atmosphere during the Mesoproterozoic.
- Several glaciations, including the hypothesized Snowball Earth during the Cryogenian period in the late Neoproterozoic.
- The Ediacaran Period (635 to 542 Ma) which is characterized by the evolution of abundant soft-bodied multicellular organisms.

The geoloic record of the Proterozoic is much better than that for the preceding Archean. In contrast to the deep-water deposits of the Archean, the Proterozoic features many strata that were laid down in extensive shallow epicontinental seas; furthermore, many of these rocks are less metamorphosed than Archean-age ones, and plenty are unaltered.

a. 1703 Genroku earthquake
c. Proterozoic Eon

b. 1700 Cascadia earthquake
d. 1509 Istanbul earthquake

9. _____ are flat or very gently sloping areas of the deep ocean basin floor. They are among the Earth's flattest and smoothest regions and the least explored. _____ cover approximately 40% of the ocean floor and reach depths between 2,200 and 5,500 m (7,200 and 18,000 ft.)

a. Eutrophication
b. Intertidal
c. AASHTO Soil Classification System
d. Abyssal plains

10. An _____ is a fan-shaped deposit formed where a fast flowing stream flattens, slows, and spreads typically at the exit of a canyon onto a flatter plain. A convergence of neighboring fans into a single apron of deposits against a slope is called a bajada, or compound _____.
   a. AL 129-1
   b. AASHTO Soil Classification System
   c. AL 333
   d. Alluvial fan

11. An _____ is a confined aquifer containing groundwater that will flow upward through a well without the need for pumping. Water may even reach the ground surface if the natural pressure is high enough, in which case the well is called a flowing artesian well. An aquifer provides the water for an artesian well.
   a. AASHTO Soil Classification System
   b. AL 129-1
   c. AL 333
   d. Artesian aquifer

12. _____ is the removal of solids (sediment, soil, rock and other particles) in the natural environment. It usually occurs due to transport by wind, water, or ice; by down-slope creep of soil and other material under the force of gravity; or by living organisms, such as burrowing animals, in the case of bioerosion.

_____ is distinguished from weathering, which is the process of chemical or physical breakdown of the minerals in the rocks, although the two processes may occur concurrently.

   a. AL 129-1
   b. AL 333
   c. AASHTO Soil Classification System
   d. Erosion

13. A _____ is a large, slow-moving mass of ice, formed from compacted layers of snow, that slowly deforms and flows in response to gravity and high pressure.

_____ ice is the largest reservoir of fresh water on Earth, and second only to oceans as the largest reservoir of total water.

   a. Glacier
   b. Keeling Curve
   c. Pacific Decadal Oscillation
   d. Little Ice Age

14. In geology, _____ refers to heat sources within the planet. _____ is technically an adjective (e.g., _____ energy) but in U.S. English the word has attained frequent use as a noun.

The planet's internal heat was originally generated during its accretion, due to gravitational binding energy, and since then additional heat has continued to be generated by decay heat from the radioactive decay of elements.

   a. Geothermal
   b. Stratification
   c. Dali
   d. Diamond Head

15. _____ is power extracted from heat stored in the earth. This geothermal energy originates from the original formation of the planet, from radioactive decay of minerals, and from solar energy absorbed at the surface. It has been used for space heating and bathing since ancient roman times, but is now better known for generating electricity.

a. Geothermal power
b. Geothermal gradient
c. Geothermal desalination
d. Hot Dry Rock Geothermal Energy

16. _____ is the naturally occurring, unconsolidated or loose covering on the Earth's surface. _____ is composed of particles of broken rock that have been altered by chemical, biological and environmental processes including weathering and erosion. _____ is different from its parent rock(s) source(s), altered by interactions between the lithosphere, hydrosphere, atmosphere, and the biosphere.
   a. Topsoil
   b. Soil
   c. 1509 Istanbul earthquake
   d. Slump

17. The _____ was the earliest of the six cratonic sequences that have occurred during the Phanerozoic (followed by the Tippecanoe, Kaskaskia, Absaroka, Zu>ñi, and Tejas.) It dates from the late Proterozoic through the early Ordovician, though the marine transgression did not begin in earnest until the middle Cambrian.

At its peak, most of North America was covered by the shallow Sauk Sea, save for parts of the Canadian Shield and the islands of the Transcontinental Arch.

   a. 1700 Cascadia earthquake
   b. Tippecanoe sequence
   c. 1509 Istanbul earthquake
   d. Sauk sequence

18. _____ is mechanical scraping of a rock surface by friction between rocks and moving particles during their transport in wind, glacier, waves, gravity or running water, after friction, the moving particles dislodge loose and weak debris from the side of the rock, these particles can be dissolved in the water source.

The intensity of _____ depends on the hardness, concentration, velocity and mass of moving particles.

A virtually smooth marine platform cut by the ocean waves at a coastline.

   a. AASHTO Soil Classification System
   b. AL 333
   c. AL 129-1
   d. Abrasion

19. The _____ Era, is the most recent of the three classic geological eras and covers the period from 65.5 million years ago to the present. It is marked by the Cretaceous-Tertiary extinction event at the end of the Cretaceous that saw the demise of the last non-avian dinosaurs and the end of the Mesozoic Era. The _____ era is ongoing.
   a. 1700 Cascadia earthquake
   b. Cenozoic
   c. 1509 Istanbul earthquake
   d. 1703 Genroku earthquake

20. _____ is a form of mechanical weathering caused by the force of moving water currents rushing into a crack in the rockface. The water compresses the air in the crack, pushing it right to the back. As the wave retreats, the highly pressurised air is suddenly released with explosive force, capable of chipping away the rockface over time.
   a. Hydraulic action
   b. Headward erosion
   c. Wave pounding
   d. Downcutting

Chapter 12. Running Water

21. _____ is caused by movement of ice, typically as glaciers. Glaciers erode predominantly by three different processes: abrasion/scouring, plucking, and ice thrusting. In an abrasion process, debris in the basal ice scrapes along the bed, polishing and gouging the underlying rocks, similar to sandpaper on wood. Glaciers can also cause pieces of bedrock to crack off in the process of plucking. In ice thrusting, the glacier freezes to its bed, then as it surges forward, it moves large sheets of frozen sediment at the base along with the glacier. This method produced some of the many thousands of lake basins that dot the edge of the Canadian Shield. These processes, combined with erosion and transport by the water network beneath the glacier, leave moraines, drumlins, eskers, ground moraine (till), kames, kame deltas, moulins, and glacial erratics in their wake, typically at the terminus or during glacier retreat.
    a. AL 129-1
    b. Ice erosion
    c. AL 333
    d. AASHTO Soil Classification System

22. _____ is soil or sediments deposited by a river or other running water. _____ is typically made up of a variety of materials, including fine particles of silt and clay and larger particles of sand and gravel.

    Flowing water associated with glaciers may also deposit _____, but deposits directly from ice are not _____ .

    a. AASHTO Soil Classification System
    b. AL 129-1
    c. Alluvium
    d. AL 333

23. In geology a _____ is the smallest division of a geologic formation or stratigraphic rock series marked by well-defined divisional planes (bedding planes) separating it from layers above and below. A _____ is the smallest lithostratigraphic unit, usually ranging in thickness from a centimeter to several meters and distinguishable from beds above and below it. Beds can be differentiated in various ways, including rock or mineral type and particle size.
    a. Sequence stratigraphy
    b. Bed
    c. Cyclostratigraphy
    d. Biozones

24. The term _____ describes particles in a flowing fluid (usually a river) that are transported along the bed. This is in opposition to suspended load and wash load which are carried entirely in suspension.

    _____ moves by a variety of methods, including rolling, sliding, traction, and saltation.

    a. Gravitational erosion
    b. Fault-block
    c. Bed load
    d. Coastal erosion

25. Two important classifications of weathering processes exist -- physical and _____. Mechanical or physical weathering involves the breakdown of rocks and soils through direct contact with atmospheric conditions, such as heat, water, ice and pressure. The second classification, _____, involves the direct effect of atmospheric chemicals or biologically produced chemicals (also known as biological weathering) in the breakdown of rocks, soils and minerals.
    a. Weathering
    b. Physical weathering
    c. 1509 Istanbul earthquake
    d. Chemical weathering

26. _____ is the term for material, especially ions from chemical weathering, that are carried in solution by a stream.
    a. Cap carbonates
    b. Palynomorph
    c. Marine clay
    d. Dissolved load

27. A _____ is flat or nearly flat land adjacent to a stream or river that experiences occasional or periodic flooding. It includes the floodway, which consists of the stream channel and adjacent areas that carry flood flows, and the flood fringe, which are areas covered by the flood, but which do not experience a strong current.

They generally contain unconsolidated sediments, often extending below the bed of the stream.

  a. 1700 Cascadia earthquake   b. 1703 Genroku earthquake
  c. 1509 Istanbul earthquake   d. Floodplain

28. _____ is the geomorphic process by which soil, regolith, and rock move downslope under the force of gravity. Types of _____ include creep, slides, flows, topples, and falls, each with its own characteristic features, and taking place over timescales from seconds to years. _____ occurs on both terrestrial and submarine slopes, and has been observed on Earth, Mars, and Venus.

  a. 1700 Cascadia earthquake   b. 1509 Istanbul earthquake
  c. Soil liquefaction   d. Mass wasting

29. In geology, _____ is a specific type of particle transport by fluids such as wind, or the denser fluid water. It occurs when loose material is removed from a bed and carried by the fluid, before being transported back to the surface. Examples include pebble transport by rivers, sand drift over desert surfaces, soil blowing over fields, or even snow drift over smooth surfaces such as those in the Arctic or Canadian Prairies.

  a. Permineralization   b. Transgression
  c. Hydrothermal circulation   d. Saltation

30. _____ is the term for the fine particles that are light enough to be carried in a stream without touching the stream bed. These particles are generally of the fine sand, silt and clay size, although they can be larger, especially in cases of high discharge, such as during floods. This is in contrast to bed load which is carried along the bottom of the stream.

  a. Suspended load   b. Tertiary
  c. Strike-slip faults   d. Valley glaciers

31. _____ is the decomposition of Earth rocks, soils and their minerals through direct contact with the planet's atmosphere. _____ occurs in situ, or 'with no movement', and thus should not be confused with erosion, which involves the movement of rocks and minerals by agents such as water, ice, wind and gravity.

Two important classifications of _____ processes exist -- physical and chemical _____.

  a. Frost disintegration   b. Weathering
  c. 1509 Istanbul earthquake   d. Physical weathering

32. The _____ is the zone of the ocean floor that separates the thin oceanic crust from thick continental crust. Continental margins constitute about 28% of the oceanic area.

The transition from continental to oceanic crust commonly occurs within the outer part of the margin, called continental rise.

Chapter 12. Running Water

a. Continental margin
b. Cuspate forelands
c. Longshore drift
d. 1509 Istanbul earthquake

33. _____ is a geological term used to describe particles of rock derived from pre-existing rock through processes of weathering and erosion. Thesel particles can consist of lithic fragments (particles of recognisable rock), or of monomineralic fragments (mineral grains.) These particles are often transported through sedimentary processes into depositional systems such as riverbeds, lakes or the ocean forming sedimentary successions.
   a. Detritus
   b. Medical geology
   c. Geomechanics
   d. Perched coastline

34. The _____ is the epoch from 1.8 million to 11550 years BP covering the world's recent period of repeated glaciations. The _____ epoch follows the Pliocene epoch and is followed by the Holocene epoch. The _____ is the third epoch of the Neogene period or 6th epoch of the Cenozoic Era. The end of the _____ corresponds with the retreat of the last continental glacier. It also corresponds with the end of the Paleolithic age used in archaeology.
   a. Late Pleistocene
   b. Tyrrhenian
   c. Pleistocene
   d. Sicilian Stage

35. The _____ was the cratonic sequence--that is, the marine transgression--that followed the Sauk sequence; it extended from roughly the middle Ordovician to the early Devonian.

After the regression of the Sauk Sea early in the Ordovician, the exposed craton for a time underwent vigorous erosion, due to being located in a tropical climate; indeed, at this point in the Phanerozoic the North American continent roughly straddled the equator.

The Tippecanoe transgression ended this period of erosion, beginning with the deposition of clean sandstones across the craton, followed by abundant carbonate deposition.

   a. 1509 Istanbul earthquake
   b. Sauk sequence
   c. Tippecanoe sequence
   d. 1700 Cascadia earthquake

36. _____ is any particulate matter that can be transported by fluid flow, and which eventually is deposited.

They are most often transported by water (fluvial processes) transported by wind (aeolian processes) and glaciers. Beach sands and river channel deposits are examples of fluvial transport and deposition, though _____ also often settles out of slow-moving or standing water in lakes and oceans.

   a. Quicksand
   b. Brickearth
   c. Sediment
   d. Bovey Beds

37. A _____ in general is a bend in a sinuous watercourse. A _____ is formed when the moving water in a river erodes the outer banks and widens its valley. A stream of any volume may assume a meandering course, alternatively eroding sediments from the outside of a bend and depositing them on the inside.
   a. 1703 Genroku earthquake
   b. 1700 Cascadia earthquake
   c. 1509 Istanbul earthquake
   d. Meander

Chapter 12. Running Water

38. A _____ is a stream that branches off and flows away from a main stream channel. They are a common feature of river deltas. The phenomenon is known as river bifurcation.
    a. 1509 Istanbul earthquake
    b. 1703 Genroku earthquake
    c. 1700 Cascadia earthquake
    d. Distributary

39. A _____ or mudslide is the most rapid (up to 80 km/h, or 50 mph) and fluid type of downhill mass wasting. It is a rapid movement of a large mass of mud formed from loose earth and water. Similar terms are mudslide (not very liquid), mud stream, debris flow (e.g. in high mountains), j>ökulhlaup, and lahar
    a. 1700 Cascadia earthquake
    b. 1509 Istanbul earthquake
    c. 1703 Genroku earthquake
    d. Mudflow

40. The _____ , usually abbreviated K for its German translation Kreide, is a geologic period and system from circa >145.5 >± 4 to >65.5 >± 0.3 million years ago . In the geologic timescale, the _____ follows on the Jurassic period and is followed by the Paleogene period. It is the youngest period of the Mesozoic era, and at 80 million years long, the longest period of the Phanerozoic eon. The end of the _____ defines the boundary between the Mesozoic and Cenozoic eras.
    a. Hauterivian
    b. Campanian
    c. Coniacian
    d. Cretaceous

41. _____ are waves that travel through the Earth or other elastic body, for example as the result of an earthquake, explosion, or some other process that imparts forces to the body. _____ are also continually excited on Earth by the incessant pounding of ocean waves (referred to as the microseism) and the wind. _____ are studied by seismologists, and measured by a seismograph, which records the output of a seismometer, or geophone.
    a. Seismic waves
    b. Maximum magnitude
    c. Harmonic tremor
    d. Shadow zone

42. The _____ is the level at which the ground water pressure is equal to atmospheric pressure. It may be conveniently visualized as the 'surface' of the ground water in a given vicinity. It usually coincides with the phreatic surface, but can be many feet above it. As water infiltrates through pore spaces in the soil, it first passes through the zone of aeration, where the soil is unsaturated. At increasing depths water fills in more spaces, until the zone of saturation is reached. The relatively horizontal plane atop this zone constitutes the _____ .
    a. Rock bolt
    b. Crosshole sonic logging
    c. Shaft construction
    d. Water table

43. _____ is the natural or artificial removal of surface and sub-surface water from an area. Many agricultural soils need _____ to improve production or to manage water supplies.

The earliest archaeological record of an advanced system of _____ comes from the Indus Valley Civilization from around 3100 BC in what is now Pakistan and North India.

    a. 1700 Cascadia earthquake
    b. 1509 Istanbul earthquake
    c. 1703 Genroku earthquake
    d. Drainage

44. A _____ is an extent of land where water from rain or snow melt drains downhill into a body of water, such as a river, lake, reservoir, estuary, wetland, sea or ocean. The _____ includes both the streams and rivers that convey the water as well as the land surfaces from which water drains into those channels, and is separated from adjacent basins by a drainage divide.

The _____ acts like a funnel, collecting all the water within the area covered by the basin and channelling it into a waterway.

   a. 1700 Cascadia earthquake
   c. 1509 Istanbul earthquake
   b. 1703 Genroku earthquake
   d. Drainage basin

45. In geomorphology, a _____ is the pattern formed by the streams, rivers, and lakes in a particular drainage basin. They are governed by the topography of the land, whether a particular region is dominated by hard or soft rocks, and the gradient of the land.

They can fall into one of several categories, depending on the topography and geology of the land:

Dendritic drainage systems are the most common form of _____.

   a. Platform
   c. Tarn
   b. Cohesion
   d. Drainage system

46. _____ are the collective effect of changes in the Earth's movements upon its climate axial tilt, and precession of the Earth's orbit determined climatic patterns on Earth, resulting in 100,000-year ice age cycles of the Quaternary glaciation over the last few million years. The Earth's axis completes one full cycle of precession approximately every 26,000 years. At the same time, the elliptical orbit rotates, more slowly, leading to a 23,000-year cycle between the seasons and the orbit.
   a. Stage
   c. Geologic record
   b. Global Standard Stratigraphic Age
   d. Milankovitch theory

47. The general term '_____' or, more precisely, 'glacial age' denotes a geological period of long-term reduction in the temperature of the Earth's surface and atmosphere, resulting in an expansion of continental ice sheets, polar ice sheets and alpine glaciers. Within a long-term _____, individual pulses of extra cold climate are termed 'glaciations'. Glaciologically, _____ implies the presence of extensive ice sheets in the northern and southern hemispheres; by this definition we are still in an _____.
   a. AL 333
   c. Ice Age
   b. AASHTO Soil Classification System
   d. AL 129-1

48. _____, also called erosional _____ or downward erosion or vertical erosion is a geological process that deepens the channel of a stream or valley by removing material from the stream's bed or the valley's floor. How fast _____ occurs depends on the stream's base level, which is the lowest point to which the stream can erode. Sea level is the ultimate base level, but many streams have a higher 'temporary' base level because they empty into another body of water that is above sea level or encounter bedrock that resists erosion.
   a. Deposition
   c. Transgression
   b. Seafloor spreading
   d. Downcutting

49. A _____ is a narrow and shallow incision into soil resulting from erosion by overland flow that has been focused into a thin thread by soil surface roughness. Rilling, the process of _____ formation, is common on agricultural land and unvegetated ground.

| a. Rill | b. Salt tectonics |
| c. Planar deformation features | d. Primordial water |

50. _____ is a fluvial process of erosion that lengthens a stream, a valley or a gully at its head and also enlarges its drainage basin. The stream erodes away at the rock and soil at its headwaters in the opposite direction that it flows. Once a stream has begun to cut back, the erosion is sped up by the steep gradient the water is flowing down. As water erodes a path from its headwaters to its mouth at a standing body of water, it tries to cut an ever-shallower path. This leads to increased erosion at the steepest parts, which is _____.

| a. Transgression | b. Mid-ocean ridge |
| c. Saltation | d. Headward erosion |

51. In stratigraphy, _____ is the native consolidated rock underlying the surface of a terrestrial planet, usually the Earth. Above the _____ is usually an area of broken and weathered unconsolidated rock in the basal subsoil. The top of the _____ is known as rockhead and identifying this, via excavations, drilling or geophysical methods, is an important task in most civil engineering projects.

| a. Biozones | b. Sequence stratigraphy |
| c. Polystrate | d. Bedrock |

52. The _____ Era is one of three geologic eras of the Phanerozoic eon. The division of time into eras dates back to Giovanni Arduino, in the 18th century, although his original name for the era now called the '_____' was 'Secondary' (making the modern era the 'Tertiary'.)

The _____ was a time of tectonic, climatic and evolutionary activity. The continents gradually shifted from a state of connectedness into their present configuration; the drifting provided for speciation and other important evolutionary developments.

| a. Mesozoic | b. 1700 Cascadia earthquake |
| c. 1509 Istanbul earthquake | d. 1703 Genroku earthquake |

Chapter 13. Groundwater

1. _____ is a sedimentary rock composed largely of the mineral calcite (calcium carbonate: $CaCO_3$.) The deposition of _____ strata is often a by-product and indicator of biological activity in the geologic record. Calcium (along with nitrogen, phosphorus, and potassium) is a key mineral to plant nutrition: soils overlying _____ bedrock tend to be pre-fertilized with calcium.

   a. 1703 Genroku earthquake
   b. 1700 Cascadia earthquake
   c. 1509 Istanbul earthquake
   d. Limestone

2. The _____ is the earliest of three geologic eras of the Phanerozoic eon. The _____ spanned from roughly 542 to 251 million years ago (ICS, 2004), and is subdivided into six geologic periods; from oldest to youngest they are: the Cambrian, Ordovician, Silurian, Devonian, Carboniferous, and Permian.

   The _____ covers the time from the first appearance of abundant, soft-shelled fossils to the time when the continents were beginning to be dominated by large, relatively sophisticated reptiles and modern plants. The lower (oldest) boundary was classically set at the first appearance of creatures known as trilobites and archeocyathids.

   a. 1509 Istanbul earthquake
   b. 1700 Cascadia earthquake
   c. 1703 Genroku earthquake
   d. Paleozoic

3. _____ is a measure of the void spaces in a material, and is measured as a fraction, between 0-1, or as a percentage between 0-100%. The term is used in multiple fields including ceramics, metallurgy, materials, manufacturing, earth sciences and construction.

   Used in geology, hydrogeology, soil science, and building science, the _____ of a porous medium (such as rock or sediment) describes the fraction of void space in the material, where the void may contain, for example, air or water.

   a. Porosity
   b. Permeability
   c. Saltwater intrusion
   d. Phreatic zone

4. _____ is the naturally occurring, unconsolidated or loose covering on the Earth's surface. _____ is composed of particles of broken rock that have been altered by chemical, biological and environmental processes including weathering and erosion. _____ is different from its parent rock(s) source(s), altered by interactions between the lithosphere, hydrosphere, atmosphere, and the biosphere.

   a. 1509 Istanbul earthquake
   b. Slump
   c. Soil
   d. Topsoil

5. _____ is an igneous rock of volcanic origin.

   They are usually fine-grained or aphanitic to glassy in texture. They often contain clasts of other rocks and phenocrysts.

   a. Petrology
   b. Large igneous provinces
   c. Volcanic rock
   d. Serpentinite

Chapter 13. Groundwater

6. An _____ is a fan-shaped deposit formed where a fast flowing stream flattens, slows, and spreads typically at the exit of a canyon onto a flatter plain. A convergence of neighboring fans into a single apron of deposits against a slope is called a bajada, or compound _____.
   a. Alluvial fan
   b. AL 129-1
   c. AL 333
   d. AASHTO Soil Classification System

7. In geology, _____ is transported rock debris overlying the solid bedrock. The term is also sometimes refers to organic debris so-transported. In the largest sense, it refers to the material left behind by retreating continental glaciers.
   a. Geodiversity
   b. Platform cover
   c. Patterned ground
   d. Drift

8. _____ is water located beneath the ground surface in soil pore spaces and in the fractures of lithologic formations. A unit of rock or an unconsolidated deposit is called an aquifer when it can yield a usable quantity of water. The depth at which soil pore spaces or fractures and voids in rock become completely saturated with water is called the water table.
   a. Depression focused recharge
   b. 1509 Istanbul earthquake
   c. 1700 Cascadia earthquake
   d. Groundwater

9. The _____ describes the continuous movement of water on, above, and below the surface of the Earth. Since the _____ is truly a 'cycle,' there is no beginning or end. Water can change states among liquid, vapor, and ice at various places in the _____.
   a. Vadose zone
   b. Water cycle
   c. Cone of depression
   d. Hydraulic conductivity

10. An _____ is an underground layer of water-bearing permeable rock or unconsolidated materials (gravel, sand, silt, or clay) from which groundwater can be usefully extracted using a water well. The study of water flow in aquifers and the characterization of aquifers is called hydrogeology. Related terms include: an aquitard, which is an impermeable layer along an _____, and an aquiclude (or aquifuge), which is a solid, impermeable area beneath an _____.
   a. AASHTO Soil Classification System
   b. AL 333
   c. AL 129-1
   d. Aquifer

11. The _____ Era, is the most recent of the three classic geological eras and covers the period from 65.5 million years ago to the present. It is marked by the Cretaceous-Tertiary extinction event at the end of the Cretaceous that saw the demise of the last non-avian dinosaurs and the end of the Mesozoic Era. The _____ era is ongoing.
   a. 1703 Genroku earthquake
   b. 1700 Cascadia earthquake
   c. 1509 Istanbul earthquake
   d. Cenozoic

12. _____ is a naturally occurring material composed primarily of fine-grained minerals, which show plasticity through a variable range of water content, and which can be hardened when dried and/or fired. _____ deposits are mostly composed of _____ minerals (phyllosilicate minerals), minerals which impart plasticity and harden when fired and/or dried, and variable amounts of water trapped in the mineral structure by polar attraction. Organic materials which do not impart plasticity may also be a part of _____ deposits.
   a. 1703 Genroku earthquake
   b. 1509 Istanbul earthquake
   c. Clay
   d. 1700 Cascadia earthquake

Chapter 13. Groundwater

13. A _____ is a rock consisting of individual stones that have become cemented together. They are sedimentary rocks consisting of rounded fragments and are thus differentiated from breccias, which consist of angular clasts. Both conglomerates and breccias are characterized by clasts larger than sand (>2 mm).
   a. Conglomerate
   b. Keystone
   c. Porcellanite
   d. Pelagic sediments

14. _____ is a geological term used to describe particles of rock derived from pre-existing rock through processes of weathering and erosion. Thesel particles can consist of lithic fragments (particles of recognisable rock), or of monomineralic fragments (mineral grains.) These particles are often transported through sedimentary processes into depositional systems such as riverbeds, lakes or the ocean forming sedimentary successions.
   a. Detritus
   b. Geomechanics
   c. Medical geology
   d. Perched coastline

15. _____ or dolomite rock is a sedimentary carbonate rock that contains a high percentage of the mineral dolomite. In old U.S.G.S. publications it was referred to as magnesian limestone. Most _____ formed as a magnesium replacement of limestone or lime mud prior to lithification.
   a. Dolostone
   b. Lithification
   c. Pelagic sediments
   d. Jasperoid

16. In geology, a _____ or _____ line is a planar fracture in rock in which the rock on one side of the fracture has moved with respect to the rock on the other side. Large faults within the Earth's crust are the result of differential or shear motion and active _____ zones are the causal locations of most earthquakes. Earthquakes are caused by energy release during rapid slippage along a _____.
   a. Combe
   b. Stack
   c. Fault
   d. Dali

17. The _____ is the geologic eon before the Archean. It started at Earth's formation about 4.6 billion years ago (4,600 Ma), and ended roughly 3.8 billion years ago, though the latter date varies according to different sources.
   a. 1509 Istanbul earthquake
   b. 1703 Genroku earthquake
   c. 1700 Cascadia earthquake
   d. Hadean

18. _____ in the earth sciences (commonly symbolized as κ a rock or k) is a measure of the ability of a material (typically unconsolidated material) to transmit fluids. It is of great importance in determining the flow characteristics of hydrocarbons in oil and gas reservoirs, and of groundwater in aquifers. It is typically measured in the lab by application of Darcy's law under steady state conditions or, more generally, by application of various solutions to the diffusion equation for unsteady flow conditions.
   a. Phreatic zone
   b. Permeability
   c. Saltwater intrusion
   d. Porosity

19. The _____ is a continental transform fault that runs a length of roughly 800 miles (1,300 km) through California in the United States. The fault's motion is right-lateral strike-slip (horizontal motion.) It forms the tectonic boundary between the Pacific Plate and the North American Plate.
   a. 1700 Cascadia earthquake
   b. 1509 Istanbul earthquake
   c. 1703 Genroku earthquake
   d. San Andreas fault

Chapter 13. Groundwater

20. _____ is a sedimentary rock composed mainly of sand-size mineral or rock grains. Most _____ is composed of quartz and/or feldspar because these are the most common minerals in the Earth's crust. Like sand, _____ may be any color, but the most common colors are tan, brown, yellow, red, gray and white.
   a. Dolostone
   b. Porcellanite
   c. Lithification
   d. Sandstone

21. _____ is one of the three main rock types (the others being igneous and metamorphic rock.) _____ is formed by deposition and consolidation of mineral and organic material and from precipitation of minerals from solution. The processes that form _____ occur at the surface of the Earth and within bodies of water.
   a. Serpentinite
   b. Petrology
   c. Rock cycle
   d. Sedimentary rock

22. _____ is a fine-grained sedimentary rock whose original constituents were clay minerals or muds. It is characterized by thin laminae breaking with an irregular curving fracture, often splintery and usually parallel to the often-indistinguishable bedding plane. This property is called fissility.
   a. Shale
   b. Mudstone
   c. Pelagic sediments
   d. Metasediment

23. _____ is the process of determining a specific date for an archaeological or palaeontological site or artifact. Some archaeologists prefer the terms chronometric or calendar dating, as use of the word 'absolute' implies a certainty and precision that is rarely possible in archaeology. _____ is usually based on the physical or chemical properties of the materials of artifacts, buildings, or other items that have been modified by humans.
   a. Absolute dating
   b. AASHTO Soil Classification System
   c. Uranium-lead dating
   d. Erathem

24. _____ refers to natural mountain building, and may be studied as a tectonic structural event, (b) as a geographical event, and (c) a chronological event. Orogenic events (a) cause distinctive structural phenomena and related tectonic activity, (b) affect certain regions of rocks and crust, and (c) happen within a specific period of time.
   a. Alice Springs Orogeny
   b. Orogeny
   c. Antler orogeny
   d. Orogenesis

25. In geology, a _____ is a place where the Earth's crust and lithosphere are being pulled apart and is an example of extensional tectonics.

Typical _____ features are a central linear downdropped fault segment, called a graben, with parallel normal faulting and _____-flank uplifts on either side forming a _____ valley, where the _____ remains above sea level. The axis of the _____ area commonly contains volcanic rocks and active volcanism is a part of many, but not all active _____ systems.

   a. 1700 Cascadia earthquake
   b. 1703 Genroku earthquake
   c. 1509 Istanbul earthquake
   d. Rift

26. The _____ is the subsurface layer in which groundwater seeps up from a water table by capillary action to fill pores. Pores at the base of the _____ are filled with water due to tension saturation. This saturated portion of the _____ is less than total capillary rise because of the presence of a mix in pore size.

a. Rockall
b. Pahoehoe lava
c. Star dunes
d. Capillary fringe

27. The _____ is the level at which the ground water pressure is equal to atmospheric pressure. It may be conveniently visualized as the 'surface' of the ground water in a given vicinity. It usually coincides with the phreatic surface, but can be many feet above it. As water infiltrates through pore spaces in the soil, it first passes through the zone of aeration, where the soil is unsaturated. At increasing depths water fills in more spaces, until the zone of saturation is reached. The relatively horizontal plane atop this zone constitutes the _____.
   a. Crosshole sonic logging
   b. Shaft construction
   c. Rock bolt
   d. Water table

28. The _____ is the area in an aquifer, below the water table, in which relatively all pores and fractures are saturated with water. The _____ may fluctuate with changes of season and during wet and dry periods.
   a. Permeability
   b. Porosity
   c. Phreatic zone
   d. Saltwater intrusion

29. A _____ is a large, slow-moving mass of ice, formed from compacted layers of snow, that slowly deforms and flows in response to gravity and high pressure.

_____ ice is the largest reservoir of fresh water on Earth, and second only to oceans as the largest reservoir of total water.

   a. Pacific Decadal Oscillation
   b. Little Ice Age
   c. Keeling Curve
   d. Glacier

30. A _____ occurs in an aquifer when groundwater is pumped from a well. In an unconfined (water table) aquifer, this is an actual depression of the water levels. In confined (artesian) aquifers, the _____ is a reduction in the pressure head surrounding the pumped well.
   a. Stemflow
   b. Water cycle
   c. Cone of depression
   d. Specific storage

31. Two important classifications of weathering processes exist -- physical and _____. Mechanical or physical weathering involves the breakdown of rocks and soils through direct contact with atmospheric conditions, such as heat, water, ice and pressure. The second classification, _____, involves the direct effect of atmospheric chemicals or biologically produced chemicals (also known as biological weathering) in the breakdown of rocks, soils and minerals.
   a. 1509 Istanbul earthquake
   b. Weathering
   c. Physical weathering
   d. Chemical weathering

Chapter 13. Groundwater

32. _____ in geology is a landform sunken or depressed below the surrounding area. Depressions may be formed by various mechanisms, and may be referred to by a variety of technical terms.

- A basin may be any large sediment filled _____. In tectonics, it may refer specifically to a circular, syncline-like _____: a geologic basin; while in sedimentology, it may refer to an area thickly filled with sediment: sedimentary basin.

- A blowout is a _____ created by wind erosion typically in either a desert sand or dry soil (such as a post-glacial loess environment.)

- A graben is a down dropped and typically linear _____ or basin created by rifting in a region under tensional tectonic forces.

- An impact crater is a _____ created by an impact such as a meteorite crater.
- A pit crater is a _____ formed by a sinking, or caving in, of the ground surface lying over a void.
- A kettle is left behind when a piece of ice left behind in glacial deposits melts.

- A _____ may be an area of subsidence caused by the collapse of an underlying structure. Examples include sinkholes above caves in karst topography, or calderas.

   a. Cohesion
   c. Depression
   b. Diamond Head
   d. Geothermal

33. _____ is the decomposition of Earth rocks, soils and their minerals through direct contact with the planet's atmosphere. _____ occurs in situ, or 'with no movement', and thus should not be confused with erosion, which involves the movement of rocks and minerals by agents such as water, ice, wind and gravity.

Two important classifications of _____ processes exist -- physical and chemical _____.

   a. 1509 Istanbul earthquake
   c. Frost disintegration
   b. Physical weathering
   d. Weathering

34. An _____ is a confined aquifer containing groundwater that will flow upward through a well without the need for pumping. Water may even reach the ground surface if the natural pressure is high enough, in which case the well is called a flowing artesian well. An aquifer provides the water for an artesian well.
   a. Artesian aquifer
   c. AASHTO Soil Classification System
   b. AL 333
   d. AL 129-1

35. The _____ is a general term for an ill-defined early Cretaceous formation of the Rocky Mountains and Great Plains. It consists of sandy, shallow-marine deposits with intermittent mud flat sediments, and occasional stream deposits. It is an important aquifer in some areas of the Great Plains. It is made of porous sandstone more than 30 meters thick.
   a. 1509 Istanbul earthquake
   c. Potomac Formation
   b. Dakota Sandstone
   d. 1700 Cascadia earthquake

Chapter 13. Groundwater

36. A _____ is a natural depression or hole in the surface topography caused by the removal of soil or bedrock, often both, by water. They may vary in size from less than a meter to several hundred meters both in diameter and depth, and vary in form from soil-lined bowls to bedrock-edged chasms. They may be formed gradually or suddenly, and are found worldwide.

   a. 1703 Genroku earthquake
   b. 1700 Cascadia earthquake
   c. Sinkhole
   d. 1509 Istanbul earthquake

37. _____ is the removal of solids (sediment, soil, rock and other particles) in the natural environment. It usually occurs due to transport by wind, water, or ice; by down-slope creep of soil and other material under the force of gravity; or by living organisms, such as burrowing animals, in the case of bioerosion.

   _____ is distinguished from weathering, which is the process of chemical or physical breakdown of the minerals in the rocks, although the two processes may occur concurrently.

   a. Erosion
   b. AL 333
   c. AASHTO Soil Classification System
   d. AL 129-1

38. A _____ is in geology an area where, as a result of metamorphism, the same combination of minerals occur in the bed rocks. These zones occur because most metamorphic minerals are only stable in certain intervals of temperature and pressure.

   The temperature and pressure at which the mineralogical composition of a rock equilibrated can vary laterally through a metamorphic terrane.

   a. Metamorphic zone
   b. Metamorphic rock
   c. Tephra
   d. Magma

39. _____ is a landscape shaped by the dissolution of a layer or layers of soluble bedrock, usually carbonate rock such as limestone or dolomite.

   Due to subterranean drainage, there may be very limited surface water, even to the absence of all rivers and lakes. Many karst regions display distinctive surface features, with sinkholes or dolines being the most common.

   a. Andrija Mohorovičić
   b. Ambulocetus
   c. Amblypoda
   d. Karst topography

40. In chemistry, a _____ is a salt or ester of carbonic acid.

   To test for the presence of the _____ anion in a salt, the addition of dilute mineral acid (e.g. hydrochloric acid) will yield carbon dioxide gas.

   _____-containing salts are industrially and mineralogically ubiquitous.

   a. Carbonate
   b. 1509 Istanbul earthquake
   c. 1703 Genroku earthquake
   d. 1700 Cascadia earthquake

41. _____ is the geological process by which material is added to a landform or land mass. Fluids such as wind and water, as well as sediment gravity flows, transport previously eroded sediment, which, at the loss of enough kinetic energy in the fluid, is deposited, building up layers of sediment.

_____ occurs when the forces responsible for sediment transportation are no longer sufficient to overcome the forces of particle weight and friction, which resist motion.

  a. Downcutting
  c. Diagenesis
  b. Deposition
  d. Headward erosion

42. _____ are flat or very gently sloping areas of the deep ocean basin floor. They are among the Earth's flattest and smoothest regions and the least explored. _____ cover approximately 40% of the ocean floor and reach depths between 2,200 and 5,500 m (7,200 and 18,000 ft.)
  a. Intertidal
  c. Eutrophication
  b. AASHTO Soil Classification System
  d. Abyssal plains

43. The _____ was a cratonic sequence that began in the mid-Devonian, peaked early in the Mississippian, and ended by mid-Mississippian time. A major unconformity separates it from the lower Tippecanoe sequence.

The basal-that is, the lowest and oldest-units of the Kaskaskia consist of clean quartz sandstones eroded from the Appalachian orogenic belt to the east, the Ozark Dome in the center of the continent, and south from the Canadian Shield.

  a. 1509 Istanbul earthquake
  c. Sauk sequence
  b. 1700 Cascadia earthquake
  d. Kaskaskia sequence

44. The _____ is the epoch from 1.8 million to 11550 years BP covering the world's recent period of repeated glaciations. The _____ epoch follows the Pliocene epoch and is followed by the Holocene epoch. The _____ is the third epoch of the Neogene period or 6th epoch of the Cenozoic Era. The end of the _____ corresponds with the retreat of the last continental glacier. It also corresponds with the end of the Paleolithic age used in archaeology.
  a. Pleistocene
  c. Late Pleistocene
  b. Tyrrhenian
  d. Sicilian Stage

45. A _____ is a type of speleothem (secondary mineral) that hangs from the ceiling or wall of limestone caves. It is sometimes referred to as dripstone.

They are formed by the deposition of calcium carbonate and other minerals, which is precipitated from mineralized water solutions.

  a. 1703 Genroku earthquake
  c. 1509 Istanbul earthquake
  b. 1700 Cascadia earthquake
  d. Stalactite

46. A _____ is a type of speleothem that rises from the floor of a limestone cave due to the dripping of mineralized solutions and the deposition of calcium carbonate.

The corresponding formation on the ceiling of a cave is known as a stalactite. If these formations grow together, the result is known as a column.

- a. 1509 Istanbul earthquake
- b. 1703 Genroku earthquake
- c. 1700 Cascadia earthquake
- d. Stalagmite

47. _____ is a sedimentary rock. It is a natural chemical precipitate of carbonate minerals; typically aragonite, but often recrystallized to, or primarily, calcite.

_____ forms as calcium carbonate is deposited from the water of mineral springs or rivulets that are saturated with dissolved calcium bicarbonate. The spring water from which the calcium carbonate precipitates can be hot, warm or cold. The rate of deposition increases with the temperature of the water, or alternatively, when biotic material accelerates the process of precipitation.

- a. 1700 Cascadia earthquake
- b. 1703 Genroku earthquake
- c. 1509 Istanbul earthquake
- d. Travertine

48. The _____ is a vast yet shallow underground water table aquifer located beneath the Great Plains in the United States. One of the world's largest aquifers, it covers an area of approximately 174,000 mi^2 in portions of the eight states of South Dakota, Nebraska, Wyoming, Colorado, Kansas, Oklahoma, New Mexico, and Texas. It was named in 1898 by N.H. Darton from its type locality near the town of Ogallala, Nebraska.
- a. AL 333
- b. AL 129-1
- c. AASHTO Soil Classification System
- d. Ogallala Aquifer

49. In geology, engineering, and surveying, _____ is the motion of a surface (usually, the Earth's surface) as it shifts downward relative to a datum such as sea-level. The opposite of _____ is uplift, which results in an increase in elevation. There are several types of _____.
- a. Pothole
- b. 1700 Cascadia earthquake
- c. Subsidence
- d. 1509 Istanbul earthquake

50. The _____ is a geological eon representing a period before the first abundant complex life on Earth. The _____ extended from 2500 Ma to 542.0 >± 1.0 Ma (million years ago), and is the most recent part of the old, informally named 'e;Precambrian'e; time.

The Proterozoic consists of 3 geologic eras, from oldest to youngest:

- Paleoproterozoic
- Mesoproterozoic
- Neoproterozoic

Chapter 13. Groundwater 159

The well-identified events were:

- The transition to an oxygenated atmosphere during the Mesoproterozoic.
- Several glaciations, including the hypothesized Snowball Earth during the Cryogenian period in the late Neoproterozoic.
- The Ediacaran Period (635 to 542 Ma) which is characterized by the evolution of abundant soft-bodied multicellular organisms.

The geoloic record of the Proterozoic is much better than that for the preceding Archean. In contrast to the deep-water deposits of the Archean, the Proterozoic features many strata that were laid down in extensive shallow epicontinental seas; furthermore, many of these rocks are less metamorphosed than Archean-age ones, and plenty are unaltered.

a. 1509 Istanbul earthquake
b. 1703 Genroku earthquake
c. 1700 Cascadia earthquake
d. Proterozoic Eon

51. _____ refers to a sediment, sedimentary rock, or soil type which is formed from or contains a high proportion of calcium carbonate in the form of calcite or aragonite.

It can also be used as an adjectival term applied to anatomical structures which are made of calcium carbonate in animals such as gastropods, when referring to such structures as the operculum, the clausilium, and the love dart.

_____ sediments are usually deposited in shallow water near land, since the carbonate is precipitated by marine organisms that need land-derived nutrients.

a. 1700 Cascadia earthquake
b. 1703 Genroku earthquake
c. 1509 Istanbul earthquake
d. Calcareous

52. The chemical compound silicon dioxide, also known as _____ , is an oxide of silicon with a chemical formula of SiO_2 and has been known for its hardness since antiquity. _____ is most commonly found in nature as sand or quartz, as well as in the cell walls of diatoms. It is a principal component of most types of glass and substances such as concrete.

a. 1700 Cascadia earthquake
b. 1703 Genroku earthquake
c. 1509 Istanbul earthquake
d. Silica

53. A _____ is a compound containing an anion in which one or more central silicon atoms are surrounded by electronegative ligands. This definition is broad enough to include species such as hexafluorosilicate ('fluorosilicate'), $[SiF_6]^{2-}$, but the _____ species that are encountered most often consist of silicon with oxygen as the ligand. _____ anions, with a negative net electrical charge, must have that charge balanced by other cations to make an electrically neutral compound.

a. Silicate
b. 1703 Genroku earthquake
c. 1700 Cascadia earthquake
d. 1509 Istanbul earthquake

Chapter 13. Groundwater

54. The _____ make up the largest and most important class of rock-forming minerals, comprising approximately 90 percent of the crust of the Earth. They are classified based on the structure of their silicate group. _____ all contain silicon and oxygen.

   a. 1509 Istanbul earthquake
   b. Mineraloid
   c. 1700 Cascadia earthquake
   d. Silicate minerals

55. _____ defines an important group of generally dark-colored rock-forming inosilicate minerals, composed of double chain SiO_4 tetrahedra, linked at the vertices and generally containing ions of iron and/or magnesium in their structures. They crystallize into two crystal systems, monoclinic and orthorhombic. In chemical composition and general characteristics they are similar to the pyroxenes. They are minerals of either igneous or metamorphic origin; in the former case occurring as constituents (hornblende) of igneous rocks, such as granite, diorite, andesite and others. Those of metamorphic origin include examples such as those developed in limestones by contact metamorphism (tremolite) and those formed by the alteration of other ferromagnesian minerals (hornblende).

   a. AL 333
   b. AL 129-1
   c. AASHTO Soil Classification System
   d. Amphibole

56. The lithosphere is broken up into what are called _____. In the case of Earth, there are eight major and many minor plates The lithospheric plates ride on the asthenosphere. These plates move in relation to one another at one of three types of plate boundaries: convergent, or collisional boundaries; divergent boundaries, also called spreading centers; and transform boundaries.

   a. Gorda Ridge
   b. Thrust fault
   c. Copperbelt Province
   d. Tectonic plates

57. In geology, _____ refers to heat sources within the planet. _____ is technically an adjective (e.g., _____ energy) but in U.S. English the word has attained frequent use as a noun.

The planet's internal heat was originally generated during its accretion, due to gravitational binding energy, and since then additional heat has continued to be generated by decay heat from the radioactive decay of elements.

   a. Stratification
   b. Geothermal
   c. Dali
   d. Diamond Head

58. _____ is power extracted from heat stored in the earth. This geothermal energy originates from the original formation of the planet, from radioactive decay of minerals, and from solar energy absorbed at the surface. It has been used for space heating and bathing since ancient roman times, but is now better known for generating electricity.

   a. Hot Dry Rock Geothermal Energy
   b. Geothermal desalination
   c. Geothermal gradient
   d. Geothermal power

Chapter 14. Glaciers and Glaciation

1. _____, originally Gondwanaland, is the name given to a southern precursor-supercontinent and then as a remnant separated from Laurasia 180-200 million years ago during the breakup of the Pangaea supercontinent that existed about 500 to 200 Ma ago into two large segments. While the corresponding northern hemisphere continent Laurasia moved further north, the nearly equal in area _____ included most of the landmasses in today's southern hemisphere, including Antarctica, South America, Africa, Madagascar, Australia-New Guinea, and New Zealand, as well as Arabia and the Indian subcontinent, which have now moved into the Northern Hemisphere.
   - a. Gondwana
   - b. 1700 Cascadia earthquake
   - c. Laurasia
   - d. 1509 Istanbul earthquake

2. The _____ is a geological epoch which began approximately 11‰700 years ago (10‰000 ^{14}C years ago). According to traditional geological thinking, the _____ continues to the present. The _____ is part of the Neogene and Quaternary periods.
   - a. 1700 Cascadia earthquake
   - b. Neoglaciation
   - c. Holocene
   - d. 1509 Istanbul earthquake

3. The general term '_____' or, more precisely, 'glacial age' denotes a geological period of long-term reduction in the temperature of the Earth's surface and atmosphere, resulting in an expansion of continental ice sheets, polar ice sheets and alpine glaciers. Within a long-term _____, individual pulses of extra cold climate are termed 'glaciations'. Glaciologically, _____ implies the presence of extensive ice sheets in the northern and southern hemispheres; by this definition we are still in an _____.
   - a. Ice Age
   - b. AASHTO Soil Classification System
   - c. AL 333
   - d. AL 129-1

4. The _____ was a period of cooling occurring after a warmer North Atlantic era known as the Medieval Warm Period. While not a true ice age, the term was introduced into scientific literature by Fran>çois E. Matthes in 1939. Climatologists and historians working with local records no longer expect to agree on either the start or end dates of this period, which varied according to local conditions.
   - a. Glacier
   - b. Pacific Decadal Oscillation
   - c. Geologic temperature record
   - d. Little Ice Age

5. The _____ or Medieval Climate Optimum was a time of warm climate in the North Atlantic region, lasting from about the tenth century to about the fourteenth century. It was followed by the a cooler period in the North Atlantic termed as the Little Ice Age. The _____ is often invoked in discussions of global warming.
   - a. Middle Bronze Age Cold Epoch
   - b. Medieval Warm Period
   - c. Paleocene-Eocene Thermal Maximum
   - d. Maunder Minimum

6. A _____ is a large, slow-moving mass of ice, formed from compacted layers of snow, that slowly deforms and flows in response to gravity and high pressure.

   _____ ice is the largest reservoir of fresh water on Earth, and second only to oceans as the largest reservoir of total water.
   - a. Keeling Curve
   - b. Little Ice Age
   - c. Glacier
   - d. Pacific Decadal Oscillation

7. The terms _____ and icehouse Earth refer to the prevailing global climate on a timescale of millions of years.

During a _____ Earth period, the planet's atmosphere contains sufficient _____ gases such as carbon dioxide and methane for ice to be entirely absent from the planet's surface.

During icehouse periods, glaciers are present in fluctuating amounts; variations in the Earth's orbit may result in many ice ages, glacials, and interglacials.

  a. 1703 Genroku earthquake
  b. Greenhouse
  c. 1700 Cascadia earthquake
  d. 1509 Istanbul earthquake

8. The _____ Era, is the most recent of the three classic geological eras and covers the period from 65.5 million years ago to the present. It is marked by the Cretaceous-Tertiary extinction event at the end of the Cretaceous that saw the demise of the last non-avian dinosaurs and the end of the Mesozoic Era. The _____ era is ongoing.
  a. 1703 Genroku earthquake
  b. 1700 Cascadia earthquake
  c. 1509 Istanbul earthquake
  d. Cenozoic

9. _____ is the geological process by which material is added to a landform or land mass. Fluids such as wind and water, as well as sediment gravity flows, transport previously eroded sediment, which, at the loss of enough kinetic energy in the fluid, is deposited, building up layers of sediment.

_____ occurs when the forces responsible for sediment transportation are no longer sufficient to overcome the forces of particle weight and friction, which resist motion.

  a. Headward erosion
  b. Downcutting
  c. Diagenesis
  d. Deposition

10. _____ is rock that is of a specific particle size range. Specifically, it is any loose rock that is larger than two millimeters (2mm) in its largest dimension (about 1/12 of an inch) and no more than 64 millimeters (about 2.5 inches.) The next smaller size class in geology is sand, which is >0.0625 mm to 2 mm in size.
  a. 1703 Genroku earthquake
  b. 1509 Istanbul earthquake
  c. 1700 Cascadia earthquake
  d. Gravel

11. The _____ is the epoch from 1.8 million to 11550 years BP covering the world's recent period of repeated glaciations. The _____ epoch follows the Pliocene epoch and is followed by the Holocene epoch. The _____ is the third epoch of the Neogene period or 6th epoch of the Cenozoic Era. The end of the _____ corresponds with the retreat of the last continental glacier. It also corresponds with the end of the Paleolithic age used in archaeology.
  a. Sicilian Stage
  b. Pleistocene
  c. Tyrrhenian
  d. Late Pleistocene

12. The _____ is a geological eon representing a period before the first abundant complex life on Earth. The _____ extended from 2500 Ma to 542.0 >± 1.0 Ma (million years ago), and is the most recent part of the old, informally named 'e;Precambrian'e; time.

The Proterozoic consists of 3 geologic eras, from oldest to youngest:

- Paleoproterozoic
- Mesoproterozoic
- Neoproterozoic

The well-identified events were:

- The transition to an oxygenated atmosphere during the Mesoproterozoic.
- Several glaciations, including the hypothesized Snowball Earth during the Cryogenian period in the late Neoproterozoic.
- The Ediacaran Period (635 to 542 Ma) which is characterized by the evolution of abundant soft-bodied multicellular organisms.

The geoloic record of the Proterozoic is much better than that for the preceding Archean. In contrast to the deep-water deposits of the Archean, the Proterozoic features many strata that were laid down in extensive shallow epicontinental seas; furthermore, many of these rocks are less metamorphosed than Archean-age ones, and plenty are unaltered.

a. 1700 Cascadia earthquake
b. 1703 Genroku earthquake
c. 1509 Istanbul earthquake
d. Proterozoic Eon

13. _____ are flat or very gently sloping areas of the deep ocean basin floor. They are among the Earth's flattest and smoothest regions and the least explored. _____ cover approximately 40% of the ocean floor and reach depths between 2,200 and 5,500 m (7,200 and 18,000 ft.)

a. Intertidal
b. AASHTO Soil Classification System
c. Abyssal plains
d. Eutrophication

14. _____ is the removal of solids (sediment, soil, rock and other particles) in the natural environment. It usually occurs due to transport by wind, water, or ice; by down-slope creep of soil and other material under the force of gravity; or by living organisms, such as burrowing animals, in the case of bioerosion.

_____ is distinguished from weathering, which is the process of chemical or physical breakdown of the minerals in the rocks, although the two processes may occur concurrently.

a. Erosion
b. AL 333
c. AASHTO Soil Classification System
d. AL 129-1

15. _____ is any particulate matter that can be transported by fluid flow, and which eventually is deposited.

They are most often transported by water (fluvial processes) transported by wind (aeolian processes) and glaciers. Beach sands and river channel deposits are examples of fluvial transport and deposition, though _____ also often settles out of slow-moving or standing water in lakes and oceans.

a. Brickearth	b. Sediment
c. Quicksand	d. Bovey Beds

16. The _____ is the layer of igneous, sedimentary, and metamorphic rocks which form the continents and the areas of shallow seabed close to their shores, known as continental shelves. This layer is sometimes called sial due to more felsic, or granitic, bulk composition, which lies in contrast to the oceanic crust, called sima due to its mafic, or basaltic rock. (Based on the change in velocity of seismic waves, it is believed that at a certain depth sial becomes close in its physical properties to sima.

a. Continental crust	b. Convergent boundary
c. Nappe	d. Tectonic plates

17. The _____ is the extended perimeter of each continent and associated coastal plain, and was part of the continent during the glacial periods, but is undersea during interglacial periods such as the current epoch by relatively shallow seas (known as shelf seas) and gulfs.

The continental rise is below the slope, but landward of the abyssal plains. Its gradient is intermediate between the slope and the shelf, on the order of 0.5-1°.

a. Continental shelf	b. 1703 Genroku earthquake
c. 1509 Istanbul earthquake	d. 1700 Cascadia earthquake

18. The _____ , usually abbreviated K for its German translation Kreide, is a geologic period and system from circa >145.5 >± 4 to >65.5 >± 0.3 million years ago . In the geologic timescale, the _____ follows on the Jurassic period and is followed by the Paleogene period. It is the youngest period of the Mesozoic era, and at 80 million years long, the longest period of the Phanerozoic eon. The end of the _____ defines the boundary between the Mesozoic and Cenozoic eras.

a. Hauterivian	b. Campanian
c. Coniacian	d. Cretaceous

19. _____ is partially-compacted n>év>é, a type of snow that has been left over from past seasons and has been recrystallized into a substance denser than n>év>é. It is ice that is at an intermediate stage between snow and glacial ice. _____ has the appearance of wet sugar, but has a hardness that makes it extremely resistant to shovelling. It generally has a density greater than 550 kg/mÂ³ and is often found underneath the snow that accumulates at the head of a glacier.

a. Bull Lake glaciation	b. Glaciolacustrine deposits
c. Firn	d. Bramertonian Stage

20. _____ is water located beneath the ground surface in soil pore spaces and in the fractures of lithologic formations. A unit of rock or an unconsolidated deposit is called an aquifer when it can yield a usable quantity of water. The depth at which soil pore spaces or fractures and voids in rock become completely saturated with water is called the water table.

a. 1509 Istanbul earthquake	b. 1700 Cascadia earthquake
c. Depression focused recharge	d. Groundwater

21. The _____ describes the continuous movement of water on, above, and below the surface of the Earth. Since the _____ is truly a 'cycle,' there is no beginning or end. Water can change states among liquid, vapor, and ice at various places in the _____ .

a. Cone of depression
b. Hydraulic conductivity
c. Vadose zone
d. Water cycle

22. _____ is an active glaciated andesitic stratovolcano in the Cascade Volcanic Arc and the North Cascades of Washington State in the United States. It is the second-most active volcano in the range after Mount Saint Helens. It is about 31 miles (50 km) due east of the city of Bellingham, Whatcom County, making it the northernmost volcano in the Cascade Range but not the northernmost of the Cascade Volcanic Arc, which extends north into the Coast Mountains.
   a. Stratovolcano
   b. Broken Top
   c. Nevado Sajama
   d. Mount Baker

23. _____ is the part of Earth's lithosphere that surfaces in the ocean basins. _____ is primarily composed of mafic rocks, or sima. It is thinner than continental crust, or sial, generally less than 10 kilometers thick, however it is denser, having a mean density of about 3.3 grams per cubic centimeter.
   a. AL 333
   b. AL 129-1
   c. Oceanic crust
   d. AASHTO Soil Classification System

24. A _____ is a compound containing an anion in which one or more central silicon atoms are surrounded by electronegative ligands. This definition is broad enough to include species such as hexafluorosilicate ('fluorosilicate'), $[SiF_6]^{2-}$, but the _____ species that are encountered most often consist of silicon with oxygen as the ligand. _____ anions, with a negative net electrical charge, must have that charge balanced by other cations to make an electrically neutral compound.
   a. 1509 Istanbul earthquake
   b. Silicate
   c. 1700 Cascadia earthquake
   d. 1703 Genroku earthquake

25. The _____ make up the largest and most important class of rock-forming minerals, comprising approximately 90 percent of the crust of the Earth. They are classified based on the structure of their silicate group. _____ all contain silicon and oxygen.
   a. 1700 Cascadia earthquake
   b. 1509 Istanbul earthquake
   c. Mineraloid
   d. Silicate minerals

26. _____ defines an important group of generally dark-colored rock-forming inosilicate minerals, composed of double chain SiO_4 tetrahedra, linked at the vertices and generally containing ions of iron and/or magnesium in their structures. They crystallize into two crystal systems, monoclinic and orthorhombic. In chemical composition and general characteristics they are similar to the pyroxenes. They are minerals of either igneous or metamorphic origin; in the former case occurring as constituents (hornblende) of igneous rocks, such as granite, diorite, andesite and others. Those of metamorphic origin include examples such as those developed in limestones by contact metamorphism (tremolite) and those formed by the alteration of other ferromagnesian minerals (hornblende).
   a. AL 333
   b. AL 129-1
   c. AASHTO Soil Classification System
   d. Amphibole

27. A _____ is an old and stable part of the continental crust that has survived the merging and splitting of continents and supercontinents for at least 500 million years. Some are over two billion years old. They are generally found in the interiors of continents and are characteristically composed of ancient crystalline basement crust of lightweight felsic igneous rock such as granite.

a. Kalahari craton
b. Superior craton
c. Sebakwe proto-craton
d. Craton

28. An _____ is an ice mass that covers less than 50 000 km² of land area (usually covering a highland area.) Masses of ice covering more than 50 000 km² are termed an ice sheet.

They are not constrained by topographical features (i.e., they will lie over the top of mountains) but their dome is usually centred on the highest point of a massif.

a. AASHTO Soil Classification System
b. AL 333
c. AL 129-1
d. Ice cap

29. The _____ was the earliest of the six cratonic sequences that have occurred during the Phanerozoic (followed by the Tippecanoe, Kaskaskia, Absaroka, Zu>ñi, and Tejas.) It dates from the late Proterozoic through the early Ordovician, though the marine transgression did not begin in earnest until the middle Cambrian.

At its peak, most of North America was covered by the shallow Sauk Sea, save for parts of the Canadian Shield and the islands of the Transcontinental Arch.

a. Sauk sequence
b. 1700 Cascadia earthquake
c. Tippecanoe sequence
d. 1509 Istanbul earthquake

30. The _____ was the cratonic sequence--that is, the marine transgression--that followed the Sauk sequence; it extended from roughly the middle Ordovician to the early Devonian.

After the regression of the Sauk Sea early in the Ordovician, the exposed craton for a time underwent vigorous erosion, due to being located in a tropical climate; indeed, at this point in the Phanerozoic the North American continent roughly straddled the equator.

The Tippecanoe transgression ended this period of erosion, beginning with the deposition of clean sandstones across the craton, followed by abundant carbonate deposition.

a. Sauk sequence
b. 1509 Istanbul earthquake
c. 1700 Cascadia earthquake
d. Tippecanoe sequence

31. Alpine glaciers form high on the mountain slopes and are niche, slope or cirque glaciers. As a mountain glacier increases in size it can begin to flow down valley, and are referred to as _____.
a. Pahoehoe lava
b. Valley glaciers
c. Tertiary
d. Star dunes

32. A _____ is a mountain rising from the ocean seafloor that does not reach to the water's surface (sea level), and thus is not an island. These are typically formed from extinct volcanoes, that rise abruptly and are usually found rising from a seafloor of 1,000-4,000 meters depth. They are defined by oceanographers as independent features that rise to at least 1,000 meters above the seafloor.

a. 1700 Cascadia earthquake
b. 1509 Istanbul earthquake
c. 1703 Genroku earthquake
d. Seamount

33. On a glacier, the _____, zone of ablation or zone of wastage is the area in which annual loss of snow through melting, evaporation, iceberg calving and sublimation exceeds annual gain of snow and ice on the surface. Of these, melting is most important in most glaciers, but the others, especially iceberg calving, can be significant. Spatially, the zone of ablation can be identified as the part of the glacier below the snowline.
   a. AASHTO Soil Classification System
   b. AL 129-1
   c. Ablation zone
   d. AL 333

34. A _____ is a huge crack formed by two glaciers colliding. Accelerations in glacier speed cause extension and can initiate a _____. Crevasses often have vertical or near-vertical walls, which can then melt and create seracs, arches, etc.; these walls sometimes expose layers that represent the glacier's stratigraphy.
   a. Predator trap
   b. Geohazard
   c. Sturzstrom
   d. Crevasse

35. _____ is a tidewater glacier in the U.S. state of Alaska and the Yukon Territory of Canada. From its source in the Yukon, the glacier stretches 122 km (76 mi) to the sea at Yakutat Bay and Disenchantment Bay. It is the longest tidewater glacier in Alaska, with an open calving face over ten kilometers (6 mi) wide.
   a. 1700 Cascadia earthquake
   b. 1703 Genroku earthquake
   c. 1509 Istanbul earthquake
   d. Hubbard Glacier

36. An _____ is a region of an ice sheet that moves significantly faster than the surrounding ice. They are significant features of the Antarctic where they account for 10% of the volume of the ice. They are up to 50 km wide, 2 km thick, can stretch for hundreds of kilometres, and account for most of the ice leaving the ice sheet.
   a. AL 333
   b. Ice stream
   c. AASHTO Soil Classification System
   d. AL 129-1

37. In stratigraphy, _____ is the native consolidated rock underlying the surface of a terrestrial planet, usually the Earth. Above the _____ is usually an area of broken and weathered unconsolidated rock in the basal subsoil. The top of the _____ is known as rockhead and identifying this, via excavations, drilling or geophysical methods, is an important task in most civil engineering projects.
   a. Biozones
   b. Polystrate
   c. Sequence stratigraphy
   d. Bedrock

38. _____ is mechanical scraping of a rock surface by friction between rocks and moving particles during their transport in wind, glacier, waves, gravity or running water, after friction, the moving particles dislodge loose and weak debris from the side of the rock, these particles can be dissolved in the water source.

The intensity of _____ depends on the hardness, concentration, velocity and mass of moving particles.

A virtually smooth marine platform cut by the ocean waves at a coastline.

   a. AL 333
   b. AL 129-1
   c. Abrasion
   d. AASHTO Soil Classification System

39. _____ consists of clay-sized particles of rock, generated by glacial erosion or by artificial grinding to a similar size. Because the material is very small, it becomes suspended in river water making the water appear cloudy.

If the river flows into a glacial lake, the lake may appear turquoise in color as a result.

- a. Cordilleran Ice Sheet
- b. Cirque glacier
- c. Glacial period
- d. Rock flour

40. _____ is caused by movement of ice, typically as glaciers. Glaciers erode predominantly by three different processes: abrasion/scouring, plucking, and ice thrusting. In an abrasion process, debris in the basal ice scrapes along the bed, polishing and gouging the underlying rocks, similar to sandpaper on wood. Glaciers can also cause pieces of bedrock to crack off in the process of plucking. In ice thrusting, the glacier freezes to its bed, then as it surges forward, it moves large sheets of frozen sediment at the base along with the glacier. This method produced some of the many thousands of lake basins that dot the edge of the Canadian Shield. These processes, combined with erosion and transport by the water network beneath the glacier, leave moraines, drumlins, eskers, ground moraine (till), kames, kame deltas, moulins, and glacial erratics in their wake, typically at the terminus or during glacier retreat.

- a. AL 333
- b. AL 129-1
- c. AASHTO Soil Classification System
- d. Ice erosion

41. A _____ is an amphitheatre-like valley formed at the head of a glacier by erosion. A _____ is also known as a coombe or coomb in England, a combe or comb in America, a corrie in Scotland and Ireland, and a cwm in Wales, although these terms apply to a specific feature of which several may be found in a _____. The term 'comb' is often found at the end of placenames such as Newcomb and Maycomb, where it is pronounced /kÉ™m/.

- a. 1509 Istanbul earthquake
- b. Cirque
- c. 1700 Cascadia earthquake
- d. 1703 Genroku earthquake

42. Geologically, a _____ is a long, narrow inlet with steep sides, created in a valley carved by glacial activity.

The seeds of a _____ are laid when a glacier cuts a U-shaped valley through abrasion of the surrounding bedrock by the sediment it carries. Many such valleys were formed during the recent ice age.

- a. 1700 Cascadia earthquake
- b. 1509 Istanbul earthquake
- c. 1703 Genroku earthquake
- d. Fjord

43. A _____ is a tributary valley with the floor at a higher relief than the main channel into which it flows. They are most commonly associated with U-shaped valleys when a tributary glacier flows into a glacier of larger volume. The main glacier erodes a deep U-shaped valley with nearly vertical sides while the tributary glacier, with a smaller volume of ice, makes a shallower U-shaped valley.

- a. 1700 Cascadia earthquake
- b. Hanging valley
- c. 1509 Istanbul earthquake
- d. 1703 Genroku earthquake

44. _____ is the geomorphic process by which soil, regolith, and rock move downslope under the force of gravity. Types of _____ include creep, slides, flows, topples, and falls, each with its own characteristic features, and taking place over timescales from seconds to years. _____ occurs on both terrestrial and submarine slopes, and has been observed on Earth, Mars, and Venus.

Chapter 14. Glaciers and Glaciation

  a. 1509 Istanbul earthquake
  c. Soil liquefaction
  b. 1700 Cascadia earthquake
  d. Mass wasting

45. _____ are the collective effect of changes in the Earth's movements upon its climate axial tilt, and precession of the Earth's orbit determined climatic patterns on Earth, resulting in 100,000-year ice age cycles of the Quaternary glaciation over the last few million years. The Earth's axis completes one full cycle of precession approximately every 26,000 years. At the same time, the elliptical orbit rotates, more slowly, leading to a 23,000-year cycle between the seasons and the orbit.
  a. Global Standard Stratigraphic Age
  c. Geologic record
  b. Milankovitch theory
  d. Stage

46. The _____ is an informal name for the supereon comprising the eons of the geologic timescale that came before the current Phanerozoic eon. It spans from the formation of Earth around 4500 Mya (million years ago) to the evolution of abundant macroscopic hard-shelled animals, which marked the beginning of the Cambrian, the first period of the first era of the Phanerozoic eon, some 542 Mya. It is named after the Roman name for Wales - Cambria - where rocks from this age were first studied.
  a. 1703 Genroku earthquake
  c. 1700 Cascadia earthquake
  b. 1509 Istanbul earthquake
  d. Precambrian

47. The _____ is the zone of the ocean floor that separates the thin oceanic crust from thick continental crust. Continental margins constitute about 28% of the oceanic area.

The transition from continental to oceanic crust commonly occurs within the outer part of the margin, called continental rise.

  a. Cuspate forelands
  c. Continental margin
  b. Longshore drift
  d. 1509 Istanbul earthquake

48. The _____ -- also called the Laurentian Plateau, or Bouclier Canadien -- is a massive geological shield covered by a thin layer of soil that forms the nucleus of the North American or Laurentia craton. It has a deep, common, joined bedrock region in eastern and central Canada and stretches North from the Great Lakes to the Arctic Ocean, covering over half of Canada; it also extends south into the northern reaches of the United States. Population is scarce, and industrial development is minimal, although the region has a large hydroelectric power potential.
  a. Gawler craton
  c. Canadian Shield
  b. Grade
  d. Yilgarn Craton

49. _____ can also be called frost shattering or frost-wedging. This type of weathering is common in mountain areas where the temperature is around freezing point. Frost induced weathering, although often attributed to the expansion of freezing water captured in cracks, is generally independent of the water-to-ice expansion. It has long been known that moist soils expand or frost heave upon freezing as a result of water migrating along from unfrozen areas via thin films to collect at growing ice lenses. This same phenomena occurs within pore spaces of rocks.
  a. Physical weathering
  c. Weathering
  b. 1509 Istanbul earthquake
  d. Frost disintegration

Chapter 14. Glaciers and Glaciation

50. A _____ is generally a large area of exposed Precambrian crystalline igneous and high-grade metamorphic rocks that form tectonically stable areas. In all cases, the age of these rocks is greater than 570 million years and sometimes dates back 2 to 3.5 billion years. They have been little affected by tectonic events following the end of the Precambrian Era, and are relatively flat regions where mountain building, faulting, and other tectonic processes are greatly diminished compared with the activity that occurs at the margins of the shields and the boundaries between tectonic plates.
    a. 1700 Cascadia earthquake
    b. 1703 Genroku earthquake
    c. 1509 Istanbul earthquake
    d. Shield

51. A _____ is a mountain lake or pool, formed in a cirque excavated by a glacier. A moraine may form a natural dam below a _____. A corrie may be called a cirque.
    a. Combe
    b. Fault
    c. Platform
    d. Tarn

52. _____ is the natural or artificial removal of surface and sub-surface water from an area. Many agricultural soils need _____ to improve production or to manage water supplies.

The earliest archaeological record of an advanced system of _____ comes from the Indus Valley Civilization from around 3100 BC in what is now Pakistan and North India.

    a. 1509 Istanbul earthquake
    b. 1700 Cascadia earthquake
    c. 1703 Genroku earthquake
    d. Drainage

53. In geology, _____ is transported rock debris overlying the solid bedrock. The term is also sometimes refers to organic debris so-transported. In the largest sense, it refers to the material left behind by retreating continental glaciers.
    a. Platform cover
    b. Patterned ground
    c. Drift
    d. Geodiversity

54. In geology, _____ refers to inclined sedimentary structures in a horizontal unit of rock. These tilted structures are deposits from bedforms such as ripples and dunes, and they indicate that the depositional environment contained a flowing fluid (typically, water or wind.) This is a case in geology when original depositional layering is tilted, and that the tilting is not a result of post-depositional deformation.
    a. Platform cover
    b. Geomicrobiology
    c. Schmidt hammer
    d. Cross-bedding

55. The _____ epoch (55.8 >± 0.2 - 33.9 >± 0.1 Ma) is a major division of the geologic timescale and the second epoch of the Palaeogene period in the Cenozoic era. The _____ spans the time from the end of the Paleocene epoch to the beginning of the Oligocene epoch. The start of the _____ is marked by the emergence of the first modern mammals.
    a. AASHTO Soil Classification System
    b. Eocene
    c. AL 333
    d. AL 129-1

56. The _____ is a geologic fault structure of the Rocky Mountains within Glacier National Park in Montana, USA and Waterton Lakes National Park in Alberta, Canada, as well as into Lewis and Clark National Forest. It provides scientific insight into geologic processes happening in other parts of the world, like the Andes and the Himalaya Mountains. Scientific study of this region is practical because the original rock characteristics were well-preserved and recently sculptured by glaciers.

a. Lewis overthrust
b. 1703 Genroku earthquake
c. 1700 Cascadia earthquake
d. 1509 Istanbul earthquake

57. _____ is a fine grained sedimentary rock whose original constituents were clays or muds. Grain size is up to 0.0625 mm with individual grains too small to be distinguished without a microscope. With increased pressure over time the platey clay minerals may become aligned, with the appearance of fissility or parallel layering.
   a. Jasperoid
   b. Diatomaceous earth
   c. Mudstone
   d. Shale

58. In geology, _____ are sedimentary structures that indicate agitation by water (current or waves) or wind. _____ formed by water consist of two basic types:

   1. Current _____ are asymmetrical in profile, with a gentle up-current slope and a steeper down-current slope. The down-current slope depends on the shape of the sediment, with 33>° being typical.
   2. Wave-formed _____ have a symmetrical, almost sinusoidal profile; they indicate an environment with weak currents where water motion is dominated by wave oscillations.

Ripples will not form in sediment larger than course sand.

   a. 1700 Cascadia earthquake
   b. 1703 Genroku earthquake
   c. 1509 Istanbul earthquake
   d. Ripple marks

59. _____ is a sedimentary rock composed mainly of sand-size mineral or rock grains. Most _____ is composed of quartz and/or feldspar because these are the most common minerals in the Earth's crust. Like sand, _____ may be any color, but the most common colors are tan, brown, yellow, red, gray and white.
   a. Porcellanite
   b. Sandstone
   c. Dolostone
   d. Lithification

60. _____ are those structures formed during sediment deposition.

_____ such as cross bedding, graded bedding and ripple marks are utilized in stratigraphic studies to indicate original position of strata in geologically complex terranes.

There are two kinds of flow regimes, which at varying speeds and velocities produce different structures.

   a. 1509 Istanbul earthquake
   b. Sedimentary structures
   c. 1703 Genroku earthquake
   d. 1700 Cascadia earthquake

61. A marine _____ is a geologic event during which sea level rises relative to the land and the shoreline moves toward higher ground, resulting in flooding. They can be caused either by the land sinking or the ocean basins filling with water (or decreasing in capacity.) Transgresssions and regressions may be caused by tectonic events such as orogenies, severe climate change such as ice ages or isostatic adjustments following removal of ice or sediment load.
   a. Stoping
   b. Transgression
   c. Wave pounding
   d. Spheroidal weathering

Chapter 14. Glaciers and Glaciation

62. A _____ is an elongated whale-shaped hill formed by glacial action. Its long axis is parallel with the movement of the ice, with the blunter end facing into the glacial movement. They may be more than 45 m (150 ft) high and more than 0.8 km (1/2 mile) long, and are often in _____ fields of similarly shaped, sized and oriented hills. They usually have layers indicating that the material was repeatedly added to a core, which may be of rock or glacial till.

   a. Sandur
   b. Monadnock
   c. 1509 Istanbul earthquake
   d. Drumlin

63. A _____ is a moraine that forms at the end of the glacier called the snout.

They mark the maximum advance of the glacier. An end moraine is at the present boundary of the glacier. They are one of the most prominent types of moraines in the Arctic. One famous _____ is the Giant's Wall in Norway.

   a. Bull Lake glaciation
   b. Firn
   c. Bramertonian Stage
   d. Terminal moraine

64. A _____ is a piece of rock that differs from the size and type of rock native to the area in which it rests. They are carried by glacial ice, often over distances of hundreds of kilometres and can range in size from pebbles to large boulders such as Big Rock (16,500 tons) in Alberta.

   a. 1700 Cascadia earthquake
   b. 1703 Genroku earthquake
   c. 1509 Istanbul earthquake
   d. Glacial erratic

65. A _____ is any glacially formed accumulation of unconsolidated glacial debris (soil and rock) which can occur in currently glaciated and formerly glaciated regions, such as those areas acted upon by a past ice age. This debris may have been plucked off the valley floor as a glacier advanced or it may have fallen off the valley walls as a result of frost wedging. Moraines may be composed of silt like glacial flour to large boulders.

   a. 1509 Istanbul earthquake
   b. 1700 Cascadia earthquake
   c. 1703 Genroku earthquake
   d. Moraine

66. The _____ is the earliest of three geologic eras of the Phanerozoic eon. The _____ spanned from roughly 542 to 251 million years ago (ICS, 2004), and is subdivided into six geologic periods; from oldest to youngest they are: the Cambrian, Ordovician, Silurian, Devonian, Carboniferous, and Permian.

The _____ covers the time from the first appearance of abundant, soft-shelled fossils to the time when the continents were beginning to be dominated by large, relatively sophisticated reptiles and modern plants. The lower (oldest) boundary was classically set at the first appearance of creatures known as trilobites and archeocyathids.

   a. 1700 Cascadia earthquake
   b. 1509 Istanbul earthquake
   c. Paleozoic
   d. 1703 Genroku earthquake

67. _____ is unsorted glacial sediment. Glacial drift is a general term for the coarsely graded and extremely heterogeneous sediments of glacial origin. Glacial _____ is that part of glacial drift which was deposited directly by the glacier. In cases where _____ has been indurated or lithified by subsequent burial into solid rock, it is known as the sedimentary rock tillite.

Chapter 14. Glaciers and Glaciation

a. 1700 Cascadia earthquake
c. 1703 Genroku earthquake
b. Till
d. 1509 Istanbul earthquake

68. A _____ is a glacial outwash plain formed of sediments deposited by meltwater at the terminus of a glacier.

_____ are found in glaciated areas, such as Svalbard, Kerguelen Islands, and Iceland. Glaciers and icecaps contain large amounts of silt and sediment, picked up as they erode the underlying rocks when they move slowly downhill, and at the snout of the glacier, meltwater can carry this sediment away from the glacier and deposit it on a broad plain.

a. Rogen moraine
c. Monadnock
b. Sandur
d. 1509 Istanbul earthquake

69. An _____ is a long winding ridge of stratified sand and gravel, examples of which occur in glaciated and formerly glaciated regions of Europe and North America. They are frequently several miles long and, because of their peculiar uniform shape, are somewhat like railroad embankments.

Most are believed to form in ice-walled tunnels by streams which flowed within (englacial) and under (subglacial) glaciers.

a. Esker
c. AASHTO Soil Classification System
b. AL 333
d. AL 129-1

70. An _____ is a fan-shaped deposit formed where a fast flowing stream flattens, slows, and spreads typically at the exit of a canyon onto a flatter plain. A convergence of neighboring fans into a single apron of deposits against a slope is called a bajada, or compound _____.

a. AL 129-1
c. AASHTO Soil Classification System
b. AL 333
d. Alluvial fan

71. _____ is a naturally occurring material composed primarily of fine-grained minerals, which show plasticity through a variable range of water content, and which can be hardened when dried and/or fired. _____ deposits are mostly composed of _____ minerals (phyllosilicate minerals), minerals which impart plasticity and harden when fired and/or dried, and variable amounts of water trapped in the mineral structure by polar attraction. Organic materials which do not impart plasticity may also be a part of _____ deposits.

a. 1700 Cascadia earthquake
c. 1509 Istanbul earthquake
b. 1703 Genroku earthquake
d. Clay

72. _____ are isolated fragments of rock found within finer-grained water-deposited sedimentary rocks. They range in size from small pebbles to boulders. The critical distinguishing feature is that there is evidence that they were not transported by normal water currents, but rather dropped in vertically through the water column.

a. 1509 Istanbul earthquake
c. 1703 Genroku earthquake
b. Dropstones
d. 1700 Cascadia earthquake

Chapter 14. Glaciers and Glaciation

73. A _____ is an annual layer of sediment or sedimentary rock. Initially, _____ was used to describe the separate components of annual layers in glacial lake sediments, but at the 1910 Geological Congress, the Swedish geologist Gerard De Geer (1858-1943) proposed a new formal definition where _____ described the whole of any annual sedimentary layer.
   a. 1703 Genroku earthquake
   b. 1700 Cascadia earthquake
   c. 1509 Istanbul earthquake
   d. Varve

74. The _____, is a geologic eon before the Proterozoic and Paleoproterozoic, before 2.5 Ga (billion years ago, or 2,500 Ma.) Instead of being based on stratigraphy, this date is defined chronometrically. The lower boundary (starting point) has not been officially recognized by the International Commission on Stratigraphy, but it is usually set to 3.8 Ga, at the end of the Hadean eon.
   a. AASHTO Soil Classification System
   b. AL 129-1
   c. AL 333
   d. Archean

75. An _____ is a geological interval of warmer global average temperature that separates glacial periods within an ice age. The current Holocene _____ has persisted since the Pleistocene, about 11,400 years ago.

During the 2.5 million year span of the Pleistocene, numerous glacials, or significant advances of continental ice sheets in North America and Europe have occurred at intervals of approximately 40,000 to 100,000 years.

   a. AL 129-1
   b. AL 333
   c. AASHTO Soil Classification System
   d. Interglacial

76. In chronostratigraphy, a _____ is a succession of rock strata laid down in an single age on the geologic timescale, which usually represents millions of years of deposition. A given _____ of rock and the corresponding age of time will by convention have the same name, and the same boundaries.
   a. Stage
   b. Chronostratigraphy
   c. Relative dating
   d. Geologic record

77. A _____ is an opening in a planet's surface or crust, which allows hot, molten rock, ash, and gases to escape from below the surface. Volcanic activity involving the extrusion of rock tends to form mountains or features like mountains over a period of time.
   a. Volcano
   b. 1509 Istanbul earthquake
   c. 1703 Genroku earthquake
   d. 1700 Cascadia earthquake

Chapter 15. The Work of Wind and Deserts

1. _____ is the naturally occurring, unconsolidated or loose covering on the Earth's surface. _____ is composed of particles of broken rock that have been altered by chemical, biological and environmental processes including weathering and erosion. _____ is different from its parent rock(s) source(s), altered by interactions between the lithosphere, hydrosphere, atmosphere, and the biosphere.
   a. Slump
   b. Soil
   c. 1509 Istanbul earthquake
   d. Topsoil

2. An _____ is a confined aquifer containing groundwater that will flow upward through a well without the need for pumping. Water may even reach the ground surface if the natural pressure is high enough, in which case the well is called a flowing artesian well. An aquifer provides the water for an artesian well.
   a. Artesian aquifer
   b. AASHTO Soil Classification System
   c. AL 333
   d. AL 129-1

3. _____ is mechanical scraping of a rock surface by friction between rocks and moving particles during their transport in wind, glacier, waves, gravity or running water, after friction, the moving particles dislodge loose and weak debris from the side of the rock, these particles can be dissolved in the water source.

   The intensity of _____ depends on the hardness, concentration, velocity and mass of moving particles.

   A virtually smooth marine platform cut by the ocean waves at a coastline.

   a. AL 129-1
   b. Abrasion
   c. AL 333
   d. AASHTO Soil Classification System

4. In geology a _____ is the smallest division of a geologic formation or stratigraphic rock series marked by well-defined divisional planes (bedding planes) separating it from layers above and below. A _____ is the smallest lithostratigraphic unit, usually ranging in thickness from a centimeter to several meters and distinguishable from beds above and below it. Beds can be differentiated in various ways, including rock or mineral type and particle size.
   a. Sequence stratigraphy
   b. Bed
   c. Cyclostratigraphy
   d. Biozones

5. The term _____ describes particles in a flowing fluid (usually a river) that are transported along the bed. This is in opposition to suspended load and wash load which are carried entirely in suspension.

   _____ moves by a variety of methods, including rolling, sliding, traction, and saltation.

   a. Bed load
   b. Coastal erosion
   c. Fault-block
   d. Gravitational erosion

6. _____ is a naturally occurring material composed primarily of fine-grained minerals, which show plasticity through a variable range of water content, and which can be hardened when dried and/or fired. _____ deposits are mostly composed of _____ minerals (phyllosilicate minerals), minerals which impart plasticity and harden when fired and/or dried, and variable amounts of water trapped in the mineral structure by polar attraction. Organic materials which do not impart plasticity may also be a part of _____ deposits.
   a. 1700 Cascadia earthquake
   b. 1703 Genroku earthquake
   c. 1509 Istanbul earthquake
   d. Clay

Chapter 15. The Work of Wind and Deserts

7. The _____ or the Dirty Thirties was a period of severe dust storms causing major ecological and agricultural damage to American and Canadian prairie lands from 1930 to 1936 (in some areas until 1940.) The phenomenon was caused by severe drought coupled with decades of extensive farming without crop rotation or other techniques to prevent erosion. Deep plowing of the virgin topsoil of the Great Plains had killed the natural grasses that normally kept the soil in place and trapped moisture even during periods of drought and high winds.

   a. 1509 Istanbul earthquake
   b. Dust Bowl
   c. 1700 Cascadia earthquake
   d. 1703 Genroku earthquake

8. In geology, _____ is a specific type of particle transport by fluids such as wind, or the denser fluid water. It occurs when loose material is removed from a bed and carried by the fluid, before being transported back to the surface. Examples include pebble transport by rivers, sand drift over desert surfaces, soil blowing over fields, or even snow drift over smooth surfaces such as those in the Arctic or Canadian Prairies.

   a. Permineralization
   b. Saltation
   c. Transgression
   d. Hydrothermal circulation

9. The _____ was the earliest of the six cratonic sequences that have occurred during the Phanerozoic (followed by the Tippecanoe, Kaskaskia, Absaroka, Zu>ñi, and Tejas.) It dates from the late Proterozoic through the early Ordovician, though the marine transgression did not begin in earnest until the middle Cambrian.

   At its peak, most of North America was covered by the shallow Sauk Sea, save for parts of the Canadian Shield and the islands of the Transcontinental Arch.

   a. Sauk sequence
   b. 1509 Istanbul earthquake
   c. 1700 Cascadia earthquake
   d. Tippecanoe sequence

10. _____ is the term for the fine particles that are light enough to be carried in a stream without touching the stream bed. These particles are generally of the fine sand, silt and clay size, although they can be larger, especially in cases of high discharge, such as during floods. This is in contrast to bed load which is carried along the bottom of the stream.

    a. Tertiary
    b. Valley glaciers
    c. Strike-slip faults
    d. Suspended load

11. _____ is the removal of solids (sediment, soil, rock and other particles) in the natural environment. It usually occurs due to transport by wind, water, or ice; by down-slope creep of soil and other material under the force of gravity; or by living organisms, such as burrowing animals, in the case of bioerosion.

    _____ is distinguished from weathering, which is the process of chemical or physical breakdown of the minerals in the rocks, although the two processes may occur concurrently.

    a. AL 129-1
    b. AL 333
    c. AASHTO Soil Classification System
    d. Erosion

Chapter 15. The Work of Wind and Deserts

12. _____ is caused by movement of ice, typically as glaciers. Glaciers erode predominantly by three different processes: abrasion/scouring, plucking, and ice thrusting. In an abrasion process, debris in the basal ice scrapes along the bed, polishing and gouging the underlying rocks, similar to sandpaper on wood. Glaciers can also cause pieces of bedrock to crack off in the process of plucking. In ice thrusting, the glacier freezes to its bed, then as it surges forward, it moves large sheets of frozen sediment at the base along with the glacier. This method produced some of the many thousands of lake basins that dot the edge of the Canadian Shield. These processes, combined with erosion and transport by the water network beneath the glacier, leave moraines, drumlins, eskers, ground moraine (till), kames, kame deltas, moulins, and glacial erratics in their wake, typically at the terminus or during glacier retreat.

   a. AL 333
   b. AASHTO Soil Classification System
   c. Ice erosion
   d. AL 129-1

13. A _____ is a large, slow-moving mass of ice, formed from compacted layers of snow, that slowly deforms and flows in response to gravity and high pressure.

   _____ ice is the largest reservoir of fresh water on Earth, and second only to oceans as the largest reservoir of total water.

   a. Little Ice Age
   b. Pacific Decadal Oscillation
   c. Keeling Curve
   d. Glacier

14. _____ is any particulate matter that can be transported by fluid flow, and which eventually is deposited.

   They are most often transported by water (fluvial processes) transported by wind (aeolian processes) and glaciers. Beach sands and river channel deposits are examples of fluvial transport and deposition, though _____ also often settles out of slow-moving or standing water in lakes and oceans.

   a. Brickearth
   b. Bovey Beds
   c. Quicksand
   d. Sediment

15. _____ pertain to the activity of the winds and more specifically, to the winds' ability to shape the surface of the Earth and other planets. Winds may erode, transport, and deposit materials, and are effective agents in regions with sparse vegetation and a large supply of unconsolidated sediments. Although water is much more powerful than wind, _____ are important in arid environments such as deserts.

   a. AASHTO Soil Classification System
   b. AL 129-1
   c. Aeolian processes
   d. AL 333

16. A _____ is a glacial outwash plain formed of sediments deposited by meltwater at the terminus of a glacier.

   _____ are found in glaciated areas, such as Svalbard, Kerguelen Islands, and Iceland. Glaciers and icecaps contain large amounts of silt and sediment, picked up as they erode the underlying rocks when they move slowly downhill, and at the snout of the glacier, meltwater can carry this sediment away from the glacier and deposit it on a broad plain.

   a. Rogen moraine
   b. Monadnock
   c. 1509 Istanbul earthquake
   d. Sandur

17. _____ are rocks that have been abraded, pitted, etched, grooved, or polished by wind-driven sand or ice crystals. These geomorphic features are most typically found in arid environments where there is little vegetation to interfere with aeolian particle transport, where there are frequently strong winds, and where there is a steady but not overwhelming supply of sand.

_____ can be abraded to eye-catching natural sculptures.

a. 1509 Istanbul earthquake
b. Ventifacts
c. Fault breccia
d. Coprolite

18. The _____ is the level at which the ground water pressure is equal to atmospheric pressure. It may be conveniently visualized as the 'surface' of the ground water in a given vicinity. It usually coincides with the phreatic surface, but can be many feet above it. As water infiltrates through pore spaces in the soil, it first passes through the zone of aeration, where the soil is unsaturated. At increasing depths water fills in more spaces, until the zone of saturation is reached. The relatively horizontal plane atop this zone constitutes the _____.

a. Crosshole sonic logging
b. Shaft construction
c. Rock bolt
d. Water table

19. A _____ is a wind-abraded ridge found in a desert environment. They are elongate features typically three or more times longer than they are wide, and when viewed from above, resemble the hull of a boat. Facing the wind is a steep, blunt face that gradually gets lower and narrower toward the lee end.

a. 1703 Genroku earthquake
b. Yardang
c. 1509 Istanbul earthquake
d. 1700 Cascadia earthquake

20. The general term '_____' or, more precisely, 'glacial age' denotes a geological period of long-term reduction in the temperature of the Earth's surface and atmosphere, resulting in an expansion of continental ice sheets, polar ice sheets and alpine glaciers. Within a long-term _____, individual pulses of extra cold climate are termed 'glaciations'. Glaciologically, _____ implies the presence of extensive ice sheets in the northern and southern hemispheres; by this definition we are still in an _____

a. AL 333
b. Ice Age
c. AL 129-1
d. AASHTO Soil Classification System

21. The _____ is the area in an aquifer, below the water table, in which relatively all pores and fractures are saturated with water. The _____ may fluctuate with changes of season and during wet and dry periods.

a. Porosity
b. Phreatic zone
c. Permeability
d. Saltwater intrusion

22. A _____ is a desert surface that is covered with closely packed, interlocking angular or rounded rock fragments of pebble and cobble size.

Several theories have been proposed for their formation. The more common theory is that they form by the gradual removal of the sand, dust and other fine grained material by the wind and intermittent rain leaving only the larger fragments behind.

Chapter 15. The Work of Wind and Deserts

a. 1703 Genroku earthquake
b. 1509 Istanbul earthquake
c. 1700 Cascadia earthquake
d. Desert pavement

23. The _____ Era, is the most recent of the three classic geological eras and covers the period from 65.5 million years ago to the present. It is marked by the Cretaceous-Tertiary extinction event at the end of the Cretaceous that saw the demise of the last non-avian dinosaurs and the end of the Mesozoic Era. The _____ era is ongoing.
a. 1509 Istanbul earthquake
b. 1700 Cascadia earthquake
c. 1703 Genroku earthquake
d. Cenozoic

24. _____ is a homogeneous, typically nonstratified, porous, friable, slightly coherent, often calcareous, fine-grained, silty, pale yellow or buff, windblown (aeolian) sediment. It generally occurs as a widespread blanket deposit that covers areas of hundreds of square kilometers and tens of meters thick. _____ often stands in either steep or vertical faces.
a. 1700 Cascadia earthquake
b. 1703 Genroku earthquake
c. 1509 Istanbul earthquake
d. Loess

25. The _____ was the cratonic sequence--that is, the marine transgression--that followed the Sauk sequence; it extended from roughly the middle Ordovician to the early Devonian.

After the regression of the Sauk Sea early in the Ordovician, the exposed craton for a time underwent vigorous erosion, due to being located in a tropical climate; indeed, at this point in the Phanerozoic the North American continent roughly straddled the equator.

The Tippecanoe transgression ended this period of erosion, beginning with the deposition of clean sandstones across the craton, followed by abundant carbonate deposition.

a. 1700 Cascadia earthquake
b. 1509 Istanbul earthquake
c. Sauk sequence
d. Tippecanoe sequence

26. _____ is the geological process by which material is added to a landform or land mass. Fluids such as wind and water, as well as sediment gravity flows, transport previously eroded sediment, which, at the loss of enough kinetic energy in the fluid, is deposited, building up layers of sediment.

_____ occurs when the forces responsible for sediment transportation are no longer sufficient to overcome the forces of particle weight and friction, which resist motion.

a. Diagenesis
b. Deposition
c. Downcutting
d. Headward erosion

27. A _____ dune is an arc-shaped sand ridge, comprising well-sorted sand. This type of dune possesses two 'horns' that face downwind, with the slip face (the downwind slope) at the angle of repose, or approximately 32 degrees. The upwind side is packed by the wind, and stands at about 15 degrees. Simple _____ dunes may stretch from meters to a hundred meters or so between the tips of the horns.
a. 1700 Cascadia earthquake
b. 1703 Genroku earthquake
c. 1509 Istanbul earthquake
d. Barchan

28. In geology, _____ refers to inclined sedimentary structures in a horizontal unit of rock. These tilted structures are deposits from bedforms such as ripples and dunes, and they indicate that the depositional environment contained a flowing fluid (typically, water or wind.) This is a case in geology when original depositional layering is tilted, and that the tilting is not a result of post-depositional deformation.
   a. Platform cover
   b. Geomicrobiology
   c. Schmidt hammer
   d. Cross-bedding

29. _____ is a naturally occurring granular material composed of finely divided rock and mineral particles.

As the term is used by geologists, _____ particles range in diameter from 0.0625 (or $>^1\!\!/\!_{16}$ mm, or 62.5 micrometers) to 2 millimeters. An individual particle in this range size is termed a _____ grain.

   a. 1703 Genroku earthquake
   b. 1509 Istanbul earthquake
   c. 1700 Cascadia earthquake
   d. Sand

30. Radially symmetrical, _____ are pyramidal sand mounds with slipfaces on three or more arms that radiate from the high center of the mound. They tend to accumulate in areas with multidirectional wind regimes. _____ grow upward rather than laterally. They dominate the Grand Erg Oriental of the Sahara. In other deserts, they occur around the margins of the sand seas, particularly near topographic barriers. In the southeast Badain Jaran Desert of China, the _____ are up to 500 meters tall and may be the tallest dunes on Earth.
   a. Loihi Seamount
   b. Star dunes
   c. Pahoehoe lava
   d. Principle of inclusions and components

31. The _____, is a geologic eon before the Proterozoic and Paleoproterozoic, before 2.5 Ga (billion years ago, or 2,500 Ma.) Instead of being based on stratigraphy, this date is defined chronometrically. The lower boundary (starting point) has not been officially recognized by the International Commission on Stratigraphy, but it is usually set to 3.8 Ga, at the end of the Hadean eon.
   a. AL 333
   b. AASHTO Soil Classification System
   c. AL 129-1
   d. Archean

32. The _____ is the epoch from 1.8 million to 11550 years BP covering the world's recent period of repeated glaciations. The _____ epoch follows the Pliocene epoch and is followed by the Holocene epoch. The _____ is the third epoch of the Neogene period or 6th epoch of the Cenozoic Era. The end of the _____ corresponds with the retreat of the last continental glacier. It also corresponds with the end of the Paleolithic age used in archaeology.
   a. Pleistocene
   b. Late Pleistocene
   c. Sicilian Stage
   d. Tyrrhenian

33. An _____ is a fan-shaped deposit formed where a fast flowing stream flattens, slows, and spreads typically at the exit of a canyon onto a flatter plain. A convergence of neighboring fans into a single apron of deposits against a slope is called a bajada, or compound _____.
   a. AL 129-1
   b. AASHTO Soil Classification System
   c. Alluvial fan
   d. AL 333

Chapter 15. The Work of Wind and Deserts

34. Two important classifications of weathering processes exist -- physical and _____. Mechanical or physical weathering involves the breakdown of rocks and soils through direct contact with atmospheric conditions, such as heat, water, ice and pressure. The second classification, _____, involves the direct effect of atmospheric chemicals or biologically produced chemicals (also known as biological weathering) in the breakdown of rocks, soils and minerals.
    a. 1509 Istanbul earthquake
    b. Weathering
    c. Chemical weathering
    d. Physical weathering

35. The _____ , usually abbreviated K for its German translation Kreide, is a geologic period and system from circa >145.5 >± 4 to >65.5 >± 0.3 million years ago . In the geologic timescale, the _____ follows on the Jurassic period and is followed by the Paleogene period. It is the youngest period of the Mesozoic era, and at 80 million years long, the longest period of the Phanerozoic eon. The end of the _____ defines the boundary between the Mesozoic and Cenozoic eras.
    a. Campanian
    b. Coniacian
    c. Cretaceous
    d. Hauterivian

36. _____ is the natural or artificial removal of surface and sub-surface water from an area. Many agricultural soils need _____ to improve production or to manage water supplies.

The earliest archaeological record of an advanced system of _____ comes from the Indus Valley Civilization from around 3100 BC in what is now Pakistan and North India.

    a. 1700 Cascadia earthquake
    b. 1703 Genroku earthquake
    c. Drainage
    d. 1509 Istanbul earthquake

37. _____ can also be called frost shattering or frost-wedging. This type of weathering is common in mountain areas where the temperature is around freezing point. Frost induced weathering, although often attributed to the expansion of freezing water captured in cracks, is generally independent of the water-to-ice expansion. It has long been known that moist soils expand or frost heave upon freezing as a result of water migrating along from unfrozen areas via thin films to collect at growing ice lenses. This same phenomena occurs within pore spaces of rocks.
    a. Frost disintegration
    b. Weathering
    c. 1509 Istanbul earthquake
    d. Physical weathering

38. _____ is water located beneath the ground surface in soil pore spaces and in the fractures of lithologic formations. A unit of rock or an unconsolidated deposit is called an aquifer when it can yield a usable quantity of water. The depth at which soil pore spaces or fractures and voids in rock become completely saturated with water is called the water table.
    a. Depression focused recharge
    b. 1700 Cascadia earthquake
    c. 1509 Istanbul earthquake
    d. Groundwater

39. The _____ was a cratonic sequence that began in the mid-Devonian, peaked early in the Mississippian, and ended by mid-Mississippian time. A major unconformity separates it from the lower Tippecanoe sequence.

The basal-that is, the lowest and oldest-units of the Kaskaskia consist of clean quartz sandstones eroded from the Appalachian orogenic belt to the east, the Ozark Dome in the center of the continent, and south from the Canadian Shield.

a. 1700 Cascadia earthquake
b. 1509 Istanbul earthquake
c. Sauk sequence
d. Kaskaskia sequence

40. _____ is the geomorphic process by which soil, regolith, and rock move downslope under the force of gravity. Types of _____ include creep, slides, flows, topples, and falls, each with its own characteristic features, and taking place over timescales from seconds to years. _____ occurs on both terrestrial and submarine slopes, and has been observed on Earth, Mars, and Venus.
  a. Soil liquefaction
  b. Mass wasting
  c. 1509 Istanbul earthquake
  d. 1700 Cascadia earthquake

41. Two important classifications of weathering processes exist -- _____ and chemical weathering. Mechanical or _____ involves the breakdown of rocks and soils through direct contact with atmospheric conditions, such as heat, water, ice and pressure. The second classification, chemical weathering, involves the direct effect of atmospheric chemicals or biologically produced chemicals (also known as biological weathering) in the breakdown of rocks, soils and minerals.
  a. Weathering
  b. 1509 Istanbul earthquake
  c. Frost disintegration
  d. Physical weathering

42. A _____ or mudslide is the most rapid (up to 80 km/h, or 50 mph) and fluid type of downhill mass wasting. It is a rapid movement of a large mass of mud formed from loose earth and water. Similar terms are mudslide (not very liquid), mud stream, debris flow (e.g. in high mountains), j>ökulhlaup, and lahar
  a. 1509 Istanbul earthquake
  b. 1703 Genroku earthquake
  c. 1700 Cascadia earthquake
  d. Mudflow

43. The _____ is an informal name for the supereon comprising the eons of the geologic timescale that came before the current Phanerozoic eon. It spans from the formation of Earth around 4500 Mya (million years ago) to the evolution of abundant macroscopic hard-shelled animals, which marked the beginning of the Cambrian, the first period of the first era of the Phanerozoic eon, some 542 Mya. It is named after the Roman name for Wales - Cambria - where rocks from this age were first studied.
  a. 1700 Cascadia earthquake
  b. 1509 Istanbul earthquake
  c. 1703 Genroku earthquake
  d. Precambrian

44. _____ is the decomposition of Earth rocks, soils and their minerals through direct contact with the planet's atmosphere. _____ occurs in situ, or 'with no movement', and thus should not be confused with erosion, which involves the movement of rocks and minerals by agents such as water, ice, wind and gravity.

Two important classifications of _____ processes exist -- physical and chemical _____.

  a. 1509 Istanbul earthquake
  b. Weathering
  c. Physical weathering
  d. Frost disintegration

45. _____ are the collective effect of changes in the Earth's movements upon its climate axial tilt, and precession of the Earth's orbit determined climatic patterns on Earth, resulting in 100,000-year ice age cycles of the Quaternary glaciation over the last few million years. The Earth's axis completes one full cycle of precession approximately every 26,000 years. At the same time, the elliptical orbit rotates, more slowly, leading to a 23,000-year cycle between the seasons and the orbit.

Chapter 15. The Work of Wind and Deserts

a. Geologic record
c. Global Standard Stratigraphic Age
b. Milankovitch theory
d. Stage

46. A _____ is a forest in which tree trunks have fossilized. That is, the wood in the trunks have turned into petrified wood, where organic cells have decomposed and are replaced by minerals, while preserving the structure of the wood.
   a. Phaneritic
   c. 1700 Cascadia earthquake
   b. 1509 Istanbul earthquake
   d. Petrified Forest

47. _____ is a geologic term for a type of topography characterized by a series of separate and parallel mountain ranges with broad valleys interposed, extending over a more or less wide area. It is typified by the topography found in the Great Basin in the western United States, which is part of a larger regional topography known as the _____ Province. _____ topography results from crustal extension.
   a. Tidal scour
   c. Rill
   b. Zechstein
   d. Basin and Range

48. The _____ is a large geologic province which includes parts of the southwestern United States and northwestern Mexico, typified by basin and range topography.

The topography of the _____ is a result of crustal extension within this part of the North American Plate. The cause of this extension is as yet not fully understood, although several hypotheses have been offered. The crust here has been stretched up to 100% of its original width. In fact, the crust underneath the _____, especially under the Great Basin, is some of the thinnest in the world.

   a. Yilgarn Craton
   c. Canadian Shield
   b. Quaternary
   d. Basin and Range Province

49. In stratigraphy, _____ is the native consolidated rock underlying the surface of a terrestrial planet, usually the Earth. Above the _____ is usually an area of broken and weathered unconsolidated rock in the basal subsoil. The top of the _____ is known as rockhead and identifying this, via excavations, drilling or geophysical methods, is an important task in most civil engineering projects.
   a. Bedrock
   c. Polystrate
   b. Biozones
   d. Sequence stratigraphy

50. A _____ is a gently inclined erosional surface carved into bedrock. It is thinly covered with Fluvial gravel that has developed at the foot of mountains. It develops when running water erodes most of the mass of the mountain. It is typically a concave surface gently sloping away from mountainous desert areas.
   a. Platform cover
   c. Karst fenster
   b. Geodiversity
   d. Pediment

51. The _____ is the zone of the ocean floor that separates the thin oceanic crust from thick continental crust. Continental margins constitute about 28% of the oceanic area.

The transition from continental to oceanic crust commonly occurs within the outer part of the margin, called continental rise.

Chapter 15. The Work of Wind and Deserts

a. Cuspate forelands
c. Longshore drift
b. 1509 Istanbul earthquake
d. Continental margin

52. _____ is a region of the Colorado Plateau characterized by a cluster of vast and iconic sandstone buttes, the largest reaching 1,000 ft (300 m) above the valley floor. It is located on the southern border of Utah with northern Arizona (around >>36>°59>'N 110>°6>'W'#20;/'#20;>36.983>°N 110.1>°W>'#20;/'#20;36.983; -110.1), near the Four Corners area. The valley lies within the range of the Navajo Nation Reservation, and is accessible from U.S. Highway 163.
   a. 1509 Istanbul earthquake
   c. Thirtynine Mile volcanic field
   b. Rano Kau
   d. Monument Valley

53. _____ is a common extrusive volcanic rock. It is usually grey to black and fine-grained due to rapid cooling of lava at the surface of a planet. It may be porphyritic containing larger crystals in a fine matrix, or vesicular, or frothy scoria.
   a. 1703 Genroku earthquake
   c. 1700 Cascadia earthquake
   b. 1509 Istanbul earthquake
   d. Basalt

54. A _____ or inselberg is an isolated rock hill, knob, ridge, or small mountain that rises abruptly from a gently sloping or virtually level surrounding plain. The term '_____' is usually used in the United States, whereas 'inselberg' is the more common international term. In southern and southern-central Africa, a similar formation of granite is known as a kopje (in fact a Dutch word) from the Afrikaans word: koppie.

_____ is an originally Native American term for an isolated hill or a lone mountain that has risen above the surrounding area, typically by surviving erosion.

   a. Monadnock
   c. 1509 Istanbul earthquake
   b. Sandur
   d. Rogen moraine

55. _____ is a sedimentary rock composed mainly of sand-size mineral or rock grains. Most _____ is composed of quartz and/or feldspar because these are the most common minerals in the Earth's crust. Like sand, _____ may be any color, but the most common colors are tan, brown, yellow, red, gray and white.
   a. Sandstone
   c. Porcellanite
   b. Lithification
   d. Dolostone

56. _____ is a sedimentary rock composed largely of the mineral calcite (calcium carbonate: $CaCO_3$.) The deposition of _____ strata is often a by-product and indicator of biological activity in the geologic record. Calcium (along with nitrogen, phosphorus, and potassium) is a key mineral to plant nutrition: soils overlying _____ bedrock tend to be pre-fertilized with calcium.
   a. Limestone
   c. 1509 Istanbul earthquake
   b. 1703 Genroku earthquake
   d. 1700 Cascadia earthquake

Chapter 16. Shorelines and Shoreline Processes

1. The _____ Era is one of three geologic eras of the Phanerozoic eon. The division of time into eras dates back to Giovanni Arduino, in the 18th century, although his original name for the era now called the '_____' was 'Secondary' (making the modern era the 'Tertiary'.)

The _____ was a time of tectonic, climatic and evolutionary activity. The continents gradually shifted from a state of connectedness into their present configuration; the drifting provided for speciation and other important evolutionary developments.

- a. 1700 Cascadia earthquake
- b. 1509 Istanbul earthquake
- c. Mesozoic
- d. 1703 Genroku earthquake

2. The _____ is an informal name for the supereon comprising the eons of the geologic timescale that came before the current Phanerozoic eon. It spans from the formation of Earth around 4500 Mya (million years ago) to the evolution of abundant macroscopic hard-shelled animals, which marked the beginning of the Cambrian, the first period of the first era of the Phanerozoic eon, some 542 Mya. It is named after the Roman name for Wales - Cambria - where rocks from this age were first studied.
- a. 1509 Istanbul earthquake
- b. 1700 Cascadia earthquake
- c. 1703 Genroku earthquake
- d. Precambrian

3. _____ are waves that travel through the Earth or other elastic body, for example as the result of an earthquake, explosion, or some other process that imparts forces to the body. _____ are also continually excited on Earth by the incessant pounding of ocean waves (referred to as the microseism) and the wind. _____ are studied by seismologists, and measured by a seismograph, which records the output of a seismometer, or geophone.
- a. Seismic waves
- b. Harmonic tremor
- c. Maximum magnitude
- d. Shadow zone

4. _____ is the geological process by which material is added to a landform or land mass. Fluids such as wind and water, as well as sediment gravity flows, transport previously eroded sediment, which, at the loss of enough kinetic energy in the fluid, is deposited, building up layers of sediment.

_____ occurs when the forces responsible for sediment transportation are no longer sufficient to overcome the forces of particle weight and friction, which resist motion.

- a. Diagenesis
- b. Headward erosion
- c. Downcutting
- d. Deposition

5. In geology, _____ is transported rock debris overlying the solid bedrock. The term is also sometimes refers to organic debris so-transported. In the largest sense, it refers to the material left behind by retreating continental glaciers.
- a. Drift
- b. Platform cover
- c. Geodiversity
- d. Patterned ground

6. The _____ is the geologic eon before the Archean. It started at Earth's formation about 4.6 billion years ago (4,600 Ma), and ended roughly 3.8 billion years ago, though the latter date varies according to different sources.
- a. 1509 Istanbul earthquake
- b. 1703 Genroku earthquake
- c. 1700 Cascadia earthquake
- d. Hadean

Chapter 16. Shorelines and Shoreline Processes

7. The _____ is the epoch from 1.8 million to 11550 years BP covering the world's recent period of repeated glaciations. The _____ epoch follows the Pliocene epoch and is followed by the Holocene epoch. The _____ is the third epoch of the Neogene period or 6th epoch of the Cenozoic Era. The end of the _____ corresponds with the retreat of the last continental glacier. It also corresponds with the end of the Paleolithic age used in archaeology.

 a. Late Pleistocene   b. Tyrrhenian
 c. Sicilian Stage   d. Pleistocene

8. The _____ is a geological eon representing a period before the first abundant complex life on Earth. The _____ extended from 2500 Ma to 542.0 >± 1.0 Ma (million years ago), and is the most recent part of the old, informally named 'e;Precambrian'e; time.

The Proterozoic consists of 3 geologic eras, from oldest to youngest:

- Paleoproterozoic
- Mesoproterozoic
- Neoproterozoic

The well-identified events were:

- The transition to an oxygenated atmosphere during the Mesoproterozoic.
- Several glaciations, including the hypothesized Snowball Earth during the Cryogenian period in the late Neoproterozoic.
- The Ediacaran Period (635 to 542 Ma) which is characterized by the evolution of abundant soft-bodied multicellular organisms.

The geoloic record of the Proterozoic is much better than that for the preceding Archean. In contrast to the deep-water deposits of the Archean, the Proterozoic features many strata that were laid down in extensive shallow epicontinental seas; furthermore, many of these rocks are less metamorphosed than Archean-age ones, and plenty are unaltered.

 a. 1509 Istanbul earthquake   b. 1703 Genroku earthquake
 c. 1700 Cascadia earthquake   d. Proterozoic Eon

9. The _____ was the earliest of the six cratonic sequences that have occurred during the Phanerozoic (followed by the Tippecanoe, Kaskaskia, Absaroka, Zu>ñi, and Tejas.) It dates from the late Proterozoic through the early Ordovician, though the marine transgression did not begin in earnest until the middle Cambrian.

At its peak, most of North America was covered by the shallow Sauk Sea, save for parts of the Canadian Shield and the islands of the Transcontinental Arch.

 a. 1509 Istanbul earthquake   b. Sauk sequence
 c. Tippecanoe sequence   d. 1700 Cascadia earthquake

Chapter 16. Shorelines and Shoreline Processes

10. _____ is the geomorphic process by which soil, regolith, and rock move downslope under the force of gravity. Types of _____ include creep, slides, flows, topples, and falls, each with its own characteristic features, and taking place over timescales from seconds to years. _____ occurs on both terrestrial and submarine slopes, and has been observed on Earth, Mars, and Venus.
   a. 1700 Cascadia earthquake
   b. Mass wasting
   c. Soil liquefaction
   d. 1509 Istanbul earthquake

11. The _____, is a geologic eon before the Proterozoic and Paleoproterozoic, before 2.5 Ga (billion years ago, or 2,500 Ma.) Instead of being based on stratigraphy, this date is defined chronometrically. The lower boundary (starting point) has not been officially recognized by the International Commission on Stratigraphy, but it is usually set to 3.8 Ga, at the end of the Hadean eon.
   a. AL 333
   b. AL 129-1
   c. AASHTO Soil Classification System
   d. Archean

12. A _____ column (or _____) is a column of rising air in the lower altitudes of the Earth's atmosphere. They are created by the uneven heating of the Earth's surface from solar radiation, and an example of convection. The Sun warms the ground, which in turn warms the air directly above it.
   a. 1703 Genroku earthquake
   b. Thermal
   c. 1509 Istanbul earthquake
   d. 1700 Cascadia earthquake

13. The _____, together with its northern extension towards Europe, the North Atlantic Drift, is a powerful, warm, and swift Atlantic ocean current that originates in the Gulf of Mexico, exits through the Strait of Florida, and follows the eastern coastlines of the United States and Newfoundland before crossing the Atlantic Ocean. The process of western intensification causes the _____ to be a northward accelerating current offshore the east coast of North America. At about 30>°W, 40>°N, it splits in two, with the northern stream crossing to northern Europe and the southern stream recirculating off West Africa.
   a. 1700 Cascadia earthquake
   b. 1509 Istanbul earthquake
   c. 1703 Genroku earthquake
   d. Gulf Stream

14. The _____ is the extended perimeter of each continent and associated coastal plain, and was part of the continent during the glacial periods, but is undersea during interglacial periods such as the current epoch by relatively shallow seas (known as shelf seas) and gulfs.

The continental rise is below the slope, but landward of the abyssal plains. Its gradient is intermediate between the slope and the shelf, on the order of 0.5-1°.

   a. Continental shelf
   b. 1703 Genroku earthquake
   c. 1509 Istanbul earthquake
   d. 1700 Cascadia earthquake

15. The _____ was the cratonic sequence--that is, the marine transgression--that followed the Sauk sequence; it extended from roughly the middle Ordovician to the early Devonian.

After the regression of the Sauk Sea early in the Ordovician, the exposed craton for a time underwent vigorous erosion, due to being located in a tropical climate; indeed, at this point in the Phanerozoic the North American continent roughly straddled the equator.

The Tippecanoe transgression ended this period of erosion, beginning with the deposition of clean sandstones across the craton, followed by abundant carbonate deposition.

- a. Sauk sequence
- b. 1509 Istanbul earthquake
- c. 1700 Cascadia earthquake
- d. Tippecanoe sequence

16. _____ is the removal of solids (sediment, soil, rock and other particles) in the natural environment. It usually occurs due to transport by wind, water, or ice; by down-slope creep of soil and other material under the force of gravity; or by living organisms, such as burrowing animals, in the case of bioerosion.

_____ is distinguished from weathering, which is the process of chemical or physical breakdown of the minerals in the rocks, although the two processes may occur concurrently.

- a. AASHTO Soil Classification System
- b. AL 333
- c. AL 129-1
- d. Erosion

17. A _____ is a large, slow-moving mass of ice, formed from compacted layers of snow, that slowly deforms and flows in response to gravity and high pressure.

_____ ice is the largest reservoir of fresh water on Earth, and second only to oceans as the largest reservoir of total water.

- a. Little Ice Age
- b. Pacific Decadal Oscillation
- c. Glacier
- d. Keeling Curve

18. In geology, a _____ or _____ line is a planar fracture in rock in which the rock on one side of the fracture has moved with respect to the rock on the other side. Large faults within the Earth's crust are the result of differential or shear motion and active _____ zones are the causal locations of most earthquakes. Earthquakes are caused by energy release during rapid slippage along a _____.

- a. Stack
- b. Dali
- c. Combe
- d. Fault

19. _____, sometimes known as shore drift, is a geological process by which sediments such as sand or other materials, move along a beach shore. It uses the process of swash to push the material up the beach and backwash down the beach; until it reaches a groyne or another obstacle.

Where waves approach the coastline at an angle, when they break their swash pushes beach material up the beach at the same angle.

- a. Swash
- b. Longshore drift
- c. Cuspate forelands
- d. 1509 Istanbul earthquake

20. The _____ is a continental transform fault that runs a length of roughly 800 miles (1,300 km) through California in the United States. The fault's motion is right-lateral strike-slip (horizontal motion.) It forms the tectonic boundary between the Pacific Plate and the North American Plate.

a. 1509 Istanbul earthquake
c. San Andreas fault
b. 1703 Genroku earthquake
d. 1700 Cascadia earthquake

21. The _____ is the maximum depth at which a water wave's passage causes significant water motion. For water depths larger than the _____, bottom sediments are no longer stirred by the wave motion above.

In deep water, the water particles are moved in a circular orbital motion when a wave passes.

a. 1703 Genroku earthquake
c. 1700 Cascadia earthquake
b. 1509 Istanbul earthquake
d. Wave base

22. A _____ is a geological phenomenon which includes a wide range of ground movement, such as rock falls, deep failure of slopes and shallow debris flows, which can occur in offshore, coastal and onshore environments. Although the action of gravity is the primary driving force for a _____ to occur, there are other contributing factors affecting the original slope stability. Typically, pre-conditional factors build up specific sub-surface conditions that make the area/slope prone to failure, whereas the actual _____ often requires a trigger before being released.

a. Mass wasting
c. 1700 Cascadia earthquake
b. 1509 Istanbul earthquake
d. Landslide

23. In geology, a _____ is a place where the Earth's crust and lithosphere are being pulled apart and is an example of extensional tectonics.

Typical _____ features are a central linear downdropped fault segment, called a graben, with parallel normal faulting and _____-flank uplifts on either side forming a _____ valley, where the _____ remains above sea level. The axis of the _____ area commonly contains volcanic rocks and active volcanism is a part of many, but not all active _____ systems.

a. Rift
c. 1700 Cascadia earthquake
b. 1509 Istanbul earthquake
d. 1703 Genroku earthquake

24. A _____ or super volcanic eruption is a volcanic eruption which is substantially larger than any volcano in historic times (generally accepted to be greater than 1,000 cubic kilometres.) They occur when magma in the Earth rises into the crust from a hotspot but is unable to break through the crust. Pressure builds in a large and growing magma pool until the crust is unable to contain the pressure.

a. Volcanic ash
c. Lapilli
b. Supervolcano
d. Pit crater

25. A _____ or sandbar is a somewhat linear landform within or extending into a body of water, typically composed of sand, silt or small pebbles. A bar is characteristically long and narrow and develops where a stream or ocean current promotes deposition of granular material, resulting in localized shallowing of the water. Bars can appear in the sea, in a lake, or in a river.

The term _____ can be applied to larger geological units that form off a coastline as part of the process of coastal erosion. These include spits and baymouth bars that form across the front of embayments and rias. A tombolo is a bar that forms an isthmus between an island or offshore rock and a mainland shore.

a. 1703 Genroku earthquake
c. 1700 Cascadia earthquake
b. 1509 Istanbul earthquake
d. Shoal

26. A _____ or sometimes ayre is a deposition landform in which an island is attached to the mainland by a narrow piece of land such as a spit or bar. They usually form because the island causes wave refraction, depositing sand and shingle moved by longshore drift in each direction around the island where the waves meet. Eustatic sea level rise may also contribute to accretion as material is pushed up with rising sea levels.
   a. Tombolo
   c. 1703 Genroku earthquake
   b. 1509 Istanbul earthquake
   d. 1700 Cascadia earthquake

27. A _____ is a mountain rising from the ocean seafloor that does not reach to the water's surface (sea level), and thus is not an island. These are typically formed from extinct volcanoes, that rise abruptly and are usually found rising from a seafloor of 1,000-4,000 meters depth. They are defined by oceanographers as independent features that rise to at least 1,000 meters above the seafloor.
   a. 1700 Cascadia earthquake
   c. 1509 Istanbul earthquake
   b. 1703 Genroku earthquake
   d. Seamount

28. The _____ was a cratonic sequence that extended from the end of the Mississippian through the Permian periods. It is the unconformity between this sequence and the preceding Kaskaskia that divides the Carboniferous into the Mississippian and Pennsylvanian periods in North America.

Like the Kaskaskia sequence, Absaroka sedimentary deposits were dominated by detrital or siliciclastic rocks.

   a. Absaroka sequence
   c. AASHTO Soil Classification System
   b. AL 333
   d. AL 129-1

29. The _____ zone is the area that is exposed to the air at low tide and submerged at high tide, for example, the area between tide marks. This area can include many different types of habitats, including steep rocky cliffs, sandy beaches, or wetlands The area can be a narrow strip, as in Pacific islands that have only a narrow tidal range, or can include many meters of shoreline where shallow beach slope interacts with high tidal excursion.
   a. Intertidal
   c. Overland flow
   b. AASHTO Soil Classification System
   d. Eutrophication

30. _____ is any particulate matter that can be transported by fluid flow, and which eventually is deposited.

They are most often transported by water (fluvial processes) transported by wind (aeolian processes) and glaciers. Beach sands and river channel deposits are examples of fluvial transport and deposition, though _____ also often settles out of slow-moving or standing water in lakes and oceans.

   a. Brickearth
   c. Sediment
   b. Quicksand
   d. Bovey Beds

31. _____ is the decomposition of Earth rocks, soils and their minerals through direct contact with the planet's atmosphere. _____ occurs in situ, or 'with no movement', and thus should not be confused with erosion, which involves the movement of rocks and minerals by agents such as water, ice, wind and gravity.

Chapter 16. Shorelines and Shoreline Processes

Two important classifications of _____ processes exist -- physical and chemical _____.

   a. 1509 Istanbul earthquake
   b. Frost disintegration
   c. Physical weathering
   d. Weathering

32. _____ are flat or very gently sloping areas of the deep ocean basin floor. They are among the Earth's flattest and smoothest regions and the least explored. _____ cover approximately 40% of the ocean floor and reach depths between 2,200 and 5,500 m (7,200 and 18,000 ft.)
   a. Eutrophication
   b. AASHTO Soil Classification System
   c. Intertidal
   d. Abyssal plains

33. _____ is the second most abundant mineral in the Earth's continental crust. It is made up of a framework of silicon-oxygen tetrahedra SiO_4, with each silicon shared between two oxygens to give the overall formula SiO_2. _____ has a hardness of 7 on the Mohs scale and a density of 2.65 g/cmÂ³.
   a. 1703 Genroku earthquake
   b. 1700 Cascadia earthquake
   c. 1509 Istanbul earthquake
   d. Quartz

34. _____ is a naturally occurring granular material composed of finely divided rock and mineral particles.

As the term is used by geologists, _____ particles range in diameter from 0.0625 (or $>^1\!\!\!>/_{16}$ mm, or 62.5 micrometers) to 2 millimeters. An individual particle in this range size is termed a _____ grain.

   a. 1703 Genroku earthquake
   b. Sand
   c. 1700 Cascadia earthquake
   d. 1509 Istanbul earthquake

35. _____ is a common extrusive volcanic rock. It is usually grey to black and fine-grained due to rapid cooling of lava at the surface of a planet. It may be porphyritic containing larger crystals in a fine matrix, or vesicular, or frothy scoria.
   a. 1703 Genroku earthquake
   b. 1509 Istanbul earthquake
   c. 1700 Cascadia earthquake
   d. Basalt

36. _____ is a naturally occurring glass formed as an extrusive igneous rock. It is produced when felsic lava extruded from a volcano cools without crystal growth. _____ is commonly found within the margins of rhyolitic lava flows known as _____ flows, where the chemical composition (high silica content) induces a high viscosity and polymerization degree of the lava.
   a. AL 333
   b. AASHTO Soil Classification System
   c. AL 129-1
   d. Obsidian

37. _____ is mechanical scraping of a rock surface by friction between rocks and moving particles during their transport in wind, glacier, waves, gravity or running water, after friction, the moving particles dislodge loose and weak debris from the side of the rock, these particles can be dissolved in the water source.

The intensity of _____ depends on the hardness, concentration, velocity and mass of moving particles.

A virtually smooth marine platform cut by the ocean waves at a coastline.

a. AL 129-1
b. AL 333
c. AASHTO Soil Classification System
d. Abrasion

38. _____ is a form of mechanical weathering caused by the force of moving water currents rushing into a crack in the rockface. The water compresses the air in the crack, pushing it right to the back. As the wave retreats, the highly pressurised air is suddenly released with explosive force, capable of chipping away the rockface over time.

a. Downcutting
b. Wave pounding
c. Headward erosion
d. Hydraulic action

39. The _____ is the earliest of three geologic eras of the Phanerozoic eon. The _____ spanned from roughly 542 to 251 million years ago (ICS, 2004), and is subdivided into six geologic periods; from oldest to youngest they are: the Cambrian, Ordovician, Silurian, Devonian, Carboniferous, and Permian.

The _____ covers the time from the first appearance of abundant, soft-shelled fossils to the time when the continents were beginning to be dominated by large, relatively sophisticated reptiles and modern plants. The lower (oldest) boundary was classically set at the first appearance of creatures known as trilobites and archeocyathids.

a. 1703 Genroku earthquake
b. 1700 Cascadia earthquake
c. 1509 Istanbul earthquake
d. Paleozoic

40. _____ is caused by movement of ice, typically as glaciers. Glaciers erode predominantly by three different processes: abrasion/scouring, plucking, and ice thrusting. In an abrasion process, debris in the basal ice scrapes along the bed, polishing and gouging the underlying rocks, similar to sandpaper on wood. Glaciers can also cause pieces of bedrock to crack off in the process of plucking. In ice thrusting, the glacier freezes to its bed, then as it surges forward, it moves large sheets of frozen sediment at the base along with the glacier. This method produced some of the many thousands of lake basins that dot the edge of the Canadian Shield. These processes, combined with erosion and transport by the water network beneath the glacier, leave moraines, drumlins, eskers, ground moraine (till), kames, kame deltas, moulins, and glacial erratics in their wake, typically at the terminus or during glacier retreat.

a. AL 129-1
b. AL 333
c. AASHTO Soil Classification System
d. Ice erosion

41. In geology, a _____ is a continental area covered by relatively flat or gently tilted, mainly sedimentary strata, which overlie a basement of consolidated igneous or metamorphic rocks of an earlier deformation. They as well as, shields and the basement rocks together constitute cratons.

It is also common practice to use the term _____ as a very general term for a sequence of shallow water carbonate _____.

a. Cleavage
b. Platform
c. Streak
d. Fault

Chapter 16. Shorelines and Shoreline Processes

42. A _____ is a natural formation (or landform) where a rock arch forms, with a natural passageway through underneath. Most natural arches form as a narrow ridge, walled by cliffs, become narrower from erosion, with a softer rock stratum under the cliff-forming stratum gradually eroding out until the rock shelters thus formed meet underneath the ridge, thus forming the arch. They commonly form where cliffs are subject to erosion from the sea, rivers or weathering (sub-aerial processes); the processes 'find' weaknesses in rocks and work on them, making them bigger until they break through.
   a. Natural arch
   b. 1509 Istanbul earthquake
   c. 1703 Genroku earthquake
   d. 1700 Cascadia earthquake

43. A _____ is a type of cave formed primarily by the wave action of the sea. The primary process involved is erosion. Sea caves are found throughout the world, actively forming along present coastlines and as relict sea caves on former coastlines.
   a. 1700 Cascadia earthquake
   b. 1509 Istanbul earthquake
   c. 1703 Genroku earthquake
   d. Sea cave

44. A _____ is a geological landform consisting of a steep and often vertical column or columns of rock in the sea near a coast. They are formed when part of a headland is eroded by hydraulic action, which is the force of the sea or water crashing against the rock. The force of the water weakens cracks in the headland, causing them to later collapse, forming free-standing stacks and even a small island.
   a. Melange
   b. Dali
   c. Cleavage
   d. Stack

45. The _____ , usually abbreviated K for its German translation Kreide, is a geologic period and system from circa >145.5 >± 4 to >65.5 >± 0.3 million years ago . In the geologic timescale, the _____ follows on the Jurassic period and is followed by the Paleogene period. It is the youngest period of the Mesozoic era, and at 80 million years long, the longest period of the Phanerozoic eon. The end of the _____ defines the boundary between the Mesozoic and Cenozoic eras.
   a. Cretaceous
   b. Coniacian
   c. Campanian
   d. Hauterivian

46. _____ is the natural or artificial removal of surface and sub-surface water from an area. Many agricultural soils need _____ to improve production or to manage water supplies.

The earliest archaeological record of an advanced system of _____ comes from the Indus Valley Civilization from around 3100 BC in what is now Pakistan and North India.

   a. 1509 Istanbul earthquake
   b. 1703 Genroku earthquake
   c. Drainage
   d. 1700 Cascadia earthquake

47. _____ was the supercontinent that is theorized to have existed during the Paleozoic and Mesozoic eras about 250 million years ago, before the component continents were separated into their current configuration.

The name was first used by the German originator of the continental drift theory, Alfred Wegener, in the 1920 edition of his book The Origin of Continents and Oceans , in which a postulated supercontinent _____ played a key role.

The single enormous ocean which surrounded Pangaea is known as Panthalassa.

a. Pangea
b. 1703 Genroku earthquake
c. 1509 Istanbul earthquake
d. 1700 Cascadia earthquake

48. In geology, engineering, and surveying, _____ is the motion of a surface (usually, the Earth's surface) as it shifts downward relative to a datum such as sea-level. The opposite of _____ is uplift, which results in an increase in elevation. There are several types of _____.
   a. 1509 Istanbul earthquake
   b. Pothole
   c. 1700 Cascadia earthquake
   d. Subsidence

49. _____ is water located beneath the ground surface in soil pore spaces and in the fractures of lithologic formations. A unit of rock or an unconsolidated deposit is called an aquifer when it can yield a usable quantity of water. The depth at which soil pore spaces or fractures and voids in rock become completely saturated with water is called the water table.
   a. 1700 Cascadia earthquake
   b. Groundwater
   c. Depression focused recharge
   d. 1509 Istanbul earthquake

50. _____ -- also known as rip rap, rubble, shot rock or rock armour -- is rock or other material used to armor shorelines, streambeds, bridge abutments, pilings and other shoreline structures against scour, water or ice erosion.

It is made from a variety of rock types, commonly granite, limestone or occasionally concrete rubble from building and paving demolition. It is used to protect coastlines and structures from erosion by the sea, rivers, or streams.

   a. Sediment trap
   b. Sediment control
   c. Sediment basin
   d. Riprap

51. _____ is an offshore rise of water associated with a low pressure weather system, typically a tropical cyclone. _____ is caused primarily by high winds pushing on the ocean's surface. The wind causes the water to pile up higher than the ordinary sea level.
   a. 1509 Istanbul earthquake
   b. Storm surge
   c. 1703 Genroku earthquake
   d. 1700 Cascadia earthquake

52. _____ is a geological term used to describe particles of rock derived from pre-existing rock through processes of weathering and erosion. Thesel particles can consist of lithic fragments (particles of recognisable rock), or of monomineralic fragments (mineral grains.) These particles are often transported through sedimentary processes into depositional systems such as riverbeds, lakes or the ocean forming sedimentary successions.
   a. Medical geology
   b. Perched coastline
   c. Detritus
   d. Geomechanics

53. Geologically, a _____ is a long, narrow inlet with steep sides, created in a valley carved by glacial activity.

The seeds of a _____ are laid when a glacier cuts a U-shaped valley through abrasion of the surrounding bedrock by the sediment it carries. Many such valleys were formed during the recent ice age.

a. 1509 Istanbul earthquake
c. Fjord
b. 1700 Cascadia earthquake
d. 1703 Genroku earthquake

54. _____ are the collective effect of changes in the Earth's movements upon its climate axial tilt, and precession of the Earth's orbit determined climatic patterns on Earth, resulting in 100,000-year ice age cycles of the Quaternary glaciation over the last few million years. The Earth's axis completes one full cycle of precession approximately every 26,000 years. At the same time, the elliptical orbit rotates, more slowly, leading to a 23,000-year cycle between the seasons and the orbit.
a. Stage
c. Milankovitch theory
b. Global Standard Stratigraphic Age
d. Geologic record

Chapter 17. Geologic Time: Concepts and Principles

1. The _____ is the first geological period of the Phanerozoic eon, lasting from 542 ± 0.3 million years ago to 488.3 ± 1.7 million years ago (ICS, 2004); it is succeeded by the Ordovician. Its subdivisions, and indeed its base, are somewhat in flux. The period was established by Adam Sedgwick, who named it after Cambria, the classical name for Wales, where Britain's _____ rocks are best exposed.

   a. 1509 Istanbul earthquake
   b. 1700 Cascadia earthquake
   c. 1703 Genroku earthquake
   d. Cambrian

2. The _____ or Cambrian radiation was the seemingly rapid appearance of most major groups of complex animals around 530 million years ago, as evidenced by the fossil record. This was accompanied by a major diversification of other organisms, including animals, phytoplankton, and calcimicrobes. Before about 580 million years ago, most organisms were simple, composed of individual cells occasionally organized into colonies.

   a. Romer's Gap
   b. Conodont Alteration Index
   c. Labyrinthodont
   d. Cambrian explosion

3. A _____ is a special-purpose map made to show geological features.

   The stratigraphic contour lines are drawn on the surface of a selected deep stratum, so that they can show the topographic trends of the strata under the ground. It is not always possible to properly show this when the strata are extremely fractured, mixed, in some discontinuities, or where they are otherwise disturbed.

   a. 1509 Istanbul earthquake
   b. Geologic map
   c. 1700 Cascadia earthquake
   d. 1703 Genroku earthquake

4. The _____ is a chronologic schema (or idealized model) relating stratigraphy to time that is used by geologists, paleontologists and other earth scientists to describe the timing and relationships between events that have occurred during the history of the Earth. The table of geologic time spans presented here agrees with the dates and nomenclature proposed by the International Commission on Stratigraphy, and uses the standard color codes of the United States Geological Survey.

   Evidence from radiometric dating indicates that the Earth is about 4.570 billion years old.

   a. 1509 Istanbul earthquake
   b. 1703 Genroku earthquake
   c. 1700 Cascadia earthquake
   d. Geologic time scale

5. The _____ is an informal name for the supereon comprising the eons of the geologic timescale that came before the current Phanerozoic eon. It spans from the formation of Earth around 4500 Mya (million years ago) to the evolution of abundant macroscopic hard-shelled animals, which marked the beginning of the Cambrian, the first period of the first era of the Phanerozoic eon, some 542 Mya. It is named after the Roman name for Wales - Cambria - where rocks from this age were first studied.

   a. 1509 Istanbul earthquake
   b. 1703 Genroku earthquake
   c. 1700 Cascadia earthquake
   d. Precambrian

6. _____ is a technique used to date materials, usually based on a comparison between the observed abundance of a naturally occurring radioactive isotope and its decay products, using known decay rates. It is the principal source of information about the absolute age of rocks and other geological features, including the age of the Earth itself, and can be used to date a wide range of natural and man-made materials. Together with stratigraphic principles, _____ methods are used in geochronology to establish the geological time scale.

a. Paleomagnetism
b. Radiometric dating
c. Chronozone
d. Global Standard Stratigraphic Age

7. _____ is the geological process by which material is added to a landform or land mass. Fluids such as wind and water, as well as sediment gravity flows, transport previously eroded sediment, which, at the loss of enough kinetic energy in the fluid, is deposited, building up layers of sediment.

_____ occurs when the forces responsible for sediment transportation are no longer sufficient to overcome the forces of particle weight and friction, which resist motion.

a. Headward erosion
b. Diagenesis
c. Downcutting
d. Deposition

8. A _____ is a type of speleothem that rises from the floor of a limestone cave due to the dripping of mineralized solutions and the deposition of calcium carbonate.

The corresponding formation on the ceiling of a cave is known as a stalactite. If these formations grow together, the result is known as a column.

a. 1700 Cascadia earthquake
b. 1509 Istanbul earthquake
c. Stalagmite
d. 1703 Genroku earthquake

9. _____ are flat or very gently sloping areas of the deep ocean basin floor. They are among the Earth's flattest and smoothest regions and the least explored. _____ cover approximately 40% of the ocean floor and reach depths between 2,200 and 5,500 m (7,200 and 18,000 ft.)
a. Abyssal plains
b. Eutrophication
c. Intertidal
d. AASHTO Soil Classification System

10. The _____, is a geologic eon before the Proterozoic and Paleoproterozoic, before 2.5 Ga (billion years ago, or 2,500 Ma.) Instead of being based on stratigraphy, this date is defined chronometrically. The lower boundary (starting point) has not been officially recognized by the International Commission on Stratigraphy, but it is usually set to 3.8 Ga, at the end of the Hadean eon.
a. AL 129-1
b. AASHTO Soil Classification System
c. AL 333
d. Archean

11. _____ or sheet joints are surface-parallel fracture systems in rock often leading to erosion of concentric slabs.
a. Exfoliation joints
b. AL 333
c. AL 129-1
d. AASHTO Soil Classification System

12. _____ is the principle that the same scientific laws and processes are constant throughout space and time. It applies specifically to sciences that require a long timescale such as geology, astronomy, and paleontology. It was first defined by Charles Lyell (1797 - 1875), who incorporated James Hutton's gradualism into the idea of _____.
a. Uniformitarianism
b. AL 333
c. AASHTO Soil Classification System
d. AL 129-1

13. An _____ is a fan-shaped deposit formed where a fast flowing stream flattens, slows, and spreads typically at the exit of a canyon onto a flatter plain. A convergence of neighboring fans into a single apron of deposits against a slope is called a bajada, or compound _____.
   a. Alluvial fan
   b. AL 333
   c. AASHTO Soil Classification System
   d. AL 129-1

14. The _____ Era, is the most recent of the three classic geological eras and covers the period from 65.5 million years ago to the present. It is marked by the Cretaceous-Tertiary extinction event at the end of the Cretaceous that saw the demise of the last non-avian dinosaurs and the end of the Mesozoic Era. The _____ era is ongoing.
   a. 1703 Genroku earthquake
   b. 1509 Istanbul earthquake
   c. Cenozoic
   d. 1700 Cascadia earthquake

15. The _____ was the earliest of the six cratonic sequences that have occurred during the Phanerozoic (followed by the Tippecanoe, Kaskaskia, Absaroka, Zu>ñi, and Tejas.) It dates from the late Proterozoic through the early Ordovician, though the marine transgression did not begin in earnest until the middle Cambrian.

At its peak, most of North America was covered by the shallow Sauk Sea, save for parts of the Canadian Shield and the islands of the Transcontinental Arch.

   a. Sauk sequence
   b. 1700 Cascadia earthquake
   c. 1509 Istanbul earthquake
   d. Tippecanoe sequence

16. _____ is the decomposition of Earth rocks, soils and their minerals through direct contact with the planet's atmosphere. _____ occurs in situ, or 'with no movement', and thus should not be confused with erosion, which involves the movement of rocks and minerals by agents such as water, ice, wind and gravity.

Two important classifications of _____ processes exist -- physical and chemical _____.

   a. Weathering
   b. Frost disintegration
   c. Physical weathering
   d. 1509 Istanbul earthquake

17. An _____ is a confined aquifer containing groundwater that will flow upward through a well without the need for pumping. Water may even reach the ground surface if the natural pressure is high enough, in which case the well is called a flowing artesian well. An aquifer provides the water for an artesian well.
   a. AASHTO Soil Classification System
   b. Artesian aquifer
   c. AL 333
   d. AL 129-1

18. _____ is the removal of solids (sediment, soil, rock and other particles) in the natural environment. It usually occurs due to transport by wind, water, or ice; by down-slope creep of soil and other material under the force of gravity; or by living organisms, such as burrowing animals, in the case of bioerosion.

_____ is distinguished from weathering, which is the process of chemical or physical breakdown of the minerals in the rocks, although the two processes may occur concurrently.

Chapter 17. Geologic Time: Concepts and Principles

    a. AASHTO Soil Classification System
    b. AL 333
    c. AL 129-1
    d. Erosion

19. A _____ is a rock consisting of individual stones that have become cemented together. They are sedimentary rocks consisting of rounded fragments and are thus differentiated from breccias, which consist of angular clasts. Both conglomerates and breccias are characterized by clasts larger than sand (>2 mm).
    a. Pelagic sediments
    b. Keystone
    c. Porcellanite
    d. Conglomerate

20. The principle of _____ states that a rock or fault is younger than any rock (or fault) through which it cuts. This principle was developed by James Hutton.

In a series of horizontal sedimentary beds, there is an igneous dyke which cuts vertically through them. The dyke is younger than the sediment beds though which it crosses, as the beds would have had to be around before the dyke could have intruded.

    a. Cross-cutting relationships
    b. Basin and Range
    c. Planar deformation features
    d. Tidal scour

21. The _____ is the geologic eon before the Archean. It started at Earth's formation about 4.6 billion years ago (4,600 Ma), and ended roughly 3.8 billion years ago, though the latter date varies according to different sources.
    a. 1700 Cascadia earthquake
    b. 1509 Istanbul earthquake
    c. 1703 Genroku earthquake
    d. Hadean

22. _____ is the process in which sediments compact under pressure, expel connate fluids, and gradually become solid rock. Essentially, _____ is a process of porosity destruction through compaction and cementation. _____ includes all the processes which convert unconsolidated sediments into sedimentary rocks.
    a. Lithification
    b. Metasediment
    c. Dolomite
    d. Jasperoid

23. The _____ Era is one of three geologic eras of the Phanerozoic eon. The division of time into eras dates back to Giovanni Arduino, in the 18th century, although his original name for the era now called the '_____' was 'Secondary' (making the modern era the 'Tertiary'.)

The _____ was a time of tectonic, climatic and evolutionary activity. The continents gradually shifted from a state of connectedness into their present configuration; the drifting provided for speciation and other important evolutionary developments.

    a. 1509 Istanbul earthquake
    b. 1703 Genroku earthquake
    c. Mesozoic
    d. 1700 Cascadia earthquake

24. The _____ states that, with sedimentary rocks, if inclusions (or clasts) are found in a formation, then the inclusions must be older than the formation that contains them. For example, in sedimentary rocks, it is common for gravel from an older formation to be ripped up and included in a newer layer. A similar situation with igneous rocks occurs when xenoliths are found. These foreign bodies are picked up as magma or lava flows, and are incorporated, later to cool in the matrix. As a result, xenoliths are older than the rock which contains them.

a. Star dunes
c. Historical geology
b. Principle of inclusions and components
d. Suspended load

25. The _____ was proposed by the Danish geological pioneer Nicholas Steno (1638-1686.) This principle states that layers of sediment are originally deposited horizontally. The principle is important to the analysis of folded and tilted strata.
   a. Cyclostratigraphy
   b. Key bed
   c. Bedrock
   d. Principle of original horizontality

26. The _____ is a key axiom based on observations of natural history that is a foundational principle of sedimentary stratigraphy and so of other geology dependent natural sciences: 'Sedimentary layers are deposited in a time sequence, with the oldest on the bottom and the youngest on the top.'

The principle was first proposed in the 11th century by the Persian geologist, Avicenna , and the law was later formulated more clearly in the 17th century by the Danish scientist Nicolas Steno.

While discussing the origins of mountains in The Book of Healing in 1027, Avicenna first outlined the principle of the superposition of strata.

   a. Global Standard Stratigraphic Age
   b. Law of superposition
   c. Geologic record
   d. Chronostratigraphy

27. The _____ is a geological eon representing a period before the first abundant complex life on Earth. The _____ extended from 2500 Ma to 542.0 >± 1.0 Ma (million years ago), and is the most recent part of the old, informally named 'e;Precambrian'e; time.

The Proterozoic consists of 3 geologic eras, from oldest to youngest:

- Paleoproterozoic
- Mesoproterozoic
- Neoproterozoic

The well-identified events were:

- The transition to an oxygenated atmosphere during the Mesoproterozoic.
- Several glaciations, including the hypothesized Snowball Earth during the Cryogenian period in the late Neoproterozoic.
- The Ediacaran Period (635 to 542 Ma) which is characterized by the evolution of abundant soft-bodied multicellular organisms.

The geoloic record of the Proterozoic is much better than that for the preceding Archean. In contrast to the deep-water deposits of the Archean, the Proterozoic features many strata that were laid down in extensive shallow epicontinental seas; furthermore, many of these rocks are less metamorphosed than Archean-age ones, and plenty are unaltered.

Chapter 17. Geologic Time: Concepts and Principles

a. 1703 Genroku earthquake
b. Proterozoic Eon
c. 1509 Istanbul earthquake
d. 1700 Cascadia earthquake

28. _____ is a sedimentary rock composed mainly of sand-size mineral or rock grains. Most _____ is composed of quartz and/or feldspar because these are the most common minerals in the Earth's crust. Like sand, _____ may be any color, but the most common colors are tan, brown, yellow, red, gray and white.
   a. Porcellanite
   b. Lithification
   c. Dolostone
   d. Sandstone

29. _____ is the geomorphic process by which soil, regolith, and rock move downslope under the force of gravity. Types of _____ include creep, slides, flows, topples, and falls, each with its own characteristic features, and taking place over timescales from seconds to years. _____ occurs on both terrestrial and submarine slopes, and has been observed on Earth, Mars, and Venus.
   a. 1700 Cascadia earthquake
   b. Mass wasting
   c. Soil liquefaction
   d. 1509 Istanbul earthquake

30. Before the advent of absolute dating in the 20th century, archaeologists and geologists were largely limited to the use of the _____ techniques. It estimates the order of prehistoric and geological events determined by using basic stratigraphic rules, and by observing where fossil organisms lay in the geological record, often in horizontal, stratified bands of rocks present throughout the world.

Though _____ can determine the sequential order in which a series of events occurred, not when they occur, it is in no way inferior to radiometric dating; in fact, _____ by biostratigraphy is the preferred method in paleontology, and is in some respects more accurate (Stanley, 167-9.)

   a. Cenomanian
   b. Geologic record
   c. Radiometric dating
   d. Relative dating

31. An _____ is a buried erosion surface separating two rock masses or strata of different ages, indicating that sediment deposition was not continuous. In general, the older layer was exposed to erosion for an interval of time before deposition of the younger, but the term is used to describe any break in the sedimentary geologic record. The phenomenon of angular unconformities was discovered by James Hutton, who found examples at Jedburgh in 1787 and at Siccar Point in 1788.
   a. AASHTO Soil Classification System
   b. AL 333
   c. AL 129-1
   d. Unconformity

32. _____ are the preserved remains or traces of animals, plants, and other organisms from the remote past. The totality of _____, both discovered and undiscovered, and their placement in fossiliferous rock formations and sedimentary layers (strata) is known as the fossil record. The study of _____ across geological time, how they were formed, and the evolutionary relationships between taxa (phylogeny) are some of the most important functions of the science of paleontology.
   a. 1700 Cascadia earthquake
   b. 1509 Istanbul earthquake
   c. 1703 Genroku earthquake
   d. Fossils

Chapter 17. Geologic Time: Concepts and Principles

33. The _____ is a physiographic region of the Intermontane Plateaus, roughly centered on the Four Corners region of the southwestern United States. The province covers an area of 337,000 km² within western Colorado, northwestern New Mexico, southern and eastern Utah, and northern Arizona. About 90% of the area is drained by the Colorado River and its main tributaries; the Green, San Juan and Little Colorado.

Development of the province has in large part been influenced by structural features in its oldest rocks. Part of the Wasatch Line and its various faults form the western edge of the province. Faults that run parallel to the Wasatch Fault that lies along the Wasatch Range form the boundaries between the plateaus in the High Plateaus Section. The Uinta Basin, Uncompahgre Uplift, and the Paradox Basin were also created by movement along structural weaknesses in the region's oldest rock.

   a. 1509 Istanbul earthquake
   b. 1703 Genroku earthquake
   c. 1700 Cascadia earthquake
   d. Colorado Plateau

34. In geology, a _____ is a widespread sedimentary layer that formed at a single time, such that it is useful for geologic correlations and dating over a large area. Examples of these are massive ashfalls, such as those produced by nearby normal volcanic eruptions, and far away in supervolcanic eruptions, as well as tills deposited by continental glaciers, and the global iridium layer deposited at the K-T boundary.
   a. Key bed
   b. Principle of original horizontality
   c. Sequence stratigraphy
   d. Bedrock

35. In geology a _____ is the smallest division of a geologic formation or stratigraphic rock series marked by well-defined divisional planes (bedding planes) separating it from layers above and below. A _____ is the smallest lithostratigraphic unit, usually ranging in thickness from a centimeter to several meters and distinguishable from beds above and below it. Beds can be differentiated in various ways, including rock or mineral type and particle size.
   a. Sequence stratigraphy
   b. Bed
   c. Cyclostratigraphy
   d. Biozones

36. _____ refers to natural mountain building, and may be studied as a tectonic structural event, (b) as a geographical event, and (c) a chronological event. Orogenic events (a) cause distinctive structural phenomena and related tectonic activity, (b) affect certain regions of rocks and crust, and (c) happen within a specific period of time.
   a. Orogeny
   b. Antler orogeny
   c. Orogenesis
   d. Alice Springs Orogeny

37. _____ are fossils used to define and identify geologic periods They work on the premise that, although different sediments may look different depending on the conditions under which they were laid down, they may include the remains of the same species of fossil. If the species concerned were short-lived, then it is certain that the sediments in question were deposited within that narrow time period.
   a. Indian bead
   b. Invertebrate paleontology
   c. Allotrioceras
   d. Index fossils

38. _____ in the earth sciences (commonly symbolized as κ a rock or k) is a measure of the ability of a material (typically unconsolidated material) to transmit fluids. It is of great importance in determining the flow characteristics of hydrocarbons in oil and gas reservoirs, and of groundwater in aquifers. It is typically measured in the lab by application of Darcy's law under steady state conditions or, more generally, by application of various solutions to the diffusion equation for unsteady flow conditions.

a. Phreatic zone
b. Saltwater intrusion
c. Permeability
d. Porosity

39. _____ is a measure of the void spaces in a material, and is measured as a fraction, between 0-1, or as a percentage between 0-100%. The term is used in multiple fields including ceramics, metallurgy, materials, manufacturing, earth sciences and construction.

Used in geology, hydrogeology, soil science, and building science, the _____ of a porous medium (such as rock or sediment) describes the fraction of void space in the material, where the void may contain, for example, air or water.

a. Porosity
b. Saltwater intrusion
c. Phreatic zone
d. Permeability

40. A _____ is a wind-abraded ridge found in a desert environment. They are elongate features typically three or more times longer than they are wide, and when viewed from above, resemble the hull of a boat. Facing the wind is a steep, blunt face that gradually gets lower and narrower toward the lee end.

a. 1509 Istanbul earthquake
b. Yardang
c. 1700 Cascadia earthquake
d. 1703 Genroku earthquake

41. _____ is the process of determining a specific date for an archaeological or palaeontological site or artifact. Some archaeologists prefer the terms chronometric or calendar dating, as use of the word 'absolute' implies a certainty and precision that is rarely possible in archaeology. _____ is usually based on the physical or chemical properties of the materials of artifacts, buildings, or other items that have been modified by humans.

a. Absolute dating
b. AASHTO Soil Classification System
c. Erathem
d. Uranium-lead dating

42. A _____ is a free neutron that is Boltzmann distributed with kT = 0.024 eV (4.0×10^{-21} J) at room temperature. This gives characteristic (not average, or median) speed of 2.2 km/s. The name 'thermal' comes from their energy being that of the room temperature gas or material they are permeating.

a. 1703 Genroku earthquake
b. 1700 Cascadia earthquake
c. Thermal neutron
d. 1509 Istanbul earthquake

43. The _____ of a quantity whose value decreases with time is the interval required for the quantity to decay to half of its initial value. The concept originated in describing how long it takes atoms to undergo radioactive decay but also applies in a wide variety of other situations.

a. 1703 Genroku earthquake
b. 1509 Istanbul earthquake
c. 1700 Cascadia earthquake
d. Half-life

44. _____ is molten rock that is found beneath the surface of the Earth, and may also exist on other terrestrial planets. Besides molten rock, _____ may also contain suspended crystals and gas bubbles. _____ often collects in a _____ chamber inside a volcano. _____ is capable of intrusion into adjacent rocks, extrusion onto the surface as lava, and explosive ejection as tephra to form pyroclastic rock.

a. Volcanic rock
b. Magma
c. Laccolith
d. Rock cycle

Chapter 17. Geologic Time: Concepts and Principles

45. _____ is one of the three main rock types (the others being igneous and metamorphic rock.) _____ is formed by deposition and consolidation of mineral and organic material and from precipitation of minerals from solution. The processes that form _____ occur at the surface of the Earth and within bodies of water.
   a. Rock cycle
   b. Serpentinite
   c. Petrology
   d. Sedimentary rock

46. _____ is one of the three main rock types (the others being sedimentary and metamorphic rock.) _____ is formed by magma (molten rock) being cooled and becoming solid . They may form with or without crystallization, either below the surface as intrusive (plutonic) rocks or on the surface as extrusive (volcanic) rocks. They make up approximately 95% of the upper part of the Earth's crust, but their great abundance is hidden on the Earth's surface by a relatively thin but widespread layer of sedimentary and metamorphic rocks.
   a. AASHTO Soil Classification System
   b. AL 333
   c. AL 129-1
   d. Igneous rock

47. A _____ is in geology an area where, as a result of metamorphism, the same combination of minerals occur in the bed rocks. These zones occur because most metamorphic minerals are only stable in certain intervals of temperature and pressure.

The temperature and pressure at which the mineralogical composition of a rock equilibrated can vary laterally through a metamorphic terrane.

   a. Magma
   b. Metamorphic rock
   c. Tephra
   d. Metamorphic zone

48. _____ is a naturally occurring material composed primarily of fine-grained minerals, which show plasticity through a variable range of water content, and which can be hardened when dried and/or fired. _____ deposits are mostly composed of _____ minerals (phyllosilicate minerals), minerals which impart plasticity and harden when fired and/or dried, and variable amounts of water trapped in the mineral structure by polar attraction. Organic materials which do not impart plasticity may also be a part of _____ deposits.
   a. 1703 Genroku earthquake
   b. 1509 Istanbul earthquake
   c. Clay
   d. 1700 Cascadia earthquake

49. _____ are hydrous aluminium phyllosilicates, sometimes with variable amounts of iron, magnesium, alkali metals, alkaline earths and other cations. Clays have structures similar to the micas and therefore form flat hexagonal sheets. _____ are common weathering products (including weathering of feldspar) and low temperature hydrothermal alteration products.
   a. Clay minerals
   b. Kaolinite
   c. 1700 Cascadia earthquake
   d. 1509 Istanbul earthquake

50. _____ is the solid-state recrystallization of pre-existing rocks due to changes in physical and chemical conditions, primarily heat, pressure, and the introduction of chemically active fluids. Both mineralogical, chemical and crystallographic changes can occur during this process.

Three types of _____ exist: dynamic, contact and regional.

a. Detritus
b. Compression
c. Reading Prong
d. Metamorphism

51. A _____ is a compound containing an anion in which one or more central silicon atoms are surrounded by electronegative ligands. This definition is broad enough to include species such as hexafluorosilicate ('fluorosilicate'), $[SiF_6]^{2-}$, but the _____ species that are encountered most often consist of silicon with oxygen as the ligand. _____ anions, with a negative net electrical charge, must have that charge balanced by other cations to make an electrically neutral compound.
   a. 1509 Istanbul earthquake
   b. Silicate
   c. 1700 Cascadia earthquake
   d. 1703 Genroku earthquake

52. The _____ make up the largest and most important class of rock-forming minerals, comprising approximately 90 percent of the crust of the Earth. They are classified based on the structure of their silicate group. _____ all contain silicon and oxygen.
   a. 1700 Cascadia earthquake
   b. Mineraloid
   c. 1509 Istanbul earthquake
   d. Silicate minerals

53. _____ defines an important group of generally dark-colored rock-forming inosilicate minerals, composed of double chain SiO_4 tetrahedra, linked at the vertices and generally containing ions of iron and/or magnesium in their structures. They crystallize into two crystal systems, monoclinic and orthorhombic. In chemical composition and general characteristics they are similar to the pyroxenes. They are minerals of either igneous or metamorphic origin; in the former case occurring as constituents (hornblende) of igneous rocks, such as granite, diorite, andesite and others. Those of metamorphic origin include examples such as those developed in limestones by contact metamorphism (tremolite) and those formed by the alteration of other ferromagnesian minerals (hornblende).
   a. Amphibole
   b. AL 333
   c. AASHTO Soil Classification System
   d. AL 129-1

54. The _____ is the epoch from 1.8 million to 11550 years BP covering the world's recent period of repeated glaciations. The _____ epoch follows the Pliocene epoch and is followed by the Holocene epoch. The _____ is the third epoch of the Neogene period or 6th epoch of the Cenozoic Era. The end of the _____ corresponds with the retreat of the last continental glacier. It also corresponds with the end of the Paleolithic age used in archaeology.
   a. Late Pleistocene
   b. Sicilian Stage
   c. Pleistocene
   d. Tyrrhenian

55. _____, is a radiometric dating method that uses the naturally occurring radioisotope carbon-14 (^{14}C) to determine the age of carbonaceous materials up to about 60,000 years. Raw, i.e. uncalibrated, radiocarbon ages are usually reported in radiocarbon years 'Before Present' (BP), 'Present' being defined as AD 1950. Such raw ages can be calibrated to give calendar dates.
   a. Stage
   b. Carbon dating
   c. Geologic record
   d. Relative dating

56. _____ or tree-ring dating is the method of scientific dating based on the analysis of tree-ring growth patterns. This technique was developed during the first half of the 20th century originally by the astronomer A. E. Douglass, the founder of the Laboratory of Tree-Ring Research at the University of Arizona. Douglass sought to better understand cycles of sunspot activity and reasoned that changes in solar activity would affect climate patterns on earth which would subsequently be recorded by tree-ring growth patterns (i.e., sunspots >→ climate >→ tree rings.)

a. 1700 Cascadia earthquake
b. 1703 Genroku earthquake
c. 1509 Istanbul earthquake
d. Dendrochronology

57. A _____ in geology is an intrusive igneous rock body that crystallized from a magma slowly cooling below the surface of the Earth. Plutons include batholiths, dikes, sills, laccoliths, lopoliths, and other igneous bodies. In practice, '_____' usually refers to a distinctive mass of igneous rock, typically kilometers in dimension, without a tabular shape like those of dikes and sills.

a. Metamorphic zone
b. Migmatite
c. Pluton
d. Vesicular texture

58. _____ is an igneous rock of volcanic origin.

They are usually fine-grained or aphanitic to glassy in texture. They often contain clasts of other rocks and phenocrysts.

a. Petrology
b. Serpentinite
c. Large igneous provinces
d. Volcanic rock

59. Biostratigraphic units or _____ are intervals of geological strata that are defined on the basis of their characteristic fossil taxa.

A biostratigraphic unit may be defined on the basis of a single taxon or combinations of taxa, on relative abundances of taxa, or variations in features related to the distribution of fossils. The same strata may be zoned differently depending on the diagnostic criteria or fossil group chosen, so there may be several, sometimes overlapping, biostratigraphic units in the same interval.

a. Bedrock
b. Biozones
c. Cyclostratigraphy
d. Sequence stratigraphy

Chapter 18. Evolution— The Theory and Its Supporting Evidence

1. A _____ is a mountain rising from the ocean seafloor that does not reach to the water's surface (sea level), and thus is not an island. These are typically formed from extinct volcanoes, that rise abruptly and are usually found rising from a seafloor of 1,000-4,000 meters depth. They are defined by oceanographers as independent features that rise to at least 1,000 meters above the seafloor.
   - a. 1703 Genroku earthquake
   - b. 1700 Cascadia earthquake
   - c. 1509 Istanbul earthquake
   - d. Seamount

2. The _____ is the first geological period of the Phanerozoic eon, lasting from 542 ± 0.3 million years ago to 488.3 ± 1.7 million years ago (ICS, 2004); it is succeeded by the Ordovician. Its subdivisions, and indeed its base, are somewhat in flux. The period was established by Adam Sedgwick, who named it after Cambria, the classical name for Wales, where Britain's _____ rocks are best exposed.
   - a. 1509 Istanbul earthquake
   - b. 1700 Cascadia earthquake
   - c. Cambrian
   - d. 1703 Genroku earthquake

3. The _____ or Cambrian radiation was the seemingly rapid appearance of most major groups of complex animals around 530 million years ago, as evidenced by the fossil record. This was accompanied by a major diversification of other organisms, including animals, phytoplankton, and calcimicrobes. Before about 580 million years ago, most organisms were simple, composed of individual cells occasionally organized into colonies.
   - a. Romer's Gap
   - b. Labyrinthodont
   - c. Conodont Alteration Index
   - d. Cambrian explosion

4. The _____ Era is one of three geologic eras of the Phanerozoic eon. The division of time into eras dates back to Giovanni Arduino, in the 18th century, although his original name for the era now called the '_____' was 'Secondary' (making the modern era the 'Tertiary'.)

   The _____ was a time of tectonic, climatic and evolutionary activity. The continents gradually shifted from a state of connectedness into their present configuration; the drifting provided for speciation and other important evolutionary developments.

   - a. 1703 Genroku earthquake
   - b. Mesozoic
   - c. 1509 Istanbul earthquake
   - d. 1700 Cascadia earthquake

5. The _____ is the earliest of three geologic eras of the Phanerozoic eon. The _____ spanned from roughly 542 to 251 million years ago (ICS, 2004), and is subdivided into six geologic periods; from oldest to youngest they are: the Cambrian, Ordovician, Silurian, Devonian, Carboniferous, and Permian.

   The _____ covers the time from the first appearance of abundant, soft-shelled fossils to the time when the continents were beginning to be dominated by large, relatively sophisticated reptiles and modern plants. The lower (oldest) boundary was classically set at the first appearance of creatures known as trilobites and archeocyathids.

   - a. Paleozoic
   - b. 1509 Istanbul earthquake
   - c. 1700 Cascadia earthquake
   - d. 1703 Genroku earthquake

6. _____ is the principle that the same scientific laws and processes are constant throughout space and time. It applies specifically to sciences that require a long timescale such as geology, astronomy, and paleontology. It was first defined by Charles Lyell (1797 - 1875), who incorporated James Hutton's gradualism into the idea of _____.

Chapter 18. Evolution— The Theory and Its Supporting Evidence

    a. AL 333
    b. AASHTO Soil Classification System
    c. Uniformitarianism
    d. AL 129-1

7. The _____, is a geologic eon before the Proterozoic and Paleoproterozoic, before 2.5 Ga (billion years ago, or 2,500 Ma.) Instead of being based on stratigraphy, this date is defined chronometrically. The lower boundary (starting point) has not been officially recognized by the International Commission on Stratigraphy, but it is usually set to 3.8 Ga, at the end of the Hadean eon.
    a. AASHTO Soil Classification System
    b. AL 333
    c. Archean
    d. AL 129-1

8. The _____ was the earliest of the six cratonic sequences that have occurred during the Phanerozoic (followed by the Tippecanoe, Kaskaskia, Absaroka, Zu>ñi, and Tejas.) It dates from the late Proterozoic through the early Ordovician, though the marine transgression did not begin in earnest until the middle Cambrian.

At its peak, most of North America was covered by the shallow Sauk Sea, save for parts of the Canadian Shield and the islands of the Transcontinental Arch.

    a. Tippecanoe sequence
    b. Sauk sequence
    c. 1509 Istanbul earthquake
    d. 1700 Cascadia earthquake

9. In the natural sciences, _____ is a theory which holds that profound change is the cumulative product of slow but continuous processes, often contrasted with catastrophism. The theory was proposed in 1795 by James Hutton, a Scottish geologist, and was later incorporated into Charles Lyell's theory of uniformitarianism.
    a. Medical geology
    b. Type locality
    c. Detritus
    d. Gradualism

10. The _____ Era, is the most recent of the three classic geological eras and covers the period from 65.5 million years ago to the present. It is marked by the Cretaceous-Tertiary extinction event at the end of the Cretaceous that saw the demise of the last non-avian dinosaurs and the end of the Mesozoic Era. The _____ era is ongoing.
    a. 1509 Istanbul earthquake
    b. 1700 Cascadia earthquake
    c. 1703 Genroku earthquake
    d. Cenozoic

11. The _____ is a geologic formation that is spread across the U.S. states of northern Arizona, Nevada, Utah, western New Mexico, and western Colorado. The _____ is controversially considered to be synonymous to Dockum Group in eastern Colorado, eastern New Mexico, southwestern Kansas, the Oklahoma panhandle, and western Texas. The _____ is sometimes colloquially used as a geologic formation within the Dockum in New Mexico and occasionally in Texas.
    a. Chinle
    b. Cohesion
    c. Diamond Head
    d. Stack

12. _____ is the geological process by which material is added to a landform or land mass. Fluids such as wind and water, as well as sediment gravity flows, transport previously eroded sediment, which, at the loss of enough kinetic energy in the fluid, is deposited, building up layers of sediment.

_____ occurs when the forces responsible for sediment transportation are no longer sufficient to overcome the forces of particle weight and friction, which resist motion.

a. Downcutting
b. Diagenesis
c. Deposition
d. Headward erosion

13. _____ are flat or very gently sloping areas of the deep ocean basin floor. They are among the Earth's flattest and smoothest regions and the least explored. _____ cover approximately 40% of the ocean floor and reach depths between 2,200 and 5,500 m (7,200 and 18,000 ft.)
   a. Abyssal plains
   b. Intertidal
   c. Eutrophication
   d. AASHTO Soil Classification System

14. _____ are the preserved remains or traces of animals, plants, and other organisms from the remote past. The totality of _____, both discovered and undiscovered, and their placement in fossiliferous rock formations and sedimentary layers (strata) is known as the fossil record. The study of _____ across geological time, how they were formed, and the evolutionary relationships between taxa (phylogeny) are some of the most important functions of the science of paleontology.
   a. 1700 Cascadia earthquake
   b. 1509 Istanbul earthquake
   c. Fossils
   d. 1703 Genroku earthquake

15. _____ theory is an obsolete concept involving vertical crustal movement that has been replaced by plate tectonics to explain crustal movement and geologic features. _____ is a term still occasionally used for a subsiding linear trough that was caused by the accumulation of sedimentary rock strata deposited in a basin and subsequently compressed, deformed, and uplifted into a mountain range, with attendant volcanism and plutonism. The filling of a _____ with tons of sediment is accompanied in the late stages of deposition by folding, crumpling, and faulting of the deposits.
   a. Doggerland
   b. Storegga Slides
   c. Geosyncline
   d. Cratonic sequence

16. _____, originally Gondwanaland, is the name given to a southern precursor-supercontinent and then as a remnant separated from Laurasia 180-200 million years ago during the breakup of the Pangaea supercontinent that existed about 500 to 200 Ma ago into two large segments. While the corresponding northern hemisphere continent Laurasia moved further north, the nearly equal in area _____ included most of the landmasses in today's southern hemisphere, including Antarctica, South America, Africa, Madagascar, Australia-New Guinea, and New Zealand, as well as Arabia and the Indian subcontinent, which have now moved into the Northern Hemisphere.
   a. 1509 Istanbul earthquake
   b. Laurasia
   c. Gondwana
   d. 1700 Cascadia earthquake

17. The _____ was a cratonic sequence that began in the mid-Devonian, peaked early in the Mississippian, and ended by mid-Mississippian time. A major unconformity separates it from the lower Tippecanoe sequence.

The basal-that is, the lowest and oldest-units of the Kaskaskia consist of clean quartz sandstones eroded from the Appalachian orogenic belt to the east, the Ozark Dome in the center of the continent, and south from the Canadian Shield.

   a. 1700 Cascadia earthquake
   b. 1509 Istanbul earthquake
   c. Sauk sequence
   d. Kaskaskia sequence

18. _____ is a common extrusive volcanic rock. It is usually grey to black and fine-grained due to rapid cooling of lava at the surface of a planet. It may be porphyritic containing larger crystals in a fine matrix, or vesicular, or frothy scoria.

a. 1703 Genroku earthquake
c. 1700 Cascadia earthquake
b. 1509 Istanbul earthquake
d. Basalt

19. The _____ is a geological eon representing a period before the first abundant complex life on Earth. The _____ extended from 2500 Ma to 542.0 >± 1.0 Ma (million years ago), and is the most recent part of the old, informally named 'e;Precambrian'e; time.

The Proterozoic consists of 3 geologic eras, from oldest to youngest:

- Paleoproterozoic
- Mesoproterozoic
- Neoproterozoic

The well-identified events were:

- The transition to an oxygenated atmosphere during the Mesoproterozoic.
- Several glaciations, including the hypothesized Snowball Earth during the Cryogenian period in the late Neoproterozoic.
- The Ediacaran Period (635 to 542 Ma) which is characterized by the evolution of abundant soft-bodied multicellular organisms.

The geoloic record of the Proterozoic is much better than that for the preceding Archean. In contrast to the deep-water deposits of the Archean, the Proterozoic features many strata that were laid down in extensive shallow epicontinental seas; furthermore, many of these rocks are less metamorphosed than Archean-age ones, and plenty are unaltered.

a. 1703 Genroku earthquake
c. 1700 Cascadia earthquake
b. Proterozoic Eon
d. 1509 Istanbul earthquake

20. Before the advent of absolute dating in the 20th century, archaeologists and geologists were largely limited to the use of the _____ techniques. It estimates the order of prehistoric and geological events determined by using basic stratigraphic rules, and by observing where fossil organisms lay in the geological record, often in horizontal, stratified bands of rocks present throughout the world.

Though _____ can determine the sequential order in which a series of events occurred, not when they occur, it is in no way inferior to radiometric dating; in fact, _____ by biostratigraphy is the preferred method in paleontology, and is in some respects more accurate (Stanley, 167-9.)

a. Radiometric dating
c. Relative dating
b. Geologic record
d. Cenomanian

21. The _____ is a geologic period and system of the Paleozoic era spanning from >416 to 359.2 million years ago (ICS, 2004.).

During the _____ Period, which occurred in the Paleozoic era, the first fish evolved legs and started to walk on land as tetrapods around 365 Ma.

- a. Devonian
- b. 1509 Istanbul earthquake
- c. Gogo Formation
- d. Xitun Formation

22. _____ are geological records of biological activity. _____ may be impressions made on the substrate by an organism: for example, burrows, borings , footprints and feeding marks, and root cavities. The term in its broadest sense also includes the remains of other organic material produced by an organism - for example coprolites or chemical markers - or sedimentological structures produced by biological means - for example, stromatolites.
- a. 1509 Istanbul earthquake
- b. 1700 Cascadia earthquake
- c. 1703 Genroku earthquake
- d. Trace fossils

23. _____ are an extinct group of marine animals of the subclass Ammonoidea in the class Cephalopoda, phylum Mollusca. They are excellent index fossils, and it is often possible to link the rock layer in which they are found to specific geological time periods.

_____' closest living relative is probably not the modern Nautilus (which they outwardly resemble), but rather the subclass Coleoidea (octopus, squid, and cuttlefish.)

- a. AL 129-1
- b. AASHTO Soil Classification System
- c. AL 333
- d. Ammonites

24. A _____ is fossilized animal dung. They are classified as trace fossils as opposed to body fossils, as they give evidence for the animal's behavior (in this case, diet) rather than morphology. They were first described by William Buckland in 1829.
- a. Coprolite
- b. 1509 Istanbul earthquake
- c. Fault breccia
- d. Ventifacts

25. In geology a _____ is the smallest division of a geologic formation or stratigraphic rock series marked by well-defined divisional planes (bedding planes) separating it from layers above and below. A _____ is the smallest lithostratigraphic unit, usually ranging in thickness from a centimeter to several meters and distinguishable from beds above and below it. Beds can be differentiated in various ways, including rock or mineral type and particle size.
- a. Sequence stratigraphy
- b. Biozones
- c. Cyclostratigraphy
- d. Bed

26. A _____ or mudslide is the most rapid (up to 80 km/h, or 50 mph) and fluid type of downhill mass wasting. It is a rapid movement of a large mass of mud formed from loose earth and water. Similar terms are mudslide (not very liquid), mud stream, debris flow (e.g. in high mountains), j>ökulhlaup, and lahar
- a. 1700 Cascadia earthquake
- b. 1703 Genroku earthquake
- c. 1509 Istanbul earthquake
- d. Mudflow

27. The _____ epoch (55.8 >± 0.2 - 33.9 >± 0.1 Ma) is a major division of the geologic timescale and the second epoch of the Palaeogene period in the Cenozoic era. The _____ spans the time from the end of the Paleocene epoch to the beginning of the Oligocene epoch. The start of the _____ is marked by the emergence of the first modern mammals.
   a. AL 129-1
   c. AL 333
   b. AASHTO Soil Classification System
   d. Eocene

28. _____ are the fossilized remains of intermediary forms of life that illustrate an evolutionary transition. They can be identified by their retention of certain primitive (plesiomorphic) traits in comparison with their more derived relatives, as they are defined in the study of cladistics. 'Missing link' is a popular term for transitional forms.
   a. Phosphatic fossilization
   c. Megabalanus
   b. Submerged forest
   d. Transitional fossils

Chapter 19. Precambrian Earth and Life History

1. The _____ is the geologic eon before the Archean. It started at Earth's formation about 4.6 billion years ago (4,600 Ma), and ended roughly 3.8 billion years ago, though the latter date varies according to different sources.
   a. 1509 Istanbul earthquake
   b. Hadean
   c. 1703 Genroku earthquake
   d. 1700 Cascadia earthquake

2. The _____ is an informal name for the supereon comprising the eons of the geologic timescale that came before the current Phanerozoic eon. It spans from the formation of Earth around 4500 Mya (million years ago) to the evolution of abundant macroscopic hard-shelled animals, which marked the beginning of the Cambrian, the first period of the first era of the Phanerozoic eon, some 542 Mya. It is named after the Roman name for Wales - Cambria - where rocks from this age were first studied.
   a. 1700 Cascadia earthquake
   b. 1509 Istanbul earthquake
   c. 1703 Genroku earthquake
   d. Precambrian

3. The _____ is a geological eon representing a period before the first abundant complex life on Earth. The _____ extended from 2500 Ma to 542.0 >± 1.0 Ma (million years ago), and is the most recent part of the old, informally named 'e;Precambrian'e; time.

The Proterozoic consists of 3 geologic eras, from oldest to youngest:

- Paleoproterozoic
- Mesoproterozoic
- Neoproterozoic

The well-identified events were:

- The transition to an oxygenated atmosphere during the Mesoproterozoic.
- Several glaciations, including the hypothesized Snowball Earth during the Cryogenian period in the late Neoproterozoic.
- The Ediacaran Period (635 to 542 Ma) which is characterized by the evolution of abundant soft-bodied multicellular organisms.

The geoloic record of the Proterozoic is much better than that for the preceding Archean. In contrast to the deep-water deposits of the Archean, the Proterozoic features many strata that were laid down in extensive shallow epicontinental seas; furthermore, many of these rocks are less metamorphosed than Archean-age ones, and plenty are unaltered.

   a. Proterozoic Eon
   b. 1509 Istanbul earthquake
   c. 1703 Genroku earthquake
   d. 1700 Cascadia earthquake

4. The _____ is a chronologic schema (or idealized model) relating stratigraphy to time that is used by geologists, paleontologists and other earth scientists to describe the timing and relationships between events that have occurred during the history of the Earth. The table of geologic time spans presented here agrees with the dates and nomenclature proposed by the International Commission on Stratigraphy, and uses the standard color codes of the United States Geological Survey.

Evidence from radiometric dating indicates that the Earth is about 4.570 billion years old.

a. 1700 Cascadia earthquake
c. 1703 Genroku earthquake
b. 1509 Istanbul earthquake
d. Geologic time scale

5. The _____, is a geologic eon before the Proterozoic and Paleoproterozoic, before 2.5 Ga (billion years ago, or 2,500 Ma.) Instead of being based on stratigraphy, this date is defined chronometrically. The lower boundary (starting point) has not been officially recognized by the International Commission on Stratigraphy, but it is usually set to 3.8 Ga, at the end of the Hadean eon.
   a. AASHTO Soil Classification System
   c. AL 333
   b. AL 129-1
   d. Archean

6. The _____ in stratigraphy, Chronostratigraphy, paleontology and other natural sciences refers to the entirety of the layers of rock strata -- depositions laid down in volcanism or by weathering detritus (clays, sands etc.) including all its fossil content and the information it yields about the history of the Earth: its past climate, geography, geology and the evolution of life on its surface. According to the Law of Superposition (first proposed in the mid-seventeenth century by the Danish naturalist Nicolas Steno) sedimentary and volcanic rocklayers are deposited on top of each other.
   a. Geologic record
   c. Paleomagnetism
   b. Relative dating
   d. Global Boundary Stratotype Section and Point

7. The _____ Era is one of three geologic eras of the Phanerozoic eon. The division of time into eras dates back to Giovanni Arduino, in the 18th century, although his original name for the era now called the '_____' was 'Secondary' (making the modern era the 'Tertiary'.)

The _____ was a time of tectonic, climatic and evolutionary activity. The continents gradually shifted from a state of connectedness into their present configuration; the drifting provided for speciation and other important evolutionary developments.

   a. 1703 Genroku earthquake
   c. 1509 Istanbul earthquake
   b. 1700 Cascadia earthquake
   d. Mesozoic

8.

A widely accepted theory of planet formation, the so-called _____ hypothesis of Viktor Safronov, states that planets form out of dust grains that collide and stick to form larger and larger bodies. When the bodies reach sizes of approximately one kilometer, then they can attract each other directly through their mutual gravity, aiding further growth into moon-sized protoplanets enormously.

   a. Planetesimal
   c. 1703 Genroku earthquake
   b. 1700 Cascadia earthquake
   d. 1509 Istanbul earthquake

9. The _____ is a rock outcrop of Archaean tonalite gneiss in the Slave craton in Northwest Territories, Canada. The rock exposed in the outcrop formed just over four billion (4×10^9) years ago; an age based on radiometric dating of zircon crystals at 4.03 Ga, which were the oldest rocks in the world at that time. It was the oldest known rock outcrop in the world until a McGill University team reported a 4.28 billion year old outcrop on the eastern shores of Hudson Bay, 40 kilometres south of Inukjuak, Quebec, Canada.

a. AL 333
b. Acasta Gneiss
c. AASHTO Soil Classification System
d. AL 129-1

10. _____ is a common extrusive volcanic rock. It is usually grey to black and fine-grained due to rapid cooling of lava at the surface of a planet. It may be porphyritic containing larger crystals in a fine matrix, or vesicular, or frothy scoria.
a. 1700 Cascadia earthquake
b. 1509 Istanbul earthquake
c. 1703 Genroku earthquake
d. Basalt

11. The _____ -- also called the Laurentian Plateau, or Bouclier Canadien -- is a massive geological shield covered by a thin layer of soil that forms the nucleus of the North American or Laurentia craton. It has a deep, common, joined bedrock region in eastern and central Canada and stretches North from the Great Lakes to the Arctic Ocean, covering over half of Canada; it also extends south into the northern reaches of the United States. Population is scarce, and industrial development is minimal, although the region has a large hydroelectric power potential.
a. Yilgarn Craton
b. Grade
c. Gawler craton
d. Canadian Shield

12. _____ is a geological term used to describe particles of rock derived from pre-existing rock through processes of weathering and erosion. Thesel particles can consist of lithic fragments (particles of recognisable rock), or of monomineralic fragments (mineral grains.) These particles are often transported through sedimentary processes into depositional systems such as riverbeds, lakes or the ocean forming sedimentary successions.
a. Geomechanics
b. Medical geology
c. Perched coastline
d. Detritus

13. _____ is a term used in geology to refer to silicate minerals, magma, and rocks which are enriched in the lighter elements such as silicon, oxygen, aluminium, sodium, and potassium. _____ minerals are usually light in color and have specific gravities less than 3. Common _____ minerals include quartz, muscovite, orthoclase, and the sodium-rich plagioclase feldspars.
a. Tephra
b. Laccolith
c. Magma
d. Felsic

14. _____ refers to a large group of dark, coarse-grained, intrusive igneous rocks chemically equivalent to basalt. The rocks are plutonic, formed when molten magma is trapped beneath the Earth's surface and cools into a crystalline mass.

The vast majority of the Earth's surface is underlain by _____ within the oceanic crust, produced by basalt magmatism at mid-ocean ridges.

a. 1509 Istanbul earthquake
b. 1700 Cascadia earthquake
c. 1703 Genroku earthquake
d. Gabbro

15. _____ is a common and widely distributed type of rock formed by high-grade regional metamorphic processes from pre-existing formations that were originally either igneous or sedimentary rocks. Gneissic rocks are usually medium to coarse foliated and largely recrystallized but do not carry large quantities of micas, chlorite or other platy minerals. Gneisses that are metamorphosed igneous rocks or their equivalent are termed granite gneisses, diorite gneisses, etc.

Chapter 19. Precambrian Earth and Life History

a. 1703 Genroku earthquake
b. 1700 Cascadia earthquake
c. 1509 Istanbul earthquake
d. Gneiss

16. The _____ was a period of mountain building in western North America, which started in the Late Cretaceous, 70 to 80 million years ago, and ended 35 to 55 million years ago. The exact duration and ages of beginning and end of the orogeny are in dispute, as is the cause. The _____ occurred in a series of pulses, with quiescent phases intervening. The major feature that was created by this orogeny was the Rocky Mountains, but evidence of this orogeny can be found from Alaska to northern Mexico, with the easternmost extent of the mountain-building represented by the Black Hills of South Dakota.
a. Kaikoura Orogeny
b. Pan-African orogeny
c. Laramide orogeny
d. Sevier orogeny

17. _____ is an adjective describing a silicate mineral or rock that is rich in magnesium and iron; the term was derived by contracting 'magnesium' and 'ferric'. Most _____ minerals are dark in color and the specific gravity is greater than 3. Common rock-forming _____ minerals include olivine, pyroxene, amphibole, and biotite.

_____ lava, before cooling, has a low viscosity, in comparison to felsic lava, due to the lower silica content in _____ magma. Water and other volatiles can more easily and gradually escape from _____ lava, so eruptions of volcanoes made of _____ lavas are less explosively violent than felsic lava eruptions.

a. Mafic
b. 1509 Istanbul earthquake
c. 1703 Genroku earthquake
d. 1700 Cascadia earthquake

18. _____ is the part of Earth's lithosphere that surfaces in the ocean basins. _____ is primarily composed of mafic rocks, or sima. It is thinner than continental crust, or sial, generally less than 10 kilometers thick, however it is denser, having a mean density of about 3.3 grams per cubic centimeter.
a. Oceanic crust
b. AL 129-1
c. AL 333
d. AASHTO Soil Classification System

19. In geology, a _____ is a continental area covered by relatively flat or gently tilted, mainly sedimentary strata, which overlie a basement of consolidated igneous or metamorphic rocks of an earlier deformation. They as well as, shields and the basement rocks together constitute cratons.

It is also common practice to use the term _____ as a very general term for a sequence of shallow water carbonate _____.

a. Platform
b. Fault
c. Cleavage
d. Streak

20. A _____ is a large emplacement of igneous intrusive rock that forms from cooled magma deep in the Earth's crust. they are almost always made mostly of felsic or intermediate rock-types, such as granite, quartz monzonite, or diorite

Although they may appear uniform, batholiths are in fact structures with complex histories and compositions.

Chapter 19. Precambrian Earth and Life History

a. Tuff
b. Batholith
c. Great Dyke
d. Flood basalt

21. A _____ is generally a large area of exposed Precambrian crystalline igneous and high-grade metamorphic rocks that form tectonically stable areas. In all cases, the age of these rocks is greater than 570 million years and sometimes dates back 2 to 3.5 billion years. They have been little affected by tectonic events following the end of the Precambrian Era, and are relatively flat regions where mountain building, faulting, and other tectonic processes are greatly diminished compared with the activity that occurs at the margins of the shields and the boundaries between tectonic plates.
    a. 1509 Istanbul earthquake
    b. 1700 Cascadia earthquake
    c. 1703 Genroku earthquake
    d. Shield

22. _____ are igneous and meta-igneous rocks with very low silica content (less than 45%), generally >18% MgO, high FeO, low potassium, and are composed of usually greater than 90% mafic minerals (dark colored, high magnesium and iron content.) The Earth's mantle is considered to be composed of _____.
    a. AL 129-1
    b. AASHTO Soil Classification System
    c. AL 333
    d. Ultramafic rocks

23. _____ is an igneous rock of volcanic origin.

They are usually fine-grained or aphanitic to glassy in texture. They often contain clasts of other rocks and phenocrysts.

   a. Petrology
   b. Volcanic rock
   c. Large igneous provinces
   d. Serpentinite

24. _____, is the process of coastal sediments returning to the visible portion of a beach or foreshore following a submersion event. A sustainable beach or foreshore often goes through a cycle of submersion during rough weather then _____ during calmer periods. If a coastline is not in a healthy sustainable condition, then erosion can be more serious and _____ does not fully restore the original volume of the visible beach or foreshore leading to permanent beach or foreshore loss.
    a. Accretion
    b. AL 333
    c. AASHTO Soil Classification System
    d. AL 129-1

25. The _____ is the layer of igneous, sedimentary, and metamorphic rocks which form the continents and the areas of shallow seabed close to their shores, known as continental shelves. This layer is sometimes called sial due to more felsic, or granitic, bulk composition, which lies in contrast to the oceanic crust, called sima due to its mafic, or basaltic rock. (Based on the change in velocity of seismic waves, it is believed that at a certain depth sial becomes close in its physical properties to sima.
    a. Convergent boundary
    b. Tectonic plates
    c. Nappe
    d. Continental crust

26. A _____ is an old and stable part of the continental crust that has survived the merging and splitting of continents and supercontinents for at least 500 million years. Some are over two billion years old. They are generally found in the interiors of continents and are characteristically composed of ancient crystalline basement crust of lightweight felsic igneous rock such as granite.

Chapter 19. Precambrian Earth and Life History

a. Craton
b. Sebakwe proto-craton
c. Kalahari craton
d. Superior craton

27. A _____ is a mountain rising from the ocean seafloor that does not reach to the water's surface (sea level), and thus is not an island. These are typically formed from extinct volcanoes, that rise abruptly and are usually found rising from a seafloor of 1,000-4,000 meters depth. They are defined by oceanographers as independent features that rise to at least 1,000 meters above the seafloor.
   a. 1700 Cascadia earthquake
   b. 1509 Istanbul earthquake
   c. 1703 Genroku earthquake
   d. Seamount

28. _____ is molten rock that is found beneath the surface of the Earth, and may also exist on other terrestrial planets. Besides molten rock, _____ may also contain suspended crystals and gas bubbles. _____ often collects in a _____ chamber inside a volcano. _____ is capable of intrusion into adjacent rocks, extrusion onto the surface as lava, and explosive ejection as tephra to form pyroclastic rock.
   a. Magma
   b. Laccolith
   c. Volcanic rock
   d. Rock cycle

29. _____ refers to natural mountain building, and may be studied as a tectonic structural event, (b) as a geographical event, and (c) a chronological event. Orogenic events (a) cause distinctive structural phenomena and related tectonic activity, (b) affect certain regions of rocks and crust, and (c) happen within a specific period of time.
   a. Orogenesis
   b. Alice Springs Orogeny
   c. Antler orogeny
   d. Orogeny

30. _____ is one of the three main rock types (the others being igneous and metamorphic rock.) _____ is formed by deposition and consolidation of mineral and organic material and from precipitation of minerals from solution. The processes that form _____ occur at the surface of the Earth and within bodies of water.
   a. Petrology
   b. Serpentinite
   c. Rock cycle
   d. Sedimentary rock

31. In geology, _____ refers to inclined sedimentary structures in a horizontal unit of rock. These tilted structures are deposits from bedforms such as ripples and dunes, and they indicate that the depositional environment contained a flowing fluid (typically, water or wind.) This is a case in geology when original depositional layering is tilted, and that the tilting is not a result of post-depositional deformation.
   a. Platform cover
   b. Geomicrobiology
   c. Schmidt hammer
   d. Cross-bedding

32. _____ is a common and widely occurring type of intrusive, felsic, igneous rock. _____ has a medium to coarse texture, occasionally with some individual crystals larger than the groundmass forming a rock known as porphyry. Granites can be pink to dark gray or even black, depending on their chemistry and mineralogy.
   a. 1509 Istanbul earthquake
   b. Granite
   c. 1703 Genroku earthquake
   d. 1700 Cascadia earthquake

33. _____ - also known as greenstone - is a general field petrologic term applied to metamorphic and/or altered mafic volcanic rock. The green is due to abundant green chlorite, actinolite and epidote minerals that dominate the rock. However, basalts may remain quite black if primary pyroxene does not revert to chlorite or actinolite.

a. Hornfels
b. Supracrustal rocks
c. Greenschist
d. Metamorphic facies

34. _____ are zones of variably metamorphosed mafic to ultramafic volcanic sequences with associated sedimentary rocks that occur within Archaean and Proterozoic cratons between granite and gneiss bodies.

The name comes from the green hue imparted by the colour of the metamorphic minerals within the mafic rocks. Chlorite, actinolite and other green amphiboles are the typical green minerals.

a. Prehnite-pumpellyite facies
b. Dalradian
c. Cataclasite
d. Greenstone belts

35. _____ is molten rock expelled by a volcano during eruption. When first expelled from a volcanic vent, it is a liquid at temperatures from 700 >°C to 1,200 >°C (1,300 >°F to 2,200 >°F.) Although _____ is quite viscous, with about 100,000 times the viscosity of water, it can flow great distances before cooling and solidifying, because of both its thixotropic and shear thinning properties.

a. Pit crater
b. Volcanic ash
c. Lava
d. Supervolcano

36. _____ are a distinctive type of rock often found in primordial sedimentary rocks. The structures consist of repeated thin layers of iron oxides, either magnetite or hematite, alternating with bands of iron-poor shale and chert. Some of the oldest known rock formations, formed around three thousand million years before present, include banded iron layers, and the banded layers are a common feature in sediments for much of the Earth's early history.

a. Superficial deposits
b. Jasperoid
c. Mudstone
d. Banded Iron Formations

37. In chemistry, a _____ is a salt or ester of carbonic acid.

To test for the presence of the _____ anion in a salt, the addition of dilute mineral acid (e.g. hydrochloric acid) will yield carbon dioxide gas.

_____-containing salts are industrially and mineralogically ubiquitous.

a. Carbonate
b. 1509 Istanbul earthquake
c. 1703 Genroku earthquake
d. 1700 Cascadia earthquake

38. _____ is a fine-grained silica-rich microcrystalline, cryptocrystalline or microfibrous sedimentary rock that may contain small fossils. It varies greatly in color (from white to black), but most often manifests as gray, brown, grayish brown and light green to rusty red; its color is an expression of trace elements present in the rock, and both red and green are most often related to traces of iron (in its oxidized and reduced forms respectively.)

_____ occurs as oval to irregular nodules in greensand, limestone, chalk, and dolostone formations as a replacement mineral, where it is formed as a result of some type of diagenesis.

a. 1703 Genroku earthquake
b. 1700 Cascadia earthquake
c. 1509 Istanbul earthquake
d. Chert

39. A _____ is a rock consisting of individual stones that have become cemented together. They are sedimentary rocks consisting of rounded fragments and are thus differentiated from breccias, which consist of angular clasts. Both conglomerates and breccias are characterized by clasts larger than sand (>2 mm).
   a. Keystone
   b. Conglomerate
   c. Porcellanite
   d. Pelagic sediments

40. _____ is the geological process by which material is added to a landform or land mass. Fluids such as wind and water, as well as sediment gravity flows, transport previously eroded sediment, which, at the loss of enough kinetic energy in the fluid, is deposited, building up layers of sediment.

    _____ occurs when the forces responsible for sediment transportation are no longer sufficient to overcome the forces of particle weight and friction, which resist motion.

   a. Diagenesis
   b. Downcutting
   c. Headward erosion
   d. Deposition

41. A _____ is a compound containing an anion in which one or more central silicon atoms are surrounded by electronegative ligands. This definition is broad enough to include species such as hexafluorosilicate ('fluorosilicate'), $[SiF_6]^{2-}$, but the _____ species that are encountered most often consist of silicon with oxygen as the ligand. _____ anions, with a negative net electrical charge, must have that charge balanced by other cations to make an electrically neutral compound.
   a. 1700 Cascadia earthquake
   b. 1509 Istanbul earthquake
   c. 1703 Genroku earthquake
   d. Silicate

42. The _____ make up the largest and most important class of rock-forming minerals, comprising approximately 90 percent of the crust of the Earth. They are classified based on the structure of their silicate group. _____ all contain silicon and oxygen.
   a. Mineraloid
   b. 1700 Cascadia earthquake
   c. Silicate minerals
   d. 1509 Istanbul earthquake

43. _____ are flat or very gently sloping areas of the deep ocean basin floor. They are among the Earth's flattest and smoothest regions and the least explored. _____ cover approximately 40% of the ocean floor and reach depths between 2,200 and 5,500 m (7,200 and 18,000 ft.)
   a. Eutrophication
   b. Intertidal
   c. AASHTO Soil Classification System
   d. Abyssal plains

44. _____ defines an important group of generally dark-colored rock-forming inosilicate minerals, composed of double chain SiO_4 tetrahedra, linked at the vertices and generally containing ions of iron and/or magnesium in their structures. They crystallize into two crystal systems, monoclinic and orthorhombic. In chemical composition and general characteristics they are similar to the pyroxenes. They are minerals of either igneous or metamorphic origin; in the former case occurring as constituents (hornblende) of igneous rocks, such as granite, diorite, andesite and others. Those of metamorphic origin include examples such as those developed in limestones by contact metamorphism (tremolite) and those formed by the alteration of other ferromagnesian minerals (hornblende).

Chapter 19. Precambrian Earth and Life History

a. AL 129-1
c. AASHTO Soil Classification System
b. AL 333
d. Amphibole

45. A _____ or dyke in geology is a type of sheet intrusion referring to any geologic body that cuts discordantly across

- planar wall rock structures, such as bedding or foliation
- massive rock formations, like igneous/magmatic intrusions and salt diapirs.

They can therefore be either intrusive or sedimentary in origin.

An intrusive _____ is an igneous body with a very high aspect ratio, which means that its thickness is usually much smaller than the other two dimensions. Thickness can vary from sub-centimeter scale to many meters and the lateral dimensions can extend over many kilometers. A _____ is an intrusion into an opening cross-cutting fissure, shouldering aside other pre-existing layers or bodies of rock; this implies that a _____ is always younger than the rocks that contain it.

a. Pneumatolysis
c. Schmidt hammer
b. Dike
d. Geopetal

46. A _____ is a special-purpose map made to show geological features.

The stratigraphic contour lines are drawn on the surface of a selected deep stratum, so that they can show the topographic trends of the strata under the ground. It is not always possible to properly show this when the strata are extremely fractured, mixed, in some discontinuities, or where they are otherwise disturbed.

a. 1703 Genroku earthquake
c. 1509 Istanbul earthquake
b. 1700 Cascadia earthquake
d. Geologic map

47. _____, like all craton land, was created as continents moved about the surface of the Earth, bumping into other continents and drifting away.

Many times in its past, _____ has been a separate continent as it is now in the form of North America. During other times in its past, _____ has been part of a supercontinent.

a. North China craton
c. South China
b. Congo craton
d. Laurentia

48. A _____ in geology is an intrusive igneous rock body that crystallized from a magma slowly cooling below the surface of the Earth. Plutons include batholiths, dikes, sills, laccoliths, lopoliths, and other igneous bodies. In practice, '_____' usually refers to a distinctive mass of igneous rock, typically kilometers in dimension, without a tabular shape like those of dikes and sills.

a. Vesicular texture
c. Pluton
b. Metamorphic zone
d. Migmatite

Chapter 19. Precambrian Earth and Life History

49. The _____ is a Canadian geological formation located in the Northwest Territories. This craton is approximately 300,000 square kilometres (120,000 sq mi) in size and forms part of the Canadian Shield. It is dominated by ca. 2.73-2.63 Ga greenstones and turbidite sequences and ca. 2.72-2.58 Ga plutonic rock, with large parts of the craton underlain by older gneiss and granitoid units.

- a. Slave craton
- b. 1509 Istanbul earthquake
- c. 1700 Cascadia earthquake
- d. 1703 Genroku earthquake

50. The _____ forms the core of both the North American continent and the Canadian Shield. It extends from Quebec in the east to eastern Manitoba in the west. The western margin extends from northern Minnesota through eastern Manitoba to northwestern Ontario.

The formation of the _____ is best explained within the context of 2.72-2.68 Ga accretion of small continental plates and trapped oceanic terranes in a tectonic regime resembling that of the rapidly changing southwestern Pacific Ocean. The craton is made up of a collage of small continental fragments of Mesoarchean age and Neoarchean oceanic plates and tracts of oceanic crust that consists of the following domains: Northern Superior, North Caribou, Winnipeg River, Marmion, Minnesota River Valley, Opatica, and Goudalie.

- a. Kalahari craton
- b. Wyoming craton
- c. Superior craton
- d. Sebakwe proto-craton

51. _____ is one of the three main rock types (the others being sedimentary and metamorphic rock.) _____ is formed by magma (molten rock) being cooled and becoming solid. They may form with or without crystallization, either below the surface as intrusive (plutonic) rocks or on the surface as extrusive (volcanic) rocks. They make up approximately 95% of the upper part of the Earth's crust, but their great abundance is hidden on the Earth's surface by a relatively thin but widespread layer of sedimentary and metamorphic rocks.

- a. AASHTO Soil Classification System
- b. AL 129-1
- c. AL 333
- d. Igneous rock

52. The _____ is the zone of the ocean floor that separates the thin oceanic crust from thick continental crust. Continental margins constitute about 28% of the oceanic area.

The transition from continental to oceanic crust commonly occurs within the outer part of the margin, called continental rise.

- a. Continental margin
- b. Longshore drift
- c. 1509 Istanbul earthquake
- d. Cuspate forelands

53. The _____ is the earliest of three geologic eras of the Phanerozoic eon. The _____ spanned from roughly 542 to 251 million years ago (ICS, 2004), and is subdivided into six geologic periods; from oldest to youngest they are: the Cambrian, Ordovician, Silurian, Devonian, Carboniferous, and Permian.

The _____ covers the time from the first appearance of abundant, soft-shelled fossils to the time when the continents were beginning to be dominated by large, relatively sophisticated reptiles and modern plants. The lower (oldest) boundary was classically set at the first appearance of creatures known as trilobites and archeocyathids.

Chapter 19. Precambrian Earth and Life History

   a. Paleozoic
   b. 1700 Cascadia earthquake
   c. 1703 Genroku earthquake
   d. 1509 Istanbul earthquake

54. In geology, a _____ is a place where the Earth's crust and lithosphere are being pulled apart and is an example of extensional tectonics.

Typical _____ features are a central linear downdropped fault segment, called a graben, with parallel normal faulting and _____-flank uplifts on either side forming a _____ valley, where the _____ remains above sea level. The axis of the _____ area commonly contains volcanic rocks and active volcanism is a part of many, but not all active _____ systems.

   a. 1703 Genroku earthquake
   b. Rift
   c. 1509 Istanbul earthquake
   d. 1700 Cascadia earthquake

55. The _____, was the major mountain building event that formed the Precambrian Canadian Shield, the North American craton, and the forging of the initial North American continent. It is the largest Paleoproterozoic orogenic belt in the world. It consists of a network of belts that were formed by Proterozoic crustal accretion and the collision of pre-existing Archean continents.
   a. Laramide orogeny
   b. Pan-African orogeny
   c. Trans-Hudson orogeny
   d. Sevier orogeny

56. The _____ is located in the west-central United States and west-central Canada -- more specifically, in Montana, Wyoming, southern Alberta, southern Saskatchewan, and parts of northern Utah. Also called the Wyoming province, it is the initial core of the continental crust of North America.

The _____ was sutured together with the Superior and Hearne-Rae cratons in the mountain-building episode that created the Trans-Hudson Suture Zone to form the core of North America (Laurentia.).

   a. Kalahari craton
   b. Craton
   c. Superior craton
   d. Wyoming craton

57. The _____ Era, is the most recent of the three classic geological eras and covers the period from 65.5 million years ago to the present. It is marked by the Cretaceous-Tertiary extinction event at the end of the Cretaceous that saw the demise of the last non-avian dinosaurs and the end of the Mesozoic Era. The _____ era is ongoing.
   a. Cenozoic
   b. 1509 Istanbul earthquake
   c. 1703 Genroku earthquake
   d. 1700 Cascadia earthquake

58. _____ is an igneous, volcanic (extrusive) rock, of felsic (silicon-rich) composition. It may have any texture from aphanitic to porphyritic. The mineral assemblage is usually quartz, alkali feldspar and plagioclase. Biotite and hornblende are common accessory minerals.

_____ can be considered as the extrusive equivalent to the plutonic granite rock, and consequently, outcroppings of it often bear a resemblance to granite. Due to their high content of silica and low iron and magnesium contents, _____ melts are highly polymerized and form highly viscous lavas.

a. Rhyolite
b. 1700 Cascadia earthquake
c. 1509 Istanbul earthquake
d. 1703 Genroku earthquake

59. The _____ was the earliest of the six cratonic sequences that have occurred during the Phanerozoic (followed by the Tippecanoe, Kaskaskia, Absaroka, Zu>ñi, and Tejas.) It dates from the late Proterozoic through the early Ordovician, though the marine transgression did not begin in earnest until the middle Cambrian.

At its peak, most of North America was covered by the shallow Sauk Sea, save for parts of the Canadian Shield and the islands of the Transcontinental Arch.

a. 1509 Istanbul earthquake
b. Sauk sequence
c. 1700 Cascadia earthquake
d. Tippecanoe sequence

60. In geology, a _____ is a landmass comprising more than one continental core, or craton. The assembly of cratons and accreted terranes that form Eurasia qualifies as a _____ today.

Most commonly, paleogeographers employ the term _____ to refer to a single landmass consisting of all the modern continents.

a. Supercontinent
b. 1509 Istanbul earthquake
c. 1700 Cascadia earthquake
d. 1703 Genroku earthquake

61. An _____ is a fan-shaped deposit formed where a fast flowing stream flattens, slows, and spreads typically at the exit of a canyon onto a flatter plain. A convergence of neighboring fans into a single apron of deposits against a slope is called a bajada, or compound _____.

a. AL 333
b. AASHTO Soil Classification System
c. Alluvial fan
d. AL 129-1

62. _____, is a phylum of bacteria that obtain their energy through photosynthesis. The name '_____' comes from the color of the bacteria . They are a significant component of the marine nitrogen cycle and an important primary producer in many areas of the ocean, but are also found in habitats other than the marine environment; in particular _____ are known to occur in both freshwater, hypersaline inland lakes and in arid areas where they are a major component of biological soil crusts.

Stromatolites of fossilized oxygen-producing _____ have been found from 2.8 billion years ago. The ability of _____ to perform oxygenic photosynthesis is thought to have converted the early reducing atmosphere into an oxidizing one, which dramatically changed the composition of life forms on Earth by provoking an explosion of biodiversity and leading to the near-extinction of oxygen-intolerant organisms.

a. 1703 Genroku earthquake
b. 1509 Istanbul earthquake
c. 1700 Cascadia earthquake
d. Cyanobacteria

63. The _____ was a series of major Neoproterozoic orogenic events (mountain building) which related to the formation of the supercontinents Gondwana and Pannotia about 900 million years ago.

a. Nevadan orogeny
b. Kaikoura Orogeny
c. Laramide orogeny
d. Pan-African orogeny

64. _____ was the supercontinent that is theorized to have existed during the Paleozoic and Mesozoic eras about 250 million years ago, before the component continents were separated into their current configuration.

The name was first used by the German originator of the continental drift theory, Alfred Wegener, in the 1920 edition of his book The Origin of Continents and Oceans, in which a postulated supercontinent _____ played a key role.

The single enormous ocean which surrounded Pangaea is known as Panthalassa.

a. 1700 Cascadia earthquake
b. 1509 Istanbul earthquake
c. 1703 Genroku earthquake
d. Pangea

65. The _____ Eon is the current eon in the geologic timescale, and the one during which abundant animal life has existed. It covers roughly 545 million years and goes back to the time when diverse hard-shelled animals first appeared.

a. 1509 Istanbul earthquake
b. 1700 Cascadia earthquake
c. 1703 Genroku earthquake
d. Phanerozoic

66. In geology, _____ are sedimentary structures that indicate agitation by water (current or waves) or wind. _____ formed by water consist of two basic types:

1. Current _____ are asymmetrical in profile, with a gentle up-current slope and a steeper down-current slope. The down-current slope depends on the shape of the sediment, with 33>° being typical.
2. Wave-formed _____ have a symmetrical, almost sinusoidal profile; they indicate an environment with weak currents where water motion is dominated by wave oscillations.

Ripples will not form in sediment larger than course sand.

a. 1509 Istanbul earthquake
b. Ripple marks
c. 1700 Cascadia earthquake
d. 1703 Genroku earthquake

67. In geology, _____ is the name of a supercontinent, a continent which contained most or all of Earth's landmass. According to plate tectonic reconstructions, _____ existed between 1100 and 750 million years ago, in the Neoproterozoic era.

In contrast with Pangaea, the last supercontinent about 300 million years ago, little is known yet about the exact configuration and geodynamic history of _____.

a. 1700 Cascadia earthquake
b. Laurasia
c. 1509 Istanbul earthquake
d. Rodinia

68. _____ is a sedimentary rock composed mainly of sand-size mineral or rock grains. Most _____ is composed of quartz and/or feldspar because these are the most common minerals in the Earth's crust. Like sand, _____ may be any color, but the most common colors are tan, brown, yellow, red, gray and white.

Chapter 19. Precambrian Earth and Life History

| a. Porcellanite | b. Dolostone |
| c. Lithification | d. Sandstone |

69. _____ are layered accretionary structures formed in shallow water by the trapping, binding and cementation of sedimentary grains by biofilms of microorganisms, especially cyanobacteria (commonly known as blue-green algae.)

A variety of stromatolite morphologies exist including conical, stratiform, branching, domal, and columnar types. _____ occur widely in the fossil record of the Precambrian, but are rare today.

| a. 1700 Cascadia earthquake | b. Stromatolites |
| c. 1703 Genroku earthquake | d. 1509 Istanbul earthquake |

70. A _____ is a large, slow-moving mass of ice, formed from compacted layers of snow, that slowly deforms and flows in response to gravity and high pressure.

_____ ice is the largest reservoir of fresh water on Earth, and second only to oceans as the largest reservoir of total water.

| a. Glacier | b. Keeling Curve |
| c. Pacific Decadal Oscillation | d. Little Ice Age |

71. In geology a _____ is the smallest division of a geologic formation or stratigraphic rock series marked by well-defined divisional planes (bedding planes) separating it from layers above and below. A _____ is the smallest lithostratigraphic unit, usually ranging in thickness from a centimeter to several meters and distinguishable from beds above and below it. Beds can be differentiated in various ways, including rock or mineral type and particle size.

| a. Sequence stratigraphy | b. Biozones |
| c. Bed | d. Cyclostratigraphy |

72. The _____ was a cratonic sequence that extended from the end of the Mississippian through the Permian periods. It is the unconformity between this sequence and the preceding Kaskaskia that divides the Carboniferous into the Mississippian and Pennsylvanian periods in North America.

Like the Kaskaskia sequence, Absaroka sedimentary deposits were dominated by detrital or siliciclastic rocks.

| a. AASHTO Soil Classification System | b. AL 129-1 |
| c. Absaroka sequence | d. AL 333 |

73. _____ is water located beneath the ground surface in soil pore spaces and in the fractures of lithologic formations. A unit of rock or an unconsolidated deposit is called an aquifer when it can yield a usable quantity of water. The depth at which soil pore spaces or fractures and voids in rock become completely saturated with water is called the water table.

| a. Groundwater | b. Depression focused recharge |
| c. 1700 Cascadia earthquake | d. 1509 Istanbul earthquake |

74. The _____ is a geologic fault structure of the Rocky Mountains within Glacier National Park in Montana, USA and Waterton Lakes National Park in Alberta, Canada, as well as into Lewis and Clark National Forest. It provides scientific insight into geologic processes happening in other parts of the world, like the Andes and the Himalaya Mountains. Scientific study of this region is practical because the original rock characteristics were well-preserved and recently sculptured by glaciers.
   a. Lewis overthrust
   b. 1700 Cascadia earthquake
   c. 1703 Genroku earthquake
   d. 1509 Istanbul earthquake

75. The _____ is the first geological period of the Phanerozoic eon, lasting from 542 ± 0.3 million years ago to 488.3 ± 1.7 million years ago (ICS, 2004); it is succeeded by the Ordovician. Its subdivisions, and indeed its base, are somewhat in flux. The period was established by Adam Sedgwick, who named it after Cambria, the classical name for Wales, where Britain's _____ rocks are best exposed.
   a. 1703 Genroku earthquake
   b. 1509 Istanbul earthquake
   c. 1700 Cascadia earthquake
   d. Cambrian

76. _____ are the preserved remains or traces of animals, plants, and other organisms from the remote past. The totality of _____, both discovered and undiscovered, and their placement in fossiliferous rock formations and sedimentary layers (strata) is known as the fossil record. The study of _____ across geological time, how they were formed, and the evolutionary relationships between taxa (phylogeny) are some of the most important functions of the science of paleontology.
   a. 1700 Cascadia earthquake
   b. 1703 Genroku earthquake
   c. 1509 Istanbul earthquake
   d. Fossils

77. An _____ is a small organic fossil, present from approximately >2,500 million years ago to the present. Their diversity reflects major ecological events such as the appearance of predation and the Cambrian explosion.

In general, any small, non-acid soluble (i.e. non-carbonate, non-siliceous) organic structure that can not otherwise be accounted for is classified as an _____.

   a. AASHTO Soil Classification System
   b. AL 129-1
   c. AL 333
   d. Acritarch

78. The _____ Period is the last geological period of the Neoproterozoic Era and of the Proterozoic Eon, immediately preceding the Cambrian Period, the first period of the Paleozoic Era and of the Phanerozoic Eon. Its status as an official geological period was ratified in 2004 by the International Union of Geological Sciences (IUGS), making it the first new geological period declared in 120 years. The type section is in the Flinders Ranges in South Australia.
   a. AL 333
   b. AL 129-1
   c. AASHTO Soil Classification System
   d. Ediacaran

79. In geology, _____ is transported rock debris overlying the solid bedrock. The term is also sometimes refers to organic debris so-transported. In the largest sense, it refers to the material left behind by retreating continental glaciers.
   a. Patterned ground
   b. Platform cover
   c. Geodiversity
   d. Drift

Chapter 19. Precambrian Earth and Life History

80. An _____ is a type of rock that contains minerals such as gemstones and metals that can be extracted through mining and refined for use. Samples of _____ in the form of exceptionally beautiful crystals, exotic layering visible when sectioned or polished or metallic presentations such as large nuggets or crystalline formations of metals such as gold or copper may command a value far beyond their value as mere _____ or raw metal for subsequent reduction to utilitarian purposes.

The grade or concentration of an _____ mineral, or metal, as well as its form of occurrence, will directly affect the costs associated with mining the _____.

   a. AL 129-1
   c. Ore
   b. AASHTO Soil Classification System
   d. Ore genesis

81. _____ is a very coarse-grained igneous rock that has a grain size of 20 mm or more; such rocks are referred to as pegmatitic.

Most _____ is composed of quartz, feldspar and mica; in essence a 'granite'. Rarer 'intermediate' and 'mafic' _____ containing amphibole, Ca-plagioclase feldspar, pyroxene and other minerals are known, found in recrystallised zones and apophyses associated with large layered intrusions.

   a. 1703 Genroku earthquake
   c. 1700 Cascadia earthquake
   b. 1509 Istanbul earthquake
   d. Pegmatite

Chapter 20. Paleozoic Earth History

1. The _____ or Cambrian radiation was the seemingly rapid appearance of most major groups of complex animals around 530 million years ago, as evidenced by the fossil record. This was accompanied by a major diversification of other organisms, including animals, phytoplankton, and calcimicrobes. Before about 580 million years ago, most organisms were simple, composed of individual cells occasionally organized into colonies.

   a. Romer's Gap
   b. Cambrian explosion
   c. Conodont Alteration Index
   d. Labyrinthodont

2. The _____ is the zone of the ocean floor that separates the thin oceanic crust from thick continental crust. Continental margins constitute about 28% of the oceanic area.

The transition from continental to oceanic crust commonly occurs within the outer part of the margin, called continental rise.

   a. Continental margin
   b. Longshore drift
   c. 1509 Istanbul earthquake
   d. Cuspate forelands

3. The _____ is the extended perimeter of each continent and associated coastal plain, and was part of the continent during the glacial periods, but is undersea during interglacial periods such as the current epoch by relatively shallow seas (known as shelf seas) and gulfs.

The continental rise is below the slope, but landward of the abyssal plains. Its gradient is intermediate between the slope and the shelf, on the order of 0.5-1°.

   a. 1700 Cascadia earthquake
   b. 1703 Genroku earthquake
   c. 1509 Istanbul earthquake
   d. Continental shelf

4. An _____ is a large shallow sea that either extends far into a continent, such as the Persian Gulf, or overlies a large part of a continent.

They are usually associated with the marine transgressions of the early Cenozoic era and may be semi-cyclic--during eras of glacial recession given a period of low mountains coupled with a warming under the influence of plate tectonics. They can be warm or cold; indeed, several were present at the end of the last Ice Age, when sea levels rose more rapidly than some areas could isostatically adjust.

   a. AASHTO Soil Classification System
   b. Epeiric sea
   c. AL 333
   d. AL 129-1

5. A _____ is a special-purpose map made to show geological features.

The stratigraphic contour lines are drawn on the surface of a selected deep stratum, so that they can show the topographic trends of the strata under the ground. It is not always possible to properly show this when the strata are extremely fractured, mixed, in some discontinuities, or where they are otherwise disturbed.

   a. Geologic map
   b. 1509 Istanbul earthquake
   c. 1703 Genroku earthquake
   d. 1700 Cascadia earthquake

Chapter 20. Paleozoic Earth History

6. The _____ is the earliest of three geologic eras of the Phanerozoic eon. The _____ spanned from roughly 542 to 251 million years ago (ICS, 2004), and is subdivided into six geologic periods; from oldest to youngest they are: the Cambrian, Ordovician, Silurian, Devonian, Carboniferous, and Permian.

The _____ covers the time from the first appearance of abundant, soft-shelled fossils to the time when the continents were beginning to be dominated by large, relatively sophisticated reptiles and modern plants. The lower (oldest) boundary was classically set at the first appearance of creatures known as trilobites and archeocyathids.

   a. 1700 Cascadia earthquake
   c. 1703 Genroku earthquake
   b. 1509 Istanbul earthquake
   d. Paleozoic

7. The _____ Eon is the current eon in the geologic timescale, and the one during which abundant animal life has existed. It covers roughly 545 million years and goes back to the time when diverse hard-shelled animals first appeared.
   a. 1700 Cascadia earthquake
   c. 1703 Genroku earthquake
   b. 1509 Istanbul earthquake
   d. Phanerozoic

8. In geology, a _____ is a continental area covered by relatively flat or gently tilted, mainly sedimentary strata, which overlie a basement of consolidated igneous or metamorphic rocks of an earlier deformation. They as well as, shields and the basement rocks together constitute cratons.

It is also common practice to use the term _____ as a very general term for a sequence of shallow water carbonate _____.

   a. Fault
   c. Cleavage
   b. Platform
   d. Streak

9. The _____ is an informal name for the supereon comprising the eons of the geologic timescale that came before the current Phanerozoic eon. It spans from the formation of Earth around 4500 Mya (million years ago) to the evolution of abundant macroscopic hard-shelled animals, which marked the beginning of the Cambrian, the first period of the first era of the Phanerozoic eon, some 542 Mya. It is named after the Roman name for Wales - Cambria - where rocks from this age were first studied.
   a. Precambrian
   c. 1509 Istanbul earthquake
   b. 1700 Cascadia earthquake
   d. 1703 Genroku earthquake

10. The _____ is a geological eon representing a period before the first abundant complex life on Earth. The _____ extended from 2500 Ma to 542.0 >± 1.0 Ma (million years ago), and is the most recent part of the old, informally named 'e;Precambrian'e; time.

The Proterozoic consists of 3 geologic eras, from oldest to youngest:

- Paleoproterozoic
- Mesoproterozoic
- Neoproterozoic

Chapter 20. Paleozoic Earth History

The well-identified events were:

- The transition to an oxygenated atmosphere during the Mesoproterozoic.
- Several glaciations, including the hypothesized Snowball Earth during the Cryogenian period in the late Neoproterozoic.
- The Ediacaran Period (635 to 542 Ma) which is characterized by the evolution of abundant soft-bodied multicellular organisms.

The geoloic record of the Proterozoic is much better than that for the preceding Archean. In contrast to the deep-water deposits of the Archean, the Proterozoic features many strata that were laid down in extensive shallow epicontinental seas; furthermore, many of these rocks are less metamorphosed than Archean-age ones, and plenty are unaltered.

a. 1700 Cascadia earthquake
b. 1509 Istanbul earthquake
c. 1703 Genroku earthquake
d. Proterozoic Eon

11. A _____ is generally a large area of exposed Precambrian crystalline igneous and high-grade metamorphic rocks that form tectonically stable areas. In all cases, the age of these rocks is greater than 570 million years and sometimes dates back 2 to 3.5 billion years. They have been little affected by tectonic events following the end of the Precambrian Era, and are relatively flat regions where mountain building, faulting, and other tectonic processes are greatly diminished compared with the activity that occurs at the margins of the shields and the boundaries between tectonic plates.

a. 1700 Cascadia earthquake
b. Shield
c. 1703 Genroku earthquake
d. 1509 Istanbul earthquake

12. In geology, a _____ is a landmass comprising more than one continental core, or craton. The assembly of cratons and accreted terranes that form Eurasia qualifies as a _____ today.

Most commonly, paleogeographers employ the term _____ to refer to a single landmass consisting of all the modern continents.

a. 1700 Cascadia earthquake
b. 1703 Genroku earthquake
c. 1509 Istanbul earthquake
d. Supercontinent

13. _____, is the process of coastal sediments returning to the visible portion of a beach or foreshore following a submersion event. A sustainable beach or foreshore often goes through a cycle of submersion during rough weather then _____ during calmer periods. If a coastline is not in a healthy sustainable condition, then erosion can be more serious and _____ does not fully restore the original volume of the visible beach or foreshore leading to permanent beach or foreshore loss.

a. Accretion
b. AASHTO Soil Classification System
c. AL 333
d. AL 129-1

14. A _____ is a large, slow-moving mass of ice, formed from compacted layers of snow, that slowly deforms and flows in response to gravity and high pressure.

_____ ice is the largest reservoir of fresh water on Earth, and second only to oceans as the largest reservoir of total water.

a. Keeling Curve
b. Pacific Decadal Oscillation
c. Little Ice Age
d. Glacier

15. _____ is a name applied by geologists to a late-Proterozoic, early-Palaeozoic continent that now includes the East European craton of northwestern Eurasia. _____ was created as an entity not earlier than 1.8 billion years ago. Before this time, the three segments/continents that now comprise the East European craton were in different places on the globe. _____ existed on a tectonic plate called the Baltic Plate.

a. Cimmeria
b. South China
c. Congo craton
d. Baltica

16. The _____ Era, is the most recent of the three classic geological eras and covers the period from 65.5 million years ago to the present. It is marked by the Cretaceous-Tertiary extinction event at the end of the Cretaceous that saw the demise of the last non-avian dinosaurs and the end of the Mesozoic Era. The _____ era is ongoing.

a. 1703 Genroku earthquake
b. 1509 Istanbul earthquake
c. 1700 Cascadia earthquake
d. Cenozoic

17. _____ is the use of the principles of geology to reconstruct and understand the history of the Earth. It focuses on geologic processes that change the Earth's surface and subsurface; and the use of stratigraphy, structural geology and paleontology to tell the sequence of these events. It also focuses on the evolution of plants and animals during different time periods in the geological timescale.

a. Historical geology
b. Strike-slip faults
c. Rockall
d. Valley glaciers

18. _____ is a small continental region in the interior of Asia. It consists of that area north and east of the Aral Sea, south of the Siberian craton and west of the Altai Mountains and Lake Balkhash. Politically, it comprises most of Kazakhstan and has a total area of around 1.3 million km^2.

It is believed that present-day _____ is chiefly a collage of early Paleozoic volcanic island arcs and some small continental terranes. These were joined together during the Ordovician to form what was at the time an isolated continent of its own.

a. 1700 Cascadia earthquake
b. Kazakhstania
c. 1509 Istanbul earthquake
d. 1703 Genroku earthquake

19. _____, like all craton land, was created as continents moved about the surface of the Earth, bumping into other continents and drifting away.

Many times in its past, _____ has been a separate continent as it is now in the form of North America. During other times in its past, _____ has been part of a supercontinent.

Chapter 20. Paleozoic Earth History

    a. North China craton
    b. Congo craton
    c. South China
    d. Laurentia

20. The _____ Era is one of three geologic eras of the Phanerozoic eon. The division of time into eras dates back to Giovanni Arduino, in the 18th century, although his original name for the era now called the '_____' was 'Secondary' (making the modern era the 'Tertiary'.)

The _____ was a time of tectonic, climatic and evolutionary activity. The continents gradually shifted from a state of connectedness into their present configuration; the drifting provided for speciation and other important evolutionary developments.

    a. Mesozoic
    b. 1703 Genroku earthquake
    c. 1700 Cascadia earthquake
    d. 1509 Istanbul earthquake

21. _____, partially synonymous with microcontinents, are fragments of continents thought to have been broken off from the main continental mass forming distinct islands, possibly several hundred kilometers from their place of origin. All continents are fragments; the terms 'continental fragment' and 'microcontinent' are restricted to those smaller than Sahul (Australia-New Guinea.) Other than perhaps Zealandia, they are not known to contain a craton or fragment of a craton.

    a. Continental crustal fragments
    b. 1509 Istanbul earthquake
    c. 1700 Cascadia earthquake
    d. 1703 Genroku earthquake

22. _____ was the supercontinent that is theorized to have existed during the Paleozoic and Mesozoic eras about 250 million years ago, before the component continents were separated into their current configuration.

The name was first used by the German originator of the continental drift theory, Alfred Wegener, in the 1920 edition of his book The Origin of Continents and Oceans , in which a postulated supercontinent _____ played a key role.

The single enormous ocean which surrounded Pangaea is known as Panthalassa.

    a. Pangea
    b. 1700 Cascadia earthquake
    c. 1703 Genroku earthquake
    d. 1509 Istanbul earthquake

23. In geology a _____ is the smallest division of a geologic formation or stratigraphic rock series marked by well-defined divisional planes (bedding planes) separating it from layers above and below. A _____ is the smallest lithostratigraphic unit, usually ranging in thickness from a centimeter to several meters and distinguishable from beds above and below it. Beds can be differentiated in various ways, including rock or mineral type and particle size.

    a. Bed
    b. Cyclostratigraphy
    c. Biozones
    d. Sequence stratigraphy

24. A _____ is a mountain rising from the ocean seafloor that does not reach to the water's surface (sea level), and thus is not an island. These are typically formed from extinct volcanoes, that rise abruptly and are usually found rising from a seafloor of 1,000-4,000 meters depth. They are defined by oceanographers as independent features that rise to at least 1,000 meters above the seafloor.

a. 1703 Genroku earthquake
c. 1509 Istanbul earthquake
b. Seamount
d. 1700 Cascadia earthquake

25. The _____ is the rigid outermost shell of a rocky planet.

In the Earth, the _____ includes the crust and the uppermost mantle, which constitute the hard and rigid outer layer of the planet. The _____ is underlain by the asthenosphere, the weaker, hotter, and deeper part of the upper mantle.

a. Juan de Fuca Ridge
c. Gorda Ridge
b. Lithosphere
d. Continental drift

26. The _____ is a middle Paleozoic mountain building event (orogeny), especially in the northern Appalachians, between New York and Newfoundland. The _____ most greatly affected the Northern Appalachian region (New England northeastward into the Gasp>é region of Canada.) The _____ should not be regarded as a single tectonic event, but rather as an orogenic era.
a. Orogenesis
c. Alice Springs Orogeny
b. Acadian orogeny
d. Alpine orogeny

27. The _____ is a mountain-building episode that extensively deformed Paleozoic rocks of the Great Basin in Nevada and western Utah during Late Devonian and Early Mississippian time. In the late Devonian, the Antler volcanic island arc terrane collided with was then the west coast of North America in the vicinity of today's border between Utah and Nevada.
a. Orogeny
c. Alleghenian orogeny
b. Orogenesis
d. Antler orogeny

28. The _____ is the first geological period of the Phanerozoic eon, lasting from 542 ± 0.3 million years ago to 488.3 ± 1.7 million years ago (ICS, 2004); it is succeeded by the Ordovician. Its subdivisions, and indeed its base, are somewhat in flux. The period was established by Adam Sedgwick, who named it after Cambria, the classical name for Wales, where Britain's _____ rocks are best exposed.
a. 1700 Cascadia earthquake
c. 1703 Genroku earthquake
b. 1509 Istanbul earthquake
d. Cambrian

29. The _____ is a geologic period and system of the Paleozoic era spanning from >416 to 359.2 million years ago (ICS, 2004.).

During the _____ Period, which occurred in the Paleozoic era, the first fish evolved legsand started to walk on land as tetrapods around 365 Ma.

a. Xitun Formation
c. Devonian
b. 1509 Istanbul earthquake
d. Gogo Formation

30. The _____ was an ocean that existed in the Neoproterozoic and Paleozoic eras of the geologic timescale (between 600 and 400 million years ago.) The _____ was situated in the southern hemisphere, between the paleocontinents of Laurentia, Baltica and Avalonia. The ocean disappeared with the Caledonian, Taconic and Acadian orogenies, when these three continents joined to form one big landmass called Laurussia.

a. AL 129-1
b. AASHTO Soil Classification System
c. AL 333
d. Iapetus Ocean

31. The _____ was a cratonic sequence that began in the mid-Devonian, peaked early in the Mississippian, and ended by mid-Mississippian time. A major unconformity separates it from the lower Tippecanoe sequence.

The basal-that is, the lowest and oldest-units of the Kaskaskia consist of clean quartz sandstones eroded from the Appalachian orogenic belt to the east, the Ozark Dome in the center of the continent, and south from the Canadian Shield.

a. 1700 Cascadia earthquake
b. 1509 Istanbul earthquake
c. Sauk sequence
d. Kaskaskia sequence

32. _____ was a supercontinent that most recently existed as a part of the split of the Pangaean supercontinent in the late Mesozoic era. It included most of the landmasses which make up today's continents of the northern hemisphere, chiefly Laurentia (the name given to the North American craton), Baltica, Siberia, Kazakhstania, and the North China and East China cratons.

a. 1700 Cascadia earthquake
b. Rodinia
c. 1509 Istanbul earthquake
d. Laurasia

33. The _____ is a British rock formation of considerable importance to early paleontology. Hutton's angular unconformity at Siccar Point where 345 million year old Devonian _____ overlies 425 million year old Silurian greywacke.

The _____ describes a suite of rocks deposited in a variety of environments during the Devonian period but extending back into the late Silurian period and forward into the earliest part of the Carboniferous period.

a. AL 129-1
b. AL 333
c. Old Red Sandstone
d. AASHTO Soil Classification System

34. _____ is a sedimentary rock composed mainly of sand-size mineral or rock grains. Most _____ is composed of quartz and/or feldspar because these are the most common minerals in the Earth's crust. Like sand, _____ may be any color, but the most common colors are tan, brown, yellow, red, gray and white.

a. Lithification
b. Dolostone
c. Porcellanite
d. Sandstone

35. _____ is unsorted glacial sediment. Glacial drift is a general term for the coarsely graded and extremely heterogeneous sediments of glacial origin. Glacial _____ is that part of glacial drift which was deposited directly by the glacier. In cases where _____ has been indurated or lithified by subsequent burial into solid rock, it is known as the sedimentary rock tillite.

a. 1703 Genroku earthquake
b. 1700 Cascadia earthquake
c. Till
d. 1509 Istanbul earthquake

36. _____ are water-soluble mineral sediments that result from the evaporation of bodies of surficial water. _____ are considered sedimentary rocks.

Although all water bodies on the surface and in aquifers contain dissolved salts, the water must evaporate into the atmosphere for the minerals to precipitate.

a. AASHTO Soil Classification System
b. Evaporites
c. AL 333
d. AL 129-1

37. _____ refers to natural mountain building, and may be studied as a tectonic structural event, (b) as a geographical event, and (c) a chronological event. Orogenic events (a) cause distinctive structural phenomena and related tectonic activity, (b) affect certain regions of rocks and crust, and (c) happen within a specific period of time.
a. Orogeny
b. Antler orogeny
c. Alice Springs Orogeny
d. Orogenesis

38. The _____ or Appalachian orogeny is one of the geological mountain-forming events (orogeny) that formed the Appalachian Mountains and Allegheny Mountains. The term and spelling 'Alleghany Orogeny' (sic) originally proposed by H.P. Woodward (1957, 1958) is preferred usage. Approximately 350 million to 300 million years ago, in the Carboniferous period, the combined continents of Europe and Africa (Gondwana) collided with North America to form the supercontinent of Pangaea.
a. Antler orogeny
b. Alice Springs Orogeny
c. Alpine orogeny
d. Alleghenian orogeny

39. The _____, is a geologic eon before the Proterozoic and Paleoproterozoic, before 2.5 Ga (billion years ago, or 2,500 Ma.) Instead of being based on stratigraphy, this date is defined chronometrically. The lower boundary (starting point) has not been officially recognized by the International Commission on Stratigraphy, but it is usually set to 3.8 Ga, at the end of the Hadean eon.
a. AL 129-1
b. AL 333
c. AASHTO Soil Classification System
d. Archean

40. A _____ refers to a very large-scale lithostratigraphic sequence that covers a complete marine transgressive-regressive cycle across a craton. They are also known as 'megasequences', 'stratigraphic sequences', or simply 'sequences.'

They were first proposed by Lawrence Sloss in 1963; each one represents a time when epeiric seas deposited sediments across the craton, while the upper and lower edges of the sequence are bounded by craton-wide unconformities eroded when the seas receded.

These sequences may in part represent eustatic or global change in sea level; however, when the proper names are used they usually refer to the North American continent.

a. Paleoseismology
b. Tyrrell Sea
c. Cornbrash
d. Cratonic sequence

41. _____ was the vast global ocean that surrounded the supercontinent Pangaea, during the late Paleozoic and the early Mesozoic eras. It included the Pacific Ocean to the west and north and the Tethys Ocean to the southeast. It became the Pacific Ocean, following the closing of the Tethys basin and the breakup of Pangaea, which created the Atlantic, Arctic, and Indian Ocean basins.

a. Gorda Ridge
b. Forearc
c. Lithosphere
d. Panthalassa

42. An _____ is a confined aquifer containing groundwater that will flow upward through a well without the need for pumping. Water may even reach the ground surface if the natural pressure is high enough, in which case the well is called a flowing artesian well. An aquifer provides the water for an artesian well.
   a. AL 129-1
   b. AASHTO Soil Classification System
   c. AL 333
   d. Artesian aquifer

43. The _____ was the earliest of the six cratonic sequences that have occurred during the Phanerozoic (followed by the Tippecanoe, Kaskaskia, Absaroka, Zu>ñi, and Tejas.) It dates from the late Proterozoic through the early Ordovician, though the marine transgression did not begin in earnest until the middle Cambrian.

At its peak, most of North America was covered by the shallow Sauk Sea, save for parts of the Canadian Shield and the islands of the Transcontinental Arch.

   a. Sauk sequence
   b. 1700 Cascadia earthquake
   c. Tippecanoe sequence
   d. 1509 Istanbul earthquake

44. _____ is a relatively new branch of geology that attempts to link subdivide sedimentary deposits into unconformity bound units on a variety of scales and explain these stratal units in terms of control by relative sea-level changes and variations in sediment supply. The essence of the method is mapping of strata based on identification of surfaces which are assumed to represent time lines (e.g. subaerial unconformities, maximum flooding surfaces), and therefore placing stratigraphy in chronostratigraphic framework. _____ is sometimes a useful alternative to a lithostratigraphic approach, which emphasizes similarity of aspect of rocks rather than time significance, but suffers from issues of testibility and the non-uniqueness of many of the predicted stratal geometries.
   a. Cyclostratigraphy
   b. Biozones
   c. Sequence stratigraphy
   d. Bed

45. The _____ -- also called the Laurentian Plateau, or Bouclier Canadien -- is a massive geological shield covered by a thin layer of soil that forms the nucleus of the North American or Laurentia craton. It has a deep, common, joined bedrock region in eastern and central Canada and stretches North from the Great Lakes to the Arctic Ocean, covering over half of Canada; it also extends south into the northern reaches of the United States. Population is scarce, and industrial development is minimal, although the region has a large hydroelectric power potential.
   a. Yilgarn Craton
   b. Canadian Shield
   c. Gawler craton
   d. Grade

46. In chemistry, a _____ is a salt or ester of carbonic acid.

To test for the presence of the _____ anion in a salt, the addition of dilute mineral acid (e.g. hydrochloric acid) will yield carbon dioxide gas.

_____-containing salts are industrially and mineralogically ubiquitous.

a. Carbonate	b. 1703 Genroku earthquake
c. 1509 Istanbul earthquake	d. 1700 Cascadia earthquake

47. In geology, _____ refers to inclined sedimentary structures in a horizontal unit of rock. These tilted structures are deposits from bedforms such as ripples and dunes, and they indicate that the depositional environment contained a flowing fluid (typically, water or wind.) This is a case in geology when original depositional layering is tilted, and that the tilting is not a result of post-depositional deformation.

a. Platform cover	b. Schmidt hammer
c. Geomicrobiology	d. Cross-bedding

48. _____ is a geological term used to describe particles of rock derived from pre-existing rock through processes of weathering and erosion. Thesel particles can consist of lithic fragments (particles of recognisable rock), or of monomineralic fragments (mineral grains.) These particles are often transported through sedimentary processes into depositional systems such as riverbeds, lakes or the ocean forming sedimentary successions.

a. Medical geology	b. Perched coastline
c. Detritus	d. Geomechanics

49. In geology, _____ are sedimentary structures that indicate agitation by water (current or waves) or wind. _____ formed by water consist of two basic types:

1. Current _____ are asymmetrical in profile, with a gentle up-current slope and a steeper down-current slope. The down-current slope depends on the shape of the sediment, with 33>° being typical.
2. Wave-formed _____ have a symmetrical, almost sinusoidal profile; they indicate an environment with weak currents where water motion is dominated by wave oscillations.

Ripples will not form in sediment larger than course sand.

a. 1703 Genroku earthquake	b. 1700 Cascadia earthquake
c. 1509 Istanbul earthquake	d. Ripple marks

50. _____ are those structures formed during sediment deposition.

_____ such as cross bedding, graded bedding and ripple marks are utilized in stratigraphic studies to indicate original position of strata in geologically complex terranes.

There are two kinds of flow regimes, which at varying speeds and velocities produce different structures.

a. Sedimentary structures	b. 1703 Genroku earthquake
c. 1509 Istanbul earthquake	d. 1700 Cascadia earthquake

51. _____ are layered accretionary structures formed in shallow water by the trapping, binding and cementation of sedimentary grains by biofilms of microorganisms, especially cyanobacteria (commonly known as blue-green algae.)

A variety of stromatolite morphologies exist including conical, stratiform, branching, domal, and columnar types. _____ occur widely in the fossil record of the Precambrian, but are rare today.

Chapter 20. Paleozoic Earth History

a. Stromatolites
c. 1703 Genroku earthquake
b. 1509 Istanbul earthquake
d. 1700 Cascadia earthquake

52. _____ is any particulate matter that can be transported by fluid flow, and which eventually is deposited.

They are most often transported by water (fluvial processes) transported by wind (aeolian processes) and glaciers. Beach sands and river channel deposits are examples of fluvial transport and deposition, though _____ also often settles out of slow-moving or standing water in lakes and oceans.

a. Quicksand
c. Brickearth
b. Sediment
d. Bovey Beds

53. A marine _____ is a geologic event during which sea level rises relative to the land and the shoreline moves toward higher ground, resulting in flooding. They can be caused either by the land sinking or the ocean basins filling with water (or decreasing in capacity.) Transgresssions and regressions may be caused by tectonic events such as orogenies, severe climate change such as ice ages or isostatic adjustments following removal of ice or sediment load.

a. Wave pounding
c. Stoping
b. Transgression
d. Spheroidal weathering

54. _____ or dolomite rock is a sedimentary carbonate rock that contains a high percentage of the mineral dolomite. In old U.S.G.S. publications it was referred to as magnesian limestone. Most _____ formed as a magnesium replacement of limestone or lime mud prior to lithification.

a. Dolostone
c. Pelagic sediments
b. Lithification
d. Jasperoid

55. The _____ is a geologic period and system, the second of six of the Paleozoic era, and covers the time between 488.3>±1.7 to 443.7>±1.5 million years ago (ICS, 2004.) It follows the Cambrian period and is followed by the Silurian period. The _____ was defined by Charles Lapworth in 1879, to resolve a dispute between followers of Adam Sedgwick and Roderick Murchison, who were placing the same rock beds in northern Wales into the Cambrian and Silurian periods respectively.

a. AL 333
c. AL 129-1
b. AASHTO Soil Classification System
d. Ordovician

56. The _____ was the cratonic sequence--that is, the marine transgression--that followed the Sauk sequence; it extended from roughly the middle Ordovician to the early Devonian.

After the regression of the Sauk Sea early in the Ordovician, the exposed craton for a time underwent vigorous erosion, due to being located in a tropical climate; indeed, at this point in the Phanerozoic the North American continent roughly straddled the equator.

The Tippecanoe transgression ended this period of erosion, beginning with the deposition of clean sandstones across the craton, followed by abundant carbonate deposition.

a. 1509 Istanbul earthquake
c. 1700 Cascadia earthquake
b. Tippecanoe sequence
d. Sauk sequence

57. In geology, _____ are a body of rock with specified characteristics. Ideally, a _____ is a distinctive rock unit that forms under certain conditions of sedimentation, reflecting a particular process or environment.

The term _____ was introduced by the Swiss geologist Amanz Gressly in 1838 and was part of his significant contribution to the foundations of modern stratigraphy, [Cross and Homewood (1997)] which replaced the earlier notions of Neptunism.

a. Schist
b. Facies
c. Granulites
d. Mylonite

58. _____ is a geological process occurring when areas of submerged seafloor are exposed above the sea level. The opposite event, marine transgression, occurs when flooding from the sea covers previously exposed land.

Evidence of _____ and transgression occurs throughout the fossil record, and these fluctuations are thought to have caused (or contributed to) several mass extinctions, among them the Permian-Triassic extinction event (250 million years ago) and Cretaceous-Tertiary extinction event (65 Ma.)

a. 1700 Cascadia earthquake
b. 1703 Genroku earthquake
c. 1509 Istanbul earthquake
d. Marine regression

59. _____ is the second most abundant mineral in the Earth's continental crust. It is made up of a framework of silicon-oxygen tetrahedra SiO_4, with each silicon shared between two oxygens to give the overall formula SiO_2. _____ has a hardness of 7 on the Mohs scale and a density of 2.65 g/cmÂ³.

a. 1700 Cascadia earthquake
b. Quartz
c. 1703 Genroku earthquake
d. 1509 Istanbul earthquake

60. _____ refers to a sediment, sedimentary rock, or soil type which is formed from or contains a high proportion of calcium carbonate in the form of calcite or aragonite.

It can also be used as an adjectival term applied to anatomical structures which are made of calcium carbonate in animals such as gastropods, when referring to such structures as the operculum, the clausilium, and the love dart.

_____ sediments are usually deposited in shallow water near land, since the carbonate is precipitated by marine organisms that need land-derived nutrients.

a. 1700 Cascadia earthquake
b. 1703 Genroku earthquake
c. Calcareous
d. 1509 Istanbul earthquake

61. _____ is a fine-grained sedimentary rock whose original constituents were clay minerals or muds. It is characterized by thin laminae breaking with an irregular curving fracture, often splintery and usually parallel to the often-indistinguishable bedding plane. This property is called fissility.

a. Pelagic sediments
b. Metasediment
c. Shale
d. Mudstone

Chapter 20. Paleozoic Earth History

62. In geology, engineering, and surveying, _____ is the motion of a surface (usually, the Earth's surface) as it shifts downward relative to a datum such as sea-level. The opposite of _____ is uplift, which results in an increase in elevation. There are several types of _____.
   a. 1509 Istanbul earthquake
   b. Pothole
   c. 1700 Cascadia earthquake
   d. Subsidence

63. The _____ was a cratonic sequence that extended from the end of the Mississippian through the Permian periods. It is the unconformity between this sequence and the preceding Kaskaskia that divides the Carboniferous into the Mississippian and Pennsylvanian periods in North America.

Like the Kaskaskia sequence, Absaroka sedimentary deposits were dominated by detrital or siliclastic rocks.

   a. AL 333
   b. Absaroka sequence
   c. AASHTO Soil Classification System
   d. AL 129-1

64. _____ is one of the three main rock types (the others being igneous and metamorphic rock.) _____ is formed by deposition and consolidation of mineral and organic material and from precipitation of minerals from solution. The processes that form _____ occur at the surface of the Earth and within bodies of water.
   a. Petrology
   b. Rock cycle
   c. Serpentinite
   d. Sedimentary rock

65. An _____ is a buried erosion surface separating two rock masses or strata of different ages, indicating that sediment deposition was not continuous. In general, the older layer was exposed to erosion for an interval of time before deposition of the younger, but the term is used to describe any break in the sedimentary geologic record. The phenomenon of angular unconformities was discovered by James Hutton, who found examples at Jedburgh in 1787 and at Siccar Point in 1788.
   a. AASHTO Soil Classification System
   b. AL 129-1
   c. AL 333
   d. Unconformity

66. An _____ is a small organic fossil, present from approximately >2,500 million years ago to the present. Their diversity reflects major ecological events such as the appearance of predation and the Cambrian explosion.

In general, any small, non-acid soluble (i.e. non-carbonate, non-siliceous) organic structure that can not otherwise be accounted for is classified as an _____.

   a. Acritarch
   b. AL 129-1
   c. AASHTO Soil Classification System
   d. AL 333

67. An _____ is a fan-shaped deposit formed where a fast flowing stream flattens, slows, and spreads typically at the exit of a canyon onto a flatter plain. A convergence of neighboring fans into a single apron of deposits against a slope is called a bajada, or compound _____.
   a. AASHTO Soil Classification System
   b. Alluvial fan
   c. AL 333
   d. AL 129-1

68. _____ are the preserved remains or traces of animals, plants, and other organisms from the remote past. The totality of _____, both discovered and undiscovered, and their placement in fossiliferous rock formations and sedimentary layers (strata) is known as the fossil record. The study of _____ across geological time, how they were formed, and the evolutionary relationships between taxa (phylogeny) are some of the most important functions of the science of paleontology.
   a. 1509 Istanbul earthquake
   b. 1700 Cascadia earthquake
   c. 1703 Genroku earthquake
   d. Fossils

69. The _____ is a geologic subperiod and stratigraphic subsystem of the Carboniferous Period. It is the earliest/lowermost of two divisions of the Carboniferous, lasting from roughly 359 to 318 Ma (million years ago.) As with most other geochronologic units, the rock beds that define the _____ are well identified, but the exact start and end dates are uncertain by a few million years.
   a. Mississippian
   b. Pennsylvanian
   c. Dinantian
   d. Calciferous sandstone

70. In structural geology, an _____ is a fold that is convex up and has its oldest beds at its core. The term is not to be confused with antiform, which is a purely descriptive term for any fold that is convex up. Therefore if age relationships (i.e. younging direction) between various strata are unknown, the term antiform must be used.
   a. AL 333
   b. Anticline
   c. AASHTO Soil Classification System
   d. AL 129-1

71. _____ is a sedimentary rock composed largely of the mineral calcite (calcium carbonate: $CaCO_3$.) The deposition of _____ strata is often a by-product and indicator of biological activity in the geologic record. Calcium (along with nitrogen, phosphorus, and potassium) is a key mineral to plant nutrition: soils overlying _____ bedrock tend to be pre-fertilized with calcium.
   a. 1700 Cascadia earthquake
   b. 1509 Istanbul earthquake
   c. 1703 Genroku earthquake
   d. Limestone

72. A _____ is an old and stable part of the continental crust that has survived the merging and splitting of continents and supercontinents for at least 500 million years. Some are over two billion years old. They are generally found in the interiors of continents and are characteristically composed of ancient crystalline basement crust of lightweight felsic igneous rock such as granite.
   a. Sebakwe proto-craton
   b. Kalahari craton
   c. Superior craton
   d. Craton

73. The _____ is a geologic subperiod and stratigraphic subsystem of the Carboniferous Period. It is the later subperiod of the Carboniferous, lasting from roughly 318.1>± 1.3 to 299>± 0.8 Ma (million years ago.) As with most other geochronologic units, the rock beds that define the _____ are well identified, but the exact date of the start and end are uncertain by a few million years.
   a. Calciferous sandstone
   b. Mississippian
   c. Dinantian
   d. Pennsylvanian

74. The _____ is a geologic formation that is spread across the U.S. states of northern Arizona, Nevada, Utah, western New Mexico, and western Colorado. The _____ is controversially considered to be synonymous to Dockum Group in eastern Colorado, eastern New Mexico, southwestern Kansas, the Oklahoma panhandle, and western Texas. The _____ is sometimes colloquially used as a geologic formation within the Dockum in New Mexico and occasionally in Texas.
   a. Cohesion
   b. Stack
   c. Diamond Head
   d. Chinle

75. An _____ is an animal lacking a vertebral column. The group includes 98% of all animal species -- all animals except those in the Chordate subphylum Vertebrata (fish, reptiles, amphibians, birds, and mammals.)

Carolus Linnaeus' Systema Naturae divided these animals into only two groups, the Insecta and the now-obsolete vermes (worms.)

   a. AASHTO Soil Classification System
   b. AL 333
   c. AL 129-1
   d. Invertebrate

76. The _____ , usually abbreviated K for its German translation Kreide, is a geologic period and system from circa >145.5 >± 4 to >65.5 >± 0.3 million years ago . In the geologic timescale, the _____ follows on the Jurassic period and is followed by the Paleogene period. It is the youngest period of the Mesozoic era, and at 80 million years long, the longest period of the Phanerozoic eon. The end of the _____ defines the boundary between the Mesozoic and Cenozoic eras.
   a. Hauterivian
   b. Campanian
   c. Coniacian
   d. Cretaceous

77. _____, originally Gondwanaland, is the name given to a southern precursor-supercontinent and then as a remnant separated from Laurasia 180-200 million years ago during the breakup of the Pangaea supercontinent that existed about 500 to 200 Ma ago into two large segments. While the corresponding northern hemisphere continent Laurasia moved further north, the nearly equal in area _____ included most of the landmasses in today's southern hemisphere, including Antarctica, South America, Africa, Madagascar, Australia-New Guinea, and New Zealand, as well as Arabia and the Indian subcontinent, which have now moved into the Northern Hemisphere.
   a. Gondwana
   b. Laurasia
   c. 1700 Cascadia earthquake
   d. 1509 Istanbul earthquake

78. An _____ is a geological interval of warmer global average temperature that separates glacial periods within an ice age. The current Holocene _____ has persisted since the Pleistocene, about 11,400 years ago.

During the 2.5 million year span of the Pleistocene, numerous glacials, or significant advances of continental ice sheets in North America and Europe have occurred at intervals of approximately 40,000 to 100,000 years.

   a. Interglacial
   b. AASHTO Soil Classification System
   c. AL 333
   d. AL 129-1

79. In chronostratigraphy, a _____ is a succession of rock strata laid down in an single age on the geologic timescale, which usually represents millions of years of deposition. A given _____ of rock and the corresponding age of time will by convention have the same name, and the same boundaries.

a. Stage
b. Geologic record
c. Relative dating
d. Chronostratigraphy

80. _____ is the removal of solids (sediment, soil, rock and other particles) in the natural environment. It usually occurs due to transport by wind, water, or ice; by down-slope creep of soil and other material under the force of gravity; or by living organisms, such as burrowing animals, in the case of bioerosion.

_____ is distinguished from weathering, which is the process of chemical or physical breakdown of the minerals in the rocks, although the two processes may occur concurrently.

a. AASHTO Soil Classification System
b. AL 129-1
c. Erosion
d. AL 333

81. _____ rocks are composed of fragments of pre-existing rock. The term is most commonly, but not uniquely, applied to sedimentary rocks.

_____ metamorphic rocks include breccias formed in faults, as well as some protomylonite and pseudotachylite.

a. Clastic
b. 1703 Genroku earthquake
c. 1509 Istanbul earthquake
d. 1700 Cascadia earthquake

82. The _____ a natural area in New York State northwest of New York City and southwest of Albany, are a mature dissected plateau, an uplifted region that was subsequently eroded into sharp relief. They are an eastward continuation, and the highest representation, of the Allegheny Plateau.

The history of the _____ is a geologic story come full circle, from erosion, deposition and uplift back to erosion. The _____ are more of a dissected plateau than a series of mountain ranges. The sediments that make up the rocks in the Catskills were deposited when the ancient Acadian Mountains in the east were rising and subsequently eroding. The sediments traveled westward and formed a great delta into the sea that was in the area at that time.

a. 1703 Genroku earthquake
b. 1509 Istanbul earthquake
c. Catskill Mountains
d. 1700 Cascadia earthquake

83. _____ is the decomposition of Earth rocks, soils and their minerals through direct contact with the planet's atmosphere. _____ occurs in situ, or 'with no movement', and thus should not be confused with erosion, which involves the movement of rocks and minerals by agents such as water, ice, wind and gravity.

Two important classifications of _____ processes exist -- physical and chemical _____.

a. 1509 Istanbul earthquake
b. Physical weathering
c. Weathering
d. Frost disintegration

Chapter 20. Paleozoic Earth History

84. The chemical compound silicon dioxide, also known as _____ , is an oxide of silicon with a chemical formula of SiO_2 and has been known for its hardness since antiquity. _____ is most commonly found in nature as sand or quartz, as well as in the cell walls of diatoms. It is a principal component of most types of glass and substances such as concrete.

   a. 1509 Istanbul earthquake
   b. 1700 Cascadia earthquake
   c. 1703 Genroku earthquake
   d. Silica

85. The _____ is a unit of sedimentary rock layers of Middle to Late Permian age located in the European Permian Basin which stretches from the east coast of England to northern Poland. The name _____ was formerly also used as a unit of time in the geologic timescale, but nowadays it is only used for the corresponding sedimentary deposits in Europe.

The _____ lies on top of the Rotliegend; on top of the _____ is the Buntsandstein or Bunter.

   a. Teilzone
   b. Salt tectonics
   c. Marine clay
   d. Zechstein

86. _____ is a naturally occurring granular material composed of finely divided rock and mineral particles.

As the term is used by geologists, _____ particles range in diameter from 0.0625 (or $>^1\!/_{16}$ mm, or 62.5 micrometers) to 2 millimeters. An individual particle in this range size is termed a _____ grain.

   a. 1509 Istanbul earthquake
   b. 1703 Genroku earthquake
   c. Sand
   d. 1700 Cascadia earthquake

87. _____ is a hard, compact variety of mineral coal that has a high lustre. It has the highest carbon count and contains the fewest impurities of all coals, despite its lower calorific content.

_____ is the highest of the metamorphic rank, in which the carbon content is between 92% and 98%.

   a. AL 333
   b. AL 129-1
   c. AASHTO Soil Classification System
   d. Anthracite

88. _____ is a relatively soft coal containing a tarlike substance called bitumen. It is of higher quality than lignite coal but of poorer quality than anthracite coal.

_____ is a sedimorphic rock formed by diagenetic and submetamorphic compression of peat bog material.

   a. 1700 Cascadia earthquake
   b. 1703 Genroku earthquake
   c. 1509 Istanbul earthquake
   d. Bituminous coal

89. An _____ is a type of rock that contains minerals such as gemstones and metals that can be extracted through mining and refined for use. Samples of _____ in the form of exceptionally beautiful crystals, exotic layering visible when sectioned or polished or metallic presentations such as large nuggets or crystalline formations of metals such as gold or copper may command a value far beyond their value as mere _____ or raw metal for subsequent reduction to utilitarian purposes.

The grade or concentration of an _____ mineral, or metal, as well as its form of occurrence, will directly affect the costs associated with mining the _____.

a. AASHTO Soil Classification System
c. AL 129-1
b. Ore genesis
d. Ore

Chapter 21. Paleozoic Life History

1. The _____ Formation is one of the world's most celebrated fossil localities, and is famous for the exceptional preservation of the fossils found within it, in which the soft parts are preserved. It is 505 million years (Middle Cambrian) in age, making it one of the earliest fossil beds to preserve the soft parts of animals. The pre-Cambrian fossil record of animals is sparse and ambiguous.
   - a. 1700 Cascadia earthquake
   - b. Burgess Shale
   - c. 1703 Genroku earthquake
   - d. 1509 Istanbul earthquake

2. _____ is a fine-grained sedimentary rock whose original constituents were clay minerals or muds. It is characterized by thin laminae breaking with an irregular curving fracture, often splintery and usually parallel to the often-indistinguishable bedding plane. This property is called fissility.
   - a. Pelagic sediments
   - b. Shale
   - c. Mudstone
   - d. Metasediment

3. The _____, is a geologic eon before the Proterozoic and Paleoproterozoic, before 2.5 Ga (billion years ago, or 2,500 Ma.) Instead of being based on stratigraphy, this date is defined chronometrically. The lower boundary (starting point) has not been officially recognized by the International Commission on Stratigraphy, but it is usually set to 3.8 Ga, at the end of the Hadean eon.
   - a. AL 333
   - b. AL 129-1
   - c. AASHTO Soil Classification System
   - d. Archean

4. _____ refers to a sediment, sedimentary rock, or soil type which is formed from or contains a high proportion of calcium carbonate in the form of calcite or aragonite.

It can also be used as an adjectival term applied to anatomical structures which are made of calcium carbonate in animals such as gastropods, when referring to such structures as the operculum, the clausilium, and the love dart.

_____ sediments are usually deposited in shallow water near land, since the carbonate is precipitated by marine organisms that need land-derived nutrients.

   - a. Calcareous
   - b. 1509 Istanbul earthquake
   - c. 1703 Genroku earthquake
   - d. 1700 Cascadia earthquake

5. The _____ is the first geological period of the Phanerozoic eon, lasting from 542 ± 0.3 million years ago to 488.3 ± 1.7 million years ago (ICS, 2004); it is succeeded by the Ordovician. Its subdivisions, and indeed its base, are somewhat in flux. The period was established by Adam Sedgwick, who named it after Cambria, the classical name for Wales, where Britain's _____ rocks are best exposed.
   - a. 1703 Genroku earthquake
   - b. 1509 Istanbul earthquake
   - c. 1700 Cascadia earthquake
   - d. Cambrian

6. The _____ or Cambrian radiation was the seemingly rapid appearance of most major groups of complex animals around 530 million years ago, as evidenced by the fossil record. This was accompanied by a major diversification of other organisms, including animals, phytoplankton, and calcimicrobes. Before about 580 million years ago, most organisms were simple, composed of individual cells occasionally organized into colonies.
   - a. Labyrinthodont
   - b. Conodont Alteration Index
   - c. Romer's Gap
   - d. Cambrian explosion

7. The _____ Era, is the most recent of the three classic geological eras and covers the period from 65.5 million years ago to the present. It is marked by the Cretaceous-Tertiary extinction event at the end of the Cretaceous that saw the demise of the last non-avian dinosaurs and the end of the Mesozoic Era. The _____ era is ongoing.
   a. 1509 Istanbul earthquake
   b. 1703 Genroku earthquake
   c. 1700 Cascadia earthquake
   d. Cenozoic

8. The _____ is a geologic period and system of the Paleozoic era spanning from >416 to 359.2 million years ago (ICS, 2004.).

During the _____ Period, which occurred in the Paleozoic era, the first fish evolved legsand started to walk on land as tetrapods around 365 Ma.

   a. Xitun Formation
   b. 1509 Istanbul earthquake
   c. Gogo Formation
   d. Devonian

9. The _____ Period is the last geological period of the Neoproterozoic Era and of the Proterozoic Eon, immediately preceding the Cambrian Period, the first period of the Paleozoic Era and of the Phanerozoic Eon. Its status as an official geological period was ratified in 2004 by the International Union of Geological Sciences (IUGS), making it the first new geological period declared in 120 years. The type section is in the Flinders Ranges in South Australia.
   a. AASHTO Soil Classification System
   b. AL 333
   c. Ediacaran
   d. AL 129-1

10. An _____ is a large shallow sea that either extends far into a continent, such as the Persian Gulf, or overlies a large part of a continent.

They are usually associated with the marine transgressions of the early Cenozoic era and may be semi-cyclic--during eras of glacial recession given a period of low mountains coupled with a warming under the influence of plate tectonics. They can be warm or cold; indeed, several were present at the end of the last Ice Age, when sea levels rose more rapidly than some areas could isostatically adjust.

   a. AL 333
   b. Epeiric sea
   c. AASHTO Soil Classification System
   d. AL 129-1

11. The _____ was a cratonic sequence that began in the mid-Devonian, peaked early in the Mississippian, and ended by mid-Mississippian time. A major unconformity separates it from the lower Tippecanoe sequence.

The basal-that is, the lowest and oldest-units of the Kaskaskia consist of clean quartz sandstones eroded from the Appalachian orogenic belt to the east, the Ozark Dome in the center of the continent, and south from the Canadian Shield.

   a. 1509 Istanbul earthquake
   b. 1700 Cascadia earthquake
   c. Sauk sequence
   d. Kaskaskia sequence

12. The _____ is the earliest of three geologic eras of the Phanerozoic eon. The _____ spanned from roughly 542 to 251 million years ago (ICS, 2004), and is subdivided into six geologic periods; from oldest to youngest they are: the Cambrian, Ordovician, Silurian, Devonian, Carboniferous, and Permian.

Chapter 21. Paleozoic Life History

The _____ covers the time from the first appearance of abundant, soft-shelled fossils to the time when the continents were beginning to be dominated by large, relatively sophisticated reptiles and modern plants. The lower (oldest) boundary was classically set at the first appearance of creatures known as trilobites and archeocyathids.

- a. Paleozoic
- b. 1703 Genroku earthquake
- c. 1509 Istanbul earthquake
- d. 1700 Cascadia earthquake

13. _____ was the supercontinent that is theorized to have existed during the Paleozoic and Mesozoic eras about 250 million years ago, before the component continents were separated into their current configuration.

The name was first used by the German originator of the continental drift theory, Alfred Wegener, in the 1920 edition of his book The Origin of Continents and Oceans, in which a postulated supercontinent _____ played a key role.

The single enormous ocean which surrounded Pangaea is known as Panthalassa.

- a. 1700 Cascadia earthquake
- b. 1703 Genroku earthquake
- c. 1509 Istanbul earthquake
- d. Pangea

14. The _____ is a geological eon representing a period before the first abundant complex life on Earth. The _____ extended from 2500 Ma to 542.0 >± 1.0 Ma (million years ago), and is the most recent part of the old, informally named 'e;Precambrian'e; time.

The Proterozoic consists of 3 geologic eras, from oldest to youngest:

- Paleoproterozoic
- Mesoproterozoic
- Neoproterozoic

The well-identified events were:

- The transition to an oxygenated atmosphere during the Mesoproterozoic.
- Several glaciations, including the hypothesized Snowball Earth during the Cryogenian period in the late Neoproterozoic.
- The Ediacaran Period (635 to 542 Ma) which is characterized by the evolution of abundant soft-bodied multicellular organisms.

The geoloic record of the Proterozoic is much better than that for the preceding Archean. In contrast to the deep-water deposits of the Archean, the Proterozoic features many strata that were laid down in extensive shallow epicontinental seas; furthermore, many of these rocks are less metamorphosed than Archean-age ones, and plenty are unaltered.

Chapter 21. Paleozoic Life History

a. 1509 Istanbul earthquake
c. 1703 Genroku earthquake
b. 1700 Cascadia earthquake
d. Proterozoic Eon

15. _____ is the geological process by which material is added to a landform or land mass. Fluids such as wind and water, as well as sediment gravity flows, transport previously eroded sediment, which, at the loss of enough kinetic energy in the fluid, is deposited, building up layers of sediment.

_____ occurs when the forces responsible for sediment transportation are no longer sufficient to overcome the forces of particle weight and friction, which resist motion.

a. Downcutting
c. Headward erosion
b. Deposition
d. Diagenesis

16. _____ are the preserved remains or traces of animals, plants, and other organisms from the remote past. The totality of _____, both discovered and undiscovered, and their placement in fossiliferous rock formations and sedimentary layers (strata) is known as the fossil record. The study of _____ across geological time, how they were formed, and the evolutionary relationships between taxa (phylogeny) are some of the most important functions of the science of paleontology.

a. 1703 Genroku earthquake
c. Fossils
b. 1509 Istanbul earthquake
d. 1700 Cascadia earthquake

17. An _____ is an animal lacking a vertebral column. The group includes 98% of all animal species -- all animals except those in the Chordate subphylum Vertebrata (fish, reptiles, amphibians, birds, and mammals.)

Carolus Linnaeus' Systema Naturae divided these animals into only two groups, the Insecta and the now-obsolete vermes (worms.)

a. AASHTO Soil Classification System
c. AL 129-1
b. AL 333
d. Invertebrate

18. A _____ is a large, slow-moving mass of ice, formed from compacted layers of snow, that slowly deforms and flows in response to gravity and high pressure.

_____ ice is the largest reservoir of fresh water on Earth, and second only to oceans as the largest reservoir of total water.

a. Little Ice Age
c. Keeling Curve
b. Glacier
d. Pacific Decadal Oscillation

19. _____ are the organisms which live on, in also known as the benthic zone. They live in or near marine sedimentary environments, from tidal pools along the foreshore, out to the continental shelf, and then down to the abyssal depths.

Many organisms adapted to deep-water pressure cannot survive in the upper parts of the water column.

a. Benthos
b. 1509 Istanbul earthquake
c. 1703 Genroku earthquake
d. 1700 Cascadia earthquake

20. The _____ Era is one of three geologic eras of the Phanerozoic eon. The division of time into eras dates back to Giovanni Arduino, in the 18th century, although his original name for the era now called the '_____' was 'Secondary' (making the modern era the 'Tertiary'.)

The _____ was a time of tectonic, climatic and evolutionary activity. The continents gradually shifted from a state of connectedness into their present configuration; the drifting provided for speciation and other important evolutionary developments.

a. 1703 Genroku earthquake
b. 1700 Cascadia earthquake
c. 1509 Istanbul earthquake
d. Mesozoic

21. _____ are geological records of biological activity. _____ may be impressions made on the substrate by an organism: for example, burrows, borings, footprints and feeding marks, and root cavities. The term in its broadest sense also includes the remains of other organic material produced by an organism - for example coprolites or chemical markers - or sedimentological structures produced by biological means - for example, stromatolites.

a. 1509 Istanbul earthquake
b. 1700 Cascadia earthquake
c. 1703 Genroku earthquake
d. Trace fossils

22. The _____ is a geologic period and system, the second of six of the Paleozoic era, and covers the time between 488.3>±1.7 to 443.7>±1.5 million years ago (ICS, 2004.) It follows the Cambrian period and is followed by the Silurian period. The _____ was defined by Charles Lapworth in 1879, to resolve a dispute between followers of Adam Sedgwick and Roderick Murchison, who were placing the same rock beds in northern Wales into the Cambrian and Silurian periods respectively.

a. AL 129-1
b. AL 333
c. AASHTO Soil Classification System
d. Ordovician

23. The _____ was the cratonic sequence--that is, the marine transgression--that followed the Sauk sequence; it extended from roughly the middle Ordovician to the early Devonian.

After the regression of the Sauk Sea early in the Ordovician, the exposed craton for a time underwent vigorous erosion, due to being located in a tropical climate; indeed, at this point in the Phanerozoic the North American continent roughly straddled the equator.

The Tippecanoe transgression ended this period of erosion, beginning with the deposition of clean sandstones across the craton, followed by abundant carbonate deposition.

a. Sauk sequence
b. 1509 Istanbul earthquake
c. Tippecanoe sequence
d. 1700 Cascadia earthquake

24. _____, originally Gondwanaland, is the name given to a southern precursor-supercontinent and then as a remnant separated from Laurasia 180-200 million years ago during the breakup of the Pangaea supercontinent that existed about 500 to 200 Ma ago into two large segments. While the corresponding northern hemisphere continent Laurasia moved further north, the nearly equal in area _____ included most of the landmasses in today's southern hemisphere, including Antarctica, South America, Africa, Madagascar, Australia-New Guinea, and New Zealand, as well as Arabia and the Indian subcontinent, which have now moved into the Northern Hemisphere.
   a. Gondwana
   b. Laurasia
   c. 1700 Cascadia earthquake
   d. 1509 Istanbul earthquake

25. _____ are fossils used to define and identify geologic periods They work on the premise that, although different sediments may look different depending on the conditions under which they were laid down, they may include the remains of the same species of fossil. If the species concerned were short-lived, then it is certain that the sediments in question were deposited within that narrow time period.
   a. Index fossils
   b. Indian bead
   c. Allotrioceras
   d. Invertebrate paleontology

26. The _____ was an ocean that existed in the Neoproterozoic and Paleozoic eras of the geologic timescale (between 600 and 400 million years ago.) The _____ was situated in the southern hemisphere, between the paleocontinents of Laurentia, Baltica and Avalonia. The ocean disappeared with the Caledonian, Taconic and Acadian orogenies, when these three continents joined to form one big landmass called Laurussia.
   a. AL 129-1
   b. AASHTO Soil Classification System
   c. AL 333
   d. Iapetus Ocean

27. The _____ is the epoch from 1.8 million to 11550 years BP covering the world's recent period of repeated glaciations. The _____ epoch follows the Pliocene epoch and is followed by the Holocene epoch. The _____ is the third epoch of the Neogene period or 6th epoch of the Cenozoic Era. The end of the _____ corresponds with the retreat of the last continental glacier. It also corresponds with the end of the Paleolithic age used in archaeology.
   a. Tyrrhenian
   b. Late Pleistocene
   c. Pleistocene
   d. Sicilian Stage

28. _____ refers to natural mountain building, and may be studied as a tectonic structural event, (b) as a geographical event, and (c) a chronological event. Orogenic events (a) cause distinctive structural phenomena and related tectonic activity, (b) affect certain regions of rocks and crust, and (c) happen within a specific period of time.
   a. Orogenesis
   b. Alice Springs Orogeny
   c. Antler orogeny
   d. Orogeny

29. The _____ is the extended perimeter of each continent and associated coastal plain, and was part of the continent during the glacial periods, but is undersea during interglacial periods such as the current epoch by relatively shallow seas (known as shelf seas) and gulfs.

The continental rise is below the slope, but landward of the abyssal plains. Its gradient is intermediate between the slope and the shelf, on the order of 0.5-1°.

   a. 1509 Istanbul earthquake
   b. 1703 Genroku earthquake
   c. 1700 Cascadia earthquake
   d. Continental shelf

Chapter 21. Paleozoic Life History

30. The _____ , usually abbreviated K for its German translation Kreide, is a geologic period and system from circa >145.5 >± 4 to >65.5 >± 0.3 million years ago . In the geologic timescale, the _____ follows on the Jurassic period and is followed by the Paleogene period. It is the youngest period of the Mesozoic era, and at 80 million years long, the longest period of the Phanerozoic eon. The end of the _____ defines the boundary between the Mesozoic and Cenozoic eras.
   a. Coniacian
   b. Cretaceous
   c. Campanian
   d. Hauterivian

31. The _____ is a geologic subperiod and stratigraphic subsystem of the Carboniferous Period. It is the earliest/lowermost of two divisions of the Carboniferous, lasting from roughly 359 to 318 Ma (million years ago.) As with most other geochronologic units, the rock beds that define the _____ are well identified, but the exact start and end dates are uncertain by a few million years.
   a. Pennsylvanian
   b. Calciferous sandstone
   c. Dinantian
   d. Mississippian

32. The _____ was a cratonic sequence that extended from the end of the Mississippian through the Permian periods. It is the unconformity between this sequence and the preceding Kaskaskia that divides the Carboniferous into the Mississippian and Pennsylvanian periods in North America.

Like the Kaskaskia sequence, Absaroka sedimentary deposits were dominated by detrital or siliclastic rocks.

   a. AL 333
   b. AL 129-1
   c. Absaroka sequence
   d. AASHTO Soil Classification System

33. The _____ is a geologic subperiod and stratigraphic subsystem of the Carboniferous Period. It is the later subperiod of the Carboniferous, lasting from roughly 318.1>± 1.3 to 299>± 0.8 Ma (million years ago.) As with most other geochronologic units, the rock beds that define the _____ are well identified, but the exact date of the start and end are uncertain by a few million years.
   a. Mississippian
   b. Calciferous sandstone
   c. Dinantian
   d. Pennsylvanian

34. The _____ is a geologic period and system that extends from about 251 to 199 Mya (million years ago.) As the first period of the Mesozoic Era, the _____ follows the Permian and is followed by the Jurassic. Both the start and end of the _____ are marked by major extinction events.
   a. Rhaetian
   b. 1700 Cascadia earthquake
   c. Triassic
   d. 1509 Istanbul earthquake

35. _____ is a geological term used to describe particles of rock derived from pre-existing rock through processes of weathering and erosion. Thesel particles can consist of lithic fragments (particles of recognisable rock), or of monomineralic fragments (mineral grains.) These particles are often transported through sedimentary processes into depositional systems such as riverbeds, lakes or the ocean forming sedimentary successions.
   a. Medical geology
   b. Detritus
   c. Geomechanics
   d. Perched coastline

36. _____, in structural geology and related disciplines, describes the tendency of a rock to break along preferred planes of weakness.

Rocks deformed under very low to low metamorphic grade often develop planes along which the rock can easily be split. Slates are an example of a rock with a penetrative _____ caused partly by the realignement of phyllosilicate minerals with increasing flattening strain.

- a. Cleavage
- b. Drainage system
- c. Compaction
- d. Combe

37. _____ is a common extrusive volcanic rock. It is usually grey to black and fine-grained due to rapid cooling of lava at the surface of a planet. It may be porphyritic containing larger crystals in a fine matrix, or vesicular, or frothy scoria.
    - a. 1509 Istanbul earthquake
    - b. 1703 Genroku earthquake
    - c. 1700 Cascadia earthquake
    - d. Basalt

38. _____ is an obsolete term for any member of the extinct superorder (Labyrinthodontia) of amphibians, which constituted some of the dominant animals of Late Paleozoic and Early Mesozoic times (about 350 to 210 million years ago.) The name describes the pattern of infolding of the dentine and enamel of the teeth, which are often the only part of the creatures that fossilize. They are also distinguished by a heavy solid skull , and complex vertebrae, the structure of which is useful in older classifications of the group.
    - a. Paleopedological record
    - b. Bromalites
    - c. Calcimicrobes
    - d. Labyrinthodont

39. The _____ is a British rock formation of considerable importance to early paleontology. Hutton's angular unconformity at Siccar Point where 345 million year old Devonian _____ overlies 425 million year old Silurian greywacke.

The _____ describes a suite of rocks deposited in a variety of environments during the Devonian period but extending back into the late Silurian period and forward into the earliest part of the Carboniferous period.

- a. Old Red Sandstone
- b. AASHTO Soil Classification System
- c. AL 333
- d. AL 129-1

40. _____ is a sedimentary rock composed mainly of sand-size mineral or rock grains. Most _____ is composed of quartz and/or feldspar because these are the most common minerals in the Earth's crust. Like sand, _____ may be any color, but the most common colors are tan, brown, yellow, red, gray and white.
    - a. Porcellanite
    - b. Sandstone
    - c. Dolostone
    - d. Lithification

41. An _____ is a small organic fossil, present from approximately >2,500 million years ago to the present. Their diversity reflects major ecological events such as the appearance of predation and the Cambrian explosion.

In general, any small, non-acid soluble (i.e. non-carbonate, non-siliceous) organic structure that can not otherwise be accounted for is classified as an _____.

- a. AL 129-1
- b. AASHTO Soil Classification System
- c. AL 333
- d. Acritarch

Chapter 21. Paleozoic Life History

42. _____ is the geological term used to describe a particle of a size between five and 500 micrometres, found in rock deposits (sedimentary rocks) and composed of organic material such as chitin, pseudochitin and sporopollenin.' Palynology is the study of _____ fossils and can be considered a subdiscipline of micropaleontology or paleobotany. Expressed more simply, palynology is the study of organic microfossils.

They form a geological record of importance in determining the type of prehistoric life that existed at the time the sedimentary formation was laid down.

- a. Transition zone
- b. Tidal scour
- c. Cap carbonates
- d. Palynomorph

43. _____ is one of the three main rock types (the others being igneous and metamorphic rock.) _____ is formed by deposition and consolidation of mineral and organic material and from precipitation of minerals from solution. The processes that form _____ occur at the surface of the Earth and within bodies of water.
- a. Petrology
- b. Serpentinite
- c. Rock cycle
- d. Sedimentary rock

44. _____ is the largest and best-known genus of the extinct order of seed ferns known as Glossopteridales (or in some cases as Arberiales or Dictyopteridiales.)

The Glossopteridales arose around the beginning of the Permian on the great southern continent of Gondwana. These plants went on to become the dominant elements of the southern flora through the rest of the Permian but disappeared in almost all places at the end of the Permian.

- a. 1509 Istanbul earthquake
- b. Pteridospermatophyta
- c. Petrified wood
- d. Glossopteris

Chapter 22. Mesozoic Earth and Life History

1. _____ was a supercontinent that most recently existed as a part of the split of the Pangaean supercontinent in the late Mesozoic era. It included most of the landmasses which make up today's continents of the northern hemisphere, chiefly Laurentia (the name given to the North American craton), Baltica, Siberia, Kazakhstania, and the North China and East China cratons.
   - a. 1509 Istanbul earthquake
   - b. Rodinia
   - c. 1700 Cascadia earthquake
   - d. Laurasia

2. The _____ Era is one of three geologic eras of the Phanerozoic eon. The division of time into eras dates back to Giovanni Arduino, in the 18th century, although his original name for the era now called the '_____' was 'Secondary' (making the modern era the 'Tertiary'.)

   The _____ was a time of tectonic, climatic and evolutionary activity. The continents gradually shifted from a state of connectedness into their present configuration; the drifting provided for speciation and other important evolutionary developments.

   - a. Mesozoic
   - b. 1700 Cascadia earthquake
   - c. 1509 Istanbul earthquake
   - d. 1703 Genroku earthquake

3. The _____ was a major mountain building event that took place along the western edge of ancient North America between the Mid to Late Jurassic (between about 180 and 140 million years ago.) The _____ was the first of three major mountain building episodes to transform Western North America between the Late Mesozoic and Early Cenozoic Eras, the latter two being the Sevier and Laramide orogeny, chronologically. Much like the two orogenies that followed, the Nevadan was caused by the subduction of oceanic lithosphere at a subduction zone running along the edge of the North American continent.
   - a. Kaikoura Orogeny
   - b. Nevadan orogeny
   - c. Pan-African orogeny
   - d. Sevier orogeny

4. _____ is the study of the record of the Earth's magnetic field preserved in various magnetic minerals through time. The study of _____ has demonstrated that the Earth's magnetic field varies substantially in both orientation and intensity through time. <
   - a. Paleomagnetism
   - b. Chronozone
   - c. Law of superposition
   - d. Stage

5. The _____ is the earliest of three geologic eras of the Phanerozoic eon. The _____ spanned from roughly 542 to 251 million years ago (ICS, 2004), and is subdivided into six geologic periods; from oldest to youngest they are: the Cambrian, Ordovician, Silurian, Devonian, Carboniferous, and Permian.

   The _____ covers the time from the first appearance of abundant, soft-shelled fossils to the time when the continents were beginning to be dominated by large, relatively sophisticated reptiles and modern plants. The lower (oldest) boundary was classically set at the first appearance of creatures known as trilobites and archeocyathids.

   - a. 1703 Genroku earthquake
   - b. 1700 Cascadia earthquake
   - c. 1509 Istanbul earthquake
   - d. Paleozoic

6. _____ was the supercontinent that is theorized to have existed during the Paleozoic and Mesozoic eras about 250 million years ago, before the component continents were separated into their current configuration.

Chapter 22. Mesozoic Earth and Life History

The name was first used by the German originator of the continental drift theory, Alfred Wegener, in the 1920 edition of his book The Origin of Continents and Oceans , in which a postulated supercontinent _____ played a key role.

The single enormous ocean which surrounded Pangaea is known as Panthalassa.

a. 1700 Cascadia earthquake
c. 1703 Genroku earthquake
b. 1509 Istanbul earthquake
d. Pangea

7. In geology, a _____ deposit or _____ is an accumulation of valuable minerals formed by deposition of dense mineral phases in a trap site. Types of _____ deposits include alluvium, eluvium, beach placers, and paleoplacers.

Typical locations for alluvial _____ deposits are on the inside bends of rivers and creeks, in natural hollows, at the break of slope on a stream, the base of an escarpment, waterfall or other barrier, within sand dunes, beach profiles or in gravel beds.

a. 1703 Genroku earthquake
c. 1509 Istanbul earthquake
b. 1700 Cascadia earthquake
d. Placer

8. The _____ is a geological eon representing a period before the first abundant complex life on Earth. The _____ extended from 2500 Ma to 542.0 >± 1.0 Ma (million years ago), and is the most recent part of the old, informally named 'e;Precambrian'e; time.

The Proterozoic consists of 3 geologic eras, from oldest to youngest:

- Paleoproterozoic
- Mesoproterozoic
- Neoproterozoic

The well-identified events were:

- The transition to an oxygenated atmosphere during the Mesoproterozoic.
- Several glaciations, including the hypothesized Snowball Earth during the Cryogenian period in the late Neoproterozoic.
- The Ediacaran Period (635 to 542 Ma) which is characterized by the evolution of abundant soft-bodied multicellular organisms.

The geoloic record of the Proterozoic is much better than that for the preceding Archean. In contrast to the deep-water deposits of the Archean, the Proterozoic features many strata that were laid down in extensive shallow epicontinental seas; furthermore, many of these rocks are less metamorphosed than Archean-age ones, and plenty are unaltered.

a. 1703 Genroku earthquake
c. 1509 Istanbul earthquake
b. 1700 Cascadia earthquake
d. Proterozoic Eon

9. In geology, a _____ is a landmass comprising more than one continental core, or craton. The assembly of cratons and accreted terranes that form Eurasia qualifies as a _____ today.

Most commonly, paleogeographers employ the term _____ to refer to a single landmass consisting of all the modern continents.

a. 1700 Cascadia earthquake
c. 1703 Genroku earthquake
b. 1509 Istanbul earthquake
d. Supercontinent

10. The _____ was an ocean that existed between the continents of Gondwana and Laurasia during the Mesozoic era before the opening of the Indian Ocean.

About 250 million years ago, during the Triassic, a new ocean began forming in the southern end of the Paleo-_____. A rift formed along the northern continental shelf of Southern Pangaea (Gondwana.) Over the next 60 million years, that piece of shelf, known as Cimmeria, traveled north, pushing the floor of the Paleo-_____ under the eastern end of Northern Pangaea (Laurasia). The _____ formed between Cimmeria and Gondwana, directly over where the Paleo-Tethys used to be.

a. 1700 Cascadia earthquake
c. 1509 Istanbul earthquake
b. 1703 Genroku earthquake
d. Tethys Ocean

11. The _____ is a geologic period and system that extends from about 251 to 199 Mya (million years ago.) As the first period of the Mesozoic Era, the _____ follows the Permian and is followed by the Jurassic. Both the start and end of the _____ are marked by major extinction events.
a. 1700 Cascadia earthquake
c. 1509 Istanbul earthquake
b. Rhaetian
d. Triassic

12. _____, is the process of coastal sediments returning to the visible portion of a beach or foreshore following a submersion event. A sustainable beach or foreshore often goes through a cycle of submersion during rough weather then _____ during calmer periods. If a coastline is not in a healthy sustainable condition, then erosion can be more serious and _____ does not fully restore the original volume of the visible beach or foreshore leading to permanent beach or foreshore loss.
a. AL 333
c. Accretion
b. AASHTO Soil Classification System
d. AL 129-1

13. _____ refers to natural mountain building, and may be studied as a tectonic structural event, (b) as a geographical event, and (c) a chronological event. Orogenic events (a) cause distinctive structural phenomena and related tectonic activity, (b) affect certain regions of rocks and crust, and (c) happen within a specific period of time.
a. Antler orogeny
c. Alice Springs Orogeny
b. Orogenesis
d. Orogeny

Chapter 22. Mesozoic Earth and Life History

14. _____, originally Gondwanaland, is the name given to a southern precursor-supercontinent and then as a remnant separated from Laurasia 180-200 million years ago during the breakup of the Pangaea supercontinent that existed about 500 to 200 Ma ago into two large segments. While the corresponding northern hemisphere continent Laurasia moved further north, the nearly equal in area _____ included most of the landmasses in today's southern hemisphere, including Antarctica, South America, Africa, Madagascar, Australia-New Guinea, and New Zealand, as well as Arabia and the Indian subcontinent, which have now moved into the Northern Hemisphere.
   a. Laurasia
   b. 1700 Cascadia earthquake
   c. 1509 Istanbul earthquake
   d. Gondwana

15. The _____ , usually abbreviated K for its German translation Kreide, is a geologic period and system from circa >145.5 >± 4 to >65.5 >± 0.3 million years ago . In the geologic timescale, the _____ follows on the Jurassic period and is followed by the Paleogene period. It is the youngest period of the Mesozoic era, and at 80 million years long, the longest period of the Phanerozoic eon. The end of the _____ defines the boundary between the Mesozoic and Cenozoic eras.
   a. Hauterivian
   b. Campanian
   c. Coniacian
   d. Cretaceous

16. The _____ was a cratonic sequence that extended from the end of the Mississippian through the Permian periods. It is the unconformity between this sequence and the preceding Kaskaskia that divides the Carboniferous into the Mississippian and Pennsylvanian periods in North America.

Like the Kaskaskia sequence, Absaroka sedimentary deposits were dominated by detrital or siliclastic rocks.

   a. AL 129-1
   b. AASHTO Soil Classification System
   c. AL 333
   d. Absaroka sequence

17. The _____, is a geologic eon before the Proterozoic and Paleoproterozoic, before 2.5 Ga (billion years ago, or 2,500 Ma.) Instead of being based on stratigraphy, this date is defined chronometrically. The lower boundary (starting point) has not been officially recognized by the International Commission on Stratigraphy, but it is usually set to 3.8 Ga, at the end of the Hadean eon.
   a. AL 129-1
   b. AL 333
   c. AASHTO Soil Classification System
   d. Archean

18. The _____ Era, is the most recent of the three classic geological eras and covers the period from 65.5 million years ago to the present. It is marked by the Cretaceous-Tertiary extinction event at the end of the Cretaceous that saw the demise of the last non-avian dinosaurs and the end of the Mesozoic Era. The _____ era is ongoing.
   a. 1700 Cascadia earthquake
   b. 1509 Istanbul earthquake
   c. 1703 Genroku earthquake
   d. Cenozoic

19. The _____ is a geologic period and system of the Paleozoic era spanning from >416 to 359.2 million years ago (ICS, 2004.).

During the _____ Period, which occurred in the Paleozoic era, the first fish evolved legsand started to walk on land as tetrapods around 365 Ma.

a. 1509 Istanbul earthquake
b. Gogo Formation
c. Xitun Formation
d. Devonian

20. An _____ is a large shallow sea that either extends far into a continent, such as the Persian Gulf, or overlies a large part of a continent.

They are usually associated with the marine transgressions of the early Cenozoic era and may be semi-cyclic--during eras of glacial recession given a period of low mountains coupled with a warming under the influence of plate tectonics. They can be warm or cold; indeed, several were present at the end of the last Ice Age, when sea levels rose more rapidly than some areas could isostatically adjust.

a. AASHTO Soil Classification System
b. Epeiric sea
c. AL 129-1
d. AL 333

21. _____ is the part of Earth's lithosphere that surfaces in the ocean basins. _____ is primarily composed of mafic rocks, or sima. It is thinner than continental crust, or sial, generally less than 10 kilometers thick, however it is denser, having a mean density of about 3.3 grams per cubic centimeter.

a. AASHTO Soil Classification System
b. Oceanic crust
c. AL 333
d. AL 129-1

22. _____ was the vast global ocean that surrounded the supercontinent Pangaea, during the late Paleozoic and the early Mesozoic eras. It included the Pacific Ocean to the west and north and the Tethys Ocean to the southeast. It became the Pacific Ocean, following the closing of the Tethys basin and the breakup of Pangaea, which created the Atlantic, Arctic, and Indian Ocean basins.

a. Gorda Ridge
b. Lithosphere
c. Forearc
d. Panthalassa

23. The _____ has been defined as a Late Permian to Early Triassic tectonic event that deformed Upper Paleozoic oceanic facies rocks and emplaced them over the Upper Paleozoic margin of northern Nevada.

a. Cocos Plate
b. Rivera Plate
c. Farallon Plate
d. Sonoma orogeny

24. In geology a _____ is the smallest division of a geologic formation or stratigraphic rock series marked by well-defined divisional planes (bedding planes) separating it from layers above and below. A _____ is the smallest lithostratigraphic unit, usually ranging in thickness from a centimeter to several meters and distinguishable from beds above and below it. Beds can be differentiated in various ways, including rock or mineral type and particle size.

a. Sequence stratigraphy
b. Cyclostratigraphy
c. Biozones
d. Bed

25. A _____ is a mountain rising from the ocean seafloor that does not reach to the water's surface (sea level), and thus is not an island. These are typically formed from extinct volcanoes, that rise abruptly and are usually found rising from a seafloor of 1,000-4,000 meters depth. They are defined by oceanographers as independent features that rise to at least 1,000 meters above the seafloor.

a. Seamount
b. 1509 Istanbul earthquake
c. 1703 Genroku earthquake
d. 1700 Cascadia earthquake

26. _____ is any particulate matter that can be transported by fluid flow, and which eventually is deposited.

They are most often transported by water (fluvial processes) transported by wind (aeolian processes) and glaciers. Beach sands and river channel deposits are examples of fluvial transport and deposition, though _____ also often settles out of slow-moving or standing water in lakes and oceans.

a. Sediment
c. Quicksand

b. Brickearth
d. Bovey Beds

27. A marine _____ is a geologic event during which sea level rises relative to the land and the shoreline moves toward higher ground, resulting in flooding. They can be caused either by the land sinking or the ocean basins filling with water (or decreasing in capacity.) Transgresssions and regressions may be caused by tectonic events such as orogenies, severe climate change such as ice ages or isostatic adjustments following removal of ice or sediment load.

a. Spheroidal weathering
c. Stoping

b. Wave pounding
d. Transgression

28. The _____ or Appalachian orogeny is one of the geological mountain-forming events (orogeny) that formed the Appalachian Mountains and Allegheny Mountains. The term and spelling 'Alleghany Orogeny' (sic) originally proposed by H.P. Woodward (1957, 1958) is preferred usage. Approximately 350 million to 300 million years ago, in the Carboniferous period, the combined continents of Europe and Africa (Gondwana) collided with North America to form the supercontinent of Pangaea.

a. Alice Springs Orogeny
c. Antler orogeny

b. Alleghenian orogeny
d. Alpine orogeny

29. _____ is a geological term used to describe particles of rock derived from pre-existing rock through processes of weathering and erosion. Thesel particles can consist of lithic fragments (particles of recognisable rock), or of monomineralic fragments (mineral grains.) These particles are often transported through sedimentary processes into depositional systems such as riverbeds, lakes or the ocean forming sedimentary successions.

a. Geomechanics
c. Medical geology

b. Perched coastline
d. Detritus

30. _____ landforms (mountains, hills, ridges, etc.) are created when large areas of bedrock are widely broken up by faults creating large vertical displacements of continental crust.

Vertical motion of the resulting blocks, sometimes accompanied by tilting, can then lead to high escarpments. These mountains are formed by the earth's crust being stretched and extended by tensional forces. Fault block mountains commonly accompany rifting, another indicator of tensional tectonic forces.

a. Gravitational erosion
c. Shutter ridge

b. Fault scarp
d. Fault-block

31. The _____ is an assemblage of Triassic sedimentary rocks which outcrop intermittently along the United States East Coast; the exposures extend from Massachusetts to North Carolina, with more still in Nova Scotia.

The _____ consists largely of poorly-sorted nonmarine sediments; typical rocks are conglomerate, arkose sandstone, siltstone, and shale.

Chapter 22. Mesozoic Earth and Life History

    a. 1509 Istanbul earthquake
    b. 1700 Cascadia earthquake
    c. Newark Group
    d. 1703 Genroku earthquake

32. The _____ is a mountain-building episode that extensively deformed Paleozoic rocks of the Great Basin in Nevada and western Utah during Late Devonian and Early Mississippian time. In the late Devonian, the Antler volcanic island arc terrane collided with was then the west coast of North America in the vicinity of today's border between Utah and Nevada.
    a. Orogenesis
    b. Orogeny
    c. Alleghenian orogeny
    d. Antler orogeny

33. The _____ was an ancient oceanic plate, which began subducting under the west coast of the North American Plate-- then located in modern Utah-- as Pangaea broke apart during the Jurassic period. It is named for the Farallon Islands which are located just west of San Francisco, California.

Over time the central part of the _____ was completely subducted under the southwestern part of the North American Plate. The remains of the _____ are the Juan de Fuca, Explorer and Gorda Plates, subducting under the northern part of the North American Plate, the Cocos Plate subducting under Central America and the Nazca Plate subducting under the South American Plate.

    a. Cocos Plate
    b. Fault trace
    c. Rivera Plate
    d. Farallon plate

34. The _____ is a tectonic plate covering most of North America, Greenland and part of Siberia. It extends eastward to the Mid-Atlantic Ridge and westward to the Chersky Range in eastern Siberia. The plate includes both continental and oceanic crust. The interior of the main continental landmass includes an extensive granitic core called a craton. Along most of the edges of this craton are fragments of crustal material called terranes, accreted to the craton by tectonic actions over the long span of geologic time. It is believed that much of North America west of the Rockies is composed of such terranes.
    a. Kermadec Plate
    b. Philippine Sea Plate
    c. Burma Plate
    d. North American plate

35. The lithosphere is broken up into what are called _____. In the case of Earth, there are eight major and many minor plates The lithospheric plates ride on the asthenosphere. These plates move in relation to one another at one of three types of plate boundaries: convergent, or collisional boundaries; divergent boundaries, also called spreading centers; and transform boundaries.
    a. Thrust fault
    b. Copperbelt Province
    c. Gorda Ridge
    d. Tectonic plates

36. _____ is a fine-grained silica-rich microcrystalline, cryptocrystalline or microfibrous sedimentary rock that may contain small fossils. It varies greatly in color (from white to black), but most often manifests as gray, brown, grayish brown and light green to rusty red; its color is an expression of trace elements present in the rock, and both red and green are most often related to traces of iron (in its oxidized and reduced forms respectively.)

_____ occurs as oval to irregular nodules in greensand, limestone, chalk, and dolostone formations as a replacement mineral, where it is formed as a result of some type of diagenesis.

a. 1703 Genroku earthquake
c. 1700 Cascadia earthquake
b. 1509 Istanbul earthquake
d. Chert

37. The _____ is a continental transform fault that runs a length of roughly 800 miles (1,300 km) through California in the United States. The fault's motion is right-lateral strike-slip (horizontal motion.) It forms the tectonic boundary between the Pacific Plate and the North American Plate.
   a. 1700 Cascadia earthquake
   c. 1509 Istanbul earthquake
   b. San Andreas fault
   d. 1703 Genroku earthquake

38. An _____ is the result of a sudden release of energy in the Earth's crust that creates seismic waves. They are recorded with a seismometer or the related and mostly obsolete Richter magnitude, with a magnitude 3 or lower _____ being mostly imperceptible and magnitude 7 causing serious damage over large areas.
   a. AASHTO Soil Classification System
   c. AL 333
   b. AL 129-1
   d. Earthquake

39. In geology, a _____ or _____ line is a planar fracture in rock in which the rock on one side of the fracture has moved with respect to the rock on the other side. Large faults within the Earth's crust are the result of differential or shear motion and active _____ zones are the causal locations of most earthquakes. Earthquakes are caused by energy release during rapid slippage along a _____.
   a. Fault
   c. Dali
   b. Stack
   d. Combe

40. In geology, _____ is the process that takes place at convergent boundaries by which one tectonic plate moves under another tectonic plate, sinking into the Earth's mantle, as the plates converge. A _____ zone is an area on Earth where two tectonic plates move towards one another and _____ occurs. Rates of _____ are typically measured in centimeters per year, with the average rate of convergence being approximately 2 to 8 centimeters per year (about the rate a fingernail grows.)
   a. Subduction
   c. Forearc
   b. Motagua Fault
   d. Divergent boundary

41. The _____ was a period of mountain building in western North America, which started in the Late Cretaceous, 70 to 80 million years ago, and ended 35 to 55 million years ago. The exact duration and ages of beginning and end of the orogeny are in dispute, as is the cause. The _____ occurred in a series of pulses, with quiescent phases intervening. The major feature that was created by this orogeny was the Rocky Mountains, but evidence of this orogeny can be found from Alaska to northern Mexico, with the easternmost extent of the mountain-building represented by the Black Hills of South Dakota.
   a. Kaikoura Orogeny
   c. Sevier orogeny
   b. Laramide orogeny
   d. Pan-African orogeny

42. The _____ was a mountain-building event that affected western North America from Canada to the north to Mexico to the south. This orogeny was the result of convergent boundary tectonism between approximately 140 million years (Ma) ago, and 50 Ma. This orogeny was produced by the collision of the oceanic Farallon Plate and Kula Plate, predecessors of the Pacific Plate, and their subduction underneath the continental North American Plate. The _____ was preceded by several other mountain-building events including the Nevadan orogeny, the Sonoman orogeny, and the Antler orogeny, and partially overlapped in time and space with the Laramide orogeny.

a. Sevier orogeny
b. Pan-African orogeny
c. Trans-Hudson orogeny
d. Kaikoura Orogeny

43. A _____ is a type of fault in which rocks of lower stratigraphic position are pushed up and over higher strata. They are often recognized because they place older rocks above younger. Thrust faults are the result of compressional forces.
   a. Subduction
   b. Thrust fault
   c. Juan de Fuca Ridge
   d. Convergent boundary

44. A _____ is a large emplacement of igneous intrusive rock that forms from cooled magma deep in the Earth's crust. they are almost always made mostly of felsic or intermediate rock-types, such as granite, quartz monzonite, or diorite

Although they may appear uniform, batholiths are in fact structures with complex histories and compositions.

   a. Tuff
   b. Flood basalt
   c. Great Dyke
   d. Batholith

45. In geology, a _____ is a place where the Earth's crust and lithosphere are being pulled apart and is an example of extensional tectonics.

Typical _____ features are a central linear downdropped fault segment, called a graben, with parallel normal faulting and _____-flank uplifts on either side forming a _____ valley, where the _____ remains above sea level. The axis of the _____ area commonly contains volcanic rocks and active volcanism is a part of many, but not all active _____ systems.

   a. 1700 Cascadia earthquake
   b. Rift
   c. 1703 Genroku earthquake
   d. 1509 Istanbul earthquake

46. The _____ is a geologic formation that is spread across the U.S. states of northern Arizona, Nevada, Utah, western New Mexico, and western Colorado. The _____ is controversially considered to be synonymous to Dockum Group in eastern Colorado, eastern New Mexico, southwestern Kansas, the Oklahoma panhandle, and western Texas. The _____ is sometimes colloquially used as a geologic formation within the Dockum in New Mexico and occasionally in Texas.
   a. Diamond Head
   b. Stack
   c. Chinle
   d. Cohesion

47. In geology, _____ refers to inclined sedimentary structures in a horizontal unit of rock. These tilted structures are deposits from bedforms such as ripples and dunes, and they indicate that the depositional environment contained a flowing fluid (typically, water or wind.) This is a case in geology when original depositional layering is tilted, and that the tilting is not a result of post-depositional deformation.
   a. Geomicrobiology
   b. Schmidt hammer
   c. Platform cover
   d. Cross-bedding

48. A _____ is a forest in which tree trunks have fossilized. That is, the wood in the trunks have turned into petrified wood, where organic cells have decomposed and are replaced by minerals, while preserving the structure of the wood.

Chapter 22. Mesozoic Earth and Life History

a. 1509 Istanbul earthquake
c. Phaneritic
b. 1700 Cascadia earthquake
d. Petrified Forest

49. _____ is a sedimentary rock composed mainly of sand-size mineral or rock grains. Most _____ is composed of quartz and/or feldspar because these are the most common minerals in the Earth's crust. Like sand, _____ may be any color, but the most common colors are tan, brown, yellow, red, gray and white.
   a. Dolostone
   c. Sandstone
   b. Lithification
   d. Porcellanite

50. The _____ is a western North American sequence of Upper Jurassic age marine shales, sandy shales, and sandstones. The formation underlies the western North American Morrison Formation, the most fertile source of dinosaur fossils in the Americas, and is separated by a disconformity from the underlying Upper Triassic Chugwater Formation red beds. The _____ is known for fossils of an extinct species of marine cephalopod, Belemnites densus.
   a. 1509 Istanbul earthquake
   c. 1700 Cascadia earthquake
   b. Sundance Formation
   d. 1703 Genroku earthquake

51. The _____ was an epeiric sea which existed in North America during the mid to late Jurassic Period of the Mesozoic Era. It was an arm of what is now the Arctic Ocean, and extended through what is now western Canada into the central western United States. The sea receded when highlands to the west began to rise.

The _____ did not occur at a single time; geological evidence suggests that the Sea was actually a series of five successive marine transgressions--each separated by an erosional hiatus--which advanced and receded from the middle Jurassic onward.
   a. Pan-African Ocean
   c. Proto-Tethys Ocean
   b. Paratethys
   d. Sundance Sea

52. The _____ is a distinctive sequence of Late Jurassic sedimentary rock that is found in the western United States, which has been the most fertile source of dinosaur fossils in North America. It is composed of mudstone, sandstone, siltstone and limestone and is light grey, greenish gray, or red. Most of the fossils occur in the green siltstone beds and lower sandstones, relics of the rivers and floodplains of the Jurassic period.
   a. 1509 Istanbul earthquake
   c. 1703 Genroku earthquake
   b. Morrison Formation
   d. 1700 Cascadia earthquake

53. _____ refers to a type of limestone quarried in the Florida Keys, in particular from Windley Key fossil quarry, which is now a State Park of Florida. The limestone is Pleistocene in age, and the rock primarily consists of scleractinian coral, such as Elkhorn coral and Brain coral.
   a. Sandstone
   c. Keystone
   b. Superficial deposits
   d. Mudstone

54. In geology, _____ are a body of rock with specified characteristics. Ideally, a _____ is a distinctive rock unit that forms under certain conditions of sedimentation, reflecting a particular process or environment.

The term _____ was introduced by the Swiss geologist Amanz Gressly in 1838 and was part of his significant contribution to the foundations of modern stratigraphy, [Cross and Homewood (1997)] which replaced the earlier notions of Neptunism.

a. Schist
b. Facies
c. Granulites
d. Mylonite

55. In geology, a _____ is a location on the Earth's surface that has experienced active volcanism for a long period of time.

J. Tuzo Wilson came up with the idea in 1963 that volcanic chains like the Hawaiian Islands result from the slow movement of a tectonic plate across a 'fixed' _____ deep beneath the surface of the planet.

a. Hotspot
b. 1509 Istanbul earthquake
c. 1700 Cascadia earthquake
d. 1703 Genroku earthquake

56. The _____ is a mid-ocean ridge, a divergent tectonic plate boundary located along the floor of the Atlantic Ocean, and the longest mountain range in the world. It separates the Eurasian Plate and North American Plate in the North Atlantic, and the African Plate from the South American Plate in the South Atlantic. The MAR extends from a junction with the Gakkel Ridge (Mid-Arctic Ridge) northeast of Greenland southward to the Bouvet Triple Junction in the South Atlantic.

a. 1700 Cascadia earthquake
b. 1509 Istanbul earthquake
c. Mid-Atlantic Ridge
d. 1703 Genroku earthquake

57. _____ is a hard, compact variety of mineral coal that has a high lustre. It has the highest carbon count and contains the fewest impurities of all coals, despite its lower calorific content.

_____ is the highest of the metamorphic rank, in which the carbon content is between 92% and 98%.

a. AL 129-1
b. AASHTO Soil Classification System
c. AL 333
d. Anthracite

58. _____ is a relatively soft coal containing a tarlike substance called bitumen. It is of higher quality than lignite coal but of poorer quality than anthracite coal.

_____ is a sedimorphic rock formed by diagenetic and submetamorphic compression of peat bog material.

a. 1700 Cascadia earthquake
b. 1703 Genroku earthquake
c. Bituminous coal
d. 1509 Istanbul earthquake

59. The _____ is a physiographic region of the Intermontane Plateaus, roughly centered on the Four Corners region of the southwestern United States. The province covers an area of 337,000 km² within western Colorado, northwestern New Mexico, southern and eastern Utah, and northern Arizona. About 90% of the area is drained by the Colorado River and its main tributaries; the Green, San Juan and Little Colorado.

Development of the province has in large part been influenced by structural features in its oldest rocks. Part of the Wasatch Line and its various faults form the western edge of the province. Faults that run parallel to the Wasatch Fault that lies along the Wasatch Range form the boundaries between the plateaus in the High Plateaus Section. The Uinta Basin, Uncompahgre Uplift, and the Paradox Basin were also created by movement along structural weaknesses in the region's oldest rock.

Chapter 22. Mesozoic Earth and Life History

a. 1703 Genroku earthquake
b. Colorado Plateau
c. 1700 Cascadia earthquake
d. 1509 Istanbul earthquake

60. The _____ is a geologic subperiod and stratigraphic subsystem of the Carboniferous Period. It is the later subperiod of the Carboniferous, lasting from roughly 318.1>± 1.3 to 299>± 0.8 Ma (million years ago.) As with most other geochronologic units, the rock beds that define the _____ are well identified, but the exact date of the start and end are uncertain by a few million years.
   a. Calciferous sandstone
   b. Pennsylvanian
   c. Dinantian
   d. Mississippian

61. The _____ is an informal name for the supereon comprising the eons of the geologic timescale that came before the current Phanerozoic eon. It spans from the formation of Earth around 4500 Mya (million years ago) to the evolution of abundant macroscopic hard-shelled animals, which marked the beginning of the Cambrian, the first period of the first era of the Phanerozoic eon, some 542 Mya. It is named after the Roman name for Wales - Cambria - where rocks from this age were first studied.
   a. 1700 Cascadia earthquake
   b. 1509 Istanbul earthquake
   c. Precambrian
   d. 1703 Genroku earthquake

62. _____ are an extinct group of marine animals of the subclass Ammonoidea in the class Cephalopoda, phylum Mollusca. They are excellent index fossils, and it is often possible to link the rock layer in which they are found to specific geological time periods.

   _____' closest living relative is probably not the modern Nautilus (which they outwardly resemble), but rather the subclass Coleoidea (octopus, squid, and cuttlefish.)

   a. AL 129-1
   b. Ammonites
   c. AASHTO Soil Classification System
   d. AL 333

63. _____ are a distinctive type of rock often found in primordial sedimentary rocks. The structures consist of repeated thin layers of iron oxides, either magnetite or hematite, alternating with bands of iron-poor shale and chert. Some of the oldest known rock formations, formed around three thousand million years before present, include banded iron layers, and the banded layers are a common feature in sediments for much of the Earth's early history.
   a. Banded Iron Formations
   b. Mudstone
   c. Jasperoid
   d. Superficial deposits

64. _____ are fossils used to define and identify geologic periods They work on the premise that, although different sediments may look different depending on the conditions under which they were laid down, they may include the remains of the same species of fossil. If the species concerned were short-lived, then it is certain that the sediments in question were deposited within that narrow time period.
   a. Indian bead
   b. Invertebrate paleontology
   c. Allotrioceras
   d. Index fossils

65. _____ is a type of potassic volcanic rock best known for sometimes containing diamonds. It is named after the town of Kimberley in South Africa, where the discovery of an 83.5 carats (16.7 g) diamond in 1871 spawned a diamond rush, eventually creating the Big Hole.

_____ occurs in the Earth's crust in vertical structures known as _____ pipes.

a. Kimberlite
c. 1703 Genroku earthquake
b. 1509 Istanbul earthquake
d. 1700 Cascadia earthquake

66. _____ are the preserved remains or traces of animals, plants, and other organisms from the remote past. The totality of _____, both discovered and undiscovered, and their placement in fossiliferous rock formations and sedimentary layers (strata) is known as the fossil record. The study of _____ across geological time, how they were formed, and the evolutionary relationships between taxa (phylogeny) are some of the most important functions of the science of paleontology.

a. 1700 Cascadia earthquake
c. 1509 Istanbul earthquake
b. 1703 Genroku earthquake
d. Fossils

67. An _____ is an animal lacking a vertebral column. The group includes 98% of all animal species -- all animals except those in the Chordate subphylum Vertebrata (fish, reptiles, amphibians, birds, and mammals.)

Carolus Linnaeus' Systema Naturae divided these animals into only two groups, the Insecta and the now-obsolete vermes (worms.)

a. AL 129-1
c. AASHTO Soil Classification System
b. Invertebrate
d. AL 333

68. An _____ is a type of rock that contains minerals such as gemstones and metals that can be extracted through mining and refined for use. Samples of _____ in the form of exceptionally beautiful crystals, exotic layering visible when sectioned or polished or metallic presentations such as large nuggets or crystalline formations of metals such as gold or copper may command a value far beyond their value as mere _____ or raw metal for subsequent reduction to utilitarian purposes.

The grade or concentration of an _____ mineral, or metal, as well as its form of occurrence, will directly affect the costs associated with mining the _____.

a. AASHTO Soil Classification System
c. Ore genesis
b. AL 129-1
d. Ore

69. The _____ is the first geological period of the Phanerozoic eon, lasting from 542 ± 0.3 million years ago to 488.3 ± 1.7 million years ago (ICS, 2004); it is succeeded by the Ordovician. Its subdivisions, and indeed its base, are somewhat in flux. The period was established by Adam Sedgwick, who named it after Cambria, the classical name for Wales, where Britain's _____ rocks are best exposed.

a. 1700 Cascadia earthquake
c. 1509 Istanbul earthquake
b. 1703 Genroku earthquake
d. Cambrian

70. The _____ or Cambrian radiation was the seemingly rapid appearance of most major groups of complex animals around 530 million years ago, as evidenced by the fossil record. This was accompanied by a major diversification of other organisms, including animals, phytoplankton, and calcimicrobes. Before about 580 million years ago, most organisms were simple, composed of individual cells occasionally organized into colonies.

Chapter 22. Mesozoic Earth and Life History

a. Labyrinthodont
b. Cambrian explosion
c. Romer's Gap
d. Conodont Alteration Index

71. _____ are single-celled algae, protists and phytoplankton belonging to the division haptophytes. They are distinguished by special calcium carbonate plates of uncertain function called coccoliths, which are important microfossils. _____ are almost exclusively marine and are found in large numbers throughout the surface euphotic zone of the ocean.
a. 1703 Genroku earthquake
b. 1700 Cascadia earthquake
c. 1509 Istanbul earthquake
d. Coccolithophores

72. _____ is one of the two orders, or basic divisions of dinosaurs. In 1888, Harry Seeley classified dinosaurs into two orders, based on their hip structure. Saurischians ('lizard-hipped') are distinguished from the ornithischians ('bird-hipped') by retaining the ancestral configuration of bones in the hip.
a. 1509 Istanbul earthquake
b. 1703 Genroku earthquake
c. Saurischia
d. 1700 Cascadia earthquake

73. A _____ is any geological stratum or deposit that contains bones of whatever kind. Inevitably, such deposits are sedimentary in nature. Not a formal term, it tends to be used more to describe especially dense collections. It is also applied to brecciated and stalagmitic deposits on the floor of caves, which frequently contain osseous remains.
a. Compression fossil
b. Bone bed
c. Fossil wood
d. Copalite

74. _____ is a sedimentary rock composed largely of the mineral calcite (calcium carbonate: $CaCO_3$.) The deposition of _____ strata is often a by-product and indicator of biological activity in the geologic record. Calcium (along with nitrogen, phosphorus, and potassium) is a key mineral to plant nutrition: soils overlying _____ bedrock tend to be pre-fertilized with calcium.
a. 1700 Cascadia earthquake
b. 1509 Istanbul earthquake
c. 1703 Genroku earthquake
d. Limestone

75. The _____ was a cratonic sequence that began in the mid-Devonian, peaked early in the Mississippian, and ended by mid-Mississippian time. A major unconformity separates it from the lower Tippecanoe sequence.

The basal-that is, the lowest and oldest-units of the Kaskaskia consist of clean quartz sandstones eroded from the Appalachian orogenic belt to the east, the Ozark Dome in the center of the continent, and south from the Canadian Shield.

a. 1509 Istanbul earthquake
b. Kaskaskia sequence
c. 1700 Cascadia earthquake
d. Sauk sequence

76. _____ is the second most abundant mineral in the Earth's continental crust. It is made up of a framework of silicon-oxygen tetrahedra SiO_4, with each silicon shared between two oxygens to give the overall formula SiO_2. _____ has a hardness of 7 on the Mohs scale and a density of 2.65 g/cmÂ³.
a. 1703 Genroku earthquake
b. 1700 Cascadia earthquake
c. Quartz
d. 1509 Istanbul earthquake

77. _____ is a form of quartz that has a microscopic structure that is different from normal quartz. Under intense pressure (but limited temperature), the crystalline structure of quartz will be deformed along planes inside the crystal. These planes, which show up as lines under a microscope, are called planar deformation features (PDFs), or shock lamellae.
  a. Shocked quartz
  b. 1700 Cascadia earthquake
  c. 1703 Genroku earthquake
  d. 1509 Istanbul earthquake

Chapter 23. Cenozoic Earth and Life History

1. The _____ is a geological epoch which began approximately 11‰700 years ago (10‰000 ^{14}C years ago). According to traditional geological thinking, the _____ continues to the present. The _____ is part of the Neogene and Quaternary periods.
   a. 1509 Istanbul earthquake
   b. 1700 Cascadia earthquake
   c. Holocene
   d. Neoglaciation

2. The _____ was a period of mountain building in western North America, which started in the Late Cretaceous, 70 to 80 million years ago, and ended 35 to 55 million years ago. The exact duration and ages of beginning and end of the orogeny are in dispute, as is the cause. The _____ occurred in a series of pulses, with quiescent phases intervening. The major feature that was created by this orogeny was the Rocky Mountains, but evidence of this orogeny can be found from Alaska to northern Mexico, with the easternmost extent of the mountain-building represented by the Black Hills of South Dakota.
   a. Sevier orogeny
   b. Pan-African orogeny
   c. Kaikoura Orogeny
   d. Laramide orogeny

3. The _____ Era is one of three geologic eras of the Phanerozoic eon. The division of time into eras dates back to Giovanni Arduino, in the 18th century, although his original name for the era now called the '_____' was 'Secondary' (making the modern era the 'Tertiary'.)

   The _____ was a time of tectonic, climatic and evolutionary activity. The continents gradually shifted from a state of connectedness into their present configuration; the drifting provided for speciation and other important evolutionary developments.

   a. Mesozoic
   b. 1700 Cascadia earthquake
   c. 1703 Genroku earthquake
   d. 1509 Istanbul earthquake

4. The _____ is a geologic period and system that began 65.5 ± 0.3 and ended 23.03 ± 0.05 million years ago and comprises the first part of the Cenozoic era. Lasting 42 million years, the _____ is most notable as being the time in which mammals evolved from relatively small, simple forms into a plethora of diverse animals in the wake of the mass extinction that ended the preceding Cretaceous Period. Some of these mammals would evolve into large forms that would dominate the land, while others would become capable of living in marine, specialized terrestrial and even airborne environments.
   a. Sharamurunian
   b. Casamayoran
   c. Paleogene
   d. Peligran

5. The _____ is the earliest of three geologic eras of the Phanerozoic eon. The _____ spanned from roughly 542 to 251 million years ago (ICS, 2004), and is subdivided into six geologic periods; from oldest to youngest they are: the Cambrian, Ordovician, Silurian, Devonian, Carboniferous, and Permian.

   The _____ covers the time from the first appearance of abundant, soft-shelled fossils to the time when the continents were beginning to be dominated by large, relatively sophisticated reptiles and modern plants. The lower (oldest) boundary was classically set at the first appearance of creatures known as trilobites and archeocyathids.

   a. 1509 Istanbul earthquake
   b. 1703 Genroku earthquake
   c. Paleozoic
   d. 1700 Cascadia earthquake

Chapter 23. Cenozoic Earth and Life History

6. The _____ is the epoch from 1.8 million to 11550 years BP covering the world's recent period of repeated glaciations. The _____ epoch follows the Pliocene epoch and is followed by the Holocene epoch. The _____ is the third epoch of the Neogene period or 6th epoch of the Cenozoic Era. The end of the _____ corresponds with the retreat of the last continental glacier. It also corresponds with the end of the Paleolithic age used in archaeology.

   a. Pleistocene
   b. Late Pleistocene
   c. Sicilian Stage
   d. Tyrrhenian

7. The _____ is a geological eon representing a period before the first abundant complex life on Earth. The _____ extended from 2500 Ma to 542.0 >± 1.0 Ma (million years ago), and is the most recent part of the old, informally named 'e;Precambrian'e; time.

The Proterozoic consists of 3 geologic eras, from oldest to youngest:

- Paleoproterozoic
- Mesoproterozoic
- Neoproterozoic

The well-identified events were:

- The transition to an oxygenated atmosphere during the Mesoproterozoic.
- Several glaciations, including the hypothesized Snowball Earth during the Cryogenian period in the late Neoproterozoic.
- The Ediacaran Period (635 to 542 Ma) which is characterized by the evolution of abundant soft-bodied multicellular organisms.

The geoloic record of the Proterozoic is much better than that for the preceding Archean. In contrast to the deep-water deposits of the Archean, the Proterozoic features many strata that were laid down in extensive shallow epicontinental seas; furthermore, many of these rocks are less metamorphosed than Archean-age ones, and plenty are unaltered.

   a. 1700 Cascadia earthquake
   b. 1509 Istanbul earthquake
   c. 1703 Genroku earthquake
   d. Proterozoic Eon

8. The _____ Period is the geologic time period after the Neogene Period, spanning 1.805 +/- 0.005 million years ago to the present. The _____ includes two geologic epochs: the Pleistocene and the Holocene Epoch.

There is an ongoing debate of the status of _____ -- a recent proposal from International Commission on Stratigraphy (ICS) was to make _____ a subperiod under Neogene, but that was retracted after criticism from International Union for _____ Research (INQUA), so instead ICS and INQUA agreed to erect _____ as an Era, above Neogene, and to place the base for _____ at 2.588 >± 3.005, the base for Gelasian Stage.

   a. Musgrave Block
   b. Quaternary
   c. Grade
   d. Gawler craton

Chapter 23. Cenozoic Earth and Life History

9. The _____ is a a term for a geologic period 65 million to 1.8 million years ago. The _____ covered the time span between the superseded Secondary period and an out-of-date definition of the Quaternary period. The period began with the demise of the non-avian dinosaurs in the Cretaceous-_____ extinction event, at start of the Cenozoic era, spanning to beginning of the most recent Ice Age, at the end of the Pliocene epoch.
   a. Rockall
   b. Historical geology
   c. Tertiary
   d. Star dunes

10. The _____ is a chronologic schema (or idealized model) relating stratigraphy to time that is used by geologists, paleontologists and other earth scientists to describe the timing and relationships between events that have occurred during the history of the Earth. The table of geologic time spans presented here agrees with the dates and nomenclature proposed by the International Commission on Stratigraphy, and uses the standard color codes of the United States Geological Survey.

Evidence from radiometric dating indicates that the Earth is about 4.570 billion years old.

   a. Geologic time scale
   b. 1703 Genroku earthquake
   c. 1509 Istanbul earthquake
   d. 1700 Cascadia earthquake

11. A _____ is a large, slow-moving mass of ice, formed from compacted layers of snow, that slowly deforms and flows in response to gravity and high pressure.

_____ ice is the largest reservoir of fresh water on Earth, and second only to oceans as the largest reservoir of total water.

   a. Glacier
   b. Keeling Curve
   c. Little Ice Age
   d. Pacific Decadal Oscillation

12. An _____ is an animal lacking a vertebral column. The group includes 98% of all animal species -- all animals except those in the Chordate subphylum Vertebrata (fish, reptiles, amphibians, birds, and mammals.)

Carolus Linnaeus' Systema Naturae divided these animals into only two groups, the Insecta and the now-obsolete vermes (worms.)

   a. AL 129-1
   b. AASHTO Soil Classification System
   c. AL 333
   d. Invertebrate

13. _____ refers to natural mountain building, and may be studied as a tectonic structural event, (b) as a geographical event, and (c) a chronological event. Orogenic events (a) cause distinctive structural phenomena and related tectonic activity, (b) affect certain regions of rocks and crust, and (c) happen within a specific period of time.
   a. Orogeny
   b. Orogenesis
   c. Alice Springs Orogeny
   d. Antler orogeny

14. The _____ is a tectonic plate which includes the continent of Africa, as well as oceanic crust which lies between the continent and various surrounding ocean ridges.

The westerly side is a divergent boundary with the North American Plate to the north and the South American Plate to the south forming the central and southern part of the Mid-Atlantic Ridge. The _____ is bounded on the northeast by the Arabian Plate, the southeast by the Indo-Australian Plate, the north by the Eurasian Plate and the Anatolian Plate, and on the south by the Antarctic Plate.

   a. Arabian Plate
   c. Easter Plate
   b. Eurasian Plate
   d. African plate

   15. The _____ is an orogenic phase in the Tertiary that formed the mountain ranges of the Alpide belt. These mountains include the Atlas, the Pyrenees, the Alps, the Dinaric Alps, the Hellenides, the Carpathians, the Balkan, the Taurus, the Caucasus, the Alborz, the Zagros, the Hindu Kush, the Pamir, the Karakoram, and the Himalayas. Sometimes other names occur to describe the formation of separate mountain ranges: for example Carpathean orogeny for the Carpathians, Hellenic orogeny for the Hellenides or the Himalayan orogeny for the Himalayas.
   a. Antler orogeny
   c. Alpine orogeny
   b. Orogeny
   d. Alleghenian orogeny

   16. The _____ Era, is the most recent of the three classic geological eras and covers the period from 65.5 million years ago to the present. It is marked by the Cretaceous-Tertiary extinction event at the end of the Cretaceous that saw the demise of the last non-avian dinosaurs and the end of the Mesozoic Era. The _____ era is ongoing.
   a. 1700 Cascadia earthquake
   c. Cenozoic
   b. 1703 Genroku earthquake
   d. 1509 Istanbul earthquake

   17. The _____ is an oceanic tectonic plate beneath the Pacific Ocean off the west coast of Central America which rides upon it.

The _____ is created by sea floor spreading along the East Pacific Rise and the Cocos Ridge, specifically in a complicated area geologists call the Cocos-Nazca spreading system. From the rise the plate is pushed eastward and pushed or dragged (perhaps both) under the less dense overriding Caribbean Plate, in the process called subduction.

   a. Cocos plate
   c. Farallon Plate
   b. Rivera Plate
   d. Fault trace

   18. An _____ is the result of a sudden release of energy in the Earth's crust that creates seismic waves. They are recorded with a seismometer or the related and mostly obsolete Richter magnitude, with a magnitude 3 or lower _____ being mostly imperceptible and magnitude 7 causing serious damage over large areas.
   a. AL 129-1
   c. Earthquake
   b. AASHTO Soil Classification System
   d. AL 333

   19. The _____ is a mid-oceanic ridge, a divergent tectonic plate boundary located along the floor of the Pacific Ocean. It separates the Pacific Plate to the west from (north to south) the North American Plate, the Rivera Plate, the Cocos Plate, the Nazca Plate, and the Antarctic Plate. It runs from an undefined point near Antarctica in the south northward to its termination at the northern end of the Gulf of California in the Salton Sea basin in southern California.

Chapter 23. Cenozoic Earth and Life History

a. Elastic rebound theory
c. East Pacific Rise
b. Obduction
d. Azores-Gibraltar Transform Fault

20. The _____ epoch (55.8 >± 0.2 - 33.9 >± 0.1 Ma) is a major division of the geologic timescale and the second epoch of the Palaeogene period in the Cenozoic era. The _____ spans the time from the end of the Paleocene epoch to the beginning of the Oligocene epoch. The start of the _____ is marked by the emergence of the first modern mammals.
    a. AASHTO Soil Classification System
    c. AL 129-1
    b. AL 333
    d. Eocene

21. The _____ was an ancient oceanic plate, which began subducting under the west coast of the North American Plate-- then located in modern Utah-- as Pangaea broke apart during the Jurassic period. It is named for the Farallon Islands which are located just west of San Francisco, California.

Over time the central part of the _____ was completely subducted under the southwestern part of the North American Plate. The remains of the _____ are the Juan de Fuca, Explorer and Gorda Plates, subducting under the northern part of the North American Plate, the Cocos Plate subducting under Central America and the Nazca Plate subducting under the South American Plate.

   a. Fault trace
   c. Cocos Plate
   b. Rivera Plate
   d. Farallon plate

22. The _____ is an oceanic tectonic plate in the eastern Pacific Ocean basin off the west coast of South America.

The eastern margin is a convergent boundary subduction zone under the South American Plate and the Andes Mountains, forming the Peru-Chile Trench. The southern side is a divergent boundary with the Antarctic Plate, the Chile Rise, where seafloor spreading permits magma to rise.

   a. Conway Reef Plate
   c. Nazca plate
   b. Timor Plate
   d. Juan de Fuca Plate

23. The _____ was a major mountain building event that took place along the western edge of ancient North America between the Mid to Late Jurassic (between about 180 and 140 million years ago.) The _____ was the first of three major mountain building episodes to transform Western North America between the Late Mesozoic and Early Cenozoic Eras, the latter two being the Sevier and Laramide orogeny, chronologically. Much like the two orogenies that followed, the Nevadan was caused by the subduction of oceanic lithosphere at a subduction zone running along the edge of the North American continent.
   a. Pan-African orogeny
   c. Kaikoura Orogeny
   b. Sevier orogeny
   d. Nevadan orogeny

24. _____ was the supercontinent that is theorized to have existed during the Paleozoic and Mesozoic eras about 250 million years ago, before the component continents were separated into their current configuration.

The name was first used by the German originator of the continental drift theory, Alfred Wegener, in the 1920 edition of his book The Origin of Continents and Oceans , in which a postulated supercontinent _____ played a key role.

The single enormous ocean which surrounded Pangaea is known as Panthalassa.

   a. 1509 Istanbul earthquake
   b. 1700 Cascadia earthquake
   c. 1703 Genroku earthquake
   d. Pangea

25. The _____ was a mountain-building event that affected western North America from Canada to the north to Mexico to the south. This orogeny was the result of convergent boundary tectonism between approximately 140 million years (Ma) ago, and 50 Ma. This orogeny was produced by the collision of the oceanic Farallon Plate and Kula Plate, predecessors of the Pacific Plate, and their subduction underneath the continental North American Plate. The _____ was preceded by several other mountain-building events including the Nevadan orogeny, the Sonoman orogeny, and the Antler orogeny, and partially overlapped in time and space with the Laramide orogeny.
   a. Kaikoura Orogeny
   b. Trans-Hudson orogeny
   c. Pan-African orogeny
   d. Sevier orogeny

26. The _____ is a tectonic plate covering the continent of South America and extending eastward to the Mid-Atlantic Ridge.

The easterly side is a divergent boundary with the African Plate forming the southern part of the Mid-Atlantic Ridge. The southerly side is a complex boundary with the Antarctic Plate and the Scotia Plate.

   a. South American plate
   b. Lhasa Plate
   c. Mariana Plate
   d. Juan de Fuca Plate

27. The _____ is a geologic period and system that extends from about 251 to 199 Mya (million years ago.) As the first period of the Mesozoic Era, the _____ follows the Permian and is followed by the Jurassic. Both the start and end of the _____ are marked by major extinction events.
   a. Triassic
   b. Rhaetian
   c. 1509 Istanbul earthquake
   d. 1700 Cascadia earthquake

28. An _____ is a confined aquifer containing groundwater that will flow upward through a well without the need for pumping. Water may even reach the ground surface if the natural pressure is high enough, in which case the well is called a flowing artesian well. An aquifer provides the water for an artesian well.
   a. AL 333
   b. AL 129-1
   c. AASHTO Soil Classification System
   d. Artesian aquifer

29. A _____ is an old and stable part of the continental crust that has survived the merging and splitting of continents and supercontinents for at least 500 million years. Some are over two billion years old. They are generally found in the interiors of continents and are characteristically composed of ancient crystalline basement crust of lightweight felsic igneous rock such as granite.
   a. Superior craton
   b. Sebakwe proto-craton
   c. Kalahari craton
   d. Craton

30. A _____ is a mountain rising from the ocean seafloor that does not reach to the water's surface (sea level), and thus is not an island. These are typically formed from extinct volcanoes, that rise abruptly and are usually found rising from a seafloor of 1,000-4,000 meters depth. They are defined by oceanographers as independent features that rise to at least 1,000 meters above the seafloor.

   a. Seamount
   b. 1703 Genroku earthquake
   c. 1509 Istanbul earthquake
   d. 1700 Cascadia earthquake

31. The lithosphere is broken up into what are called _____. In the case of Earth, there are eight major and many minor plates The lithospheric plates ride on the asthenosphere. These plates move in relation to one another at one of three types of plate boundaries: convergent, or collisional boundaries; divergent boundaries, also called spreading centers; and transform boundaries.

   a. Thrust fault
   b. Gorda Ridge
   c. Copperbelt Province
   d. Tectonic plates

32. _____ is a geologic term for a type of topography characterized by a series of separate and parallel mountain ranges with broad valleys interposed, extending over a more or less wide area. It is typified by the topography found in the Great Basin in the western United States, which is part of a larger regional topography known as the _____ Province. _____ topography results from crustal extension.

   a. Tidal scour
   b. Rill
   c. Zechstein
   d. Basin and Range

33. The _____ is a large geologic province which includes parts of the southwestern United States and northwestern Mexico, typified by basin and range topography.

The topography of the _____ is a result of crustal extension within this part of the North American Plate. The cause of this extension is as yet not fully understood, although several hypotheses have been offered. The crust here has been stretched up to 100% of its original width. In fact, the crust underneath the _____, especially under the Great Basin, is some of the thinnest in the world.

   a. Quaternary
   b. Yilgarn Craton
   c. Canadian Shield
   d. Basin and Range Province

34. A _____ is a large emplacement of igneous intrusive rock that forms from cooled magma deep in the Earth's crust. they are almost always made mostly of felsic or intermediate rock-types, such as granite, quartz monzonite, or diorite

Although they may appear uniform, batholiths are in fact structures with complex histories and compositions.

   a. Tuff
   b. Flood basalt
   c. Batholith
   d. Great Dyke

35. The _____ is a physiographic region of the Intermontane Plateaus, roughly centered on the Four Corners region of the southwestern United States. The province covers an area of 337,000 km^2 within western Colorado, northwestern New Mexico, southern and eastern Utah, and northern Arizona. About 90% of the area is drained by the Colorado River and its main tributaries; the Green, San Juan and Little Colorado.

Development of the province has in large part been influenced by structural features in its oldest rocks. Part of the Wasatch Line and its various faults form the western edge of the province. Faults that run parallel to the Wasatch Fault that lies along the Wasatch Range form the boundaries between the plateaus in the High Plateaus Section. The Uinta Basin, Uncompahgre Uplift, and the Paradox Basin were also created by movement along structural weaknesses in the region's oldest rock.

- a. 1509 Istanbul earthquake
- b. 1703 Genroku earthquake
- c. 1700 Cascadia earthquake
- d. Colorado Plateau

36. The _____ is a tectonic plate arising from the Juan de Fuca Ridge, and subducting under the northerly portion of the western side of the North American Plate at the Cascadia subduction zone. It is bounded on the south by the Blanco Fracture Zone, on the north by the Nootka Fault, and along the west by the Pacific Plate. The _____ was originally part of the once-vast Farallon Plate, now largely subducted under the North American Plate, and has since fractured into three pieces.
- a. Lhasa Plate
- b. North American Plate
- c. Kermadec Plate
- d. Juan de Fuca plate

37. _____ are the collective effect of changes in the Earth's movements upon its climate axial tilt, and precession of the Earth's orbit determined climatic patterns on Earth, resulting in 100,000-year ice age cycles of the Quaternary glaciation over the last few million years. The Earth's axis completes one full cycle of precession approximately every 26,000 years. At the same time, the elliptical orbit rotates, more slowly, leading to a 23,000-year cycle between the seasons and the orbit.
- a. Stage
- b. Global Standard Stratigraphic Age
- c. Geologic record
- d. Milankovitch theory

38. The _____ is a tectonic plate covering most of North America, Greenland and part of Siberia. It extends eastward to the Mid-Atlantic Ridge and westward to the Chersky Range in eastern Siberia. The plate includes both continental and oceanic crust. The interior of the main continental landmass includes an extensive granitic core called a craton. Along most of the edges of this craton are fragments of crustal material called terranes, accreted to the craton by tectonic actions over the long span of geologic time. It is believed that much of North America west of the Rockies is composed of such terranes.
- a. Burma Plate
- b. Philippine Sea Plate
- c. Kermadec Plate
- d. North American plate

39. The _____ is a former mid-ocean ridge that existed between the Pacific and Farallon plates in the Pacific Ocean during the Tertiary period. Its appearance was in a north-south direction. About 60 million years ago, it might have extended at least 10,000 km (6,214 mi). Remnants of the _____ include the Explorer, Gorda, Juan de Fuca and the East Pacific ridges.
- a. Kula-Farallon Ridge
- b. Pacific-Kula Ridge
- c. Pacific-Farallon Ridge
- d. Nazca Ridge

40. The _____ is an active transform fault, located between the North American Plate and the Pacific Plate, Canada's equivalent of the San Andreas Fault. The _____ forms a triple junction on its south with the Cascadia subduction zone and the Explorer Ridge (the Queen Charlotte Triple Junction.) The fault is named for Queen Charlotte Island which lies just north of the triple junction.

a. 1509 Istanbul earthquake
c. 1703 Genroku earthquake

b. 1700 Cascadia earthquake
d. Queen Charlotte fault

41. The _____ is a continental transform fault that runs a length of roughly 800 miles (1,300 km) through California in the United States. The fault's motion is right-lateral strike-slip (horizontal motion.) It forms the tectonic boundary between the Pacific Plate and the North American Plate.
    a. San Andreas fault
    c. 1700 Cascadia earthquake

    b. 1703 Genroku earthquake
    d. 1509 Istanbul earthquake

42. _____ is a common extrusive volcanic rock. It is usually grey to black and fine-grained due to rapid cooling of lava at the surface of a planet. It may be porphyritic containing larger crystals in a fine matrix, or vesicular, or frothy scoria.
    a. 1703 Genroku earthquake
    c. 1509 Istanbul earthquake

    b. 1700 Cascadia earthquake
    d. Basalt

43. In geology, a _____ or _____ line is a planar fracture in rock in which the rock on one side of the fracture has moved with respect to the rock on the other side. Large faults within the Earth's crust are the result of differential or shear motion and active _____ zones are the causal locations of most earthquakes. Earthquakes are caused by energy release during rapid slippage along a _____.
    a. Dali
    c. Fault

    b. Stack
    d. Combe

44. The _____ or Palaeocene, 'early dawn of the recent' is a geologic epoch that lasted from 65.5 >± 0.3 Ma to 55.8 >± 0.2 Ma (million years ago.) It is the first epoch of the Palaeogene Period in the modern Cenozoic era. As with most other older geologic periods, the strata that define the epoch's beginning and end are well identified but the exact date of the end is uncertain.
    a. 1703 Genroku earthquake
    c. Paleocene

    b. 1509 Istanbul earthquake
    d. 1700 Cascadia earthquake

45. An _____ is a large shallow sea that either extends far into a continent, such as the Persian Gulf, or overlies a large part of a continent.

They are usually associated with the marine transgressions of the early Cenozoic era and may be semi-cyclic--during eras of glacial recession given a period of low mountains coupled with a warming under the influence of plate tectonics. They can be warm or cold; indeed, several were present at the end of the last Ice Age, when sea levels rose more rapidly than some areas could isostatically adjust.

a. Epeiric sea
c. AL 333

b. AASHTO Soil Classification System
d. AL 129-1

46. In geology, _____ are a body of rock with specified characteristics. Ideally, a _____ is a distinctive rock unit that forms under certain conditions of sedimentation, reflecting a particular process or environment.

The term _____ was introduced by the Swiss geologist Amanz Gressly in 1838 and was part of his significant contribution to the foundations of modern stratigraphy, [Cross and Homewood (1997)] which replaced the earlier notions of Neptunism.

a. Schist
b. Facies
c. Mylonite
d. Granulites

47. In chemistry, a _____ is a salt or ester of carbonic acid.

To test for the presence of the _____ anion in a salt, the addition of dilute mineral acid (e.g. hydrochloric acid) will yield carbon dioxide gas.

_____-containing salts are industrially and mineralogically ubiquitous.

a. 1509 Istanbul earthquake
b. Carbonate
c. 1703 Genroku earthquake
d. 1700 Cascadia earthquake

48. _____ is any particulate matter that can be transported by fluid flow, and which eventually is deposited.

They are most often transported by water (fluvial processes) transported by wind (aeolian processes) and glaciers. Beach sands and river channel deposits are examples of fluvial transport and deposition, though _____ also often settles out of slow-moving or standing water in lakes and oceans.

a. Quicksand
b. Bovey Beds
c. Brickearth
d. Sediment

49. A marine _____ is a geologic event during which sea level rises relative to the land and the shoreline moves toward higher ground, resulting in flooding. They can be caused either by the land sinking or the ocean basins filling with water (or decreasing in capacity.) Transgresssions and regressions may be caused by tectonic events such as orogenies, severe climate change such as ice ages or isostatic adjustments following removal of ice or sediment load.

a. Stoping
b. Spheroidal weathering
c. Wave pounding
d. Transgression

50. The _____ is the zone of the ocean floor that separates the thin oceanic crust from thick continental crust. Continental margins constitute about 28% of the oceanic area.

The transition from continental to oceanic crust commonly occurs within the outer part of the margin, called continental rise.

a. Longshore drift
b. Cuspate forelands
c. 1509 Istanbul earthquake
d. Continental margin

51. The _____ was the earliest of the six cratonic sequences that have occurred during the Phanerozoic (followed by the Tippecanoe, Kaskaskia, Absaroka, Zu>ñi, and Tejas.) It dates from the late Proterozoic through the early Ordovician, though the marine transgression did not begin in earnest until the middle Cambrian.

At its peak, most of North America was covered by the shallow Sauk Sea, save for parts of the Canadian Shield and the islands of the Transcontinental Arch.

a. 1509 Istanbul earthquake
b. 1700 Cascadia earthquake
c. Sauk sequence
d. Tippecanoe sequence

52. _____ is the removal of solids (sediment, soil, rock and other particles) in the natural environment. It usually occurs due to transport by wind, water, or ice; by down-slope creep of soil and other material under the force of gravity; or by living organisms, such as burrowing animals, in the case of bioerosion.

_____ is distinguished from weathering, which is the process of chemical or physical breakdown of the minerals in the rocks, although the two processes may occur concurrently.

a. Erosion
b. AL 129-1
c. AL 333
d. AASHTO Soil Classification System

53. An _____ is an underground layer of water-bearing permeable rock or unconsolidated materials (gravel, sand, silt, or clay) from which groundwater can be usefully extracted using a water well. The study of water flow in aquifers and the characterization of aquifers is called hydrogeology. Related terms include: an aquitard, which is an impermeable layer along an _____, and an aquiclude (or aquifuge), which is a solid, impermeable area beneath an _____.

a. AL 129-1
b. Aquifer
c. AASHTO Soil Classification System
d. AL 333

54. In geology, engineering, and surveying, _____ is the motion of a surface (usually, the Earth's surface) as it shifts downward relative to a datum such as sea-level. The opposite of _____ is uplift, which results in an increase in elevation. There are several types of _____.

a. 1700 Cascadia earthquake
b. Subsidence
c. Pothole
d. 1509 Istanbul earthquake

55. The _____, is a geologic eon before the Proterozoic and Paleoproterozoic, before 2.5 Ga (billion years ago, or 2,500 Ma.) Instead of being based on stratigraphy, this date is defined chronometrically. The lower boundary (starting point) has not been officially recognized by the International Commission on Stratigraphy, but it is usually set to 3.8 Ga, at the end of the Hadean eon.

a. AASHTO Soil Classification System
b. AL 333
c. AL 129-1
d. Archean

56. In stratigraphy, _____ is the native consolidated rock underlying the surface of a terrestrial planet, usually the Earth. Above the _____ is usually an area of broken and weathered unconsolidated rock in the basal subsoil. The top of the _____ is known as rockhead and identifying this, via excavations, drilling or geophysical methods, is an important task in most civil engineering projects.

a. Biozones
b. Sequence stratigraphy
c. Bedrock
d. Polystrate

57. A _____ is a cauldron-like volcanic feature usually formed by the collapse of land following a volcanic eruption such as the one at Yellowstone National Park. They are sometimes confused with volcanic craters.

a. 1509 Istanbul earthquake
b. 1700 Cascadia earthquake
c. 1703 Genroku earthquake
d. Caldera

Chapter 23. Cenozoic Earth and Life History

58. The _____ is the extended perimeter of each continent and associated coastal plain, and was part of the continent during the glacial periods, but is undersea during interglacial periods such as the current epoch by relatively shallow seas (known as shelf seas) and gulfs.

The continental rise is below the slope, but landward of the abyssal plains. Its gradient is intermediate between the slope and the shelf, on the order of 0.5-1°.

a. 1700 Cascadia earthquake
b. 1703 Genroku earthquake
c. Continental shelf
d. 1509 Istanbul earthquake

59. The _____ , usually abbreviated K for its German translation Kreide, is a geologic period and system from circa >145.5 >± 4 to >65.5 >± 0.3 million years ago . In the geologic timescale, the _____ follows on the Jurassic period and is followed by the Paleogene period. It is the youngest period of the Mesozoic era, and at 80 million years long, the longest period of the Phanerozoic eon. The end of the _____ defines the boundary between the Mesozoic and Cenozoic eras.

a. Campanian
b. Coniacian
c. Cretaceous
d. Hauterivian

60. A _____ is a piece of rock that differs from the size and type of rock native to the area in which it rests. They are carried by glacial ice, often over distances of hundreds of kilometres and can range in size from pebbles to large boulders such as Big Rock (16,500 tons) in Alberta.

a. 1700 Cascadia earthquake
b. 1703 Genroku earthquake
c. 1509 Istanbul earthquake
d. Glacial erratic

61. _____ is rock that is of a specific particle size range. Specifically, it is any loose rock that is larger than two millimeters (2mm) in its largest dimension (about 1/12 of an inch) and no more than 64 millimeters (about 2.5 inches.) The next smaller size class in geology is sand, which is >0.0625 mm to 2 mm in size.

a. 1509 Istanbul earthquake
b. 1703 Genroku earthquake
c. 1700 Cascadia earthquake
d. Gravel

62. An _____ is a geological interval of warmer global average temperature that separates glacial periods within an ice age. The current Holocene _____ has persisted since the Pleistocene, about 11,400 years ago.

During the 2.5 million year span of the Pleistocene, numerous glacials, or significant advances of continental ice sheets in North America and Europe have occurred at intervals of approximately 40,000 to 100,000 years.

a. Interglacial
b. AL 333
c. AL 129-1
d. AASHTO Soil Classification System

63. The _____ is an oceanic tectonic plate beneath the Pacific Ocean.

To the north the easterly side is a divergent boundary with the Explorer Plate, the Juan de Fuca Plate and the Gorda Plate forming respectively the Explorer Ridge, the Juan de Fuca Ridge and the Gorda Ridge. In the middle the easterly side is a transform boundary with the North American Plate along the San Andreas Fault and a boundary with the Cocos Plate.

a. Gorda Plate
b. Pacific plate
c. Conway Reef Plate
d. Somali Plate

64. Alpine glaciers form high on the mountain slopes and are niche, slope or cirque glaciers. As a mountain glacier increases in size it can begin to flow down valley, and are referred to as _____.
   a. Pahoehoe lava
   b. Star dunes
   c. Valley glaciers
   d. Tertiary

65. _____ is the geological process by which material is added to a landform or land mass. Fluids such as wind and water, as well as sediment gravity flows, transport previously eroded sediment, which, at the loss of enough kinetic energy in the fluid, is deposited, building up layers of sediment.

_____ occurs when the forces responsible for sediment transportation are no longer sufficient to overcome the forces of particle weight and friction, which resist motion.

   a. Deposition
   b. Headward erosion
   c. Downcutting
   d. Diagenesis

66. In chronostratigraphy, a _____ is a succession of rock strata laid down in an single age on the geologic timescale, which usually represents millions of years of deposition. A given _____ of rock and the corresponding age of time will by convention have the same name, and the same boundaries.
   a. Chronostratigraphy
   b. Geologic record
   c. Relative dating
   d. Stage

67. The _____ is the layer of igneous, sedimentary, and metamorphic rocks which form the continents and the areas of shallow seabed close to their shores, known as continental shelves. This layer is sometimes called sial due to more felsic, or granitic, bulk composition, which lies in contrast to the oceanic crust, called sima due to its mafic, or basaltic rock. (Based on the change in velocity of seismic waves, it is believed that at a certain depth sial becomes close in its physical properties to sima.
   a. Nappe
   b. Convergent boundary
   c. Tectonic plates
   d. Continental crust

68. A _____ is an elongated whale-shaped hill formed by glacial action. Its long axis is parallel with the movement of the ice, with the blunter end facing into the glacial movement. They may be more than 45 m (150 ft) high and more than 0.8 km (1/2 mile) long, and are often in _____ fields of similarly shaped, sized and oriented hills. They usually have layers indicating that the material was repeatedly added to a core, which may be of rock or glacial till.
   a. Monadnock
   b. 1509 Istanbul earthquake
   c. Sandur
   d. Drumlin

69. The _____ was part of an early conceptual climatic and chronological framework composed of four glacial and interglacial stages used by early geomorphologists and Quaternary geologists to subdivide glacial and nonglacial deposits within north-central United States. From youngest to oldest, they were the Wisconsin (glacial), Sangamonian (interglacial), Illinoian (glacial), Yarmouthian (Yarmouth)(interglacial), Kansan (glacial), Aftonian (interglacial), and Nebraskan (glacial) stages. As developed between 1894 and 1909, the Kansan Stage was based on a model that assumed that the Pleistocene deposits contained only two glacial tills and one volcanic ash bed within Nebraska and Kansas.

a. 1703 Genroku earthquake
c. Kansan glaciation
b. 1509 Istanbul earthquake
d. 1700 Cascadia earthquake

70. _____ was a prehistoric pluvial lake that covered much of North America's Great Basin region. Most of the territory it covered was in present-day Utah, though parts of the lake extended into present-day Idaho and Nevada. Formed about 32,000 years ago, it existed until about 16,800 years ago, when a large portion of the lake was released through the Red Rock Pass in Idaho.

Like most, if not all, of the ice age pluvial lakes of the American West, _____ was a result of the combination of lower temperatures, decreased evaporation, and higher precipitation that then prevailed in the region, perhaps due to a more southerly jet stream than today's. The lake was probably not a singular entity either; geologic evidence suggests that it may have evaporated and reformed as many as 28 times in the last 3 million years.

a. 1509 Istanbul earthquake
c. 1703 Genroku earthquake
b. 1700 Cascadia earthquake
d. Lake Bonneville

71. _____ is the part of Earth's lithosphere that surfaces in the ocean basins. _____ is primarily composed of mafic rocks, or sima. It is thinner than continental crust, or sial, generally less than 10 kilometers thick, however it is denser, having a mean density of about 3.3 grams per cubic centimeter.
a. Oceanic crust
c. AL 333
b. AL 129-1
d. AASHTO Soil Classification System

72. A _____ is a moraine that forms at the end of the glacier called the snout.

They mark the maximum advance of the glacier. An end moraine is at the present boundary of the glacier. They are one of the most prominent types of moraines in the Arctic. One famous _____ is the Giant's Wall in Norway.

a. Bull Lake glaciation
c. Firn
b. Terminal moraine
d. Bramertonian Stage

73. An _____ is a fan-shaped deposit formed where a fast flowing stream flattens, slows, and spreads typically at the exit of a canyon onto a flatter plain. A convergence of neighboring fans into a single apron of deposits against a slope is called a bajada, or compound _____.
a. AL 333
c. AL 129-1
b. AASHTO Soil Classification System
d. Alluvial fan

74. A _____ is any glacially formed accumulation of unconsolidated glacial debris (soil and rock) which can occur in currently glaciated and formerly glaciated regions, such as those areas acted upon by a past ice age. This debris may have been plucked off the valley floor as a glacier advanced or it may have fallen off the valley walls as a result of frost wedging. Moraines may be composed of silt like glacial flour to large boulders.
a. 1700 Cascadia earthquake
c. 1703 Genroku earthquake
b. Moraine
d. 1509 Istanbul earthquake

Chapter 23. Cenozoic Earth and Life History

75. A _____, sometimes called a composite volcano, is a tall, conical volcano with many layers (strata) of hardened lava, tephra, and volcanic ash. They are characterized by a steep profile and periodic, explosive eruptions. The lava that flows from a _____ tends to be viscous; it cools and hardens before spreading far.
   a. Stratovolcano
   b. Broken Top
   c. Mount Baker
   d. Mount Overlord

76. A _____ is an opening in a planet's surface or crust, which allows hot, molten rock, ash, and gases to escape from below the surface. Volcanic activity involving the extrusion of rock tends to form mountains or features like mountains over a period of time.
   a. 1509 Istanbul earthquake
   b. 1703 Genroku earthquake
   c. 1700 Cascadia earthquake
   d. Volcano

77. A _____ is a pyroclastic material. They are extrusive igneous rocks, and are similar to pumice, which has so many cavities and is such low-density that it can float on water.
   a. Pit crater
   b. Cinder
   c. Wadati-Benioff zone
   d. Pyroclastic flow

78. A _____ or scoria cone is a steep conical hill of volcanic fragments that accumulate around and downwind from a volcanic vent. The rock fragments, often called cinders or scoria, are glassy and contain numerous gas bubbles 'frozen' into place as magma exploded into the air and then cooled quickly. Cinder cones range in size from tens to hundreds of meters tall.
   a. 1700 Cascadia earthquake
   b. 1703 Genroku earthquake
   c. 1509 Istanbul earthquake
   d. Cinder cone

79. In geology and climatology, a _____ was an extended period of abundant rainfall lasting many thousands of years. The term is especially applied to such periods during the Pleistocene Epoch. A minor, short _____ may be termed a 'subpluvial'.
   a. 1700 Cascadia earthquake
   b. Pluvial
   c. 1703 Genroku earthquake
   d. 1509 Istanbul earthquake

80. A _____ is a lake that experiences significant increase in depth and extent as a result of increased precipitation and reduced evaporation. Such lakes are likely to be endorheic.

They represent changes in the hydrological cycle -- wet cycles generate large lakes, whereas dry cycles cause the lakes to dry up leaving large flat plains.

   a. 1700 Cascadia earthquake
   b. 1703 Genroku earthquake
   c. 1509 Istanbul earthquake
   d. Pluvial lake

81. _____ is water located beneath the ground surface in soil pore spaces and in the fractures of lithologic formations. A unit of rock or an unconsolidated deposit is called an aquifer when it can yield a usable quantity of water. The depth at which soil pore spaces or fractures and voids in rock become completely saturated with water is called the water table.
   a. Depression focused recharge
   b. 1509 Istanbul earthquake
   c. 1700 Cascadia earthquake
   d. Groundwater

82. In geology, a _____ is a location on the Earth's surface that has experienced active volcanism for a long period of time.

J. Tuzo Wilson came up with the idea in 1963 that volcanic chains like the Hawaiian Islands result from the slow movement of a tectonic plate across a 'fixed' _____ deep beneath the surface of the planet.

   a. 1703 Genroku earthquake
   c. 1509 Istanbul earthquake
   b. 1700 Cascadia earthquake
   d. Hotspot

83. A _____ is an upwelling of abnormally hot rock within the Earth's mantle. As the heads of mantle plumes can partly melt when they reach shallow depths, they are thought to be the cause of volcanic centers known as hotspots and probably also to have caused flood basalts. It is a secondary way that Earth loses heat, much less important in this regard than is heat loss at plate margins.
   a. Strainmeter
   c. Mazuku
   b. Seismic refraction
   d. Mantle plume

84. A _____ or super volcanic eruption is a volcanic eruption which is substantially larger than any volcano in historic times (generally accepted to be greater than 1,000 cubic kilometres.) They occur when magma in the Earth rises into the crust from a hotspot but is unable to break through the crust. Pressure builds in a large and growing magma pool until the crust is unable to contain the pressure.
   a. Supervolcano
   c. Lapilli
   b. Volcanic ash
   d. Pit crater

85. _____ is a type of rock consisting of consolidated volcanic ash ejected from vents during a volcanic eruption. _____ is sometimes called tufa, particularly when used as construction material, although tufa also refers to a quite different rock.

The products of a volcanic eruption are volcanic gases, lava, steam, and tephra. Magma is blown apart when it interacts violently with volcanic gases and steam. Solid material produced and thrown into the air by such volcanic eruptions is called tephra, regardless of composition or fragment size. If the resulting pieces of ejecta are small enough, the material is called volcanic ash, defined as such particles less than 2 mm in diameter, sand-sized or smaller.

   a. Pyroclastic rocks
   c. Coldwell Complex
   b. Country rock
   d. Tuff

86. _____ - also known as diatomite, diahydro, kieselguhr, kieselgur or celite - is a naturally occurring, soft, chalk-like sedimentary rock that is easily crumbled into a fine white to off-white powder. This powder has an abrasive feel, similar to pumice powder, and is very light, due to its high porosity. The typical chemical composition of _____ is 86% silica, 5% sodium, 3% magnesium and 2% iron. _____ consists of fossilized remains of diatoms, a type of hard-shelled algae.
   a. Jasperoid
   c. Diatomaceous earth
   b. Dolomite
   d. Porcellanite

87. _____ are water-soluble mineral sediments that result from the evaporation of bodies of surficial water. _____ are considered sedimentary rocks.

Although all water bodies on the surface and in aquifers contain dissolved salts, the water must evaporate into the atmosphere for the minerals to precipitate.

 a. AL 129-1
 b. AL 333
 c. AASHTO Soil Classification System
 d. Evaporites

88. The _____ is an Eocene geologic formation that records the sedimentation in a series of intermountain lakes. The sedimentary layers were formed in a large area of interconnecting lakes a tributary of the Colorado River. The area of the formation exists as three separate basins around the Uinta Mountains of northeastern Utah: an area in northwestern Colorado east of the Uintas, a larger area in the southwest corner of Wyoming just north of the Uintas known as Lake Gosiute, and the largest area, which lies in northeastern Utah and western Colorado south of the Uintas, known as Lake Uinta.
 a. Green River Formation
 b. 1700 Cascadia earthquake
 c. 1703 Genroku earthquake
 d. 1509 Istanbul earthquake

89. In geology, a _____ deposit or _____ is an accumulation of valuable minerals formed by deposition of dense mineral phases in a trap site. Types of _____ deposits include alluvium, eluvium, beach placers, and paleoplacers.

Typical locations for alluvial _____ deposits are on the inside bends of rivers and creeks, in natural hollows, at the break of slope on a stream, the base of an escarpment, waterfall or other barrier, within sand dunes, beach profiles or in gravel beds.

 a. 1703 Genroku earthquake
 b. 1509 Istanbul earthquake
 c. 1700 Cascadia earthquake
 d. Placer

90. _____ are flat or very gently sloping areas of the deep ocean basin floor. They are among the Earth's flattest and smoothest regions and the least explored. _____ cover approximately 40% of the ocean floor and reach depths between 2,200 and 5,500 m (7,200 and 18,000 ft.)
 a. Intertidal
 b. AASHTO Soil Classification System
 c. Eutrophication
 d. Abyssal plains

91. _____ is a naturally occurring material composed primarily of fine-grained minerals, which show plasticity through a variable range of water content, and which can be hardened when dried and/or fired. _____ deposits are mostly composed of _____ minerals (phyllosilicate minerals), minerals which impart plasticity and harden when fired and/or dried, and variable amounts of water trapped in the mineral structure by polar attraction. Organic materials which do not impart plasticity may also be a part of _____ deposits.
 a. 1700 Cascadia earthquake
 b. 1509 Istanbul earthquake
 c. 1703 Genroku earthquake
 d. Clay

92. An _____ is a long winding ridge of stratified sand and gravel, examples of which occur in glaciated and formerly glaciated regions of Europe and North America. They are frequently several miles long and, because of their peculiar uniform shape, are somewhat like railroad embankments.

Most are believed to form in ice-walled tunnels by streams which flowed within (englacial) and under (subglacial) glaciers.

a. AASHTO Soil Classification System
b. Esker
c. AL 333
d. AL 129-1

93. _____ is an accumulation of partially decayed vegetation matter. _____ forms in wetlands or peatlands, variously called bogs, moors, muskegs, pocosins, mires, and _____ swamp forests. By volume there are about 4 trillion mÂÂ³ of _____ in the world covering a total of around 2% of global land mass (about 3 million km^2), containing about 8 billion terajoules of energy.

a. 1509 Istanbul earthquake
b. Peat
c. 1703 Genroku earthquake
d. 1700 Cascadia earthquake

94. _____ are an extinct group of marine animals of the subclass Ammonoidea in the class Cephalopoda, phylum Mollusca. They are excellent index fossils, and it is often possible to link the rock layer in which they are found to specific geological time periods.

_____' closest living relative is probably not the modern Nautilus (which they outwardly resemble), but rather the subclass Coleoidea (octopus, squid, and cuttlefish.)

a. AL 129-1
b. Ammonites
c. AL 333
d. AASHTO Soil Classification System

95. _____ are single-celled algae, protists and phytoplankton belonging to the division haptophytes. They are distinguished by special calcium carbonate plates of uncertain function called coccoliths, which are important microfossils. _____ are almost exclusively marine and are found in large numbers throughout the surface euphotic zone of the ocean.

a. 1703 Genroku earthquake
b. Coccolithophores
c. 1509 Istanbul earthquake
d. 1700 Cascadia earthquake

96. The _____ is a geologic period and system of the Paleozoic era spanning from >416 to 359.2 million years ago (ICS, 2004.).

During the _____ Period, which occurred in the Paleozoic era, the first fish evolved legsand started to walk on land as tetrapods around 365 Ma.

a. Xitun Formation
b. Gogo Formation
c. 1509 Istanbul earthquake
d. Devonian

97. The chemical compound silicon dioxide, also known as _____ , is an oxide of silicon with a chemical formula of SiO_2 and has been known for its hardness since antiquity. _____ is most commonly found in nature as sand or quartz, as well as in the cell walls of diatoms. It is a principal component of most types of glass and substances such as concrete.

a. 1509 Istanbul earthquake
b. 1700 Cascadia earthquake
c. 1703 Genroku earthquake
d. Silica

98. The _____ was an ocean that existed between the continents of Gondwana and Laurasia during the Mesozoic era before the opening of the Indian Ocean.

About 250 million years ago, during the Triassic, a new ocean began forming in the southern end of the Paleo-_____. A rift formed along the northern continental shelf of Southern Pangaea (Gondwana.) Over the next 60 million years, that piece of shelf, known as Cimmeria, traveled north, pushing the floor of the Paleo-_____ under the eastern end of Northern Pangaea (Laurasia). The _____ formed between Cimmeria and Gondwana, directly over where the Paleo-Tethys used to be.

   a. Tethys Ocean
   c. 1700 Cascadia earthquake
   b. 1509 Istanbul earthquake
   d. 1703 Genroku earthquake

99. _____ are the preserved remains or traces of animals, plants, and other organisms from the remote past. The totality of _____, both discovered and undiscovered, and their placement in fossiliferous rock formations and sedimentary layers (strata) is known as the fossil record. The study of _____ across geological time, how they were formed, and the evolutionary relationships between taxa (phylogeny) are some of the most important functions of the science of paleontology.
   a. 1703 Genroku earthquake
   c. 1700 Cascadia earthquake
   b. 1509 Istanbul earthquake
   d. Fossils

100. _____, originally Gondwanaland, is the name given to a southern precursor-supercontinent and then as a remnant separated from Laurasia 180-200 million years ago during the breakup of the Pangaea supercontinent that existed about 500 to 200 Ma ago into two large segments. While the corresponding northern hemisphere continent Laurasia moved further north, the nearly equal in area _____ included most of the landmasses in today's southern hemisphere, including Antarctica, South America, Africa, Madagascar, Australia-New Guinea, and New Zealand, as well as Arabia and the Indian subcontinent, which have now moved into the Northern Hemisphere.
   a. 1509 Istanbul earthquake
   c. 1700 Cascadia earthquake
   b. Laurasia
   d. Gondwana

101. _____ is an extinct species of the genus Homo, believed to have been the first hominin to leave Africa.

_____ originally migrated from Africa during the Early Pleistocene, possibly as a result of the operation of the Saharan pump, around 2.0 million years ago, and dispersed throughout most of the Old World.

   a. Homo erectus
   c. 1509 Istanbul earthquake
   b. 1703 Genroku earthquake
   d. 1700 Cascadia earthquake

102. The _____ is an extinct member of the Homo genus that is known from Pleistocene specimens found in Europe and parts of western and central Asia. Neanderthals are either classified as a subspecies of humans (Homo sapiens neanderthalensis) or as a separate species (Homo neanderthalensis.) The first proto-_____ traits appeared in Europe as early as 600,000-350,000 years ago.
   a. 1509 Istanbul earthquake
   c. 1703 Genroku earthquake
   b. Neanderthal
   d. 1700 Cascadia earthquake

103. The _____ was a cratonic sequence that began in the mid-Devonian, peaked early in the Mississippian, and ended by mid-Mississippian time. A major unconformity separates it from the lower Tippecanoe sequence.

The basal-that is, the lowest and oldest-units of the Kaskaskia consist of clean quartz sandstones eroded from the Appalachian orogenic belt to the east, the Ozark Dome in the center of the continent, and south from the Canadian Shield.

a. Sauk sequence
b. 1700 Cascadia earthquake
c. Kaskaskia sequence
d. 1509 Istanbul earthquake

Chapter 24. Physical and Historical Geology in Perspective

1. _____ is the use of the principles of geology to reconstruct and understand the history of the Earth . It focuses on geologic processes that change the Earth's surface and subsurface; and the use of stratigraphy, structural geology and paleontology to tell the sequence of these events. It also focuses on the evolution of plants and animals during different time periods in the geological timescale.
   a. Historical geology
   b. Rockall
   c. Valley glaciers
   d. Strike-slip faults

2. An _____ is the result of a sudden release of energy in the Earth's crust that creates seismic waves. They are recorded with a seismometer or the related and mostly obsolete Richter magnitude, with a magnitude 3 or lower _____ being mostly imperceptible and magnitude 7 causing serious damage over large areas.
   a. AASHTO Soil Classification System
   b. AL 333
   c. Earthquake
   d. AL 129-1

3. The _____ Era, is the most recent of the three classic geological eras and covers the period from 65.5 million years ago to the present. It is marked by the Cretaceous-Tertiary extinction event at the end of the Cretaceous that saw the demise of the last non-avian dinosaurs and the end of the Mesozoic Era. The _____ era is ongoing.
   a. 1700 Cascadia earthquake
   b. 1703 Genroku earthquake
   c. 1509 Istanbul earthquake
   d. Cenozoic

4. A _____ is a geological phenomenon which includes a wide range of ground movement, such as rock falls, deep failure of slopes and shallow debris flows, which can occur in offshore, coastal and onshore environments. Although the action of gravity is the primary driving force for a _____ to occur, there are other contributing factors affecting the original slope stability. Typically, pre-conditional factors build up specific sub-surface conditions that make the area/slope prone to failure, whereas the actual _____ often requires a trigger before being released.
   a. 1509 Istanbul earthquake
   b. 1700 Cascadia earthquake
   c. Mass wasting
   d. Landslide

5. _____ is the geomorphic process by which soil, regolith, and rock move downslope under the force of gravity. Types of _____ include creep, slides, flows, topples, and falls, each with its own characteristic features, and taking place over timescales from seconds to years. _____ occurs on both terrestrial and submarine slopes, and has been observed on Earth, Mars, and Venus.
   a. Soil liquefaction
   b. 1700 Cascadia earthquake
   c. 1509 Istanbul earthquake
   d. Mass wasting

6. The _____ is a continental transform fault that runs a length of roughly 800 miles (1,300 km) through California in the United States. The fault's motion is right-lateral strike-slip (horizontal motion.) It forms the tectonic boundary between the Pacific Plate and the North American Plate.
   a. 1703 Genroku earthquake
   b. San Andreas fault
   c. 1509 Istanbul earthquake
   d. 1700 Cascadia earthquake

7. _____ is the naturally occurring, unconsolidated or loose covering on the Earth's surface. _____ is composed of particles of broken rock that have been altered by chemical, biological and environmental processes including weathering and erosion. _____ is different from its parent rock(s) source(s), altered by interactions between the lithosphere, hydrosphere, atmosphere, and the biosphere.
   a. Topsoil
   b. 1509 Istanbul earthquake
   c. Soil
   d. Slump

8. The _____ is a geologic period and system that extends from about 251 to 199 Mya (million years ago.) As the first period of the Mesozoic Era, the _____ follows the Permian and is followed by the Jurassic. Both the start and end of the _____ are marked by major extinction events.
   a. 1509 Istanbul earthquake
   b. 1700 Cascadia earthquake
   c. Rhaetian
   d. Triassic

9. In geology, a _____ or _____ line is a planar fracture in rock in which the rock on one side of the fracture has moved with respect to the rock on the other side. Large faults within the Earth's crust are the result of differential or shear motion and active _____ zones are the causal locations of most earthquakes. Earthquakes are caused by energy release during rapid slippage along a _____.
   a. Fault
   b. Stack
   c. Dali
   d. Combe

10. The _____ or the Dirty Thirties was a period of severe dust storms causing major ecological and agricultural damage to American and Canadian prairie lands from 1930 to 1936 (in some areas until 1940.) The phenomenon was caused by severe drought coupled with decades of extensive farming without crop rotation or other techniques to prevent erosion. Deep plowing of the virgin topsoil of the Great Plains had killed the natural grasses that normally kept the soil in place and trapped moisture even during periods of drought and high winds.
   a. 1700 Cascadia earthquake
   b. 1703 Genroku earthquake
   c. 1509 Istanbul earthquake
   d. Dust Bowl

11. _____ is water located beneath the ground surface in soil pore spaces and in the fractures of lithologic formations. A unit of rock or an unconsolidated deposit is called an aquifer when it can yield a usable quantity of water. The depth at which soil pore spaces or fractures and voids in rock become completely saturated with water is called the water table.
   a. 1700 Cascadia earthquake
   b. Groundwater
   c. Depression focused recharge
   d. 1509 Istanbul earthquake

12. The _____ is an informal name for the supereon comprising the eons of the geologic timescale that came before the current Phanerozoic eon. It spans from the formation of Earth around 4500 Mya (million years ago) to the evolution of abundant macroscopic hard-shelled animals, which marked the beginning of the Cambrian, the first period of the first era of the Phanerozoic eon, some 542 Mya. It is named after the Roman name for Wales - Cambria - where rocks from this age were first studied.
   a. 1700 Cascadia earthquake
   b. 1509 Istanbul earthquake
   c. 1703 Genroku earthquake
   d. Precambrian

13. _____, is a phylum of bacteria that obtain their energy through photosynthesis. The name '_____' comes from the color of the bacteria . They are a significant component of the marine nitrogen cycle and an important primary producer in many areas of the ocean, but are also found in habitats other than the marine environment; in particular _____ are known to occur in both freshwater, hypersaline inland lakes and in arid areas where they are a major component of biological soil crusts.

Stromatolites of fossilized oxygen-producing _____ have been found from 2.8 billion years ago. The ability of _____ to perform oxygenic photosynthesis is thought to have converted the early reducing atmosphere into an oxidizing one, which dramatically changed the composition of life forms on Earth by provoking an explosion of biodiversity and leading to the near-extinction of oxygen-intolerant organisms.

a. 1703 Genroku earthquake
c. 1509 Istanbul earthquake
b. Cyanobacteria
d. 1700 Cascadia earthquake

Chapter 1

1. d	2. a	3. c	4. c	5. a	6. d	7. b	8. c	9. a	10. d
11. b	12. d	13. a	14. d	15. b	16. b	17. d	18. d	19. d	20. d
21. d	22. d	23. d	24. d	25. b	26. b	27. b	28. b	29. c	30. d
31. c	32. d	33. d	34. c	35. b	36. a	37. c	38. d	39. c	40. d
41. d	42. d	43. d	44. d	45. b	46. a	47. b	48. d		

Chapter 2

1. d	2. d	3. a	4. d	5. d	6. d	7. d	8. c	9. d	10. d
11. a	12. c	13. c	14. a	15. d	16. a	17. d	18. d	19. d	20. d
21. a	22. a	23. b	24. d	25. c	26. d	27. a	28. d	29. c	30. d
31. c	32. d	33. d	34. b	35. a	36. c	37. b	38. d	39. d	40. d
41. d	42. a	43. b	44. d	45. d	46. d	47. d	48. c	49. d	50. d
51. a	52. d	53. a	54. d	55. a	56. d	57. b	58. a	59. d	60. c
61. d	62. c	63. d	64. d	65. d	66. d	67. d			

Chapter 3

1. d	2. d	3. a	4. d	5. d	6. c	7. d	8. d	9. a	10. c
11. d	12. b	13. d	14. a	15. b	16. d	17. c	18. b	19. d	20. c
21. b	22. c	23. d	24. a	25. d	26. d	27. c	28. a	29. d	30. d
31. d	32. d	33. d	34. d	35. d	36. d	37. d	38. d	39. b	40. c
41. d	42. d	43. d	44. d	45. a	46. b				

Chapter 4

1. d	2. c	3. c	4. b	5. c	6. d	7. c	8. d	9. d	10. a
11. d	12. d	13. d	14. a	15. b	16. a	17. b	18. d	19. c	20. a
21. b	22. d	23. d	24. d	25. b	26. d	27. c	28. b	29. d	30. d
31. d	32. d	33. c	34. d	35. d	36. d	37. b	38. d	39. a	40. c
41. d	42. b	43. b	44. d	45. c	46. d	47. d	48. d	49. d	50. b
51. c	52. d	53. a	54. d	55. c	56. c	57. d	58. d	59. d	60. a
61. d	62. c	63. d	64. d	65. b	66. d	67. d	68. d	69. c	

Chapter 5

1. c	2. b	3. d	4. d	5. b	6. d	7. b	8. a	9. d	10. d
11. a	12. c	13. c	14. a	15. d	16. d	17. b	18. d	19. c	20. d
21. a	22. b	23. d	24. a	25. a	26. c	27. d	28. d	29. b	30. d
31. d	32. a	33. d	34. d	35. b	36. b	37. d	38. d	39. d	40. d
41. d	42. d	43. d	44. b	45. d	46. b	47. b	48. b		

ANSWER KEY

Chapter 6

1. d	2. d	3. c	4. a	5. d	6. d	7. a	8. d	9. b	10. a
11. d	12. d	13. a	14. d	15. b	16. d	17. c	18. b	19. d	20. d
21. b	22. d	23. b	24. d	25. b	26. a	27. d	28. a	29. d	30. d
31. c	32. b	33. d	34. a	35. b	36. d	37. c	38. d	39. d	40. a
41. d	42. a	43. d	44. d	45. d	46. d	47. d	48. d	49. a	50. d
51. b	52. c	53. c	54. d	55. d	56. c	57. b	58. b	59. c	60. a
61. d	62. b	63. b	64. c	65. d	66. d	67. b	68. a	69. d	70. b
71. d	72. b	73. d	74. d	75. a	76. d	77. b	78. b	79. b	80. d
81. d	82. a	83. a	84. d	85. c	86. a	87. d	88. c	89. d	90. a
91. d	92. c	93. c	94. a	95. d	96. c	97. c	98. b	99. d	100. d
101. c	102. d	103. d	104. d	105. d	106. d	107. b	108. d	109. c	110. d
111. c	112. b	113. d	114. b	115. d	116. d				

Chapter 7

1. a	2. d	3. d	4. d	5. a	6. d	7. d	8. d	9. a	10. a
11. d	12. b	13. a	14. d	15. d	16. d	17. b	18. d	19. a	20. b
21. d	22. d	23. b	24. d	25. d	26. b	27. b	28. c	29. d	30. d
31. b	32. d	33. d	34. d	35. d	36. d	37. d	38. a	39. d	40. c
41. c	42. b	43. d	44. b	45. d	46. d	47. a	48. d	49. a	50. a
51. d	52. d	53. a	54. d	55. a	56. c	57. b	58. d	59. d	60. a
61. d	62. d	63. d	64. d	65. c	66. a	67. b	68. a	69. b	70. c
71. a	72. d	73. a	74. d						

Chapter 8

1. c	2. d	3. a	4. c	5. c	6. c	7. d	8. c	9. d	10. d
11. d	12. c	13. b	14. d	15. c	16. d	17. c	18. a	19. d	20. d
21. d	22. d	23. d	24. d	25. b	26. a	27. d	28. d	29. c	30. d
31. c	32. d	33. b	34. b	35. d	36. c	37. b	38. d	39. d	40. d
41. b	42. d	43. a	44. c	45. b	46. b	47. d	48. c	49. d	50. d
51. c	52. c	53. d	54. d	55. a	56. b	57. b	58. d	59. d	60. a
61. c	62. d								

Chapter 9

1. d	2. d	3. c	4. c	5. c	6. d	7. d	8. d	9. c	10. a
11. d	12. d	13. b	14. a	15. a	16. d	17. d	18. b	19. b	20. b
21. a	22. c	23. b	24. d	25. b	26. c	27. d	28. d	29. a	30. c
31. d	32. b	33. c	34. d	35. d	36. a	37. d	38. a	39. d	40. d
41. d	42. b	43. d	44. b	45. d	46. b	47. c	48. d	49. d	50. b
51. d	52. d	53. d	54. a	55. d	56. c	57. a	58. a	59. a	60. d
61. b	62. d	63. c	64. d	65. a	66. d	67. b	68. d	69. c	70. d
71. b	72. d								

Chapter 10

1. d	2. d	3. a	4. d	5. d	6. a	7. d	8. d	9. c	10. d
11. b	12. b	13. a	14. d	15. d	16. a	17. b	18. a	19. d	20. d
21. b	22. b	23. a	24. d	25. b	26. c	27. c	28. a	29. a	30. d
31. b	32. b	33. c	34. a	35. d	36. d	37. a	38. d	39. c	40. d
41. c	42. b	43. d	44. d	45. a	46. a	47. d	48. d	49. c	50. d
51. d	52. c	53. d	54. d	55. d	56. d	57. d	58. d	59. a	60. a
61. d	62. c	63. c	64. c	65. a	66. d	67. a	68. d	69. d	70. d
71. c	72. d	73. b	74. d	75. d	76. d	77. d	78. d	79. a	

Chapter 11

1. b	2. d	3. b	4. d	5. d	6. c	7. d	8. a	9. a	10. a
11. a	12. d	13. b	14. d	15. d	16. d	17. c	18. d	19. a	20. d
21. d	22. b	23. b	24. a	25. c	26. d	27. b	28. a	29. d	30. b
31. a	32. d	33. c	34. d	35. b	36. d	37. b	38. b	39. b	40. a
41. d	42. d	43. d	44. a	45. a	46. d	47. c	48. d	49. d	50. d
51. d	52. a								

Chapter 12

1. c	2. d	3. d	4. a	5. b	6. c	7. d	8. c	9. d	10. d
11. d	12. d	13. a	14. a	15. a	16. b	17. d	18. d	19. b	20. a
21. b	22. c	23. b	24. c	25. d	26. d	27. d	28. d	29. d	30. a
31. b	32. a	33. a	34. c	35. c	36. c	37. d	38. d	39. d	40. d
41. a	42. d	43. d	44. d	45. d	46. d	47. c	48. d	49. a	50. d
51. d	52. a								

Chapter 13

1. d	2. d	3. a	4. c	5. c	6. a	7. d	8. d	9. b	10. d
11. d	12. c	13. a	14. a	15. a	16. c	17. d	18. b	19. d	20. d
21. d	22. a	23. a	24. b	25. d	26. d	27. d	28. c	29. d	30. c
31. d	32. c	33. d	34. a	35. b	36. c	37. a	38. a	39. d	40. a
41. b	42. d	43. d	44. a	45. d	46. d	47. d	48. d	49. c	50. d
51. d	52. d	53. a	54. d	55. d	56. d	57. b	58. d		

Chapter 14

1. a	2. c	3. a	4. d	5. b	6. c	7. b	8. d	9. d	10. d
11. b	12. d	13. c	14. a	15. b	16. a	17. a	18. d	19. c	20. d
21. d	22. d	23. c	24. b	25. d	26. d	27. d	28. d	29. a	30. d
31. b	32. d	33. c	34. d	35. d	36. b	37. d	38. c	39. d	40. d
41. b	42. d	43. b	44. d	45. b	46. d	47. c	48. c	49. d	50. d
51. d	52. d	53. c	54. d	55. b	56. a	57. c	58. d	59. b	60. b
61. b	62. d	63. d	64. d	65. d	66. c	67. b	68. b	69. a	70. d
71. d	72. b	73. d	74. d	75. d	76. a	77. a			

ANSWER KEY

Chapter 15
1. b	2. a	3. b	4. b	5. a	6. d	7. b	8. b	9. a	10. d
11. d	12. c	13. d	14. d	15. c	16. d	17. b	18. d	19. b	20. b
21. b	22. d	23. d	24. d	25. d	26. b	27. d	28. d	29. d	30. b
31. d	32. a	33. c	34. c	35. c	36. c	37. a	38. d	39. d	40. b
41. d	42. d	43. d	44. b	45. b	46. d	47. d	48. d	49. a	50. d
51. d	52. d	53. d	54. a	55. a	56. a				

Chapter 16
1. c	2. d	3. a	4. d	5. a	6. d	7. d	8. d	9. b	10. b
11. d	12. b	13. d	14. a	15. d	16. d	17. c	18. d	19. b	20. c
21. d	22. d	23. a	24. b	25. d	26. a	27. d	28. a	29. a	30. c
31. d	32. d	33. d	34. b	35. d	36. d	37. d	38. d	39. d	40. d
41. b	42. a	43. d	44. d	45. a	46. c	47. a	48. d	49. b	50. d
51. b	52. c	53. c	54. c						

Chapter 17
1. d	2. d	3. b	4. d	5. d	6. b	7. d	8. c	9. a	10. d
11. a	12. a	13. a	14. c	15. a	16. a	17. b	18. d	19. d	20. a
21. d	22. a	23. c	24. b	25. d	26. b	27. b	28. d	29. b	30. d
31. d	32. d	33. d	34. a	35. b	36. a	37. d	38. c	39. a	40. b
41. a	42. c	43. d	44. b	45. d	46. d	47. d	48. c	49. a	50. d
51. b	52. d	53. a	54. c	55. b	56. d	57. c	58. d	59. b	

Chapter 18
1. d	2. c	3. d	4. b	5. a	6. c	7. c	8. b	9. d	10. d
11. a	12. c	13. a	14. c	15. c	16. c	17. d	18. d	19. b	20. c
21. a	22. d	23. d	24. a	25. d	26. d	27. d	28. d		

Chapter 19
1. b	2. d	3. a	4. d	5. d	6. a	7. d	8. a	9. b	10. d
11. d	12. d	13. d	14. d	15. d	16. c	17. a	18. a	19. a	20. b
21. d	22. d	23. b	24. a	25. d	26. a	27. d	28. a	29. d	30. d
31. d	32. b	33. c	34. d	35. c	36. d	37. a	38. d	39. b	40. d
41. d	42. c	43. d	44. d	45. b	46. d	47. d	48. c	49. a	50. c
51. d	52. a	53. a	54. b	55. c	56. d	57. a	58. a	59. b	60. a
61. c	62. d	63. d	64. d	65. d	66. b	67. d	68. d	69. b	70. a
71. c	72. c	73. a	74. a	75. d	76. d	77. d	78. d	79. d	80. c
81. d									

Chapter 20

1. b	2. a	3. d	4. b	5. a	6. d	7. d	8. b	9. a	10. d
11. b	12. d	13. a	14. d	15. d	16. d	17. a	18. b	19. d	20. a
21. a	22. a	23. a	24. b	25. b	26. b	27. d	28. d	29. c	30. d
31. d	32. d	33. c	34. d	35. c	36. b	37. a	38. d	39. d	40. d
41. d	42. d	43. a	44. c	45. b	46. a	47. d	48. c	49. d	50. a
51. a	52. b	53. b	54. a	55. d	56. b	57. b	58. d	59. b	60. c
61. c	62. d	63. b	64. d	65. d	66. a	67. b	68. d	69. a	70. b
71. d	72. d	73. d	74. d	75. d	76. d	77. a	78. a	79. a	80. c
81. a	82. c	83. c	84. d	85. d	86. c	87. d	88. d	89. d	

Chapter 21

1. b	2. b	3. d	4. a	5. d	6. d	7. d	8. d	9. c	10. b
11. d	12. a	13. d	14. d	15. b	16. c	17. d	18. b	19. a	20. d
21. d	22. d	23. c	24. a	25. a	26. d	27. c	28. d	29. d	30. b
31. d	32. c	33. d	34. c	35. b	36. a	37. d	38. d	39. a	40. b
41. d	42. d	43. d	44. d						

Chapter 22

1. d	2. a	3. b	4. a	5. d	6. d	7. d	8. d	9. d	10. d
11. d	12. c	13. d	14. d	15. d	16. d	17. d	18. d	19. d	20. b
21. b	22. d	23. d	24. d	25. a	26. a	27. d	28. b	29. d	30. d
31. c	32. d	33. d	34. d	35. d	36. d	37. b	38. d	39. a	40. a
41. b	42. a	43. b	44. d	45. b	46. c	47. d	48. d	49. c	50. b
51. d	52. b	53. c	54. b	55. a	56. c	57. d	58. c	59. b	60. b
61. c	62. b	63. a	64. d	65. a	66. d	67. b	68. d	69. d	70. b
71. d	72. c	73. b	74. d	75. b	76. c	77. a			

Chapter 23

1. c	2. d	3. a	4. c	5. c	6. a	7. d	8. b	9. c	10. a
11. a	12. d	13. a	14. d	15. c	16. c	17. a	18. c	19. c	20. d
21. d	22. c	23. d	24. d	25. d	26. a	27. a	28. d	29. d	30. a
31. d	32. d	33. d	34. c	35. d	36. d	37. d	38. d	39. c	40. d
41. a	42. d	43. c	44. c	45. a	46. b	47. b	48. d	49. d	50. d
51. c	52. a	53. b	54. b	55. d	56. c	57. d	58. c	59. c	60. d
61. d	62. a	63. b	64. c	65. a	66. d	67. d	68. d	69. c	70. d
71. a	72. b	73. d	74. b	75. a	76. d	77. b	78. d	79. b	80. d
81. d	82. d	83. d	84. a	85. d	86. c	87. d	88. a	89. d	90. d
91. d	92. b	93. b	94. b	95. b	96. d	97. d	98. a	99. d	100. d
101. a	102. b	103. c							

Chapter 24

1. a	2. c	3. d	4. d	5. d	6. b	7. c	8. d	9. a	10. d
11. b	12. d	13. b							

www.ingramcontent.com/pod-product-compliance
Lightning Source LLC
Chambersburg PA
CBHW080544230426
43663CB00015B/2701